"David Ayers does a mast[...] [c]lassical Christian wisdom, hi[s...]eff to Bellah, it's all there. I especially appreciate his rejection [...] eutic character of many contemporary relationships, Ayers' ability to discuss marriage's connection to health, his use of the General Social Survey and National Survey of Family Growth, his appreciation of the power of generosity, and the challenging discussion of divorce."

—W. Bradford Wilcox, professor of sociology, University of Virginia; director, National Marriage Project; senior fellow, Institute for Family Studies; visiting scholar, American Enterprise Institute

"David Ayers has done the church a favor by writing this book. Hundreds of footnotes quoting and using various confessional documents, modern research, scholars in social psychology and family practice, and recognized theologians from church history are very impressive. He delves into issues the church needs to be discussing, and you will find his insights helpful and challenging. It is a fascinating book, and I highly recommend it."

—Jerry O'Neill, president and professor of pastoral theology emeritus, Reformed Presbyterian Theological Seminary (Pittsburgh, PA)

"If you are interested in—or interested in living out—the evangelical Christian view of marriage, buy this book. It is a remarkable exploration of the meaning of marriage that will warm your heart, sharpen your intellect, and spark your imagination."

—Maggie Gallagher, coauthor of *The Case for Marriage*; former president of the National Organization for Marriage and of the Institute for Marriage and Family Policy; nationally syndicated columnist

"Ayers has done a service for Christian institutions everywhere by presenting this well-crafted treatise on marriage and the family. This book presents an orthodox biblical view and is supported by scholarly research; it is a valuable work for anyone seeking resources for premarital counseling, church classes, or college and seminary courses. Although articles and narrow, topical books have been written on these issues, it is rare to find a comprehensive and trustworthy volume like this. The time is now for the church to provide compelling answers to the troubling issues surrounding marriage, and Ayers' book is much needed."

—Robert Daniels, associate professor of sociology, Bethel College (IN)

"The attack on traditional marriage in our time seems unprecedented. It certainly is unwarranted, especially when we consider how beneficial marriage is to society. Dr. David Ayers has written an excellent book in defense of biblical marriage, filled with good research, scriptural evidence, and powerful and practical conclusions."

—Jerry Newcombe, senior producer, on-air host, and columnist for D. James Kennedy Ministries; coauthor (with Peter Lillback) of *George Washington's Sacred Fire*

"Christians don't lack for books on marriage, but *Christian Marriage* is unlike any other book I've seen on the topic. Combining theology, sociology, and historical analysis, David Ayers has provided readers with a clear, thorough, and eminently practical study on God's good design for marriage. This is a book to which I anticipate returning regularly for helpful insight on a critical subject."

—Matthew J. Hall, dean, Boyce College; senior vice president, The Southern Baptist Theological Seminary

"I am grateful to Professor Ayers for providing a sociologically grounded— yet biblically informed—book for those of us who teach undergraduate sociology courses in marriage and the family on Catholic and Christian campuses. It is much needed. In the past I have had to create readers for my courses in marriage and the family in order to provide the needed data and theory on dating and mate selection, single-parent families, divorce outcomes, and the demographics surrounding all aspects of marriage and the family. This new book will surely facilitate course design for faculty. But more importantly, students will appreciate the engaging narrative, which, while filled with sociological data and theories, will capture their attention—and their hearts."

—Anne Hendershott, professor of sociology and director of the Veritas Center for Ethics in Public Life at Franciscan University of Steubenville, Ohio

"This book comes as an excellent complement to the many fine books on marriage. One of the many helpful things that strikes me about Dr. Ayers' work is the overwhelming sociological evidence for the negative consequences when one steps outside God's created order for marriage, family, and overall happiness. One does not need the cosmological argument for the existence of God. I highly recommend this book as an excellent resource on the subject of marriage."

—Robert G. Hall, co-pastor, The Bronx Household of Faith; part-time instructor in practical theology, Westminster Seminary–Philadelphia

"Marriage is an institution established by God to help men and women flourish. Well-ordered marriages produce well-ordered lives, communities, and cultures, while disordered marriages create disorder for everyone. Our culture's understanding of marriage is disordered, and the church must rely upon wise guides as we seek to reaffirm God's design for marriage. Dr. Ayers is such a guide who brings to his scholarship strong biblical fidelity, sound theological insight, and the greatest of pastoral sensitivity. *Christian Marriage* helps the church to understand, maintain, and promote God's design for marriage in an age of confusion."

—Nathanael Devlin, associate pastor, Beverly Heights Presbyterian Church; moderator of the Presbytery of the Alleghenies (EPC)

"I've known Dr. Ayers for more than twenty years, and I know that this book has been a labor of love for him for much of that time. It is close to his heart, his mind, his soul. I am thrilled with the final product. This is a beautiful work on the beautiful—and biblical and natural—order of Christian marriage. It is a testimony to marriage and family in the way that the laws of nature and of nature's God intended from the beginning, from its literal genesis. Sadly, this book will be attacked by intolerant people from the political-cultural left and the LGBTQ movement. That is a shame, a regrettable reflection of the anger and animosity that fuel too many of those in that movement. In truth, this is a book that goes way beyond so-called gay issues. Dr. Ayers spends far more time on matters such as divorce, single-parent families, marital infidelity, pre-marital sex, dating, procreation, and problems almost exclusively of a heterosexual nature. And most important, all of this information is backed up by hard data—as this book is as much a sociological analysis as a biblical one. Equally notable, it is also an ecumenical analysis, tackling a variety of faiths in the Judeo-Christian tradition and accessible and applicable to Protestants and Catholics alike. Kudos to Dr. Ayers for having the knowledge, the insight, the experience, the wisdom, and the courage to write this important book that couldn't be more badly needed in our culture today."

—Paul Kengor, professor of political science, Grove City College; bestselling author of over a dozen books, including *Takedown: How the Left Has Sabotaged Family and Marriage*

"David Ayers is a brilliant scholar who makes enormous contributions to our understanding of Christian marriage with this important book. As a distinguished sociologist, Ayers understands the cultural terrain from which our current confusion emanates. He unpacks with great wisdom, clarity, sensitivity, and profound biblical insight into that confusion, helping Christians to better understand God's design for marriage and its proper role in a well-ordered society. *Christian Marriage* provides useful instruction, practical advice, pastoral counsel, relevant research, and sound biblical principles. Every Christian should read and savor this timely and trenchant book!"

—Thomas O'Boyle, media executive, author, teacher, and former writer for *The Wall Street Journal*

"With *Christian Marriage*, Dr. Ayers has written his magnum opus. As a Christian sociologist, Ayers deftly assimilates the mound of data and statistics from studies related to marriage into a thoroughly biblical approach. But this is no research-heavy tome alone. *Christian Marriage* has a practical angle often missed in other Christian publications dealing with marriage and its unfortunate demise in many societies around the world. Ayers provides much-needed guidance for how we can recapture the beauty and purpose of this divine institution. This book will benefit everyone: singles considering marriage, engaged couples on the verge of wedlock, parents who want to counsel their children, pastors and university professors who will preach and teach on the topic. Even after twenty-six years of marriage, I found *Christian Marriage* extremely helpful. Honest, forthright, comprehensive, insightful, practical, and most importantly, biblical, *Christian Marriage* is Dr. Ayers's gift to us that, if heeded, will only help strengthen the institution of marriage, this glue of society so often under attack today."

—Victor Kuligin, lecturer at Bible Institute of South Africa; author
of *Snubbing God: The High Cost of Rejecting God's Created Order*

CHRISTIAN MARRIAGE

A Comprehensive Introduction

DAVID J. AYERS

LEXHAM PRESS

Christian Marriage: A Comprehensive Introduction
Copyright 2018 David J. Ayers

Lexham Press, 1313 Commercial St., Bellingham, WA 98225
LexhamPress.com

ISBN: 9781683592549
EPUB: 9781683592556

Lexham Editorial Team: Jim Weaver, Elliot Ritzema, Jennifer Edwards, Sarah Awa
Cover Design: Whantai Park
Typesetting: Scribe Inc.

I dedicate this book to my wife of more than thirty-five years and best friend for longer than that, Kathleen Burd Ayers.

She was that cute, interesting, popular Hermitage House social-work intern who took a chance on this eccentric, uncool, ex-hippy born-again who was not quite out of the woods. Through adventures and trials across six states, we have built a family and a legacy together under the care and lordship of Jesus Christ. Kathy has had to encourage me far more often than should have been necessary, but she never gave up doing so. She always points me back to God as my anchor, confidence, and hope in good times and bad. Kathy is my steady source of words "fitly spoken" that are like "apples of gold in a setting of silver" (Prov 25:11). This book would not have been finished but for her.

CONTENTS

PART 3: DIVORCE AND REMARRIAGE

PART 4: MARITAL HAPPINESS AND SUCCESS

PREFACE

A s I write this, I am absorbing news of yet one more shocking defection from biblical teaching on marriage and sexuality by someone I have known for years—up until recently a conservative office-holder in an established church with a sound confession. The departure of professing Christian individuals and institutions from orthodoxy in these areas, such as his, has become common, but I have not become numb to it. Long-term Christian acquaintances or friends whose children, raised in professing churches with solid gospel preaching, have come out as gay, transgender, and even actively bisexual and polyamorous are on my mind and in my prayers. There are many these days. The pace of change accelerates. I know I am not the only grandparent wondering how his children are going to raise his grandchildren to be faithful, effective believers in our increasingly post-Christian, and even aggressively anti-Christian, Western culture. I feel for them. I pray to God to guide and strengthen them.

We are a people who have never been healthier or more prosperous, our lives infused by a dazzling abundance of technological marvels. Yet two married parents will not raise most of our children from cradle to adulthood. The deaths of their mothers or fathers do not normally deprive them of this incredibly valuable gift. Rather, it is usually because, for whatever reasons, their parents did not enter into or maintain healthy, deeply committed, covenant marriages.

Meanwhile, most of our cultural and policy responses have not involved rededicating ourselves to strengthening these sacred unions. Rather, they have weakened marriage further, blurring the boundaries of matrimony and knocking down every distinction between it and a host of lesser, or even immoral, relational arrangements. Yesterday it was the casual acceptance of premarital sex, out-of-wedlock birth, no-fault divorce, cohabitation, and same-sex marriage. Polyamory, sometimes involving odd mixtures of sexual orientations and gender identities, seems to be the next thing on the horizon, but who knows?

For professing Christians, these problems are not "out there somewhere" afflicting only the overtly pagan, secular, or liberal. Many of those within the boundaries of the historically orthodox are moving in the same direction. They are sometimes one or two steps behind, but in other ways are keeping up. Already, in many key areas related to marital and sexual practices, there is little difference between professing believers and the world. For many of us these are not sterile statistics—we see it in our congregations and among our friends every day.

Yet I am also typing these words only a few days before Christmas, the time when we celebrate that the incarnate God was born to a virgin peasant woman betrothed to a Jewish carpenter, in the midst of an unbelievably corrupt and cruel civilization built on bloody war and the backs of slaves. Light burst forth into the darkness, witnessed by shepherds and announced by angels. "The people who walked in darkness have seen a great light; those who dwelt in a land of deep darkness, on them has light shone" (Isa 9:2). Here was hope for the hopeless, justice for the oppressed, comfort for the afflicted, wisdom for the foolish, sight for the blind, and salvation for lost sinners. Here was cause for confident anticipation—not because the world had suddenly become a great place filled with wise and righteous people, but because he was now in it, redeeming all things. In the shadow of the moral depredations of Herod's court, here was the author of marriage preparing to become the faithful son of a simple couple heading a working-class family, destined not only to sit on David's throne but also to be the flawless and triumphant husband of his eternal bride prepared from before time, the church.

When we look at the state of marriage and its trajectory, we can be tempted to despair and retreat. The more we understand the vital importance of this most original of all human institutions to so much else in God's plan for humankind, the greater our despondency can be. However, when we look to the God who entered human history on that night in Palestine, all he has done and all he is—his love, wisdom, faithfulness, and power— there is no longer cause for hopelessness and fear. If he who entered the world to redeem us, who was not only born of a virgin but rose from the dead, is for us, then nothing can stand against us (Rom 8:31).

With this confidence and hope, trusting not in our own strength and wisdom but his, we can now rededicate ourselves as the people of God to strengthen and advance what so much of the West has now abandoned— the beautiful order of Christian marriage. This has increasingly been my passion as a layperson, Sunday school teacher, and evangelical sociology professor for decades now. It has animated much of my research, reading, thought, and now, this book.

Writing this has been a delight but often quite difficult as well. The amount of research and the challenge of distilling complex realities into clear, succinct, orderly text has certainly accounted for many of my struggles in authoring this, and more than one sleepless night. However, most of my discomfort has come from confronting the gap between the biblical ideals I am often trying to present and my own weaknesses, shortcomings, and failings. It is hard to be an honest parent writing a book on Christian childrearing, and it is equally hard being a reflective but sinful married person writing about godly marriage. Close behind that are the vastness and importance of the subject versus the limitations of any book that seeks to adequately address it.

Thus, I present this book in the hopes that, despite its limitations and mine, it can be of service to Christian individuals and churches in recovering sound marital doctrine and practice. I also offer it with the intention of helping us to see not only the moral and practical truth of Christian marriage, but also its loveliness. With my sincere prayer and expectation that the chapters to follow will bear fruit by the grace of God, I offer this to you.

ACKNOWLEDGMENTS

Writing means spending a lot of time alone, and yet it is not something we can do well on our own. That was certainly true with this manuscript.

First, I am grateful to Jim Weaver for taking a chance on this project and me, providing excellent encouragement, guidance, and suggestions. My wife, Kathy, read every word for a man who was not always the best at accepting critical advice. My old pastor from the Bronx Household of Faith, Reverend Robert Hall, and his wife, Jeannie, reviewed every chapter together and were meticulous in identifying problems but also quick with a needed pat on the back. Likewise, Reverend Nathanael Devlin, associate pastor of Beverly Heights Presbyterian Church in Pittsburgh, went through every chapter carefully and gave me excellent supportive and critical feedback through several long but thoroughly enjoyable lunch meetings. My oldest daughter, Leah, and her husband, Andy Stapleton, a Westminster Seminary graduate and classical Christian school faculty member at Mars Hill Christian Academy in Mason, Ohio, went thoroughly through the early chapters and inspired significant revision and reorientation, until the birth of their son Teddy rerouted their time and attentions to more important things. The team at Lexham Press, including Elliot Ritzema, Jennifer Edwards, Justin Marr, Brannon Ellis, and others, have been consistently professional, insightful, helpful, and encouraging.

The library staff at Grove City College's Buhl Library have been incredibly helpful and unfailingly cheerful in the process. They helped me track down elusive manuscripts and obtained books for me, by purchase or loan, at lightning speed. Special thanks go to Kim Marks, Amy Cavanaugh, Conni Shaw, and Joyce Kebert. I also wish to thank Lee Wishing and The Center for Vision and Values for providing monetary support with transcription services early on.

Earlier in the project, I benefited from encouragement and support from those who gave me key support in getting my proposal accepted. These included my friend and prolific author, Grove City College professor of political science Paul Kengor; Grove City College religion professors and ordained Presbyterian ministers James Bibza, T. David Gordon, and Paul Schaefer; *Pittsburgh Post-Gazette* senior manager of audience and former *Wall Street Journal* writer Thomas O'Boyle; Reformed Presbyterian Theological Seminary (RPTS) president Jerry O'Neill; Westminster Seminary–Philadelphia professor of Old Testament and pastor of Christ Presbyterian Church of Glenside, Pennsylvania, Iain Duguid; and Victor Kuligin, professor and academic dean of the Bible Institute in Cape Town, South Africa.

Finally, I had the privilege of developing materials for this book in the process of teaching two Sunday school classes on Christian marriage. At Covenant Orthodox Presbyterian Church of Grove City, Pennsylvania, the adult class tolerated me dealing with this material, in great depth, for about a year. Their Sunday school superintendent, Grove City College history professor Mark Graham, was good enough to allow me to do this and encouraged me continuously as I did. Meanwhile, the adult class at Beverly Heights Presbyterian put up with me teaching similar material for six weeks. In both cases, questions and insights during the classes and by email helped me a great deal.

INTRODUCTION

A PRICELESS JEWEL IN A PLAIN BROWN WRAPPER

A man shall leave his mother, and a woman leave her home. They shall travel on to where the two shall be as one. As it was in the beginning, is now until the end, woman draws her life from man and gives it back again. And there is love.

Paul Stookey[1]

The human race began as mere earth, as simple dust. Yes, it was good, clean, honest dirt, but still, just common clay. Yet God shaped that soil with his own hands and breathed life into it from his mouth (Gen 2:7). He then made the amazing declaration that, among all the wonderful creations that he had brought forth in that week of all weeks, this creature, made from dust, had the preeminence. Male and female he created them, invested with power, carrying the future in their loins, alone his image bearers in the dazzling splendor and glory of that world (Gen 1:26–27).

Millennia later the apostle Paul, after having already reminded the Corinthians of these humble beginnings of the human race (1 Cor 15:47), went on to tell them that they too were plain "jars of clay" (2 Cor 4:7). You are earthen vessels, he reminded them, perhaps comely in shape, but still dust that will return to dust (see Gen 3:19; Eccl 3:20; 12:7; Ps 103:14). Yet by the grace and wisdom of God, they were now pottery specially loved and filled with magnificent treasure of exquisite beauty and incredible power. They displayed the "light of the gospel of the glory of Christ, who is the image of God . . . [and] the light of the knowledge of the glory of

---

1. "Wedding Song (There Is Love)."

God in the face of Jesus Christ" (2 Cor 4:4, 6), destined to reign with Christ (2 Tim 2:12).

Marriage is like that. In its outward appearance, it is deceptively ordinary and simple. Just a man and a woman joined in lifelong sexual union, serving God together, loving and helping each other, laboring together, through good times and bad, as long as both live. Yet God personally and painstakingly created that structure and essence from the very beginning, so that male and female united that way are necessary for, and a gorgeous adornment over, all of his creation; generating, sustaining, and ordering human society.

Marriages in which God himself is both matchmaker and minister book-end the Bible (Gen 2:18–24; Rev 19:9; 21:2–3). Jesus used a Jewish wedding as the occasion to perform his first miracle (John 2:1–11). The simple vessel of covenant marriage, created before Adam's fall led to our need for redemption, reveals and symbolizes to us the mysteries of the gospel and of Christ's relationship with his covenant people (Eph 5:32). Both Isaiah (54:5–6) and Hosea (2:16–20) described the redemptive relationship of God to his people as like a husband to his wife, pointing forward to Christ. Clearly marriage, especially *Christian* marriage, is a "canvas upon which the Holy Spirit of God paints the gospel."[2] Like a geode—on the outside nothing more than a potato-like stone—inside God has filled marriage with mystery and wonder. Moreover, Scripture tells us that the simple blessings of godly marriage are among the richest gifts we can receive from God, more than money, fame, or power. David describes God's reward for the man who fears the Lord: "Your wife will be like a fruitful vine within your house; your children will be like olive shoots around your table" (Ps 128:3). In one of the most gorgeous passages in Ecclesiastes (9:9), we find this heartfelt recommendation: "Enjoy life with the wife whom you love, all the days of your vain life that he has given you under the sun, because that is your portion in life and in your toil at which you toil under the sun."

Given all that Scripture teaches about God's view of marriage and its centrality in creation, no one should claim to have an exalted view of God who holds marriage—his own or marriage in general—in low esteem. Unfortunately, throughout human history, people, including the chosen people of God, have not treated marriage with the respect, dignity, status,

---

2. Wilson, "Gresham and Emily."

and deference it deserves and that God expects. In the Scriptures, it is true that we can delight in the beautiful love story of Isaac and Rebekah (Gen 24) but that is after witnessing the sordid, alcohol-soaked degradation of Isaac's first cousin, Lot (Gen 19:30–38). Yes, we see Ruth the Moabite redeemed to be wife to the godly man Boaz (Ruth 3:1–4:13) but then we witness the tragedy of their great-grandson David luridly violating his own marital vows while stealing the wife of one of his most loyal warriors. In the Old Testament, the records of failure seem to outnumber those of marital loyalty and love.

Certainly, history records many high and low points in terms of fidelity to God's teachings about marriage. The American church today seems to have mired itself in another "Malachi moment." As in the days of that prophet (2:14–16), our treatment of the covenant of marriage and all it is meant to be and do has dishonored God, harmed and failed his people, and weakened our witness to the non-Christian world. We see epidemic rates of divorce, premarital sex, and out-of-wedlock birth not only in our larger culture, but also in the churches. Domestic violence, sexually transmitted diseases, abortion, adultery, lack of charity, interpersonal alienation, bitter conflict, and pornography addictions are far more common in our marriages than we care to admit or see. We are now even beginning to see professed Bible-believing evangelical laypeople and leaders celebrating and defending men leaving their wives and children in order to pursue a gay lifestyle.[3] How far downstream is that from a major Christian leader like Pat Robertson declaring that it is acceptable for men to divorce their Alzheimer-afflicted wives, provided they ensure their long-term care?[4]

It is obvious to even the casual observer that the knowledge and practice of biblical marital principles are not healthy in our culture or churches. The following chapters will document these sad realities, alongside scriptural teaching and example. I will do so using sound social-scientific research. My purpose in doing so is not to jab fingers in anyone's eyes, thump my chest, or condemn or shame anyone. I have been a human, a husband, and a parent too long to want to risk casting stones. Every one of us, even in our best moments, is a chief of sinners helping our fellow sinners as best as we have the energy and light to do. Rather, my aim is to do honest reflection

---

3. Merritt, "Christian Rock Star Comes Out as Gay."
4. Moisse and Hopper, "Pat Robertson Says Alzheimer's Makes Divorce OK."

leading to sound diagnosis, constructive solutions, and lasting change. Yes, we must sometimes probe unseemly realities and render disturbing diagnoses—but to cure, not to kill.

And yet today and throughout the history of the Christian church there have been inspiring marriages bearing lovely fruit supported by wise and caring friends, families, and churches. Moreover, in every successful marriage there will be failure and repentance. In marriage as in so many other areas, we have in history and today a "cloud of witnesses" (Heb 12:1) to inspire, instruct, encourage, and guide us. So what do we see when we examine what builds sound marriages and churches that faithfully nurture and support them? We inevitably find that most of those successful practices are not new or mysterious. The rudiments of good marriage are ordinary and commonplace.

The constructive practices I discuss in this book have to do with how we form married couples, what we teach them, how we train them, how we prevent disorder and breakdown, how we support them at each step, from courting through marriage and childbearing and aging and death. If there are surprises here, it is because of what we have lost or forgotten, not because I am presenting novel insights.

Building a sound marriage culture also means engaging the effects and aftermath of personal failure and natural calamity—things done by and to folks. Tackling these things also involves parents, churches, kin, friends, communities, schools, and even civic leaders. There are no simple prescriptions, cure-alls, or snake-oil remedies. I address those things too.

However, before considering these practical matters, we must first grasp something that is essential and foundational, namely, *design*. And there are two things we must always grasp to understand the design of anything—what it *is* and what it is intended *to do*. Marriage is no different. Thankfully, God has clearly communicated these things to us in the Bible.

So first, we must know how God has *defined* marriage. What must be present in order for God to call a human relationship "marriage"? Conversely, what are broken, or counterfeit, versions of marriage? How can we spot the fakes and recognize the genuine article?

Second, we need to grasp what God's *purposes* are for marriage. What is it designed to accomplish? If we don't know that, then how can we determine when it is "delivering the goods" and when it is not, or when we are expecting something from marriage that it was never meant to provide? If we don't know what marriage is for, then how can we detect when we, or others, are illegitimately assigning its proper functions to other institutions or entities that were never meant to bear those responsibilities?

This will move us inevitably to the hub that brings into harmonious cooperation all the parts of the wheel: the *one-flesh* reality of marriage. In marriage, the two become one flesh, for the glory of God and the welfare of the human race. In no other human relationship or institution does this happen. Like all things, this one-flesh reality begins at the beginning and appears in the second chapter of Genesis (vv. 18–19a, 20b–24). This is where, as Thomas Adams famously said, "As God by creation made two of one, so again by marriage he made one of two."[5] This uniting of man and woman as one flesh in marriage is affirmed and applied quite clearly by Christ (Matt 19:4–6) and later by the apostle Paul (Eph 5:28–32).

We will have occasion to open up these passages more fully in the first chapter. We will then consider their implications many times in this book, and yet never exhaust the full depth of meaning of marriage as one flesh.

So it makes no sense to get into "how to" and "how not to" if we do not know *what* we are trying to do and *why*, rooted in and resting upon this potent, one-flesh nature of marriage. That is what I will do in the four chapters of the first section of this book. Having done that, I then go on in the rest of the book to the practicalities of sound marriage practice and policy.

In the second section, I look at the "front end" of creating and sustaining sound, happy, and godly marriages. That is, I consider positive spiritual and practical principles for selecting a suitable spouse and preparing for marriage. I look at what churches, individuals, and parents can and should do and aspire to. By necessity, this also involves looking at the rampant premarital confusion and sinful conduct in modern professing churches, and at their causes, consequences, and solutions.

The third section of this book deals with divorce and remarriage. There are sound reasons for placing these difficult topics at this point in the overall flow of the book, which will be clear as we proceed. Here, suffice it to say that much of the motivation for seeking to build strong marriages, and for resolving to do all that we are able to do to sustain them, needs to be

---

5. Adams, *An Exposition Upon the Second Epistle General of St. Peter*, 84.

rooted in a comprehensive understanding of divorce. First, I consider how God himself sees divorce, and why, in his love for his people, he hates it so much. I then consider the complex but important issue of whether there are biblical grounds for divorce and remarriage, and if so, what those are. Second, I honestly assess divorce trends and risks, including the degree to which high divorce rates plague the modern professing church. Third, I look candidly at the destruction that divorce causes, both as a further motivation to avoid it, and as a means to enable the church to help divorced members and their families with intelligence, humility, and compassion.

In the fourth and final section of the book, I take three chapters to move into something much more positive—marital beauty, joy, and fulfillment. These include, first, getting a vision for what godly marriage can and should be, to celebrate and comprehend it as God wants us to do. This should encourage and enrich us and help us become better able to communicate this loveliness and richness to others. Then, I look at practical ways to enhance marital satisfaction and happiness across the lifespan. Throughout, I continually consider Scripture side-by-side with historical examples and modern empirical social science. The Bible, history, and social science are compatible on these matters. Taken together and applied with wisdom and discretion, they help us to succeed more consistently in our quest for blessing God's people with more joyful, fruitful, satisfying, faithful, enduring, godly marriages.

The last chapter pulls together the central discoveries, teaching, and themes of this book into a summary of clear suggestions for churches. These are practical things that your church should consider doing to help couples form excellent marital unions, prepare for married life, strengthen existing marriages, prevent divorce, and minister to those in broken marital situations. Without strong families, there will not be solid churches, and both are rooted in good marriages. In turn, marriages and families need the church.

The relationship between Christian marriage and the Christian church is a reciprocal one, for good or for ill. So why are so few churches truly intentional and strategic about nurturing sound marriages? Why do so few cultivate a healthy marriage culture? This does not have to be the case. We can do a lot better. Indeed, we must. Here is how Pope Francis put it: "When a man and a woman marry in the Lord, they participate in the missionary life of the Church, by living not only for themselves or their own family, but for all people. Therefore the life of the Church is enriched through every marriage which shows forth this beauty, and is impoverished when marriage is disfigured in any way."[6]

For many years, I have had a passionate desire to see godly marriage and family life reclaimed among professing Christians in our culture, for the honor of God and the welfare of his people. Imagine if unbelievers saw that our marriages and families truly reflected the gospel. What could happen if they saw our husbands consistently displaying the sacrificial love of Christ for their wives, who in turn display loving confidence and devotion toward their husbands? I don't think this is unrealistic. Historians frequently note that Christian practice in sexuality and marriage made a deep impression on ancient pagans. Not only their teaching but also their practices in such areas as chastity, lifelong monogamy, and marital devotion clearly distinguished them from others, even for those who rejected their beliefs.[7] This can be true for us.

Unbelievers outside the church find themselves in a rapidly declining culture that is increasingly marked by alienation and confusion with regard to gender identity, relationships, loyalty, and personal trust. They dwell in an ever-darkening relational world where they can have all the sex they want in a multitude of forms, but where it has no more meaning than any other form of entertainment,[8] while true sexual fulfillment eludes them. Their lives prior to marriage have typically involved a series of emotional connections and break-ups over many years. Their parents are often divorced, many of them repeatedly so. We know that this has left many scarred, seeking to protect themselves but often counter-productively and at great interpersonal cost.

Our marriages can and should, in humility and integrity, speak to the lost souls of our age about something far better. Our marriages should point them to something that is both earthly good and spiritually ennobling, to something that is bound to this life and yet points well beyond it to realities that have eternal weight and consequence. It is my prayer that in some small measure this book will help Christians and the church realize this dream.

---

6. Pope Francis, "General Audience on Christian Marriage."

7. See, for example, Troeltsch, *The Social Teaching of the Christian Churches*, 1:81, 129–31.

8. See remarks by sociologist Christian Smith in an interview on PBS's *Religion and Ethics Newsweekly*, "Hooking Up."

PART 1

GOD'S BOUNDARIES AND PURPOSES FOR MARRIAGE

INTRODUCTION TO PART 1

*Now it must be, that marriage, which was ordained of such an
excellent author, and in such a happy place, and of such an ancient
time, and after such a notable order, must likewise have special causes
for the ordinance of it.*

Henry Smith[1]

There is a veritable cottage industry of books and articles on subjects
such as finding the perfect spouse, preparing for marriage, and maintaining healthy lifelong conjugal partnerships. Many of these are intentionally Christian, and a lot of them are excellent. However, these often lack
any explicit grounding in not only what marriage *is* (as we have discussed),
but also what it is *for*. This is a bit like telling folks how to build the perfect
building without first establishing what this edifice is supposed to *do*. Do
we want an ideal warehouse, garage, single-family home, or office building?
The intended function has to be clear before any practical undertakings
begin.

God has set forth for us in the Scriptures what marriage is and what it
is not. We may not define it in any way we wish, nor is it just a relationship rooted in individual aspirations, will, emotional connection, or erotic
attraction. God has given it a definite shape, structure, and boundaries.
Arrangements that do not meet its requirements will not deliver the same
positive goods individually or socially. Yet as with complex doctrines like
the Trinity, the Bible does not give us all of its particulars in one place.
Because of human sin and God's accommodations to it, our full understanding of it has developed over time, though by the end of the Reformation

---

1. "A Preparative to Marriage," 12.

period, the church certainly had a solid and detailed understanding of what constitutes a true and valid marriage. These are principles that are timeless but allow for reasonable variations in practice for diverse cultures and legal orders and in different historical periods. In chapter 1, we will explore the definition of marriage, what it is and is not, in depth.

Like other social institutions, the constellation of *purposes* God designed marriage to fulfill is unique. What does he want us to achieve in and through our marital unions? If we cannot answer that, then how do we know a particular person would be the right partner for us? How can we be sure that a particular approach to courtship, marital preparation, and married life will help us to realize "better" marriages in a truly *Christian*, God-centered way?

When God called into existence the various elements of his world, he repeatedly remarked that what he had made was "good" (Gen 1:10, 18, 21, 25). After the creation of man and woman, we find the praise increased a notch: "And God saw everything that he had made, and behold, it was *very good*" (Gen 1:31, emphasis added). This goodness meant that each part of his creation was not only lovely but also suited to achieving his particular purposes for it. To God, what is "good" satisfies his perfect and holy aims. So if we want to find the "right" partner and have an "excellent" marriage, then we need to seek what best enables us—as individuals with particular gifts, callings, weaknesses, strengths, proclivities—to fulfill his purposes through our marriage. Doing so will protect, bless, and fulfill us.

The Book of Common Prayer summarizes God's *three basic purposes* for marriage in a manner that is both earthy and elegant:

> Dearly beloved, we are gathered together here in the sight of God, and in the face of this Congregation, to join together this man and this woman in holy Matrimony; which . . . is not by any to be enterprised, nor taken in hand, lightly, or wantonly, to satisfy men's carnal lusts and appetites, like brute beasts that have no understanding; but reverently, discreetly, advisedly, soberly, and in the fear of God; *duly considering the causes for which matrimony was ordained.*
>
> First, It was ordained for the *procreation of children*, to be brought up in the fear and nurture of the Lord, and to the praise of his holy Name.
>
> Secondly, It was ordained for *a remedy against sin, and to avoid fornication; that such persons as have not the gift of continence*

might marry, and keep themselves undefiled members of Christ's body.

Thirdly, It was ordained for the *mutual society, help, and comfort that the one ought to have of the other*, both in prosperity and adversity.[2]

The *Westminster Confession of Faith* agrees with these three purposes, stating them in a more succinct, if less lyrical, manner: "Marriage was ordained for the *mutual help* of husband and wife, for the *increase of mankind* with a legitimate issue, and of the church with an holy seed; and for *preventing of uncleanness*."[3] Leland Ryken notes that this "threefold purpose" represented the "unified Protestant tradition."[4] John Calvin clearly agreed.[5] It is interesting to note that the famous Finnish anthropologist and moral philosopher Edward Westermarck identifies these as "essential elements" of marriage across human cultures,[6] a demonstration of God's common grace.

What particularly meets these purposes is going to vary across individuals, subcultures, cultures, and historical periods. A modern American Baptist man who is just starting medical school will do so in very different ways than a Dutch Reformed farmer's daughter in 1634 hoping to marry someone but also needing to care for her elderly parents and her disabled younger brother. The marital choices of a newly converted Cantonese merchant man in 1841 will look quite different from either. All of these can and should have marriages that fulfill these same three basic purposes, but the types of persons they should marry to do so, and the way they will "do" marriage once they have united, are going to be quite diverse.

There are a couple of variations among Christians on this list of purposes for marriage. One is a slight Protestant modification advanced by some. The other is the Roman Catholic view.

Some Protestant theologians such as A. A. Hodge see *four* purposes, as implied by the exact wording of the *Westminster Confession of Faith*. He divides procreation into two purposes—populating the earth and blessing the church with children raised to do God's work.[7]

---

2. *The Book of Common Prayer*, 311–12 (emphasis added).

3. *Westminster Confession of Faith*, 80 (emphasis added).

4. Ryken, *Worldly Saints*, 47. A good example of a common restatement and justification of this three-purpose view is in Henry Smith's "A Preparative to Marriage," 12–14.

5. Witte, "Marriage and Family Life," 461.

6. "The Future of Marriage in Western Civilization," 26, 33.

7. Hodge, *The Westminster Confession*, 303.

It is good to highlight the special role that married Christian parents play by increasing and enriching the church with godly children. This benefits society as a whole. We are too inclined to think of the growth of the church primarily in terms of evangelism (as important as that is), and too many believers neglect their families in order to pursue "lost souls."

However, this latter purpose does not apply to marriage *generally*. All marriages can fulfill the first three purposes for marriage, and not just those between believers. Two unbelievers can provide mutual help and comfort to one another through all the joys and trials of life, find within marriage a morally permissible means of sexual fulfillment, and provide society with legitimate children, raising them well enough to contribute to good order in human society. So I would rather see the provision of legitimate offspring, for humankind as a whole and for the church, as two prongs of a single purpose.

Second, the Roman Catholic Church continues to teach that sex is only legitimated by at least the possibility of procreation, rather than its lawful fulfillment being a distinct, godly reason for marriage in itself. Thus, officially Catholics are given only two basic purposes for marriage: legitimate offspring (with sex designed to draw men and women together in marriage to have children), and the mutual help of husband and wife. Here is how the *Catechism of the Catholic Church* frames this "two-purpose" view: "The matrimonial covenant . . . is by its nature ordered toward the *good of the spouse* and the *procreation and education of offspring*."[8] A Catholic informational leaflet is even more explicit, stating that God made marriage for "two purposes," namely, "bringing children into the world and rearing them" and "the mutual help of the husband and wife."[9]

Like other Protestants, I believe that sexual fulfillment within marriage is a distinct good that does not need to be justified by the possibility of procreation.[10] Thus I am content with the three basic purposes for marriage outlined above.

In chapter 2, I will focus on *mutual help*. Then in chapters 3 and 4, respectively, I will tackle legitimate sexual fulfillment and procreation.

---

8. *Catechism of the Catholic Church*, 2nd ed., 400 (emphasis added).

9. Vaillancourt, "God Made Marriage."

10. Ryken, *Worldly Saints*, 40–42.

CHAPTER 1

WHAT IS "MARRIAGE"?

There is no such fountain on earth as marriage.

Thomas Adams[1]

The Christian religion, by confining marriage to pairs, and rendering the relation indissoluble, has by these two things done more toward the peace, happiness, settlement, and civilization of the world, than by any other part in this whole scheme of divine wisdom.

Edmund Burke[2]

In graduate school, I had a professor who used to say something like this: "Defining your terms well is about half of any research project." That really stuck with me. If you try to talk about something but you cannot clearly define it, you literally "don't know what you're talking about"! You cannot measure or describe its condition—is it increasing or decreasing, remaining static or changing, declining or improving? Deciding what particular cases fit the term you are using becomes difficult, if not impossible. How do you know if you cannot say for sure what it *is*? Imagine a biologist who cannot accurately differentiate wolves from, say, dogs or coyotes, reporting that wolf populations are getting larger.

Sadly, when it comes to marriage, it appears there is a lot of conceptual confusion, and it is getting worse. Christians who claim to accept the authority of Scripture are not immune from our culture's muddled definitions of marriage. The Bible actually says a great deal about what marriage

---

1. Quoted in Ryken, *Worldly Saints*, 43.
2. Burke, *The Works of the Right Hon. Edmund Burke*, vol. 2, 297. From a letter that was originally written in 1796.

is and is not, and it usually does so clearly, but increasingly Christians do not comprehend or accept it. For example, an April 2016 survey found that over four in ten self-identified practicing Christians agreed that premarital cohabitation is a "good idea."[3] People who adequately grasp God's claims about the essence of marriage would not say that.

To cite another illustration of this deterioration, consider the case of Rosaria Butterfield. She had been a lesbian activist and tenured Syracuse University English faculty member, then converted to evangelical Christianity, and is now a pastor's wife and homeschooling mother who frequently speaks on both secular and Christian college campuses. Butterfield reports that, surprisingly, some of her toughest experiences are at Christian colleges. Many students, faculty, and staff at these institutions defend homosexuality and gay marriage, even considering them legitimate options for born-again Christians, while professing themselves to be faithful to Christ.[4] The most elemental biblical teachings on what marriage is and is not appear to be up for grabs in many evangelical churches and institutions.

Without a doubt, biblical, doctrinal, hermeneutical, and confessional illiteracy are partly to blame for this uncertainty and misunderstanding among professing Christians. Most of this lack of clarity about God's definition of marriage, for Christians as well as for our culture as a whole, is our increasing discomfort with *exclusion*. We are enamored of the concepts of inclusion, tolerance, and diversity, however vague and contradictory our understanding of them. All useful definitions must exclude. They all set boundaries. A clear definition of marriage means that some people's actual or desired relationship can never be included in it, regardless of what they want or believe. We are not comfortable holding the line in cases like this, as many believe doing so is mean or cruel, and others are unwilling to handle the enormous pressures being brought against those who do so.

Fidelity to both love and truth requires that we say no to those who want to be considered legitimately married but can never be so in the eyes of God. This is the truly compassionate stance. Caving in to demands to continually expand our definition of marriage damages those we are trying to

---

3. Barna Group, "Majority of Americans Now Believe In Cohabitation." This was based on 1,097 respondents. "Practicing Christians" are those who self-identify as believers and attend religious services at least once per month.

4. Olasky, "Rosaria Butterfield: No Free Passes."

help, and it will ultimately erase marriage as a meaningful social entity. By doing so, we will deprive individuals and society of marriage's enormous benefits. But in a world that increasingly believes that love requires us to affirm rather than challenge lifestyles that almost everyone used to see as aberrant, maintaining these restrictions is not easy.

Embracing same-sex marriage is the most obvious example of this desire to be inclusive at the expense of holding to clear, sensible, ancient definitional boundaries. More is coming. As we shall see, pressure is increasing to "let in" incest and polyamory.[5] Having already retreated in major ways from the firm boundaries of a sound definition of marriage, how long will we say no to these other petitioners? Like ancient Jerusalem in Jeremiah's day, the walls have been broken down and it is only a matter of time.

I contemplate all this with profound grief because marriage is beautiful, necessary, and woven into the very fabric of creation by God for our good and his glory. He has given it a definite structure and form that is practical, lovely, and communicates deep truth. Biblical, natural marriage is at the center of God's nature as well as his wise plans for, and compassionate care of, the human race. The counterfeits will never know the loveliness and wholeness of marriage according to God's design and will, in fact, replace God's good and wonderful gift with things that are a mockery of it—ugly, out of joint, and destructive. Because they are fantasies, not reality, they will fail. Yet if we who belong to Christ understand and embrace marriage as he has made it and distinguished it from other human relationships, and if we will faithfully proclaim, honor, and live the truth of that out in our homes, communities, and churches in the coming years, he will shine all the brighter in the years ahead.

Cultural consensus, legal rules and categories, even the proclamations and rituals of churches and denominations about what marriage is are malleable and cannot be trusted. They change with fashion, public opinion, and political pressure. In sharp contrast, God's definition of marriage is fixed, and has been so from the garden itself. It is a firm foundation. So what is it?

---

5. That is, people having more than one partner at one time, with mutual consent, regardless of sex or gender identity. This is different in some ways from the older "polygamy," as it lacks the same kind of structure, cultural functions, and history, and may involve transgendered, homosexual, and bisexual partners in the mix.

GOD'S DEFINITION OF MARRIAGE:
FOUNDATIONS

ONE-FLESH PASSAGES

In the introduction, I pointed out that the root of our understanding of marriage is that, in it, the husband and wife become one flesh. This is creational, and God created marriage before Adam and Eve sinned. Since God started there, let's also do so, beginning with Genesis 2:18-19a, 20b-24:

> Then the LORD God said, "It is not good that the man should be alone; I will make him a helper fit for him." Now out of the ground the LORD God had formed every beast of the field and every bird of the heavens . . . But for Adam there was not found a helper fit for him. So the LORD God caused a deep sleep to fall upon the man, and while he slept took one of his ribs and closed up its place with flesh. And the rib that the LORD God had taken from the man he made into a woman and brought her to the man. Then the man said,
>
> > "This at last is *bone of my bones*
> > *and flesh of my flesh;*
> > she shall be called Woman,
> > because she was taken out of Man."
>
> Therefore a man shall leave his father and his mother and hold fast to his wife, and they shall become *one flesh*. (emphasis added)

Notice how God, in his infinite wisdom, chose to create Eve. He did not do so directly from the dust as he had the man, but instead made her from Adam's rib. The intricacy of what God did here is magnificent. He wrote into this, as we have already mentioned, the gospel itself. In verses 23 and 24, we see the first vow of marriage as Adam makes himself accountable to God to treat Eve as his own flesh, and the Lord witnesses and seals their entry into his marital covenant.[6] Every small detail here is pregnant with meaning, message, and deep spiritual reality.

---

6. Heth, "Remarriage for Adultery or Desertion," 61.

Jesus later refers to man and wife as one flesh, referring back to this precise creation account. He did so in responding to a "gotcha" question from the Pharisees about divorce: "Have you not read that he who created them at the beginning made them male and female, and said, 'Therefore a man shall leave his father and his mother and hold fast to his wife, and the two shall become *one flesh*'? So they are no longer two but *one flesh*. What therefore God has joined together, let not man separate" (Matt 19:4-6, emphasis added).

Moving on from there, the apostle Paul describes the relationship of the believer to Christ as of the same "one flesh" nature. God has symbolized and embedded this reality in marriage between man and woman. Just as Jesus applied "one flesh" to explain why men should not divorce their wives except for the gravest possible causes, Paul used this to help his readers understand how husbands should love, and never mistreat, their wives:

> In the same way husbands should love their wives as their own bodies. He who loves his wife loves himself. For no one ever *hated his own flesh,* but nourishes and cherishes it, just as Christ does the church, because we are *members of his body.* "Therefore a man shall leave his father and mother and hold fast to his wife, and the two shall become *one flesh.*" This mystery is profound, and I am saying that it refers to Christ and the church. (Eph 5:28-32, emphasis added)

Centuries later, Matthew Henry echoed Paul's application of the Genesis account: "The woman was made of a rib out of the side of Adam; not made out of his head to rule over him, nor out of his feet to be trampled upon by him, but out of his side to be equal with him, under his arm to be protected, and near his heart to be beloved."[7]

BOOK OF COMMON PRAYER

Two incredible Protestant sources are faithful to these foundational scriptural teachings and expand upon them with further biblical insights. First, let's look at the traditional wedding vows in the classic Anglican Book of

---

7. Henry, *Commentary on the Whole Bible,* 16.

Common Prayer.[8] I have inserted the names Richard and Beatrice for the bride and groom, in order to ease the flow.

"I Richard take thee Beatrice to my wedded wife, to have and to hold from this day forward, for better for worse, for richer for poorer, in sickness and in health, to love and to cherish, till death us do part, according to God's holy ordinance; and thereto I plight thee my troth."[9]

"I Beatrice take thee Richard to my wedded husband, to have and to hold from this day forward, for better for worse, for richer for poorer, in sickness and in health, to love, cherish, and to obey, till death us do part, according to God's holy ordinance; and thereto I plight thee my troth."

Following this, the groom places a ring on the bride's finger and says, "With this ring I thee wed, with my body I thee worship, and with all my worldly goods I thee endow. In the name of the Father, and of the Son, and of the Holy Ghost, Amen."

After praying, the minister declares the couple to be man and wife. "Forasmuch as Richard and Beatrice have consented together in holy wedlock, and have witnessed the same before God and this company, and thereto have given and pledged their troth to each other, and have declared the same by giving and receiving of a ring, and by joining of hands; I pronounce that they be man and wife together, In the name of the Father, and of the Son, and of the Holy Ghost. Amen."

WESTMINSTER CONFESSION OF FAITH

Chapter 24 of the *Westminster Confession of Faith* is entitled "Of Marriage and Divorce." Here I will cite just those portions that focus specifically on the definition of marriage.

> 1. Marriage is to be between one man and one woman: neither is it lawful for any man to have more than one wife, nor for any woman to have more than one husband, at the same time. . . . 3. It is lawful for all sorts of people to marry, who are able with judgment to give their consent. . . . 4. Marriage ought not to be within the degrees of consanguinity or affinity forbidden by the Word.

---

8. Book of Common Prayer, 313–14.

9. "Plight thee my troth" means making a serious and solemn oath ("plight") to be faithful ("troth").

Nor can such an incestuous marriage ever be made by any law of man or consent of parties, so as those persons may live together as man and wife.[10]

APPLYING AND UNDERSTANDING
GOD'S DEFINITION OF MARRIAGE

Now let us consider some essential points we can draw from these passages from the Bible, the Anglican Book of Common Prayer, and the *Westminster Confession of Faith*.

ORDAINED AND ORDERED BY GOD

As A. A. Hodge pointed out in his 1869 commentary, marriage is "ordained of God and thus a divine institution."[11] In fact, God himself conducted the first marriage. Humans did not invent marriage, nor did it emerge slowly from a time in which human societies did not have marriage, as so many social scientists contend. God created marriage, and it has been present from the very beginnings of the human race. Society did not create it, but rather flowed from and rested upon it. The health of society reflects the state of marriage, and always will.

With this, as the Anglican matrimonial ceremony puts it, marriage was "instituted of God in the time of man's innocency."[12] Unlike other institutions, such as political government, it was not added later to restrain sin. Controlling or discouraging evil is now a core function of marriage but not integral to its original design.

This creational understanding of marriage means that God has ordered it: "The law of marriage, the conditions of its contract, continuance and dissolution, are laid down in the Word of God."[13] No matter what innovations the cultures and governments in which we live create and demand we accept, we must be faithful to God's ordinances, individually and in the church. God did not ordain marriage and then leave it up to humans to define it in any way they choose.

---

10. *Westminster Confession of Faith*, 80–81. Sections cited here are essentially as they were originally written in the Westminster Assembly in 1643–1647.

11. Hodge, *The Westminster Confession*, 302.

12. Book of Common Prayer, 311.

13. Hodge, *The Westminster Confession*, 302.

This ordered understanding of marriage, often called "institutional," stands in sharp contrast to the post-Christian idea that marriage is primarily about psychological gratification, personal fulfillment, self-realization, spontaneity, and positive feelings. The classic Christian understanding of marriage centers upon God and others, while modern people focus more on the self. In the classic *Habits of the Heart*, Robert Bellah and his co-authors identify the latter as a "therapeutic" orientation to marriage. They point out that it exists in tension with the older view that marriage is an institution with structured roles and obligations that we cannot change by whim, and that often involve the denial of self. Americans have mixed feelings, wanting the freedom of one but the security and the stability of the other.[14] Clearly, in our culture and the modern church, therapeutic marriage is winning.[15]

MARRIAGE IS A CONTRACT AND A COVENANT

Hodge states that marriage is a "contract."[16] The anthropologist William Stephens regarded this as a near-universal condition for marriage among human cultures, noting correctly that this "contract" can be implicit or formal and explicit, always spells out the rights and duties that each partner has in relation to the other, and that each has toward any of their offspring.[17]

However, I strongly prefer identifying marriage as a solemn "covenant," a contract but something much more than that. In modern America, the word "contract" has come to have a sterile, limited meaning, denoting terms, conditions, rewards, and penalties decided upon by the parties forging it and enforced by the State. We then have millions of individual marriages bound to various extents by many different, specific contracts beyond the increasingly limited stipulations required by each state's laws. That is not what the Scriptures teach. Marriage is a covenant created by God with boundaries, structure, obligations, and rights established by him. This is true for all married people, whether they accept it or not. A bride

---

14. Bellah et al., *Habits of the Heart*, 85–112.

15. Almost twenty years before the latter classic, Philip Rieff heralded this revolution in his famous book, aptly titled *The Triumph of the Therapeutic*. See especially 232–61.

16. Hodge, *The Westminster Confession*, 302.

17. Stephens, *The Family in Cross-Cultural Perspective*, 5–7.

and groom enter into his covenant, and he witnesses, seals, enforces, and sustains it.[18]

MARRIAGE IS BOTH RELIGIOUS AND CIVIL

Moving forward from this discussion of marriage as both contract and covenant—marriage is both religious and civil. People make solemn religious vows, essentially *covenanting* before God as the Great Witness and Judge. Malachi (2:14) warned Jewish men, "The LORD was witness between you and the wife of your youth . . . though she is . . . your wife by covenant." God's active part in these vows includes the uniting of man and wife as one flesh. That prophet goes on to point out (2:15), "Did he not make them one?" However, civil society must also recognize and enforce marital *contracts*. In Western civilization, for centuries, this has meant complying with formal state requirements.

Regarding civil marriage, as Hodge correctly pointed out, the state should respect and protect marriage according to God's order.[19] This need not involve the creation of a theocracy. Marriage according to a particular design is part of God's common-grace care for the human race. Believers should want to see their non-religious fellow citizens marry, even outside the church, in a manner consistent with the created order. To advance public welfare, the state should uphold natural marriage and the obligations and rights generated by it. For example, there should be laws pertaining to the care of children produced in marriage, the ownership and disposition of property for married people, the conditions under which spouses may or may not testify against one another in court, inheritance, power of attorney, and a lot more.

For Christians who think that the civil aspects of marriage detract from its sacredness, Edmund Morgan's marvelous social history *The Puritan Family* can be instructive. Morgan pointed out that, before 1686, civil magistrates, not ministers, performed all marriages among the New England

---

18. This traditional understanding of marriage as a covenant witnessed by God, as presented in Malachi and tied back to Genesis 2–3, is ably defended in a detailed exegetical work by Hugenberger, *Marriage as a Covenant*. For example, see his opening statement on page 168. This approach was also absolutely central to John Calvin's theology of marriage, as detailed by Witte, "Marriage and Family," 456–59, and in Calvin's sermon on Deuteronomy 5:18, see *Sermons on the Ten Commandments*, 169–70.

19. Hodge, *The Westminster Confession*, 302.

Puritans. They only began allowing ministers to perform marriages after 1686 because the crown of England forced them to do so. Even then, when they moved wedding ceremonies into their churches they made few changes in ritual. Interestingly, it was at engagement, not marriage, ceremonies that Puritan preachers officiated and gave their nuptial sermons, while the wedding itself was very simple.[20] Their concept that marriage was "both a public and ecclesial affair" was also widely held by the Continental Reformers, such as Luther and Calvin.[21] Yet few if any historians would deny that the Puritans and Continental Reformers held marriage to be extraordinarily sacred.[22]

On the other hand, the relationship between the civil and religious aspects of marriage can become problematic when states violate God's order in significant ways. Here, as Hodge points out, "Christians must obey God rather than men."[23] States may forbid marriages that God allows, permit marriages that God forbids, or even penalize legal marriages so much that couples are better off without a state marriage license.[24] Indeed, modern states are increasingly defining legal marriage in ways that are clearly contrary to God's design, demanding to some degree that the public comply with these redefinitions. Christians are already facing serious challenges as private citizens, business owners, or employees. Soon this may directly affect explicitly religious entities, such as churches and religious schools. For example, many fine legal minds on both sides of the now-famous June 2015 *Obergefell* decision declaring same-sex marriage to be a constitutional right believe that the tax-exempt status of religious institutions that refuse to support or recognize same-sex marriages might be revoked.[25]

Given these trends, it may become impossible for churches to issue marriage licenses while remaining biblically faithful. In such cases, couples may decide to have civil ceremonies to obtain their licenses, then wedding ceremonies before their churches separately. This may not be ideal, but for orthodox believers, it is certainly preferable to having a wedding ceremony officiated by an ordained minister who is comfortable with same-sex marriage.

---

20. Morgan, *The Puritan Family*, 31–32.

21. Browning, *Marriage and Modernization*, 22–23.

22. Ibid.; see also Ryken, *Worldly Saints*, 42–43.

23. Hodge, *The Westminster Confession*, 302.

24. Newheiser, *Marriage, Divorce, and Remarriage*, 19–20, 22–23.

25. Bailey, "Here Are the Key Excerpts On Religious Liberty From the Supreme Court's Decision On Gay Marriage."

Churches may choose to allow couples to give their public vows and become married without the involvement of the state at all, except in enforcing whatever contracts they choose to make with each other within the scope of God's marital covenant. This does not dispense the civil or public aspect of the marriage at all, but rather, the state license. There is certainly no scriptural requirement to obtain a marriage license. Living together without one is rarely illegal, and there are civil provisions for contracts between domestic partners. Common-law marriages, which recognize couples as wedded provided they dwell together for a given period of time and present themselves as man and wife, are also recognized in many jurisdictions. There are already situations in which churches perform marriage ceremonies without state licensure, though they are rare. However, a couple should only decide to forego a marriage license after securing solid pastoral and legal counsel, and after carefully examining their motives.[26] Even in this age of same-sex marriage, I still encourage those getting married to obtain a state license if possible.

MARRIAGE IS BOTH PRIVATE AND PUBLIC

Marriage involves communal obligations and is not just an arrangement to serve private needs and ends.[27] Therefore, whether or not a wedding is simple or elaborate, or religious or secular, some public witness of the marital vows is required.[28] As Stephens points out, this requirement is almost a cultural universal.[29]

MARRIAGE REQUIRES MUTUAL CONSENT

As the Anglican service provides[30] and the *Westminster Confession of Faith* states, true marriage requires what we would call today "informed consent." It cannot be the result of force, fraud, trickery, or deceit. Neither partner can withhold from the other anything that would have, had it been known,

---

26. Cf. the excellent pastoral discussion of these issues related to churches conducting marriages outside legal licensing in Newheiser, *Marriage, Divorce, and Remarriage*, chapter 3.

27. Browning, *Marriage and Modernization*, 23.

28. There is, of course, the "two lovers on a desert island" scenario, wanting to marry but having no public to swear before. Yes, they can be married, assuming they will make their vows public at the first opportunity. See Newheiser, *Marriage, Divorce, and Remarriage*, 22.

29. Stephens, *The Family in Cross-Cultural Perspective*, 6, 11.

30. Ibid., 314.

led that partner to withdraw his or her consent. Angry fathers cannot force people to marry at the point of shotguns, as we find in old jokes and stories. Such marriages are not legally valid.[31] In fact, they are criminal in the true sense of the word, as they deprive someone of their freedom, for life, under conditions of fraud or force.

For centuries, Christians have recognized consent as necessary for marriage.[32] They did not base this in a scriptural proof text. Rather, they looked honestly at what marriage is and what its purposes are and saw that fulfilling God's design for marriage meant entering it freely and fully informed. Under normal circumstances, parents and others should be helpfully involved in the mate selection process, but they should never overrule the lawful preferences of adults who are getting married.

MARRIAGE IS FOR ALL TYPES OF PEOPLE

According to the *Westminster Confession of Faith*, "all sorts of people" can enter into the bonds of marriage.[33] Although prescriptively, Christians should only marry fellow believers (Deut 7:3-4; 1 Cor 7:39; 2 Cor 6:14-15), marriage is a gracious provision from God for all of humankind. Any marriage that fits the structure that God has laid out is a valid marriage, with all the potential protections and blessings tied to it. God unites both believers and unbelievers into one flesh when they enter a true marital covenant. This is true when one marries the other. The Bible also teaches that marriages between Christians and non-Christians experience many of the blessings of being part of God's family through the believing spouse (1 Cor 7:12-14). What Hodge says about how to view "unequal yoking" is concise and valuable: "True believers should not intermarry with the ungodly," but "marriages . . . between the converted and the unconverted are unquestionably valid, and to be respected as such."[34] We should support such couples in every way while praying that unconverted spouses embrace the gospel, and that believing spouses will be active members in strong churches, grow in Christ, and do their best to bring up their children in the faith.

---

31. FindLaw, "Marriage Requirements Basics."

32. Browning, *Marriage and Modernization*, 83. Everitt, "Ten Key Moments in the History of Marriage."

33. *Westminster Confession of Faith*, 80.

34. Hodge, *The Westminster Confession*, 305.

Meanwhile, Christians can often learn from non-Christians who have great marriages. In fact, we should praise God for providing those examples to us and learn from them.

MARRIAGE IS HETEROSEXUAL AND MONOGAMOUS

Marriage is to be between "one man and one woman."[35] Up until quite recently, in the church and legal-political spheres, the emphasis here was to reject plural marriage, or polygamy. The *Westminster Confession of Faith* states this clearly, as we have seen. To be sure, Hebrew patriarchs such as Abraham and Jacob practiced polygyny, consistent with the cultures among whom they lived. The Mosaic law permitted a man to have more than one wife at the same time; though God provided protections to limit abuse, there were many negative consequences of allowing this practice, and the Bible never mentions it positively. By the time Christ was born this had fallen into general disuse and was rare among the Jews.[36] With Jesus' direct admonitions about the exclusivity of the marriage relation, the Christian church readily embraced monogamy.[37]

Modern readers more immediately apply this "one man and one woman" stipulation to the issue of same-sex marriage, which has been enshrined by the Supreme Court as a constitutional right in the United States, and either performed or recognized in over twenty other nations. Those who wrote the *Westminster Confession of Faith,* and many others who have asserted the Christian teaching of male/female monogamy for many centuries, did not write on this much—the notion of same-sex marriage being unthinkable. The Puritans being thorough, divines like William Gouge did briefly mention the possibility of someone choosing a same-sex marriage partner only to categorically reject it before moving on to what he saw as more realistic errors.[38] In fact, even thirty years ago, most people considered same-sex marriage to be grossly immoral and outrageous.

---

35. *Westminster Confession of Faith,* 80.

36. Cf. the brief but comprehensive summary in Newheiser, *Marriage, Divorce, and Remarriage,* 25–26.

37. Nicely summarized by Hodge in *The Westminster Confession,* 303.

38. In *Of Domesticall Duties,* he was explicit that "the male must choose a female, the female a male" (185). As he went on to note, marrying someone of the same sex violated every basic purpose and design God had for marriage, not to mention specific prohibitions on homosexual relations, basically summarizing objections that orthodox believers still have to gay marriage.

In the eyes of God, a union between two biological males or females can never be true marriage in any sense. This is clear from the moment he created Eve from Adam and conducted the first wedding. Besides the clear condemnation of homosexuality in both testaments (cf. Lev 18:22; 20:13; Rom 1:26–27; 1 Cor 6:9), and the total absence of any positive mention of it, there are no places anywhere in Scripture where marriage, monogamous or polygamous, is described except in terms of being between a male and a female. In fact, the restriction of marriage to male and female and the requirement of monogamy go together. This is evident in the Genesis account, which Jesus strongly affirmed. As Kevin DeYoung pointed out, "it's because the two—male and female—are divinely designed complements each for the other that monogamy makes sense and same-sex marriage does not."[39]

I will cover another biblical aspect of marriage that renders it logically impossible for any same-sex union to be true marriage according to God's design later in this chapter. Still, the Bible also directly states and assumes that marriage is between man and woman.

Same-sex marriage threatens godly monogamy in another way. Logically, if the former is a constitutional right, it becomes harder to maintain the current restriction of marriage to two partners, as Chief Justice Roberts pointed out in his dissent to the June 2015 *Obergefell* decision. We are already seeing the pressure building just as he predicted.[40] It gets worse. If our society eventually grants plural marriage the same legal status as same-sex marriage and on roughly the same logical and legal grounds, it will be different from any form of polygamy accepted by other cultures historically. The combination of the two "rights" will mean that virtually any combination of biological sex, gender identity, and sexual orientation among the partners to such a plural union will be possible. This is not far-fetched, as news stories about homosexual "throuples" (three-way marriages) have already appeared, including a lesbian throuple in Massachusetts that had a child together.[41] No, these "marriages" have not received civil recognition . . . yet.

---

39. DeYoung, *What Does the Bible Teach About Homosexuality?*, 31. See also the fine, concise discussion in Cherlin, *Marriage, Divorce, Remarriage*, 30–35.

40. DeBoer, "It's Time to Legalize Polygamy."

41. Haque, "Meet the World's First Gay Married Throuple"; Li, "Married Lesbian 'Throuple' Expecting First Child."

Biblical Christians will differ in how to respond to state recognition of same-sex unions as marriage, including to state pressures on those who have religious objections to them, as we have already discussed. There will be agonizing issues, not the least of which will be our concern not to reject or alienate children raised by homosexual parents, and our desire to engage homosexual people in loving ways. Some will be our own children. It will not be easy, but we must never affirm that same-sex marriage is legitimate before God. To do so is to reject something that God placed at the center of created order, and ultimately, to do a grave disservice to homosexual people, their families, and larger society.

MARRIAGE CANNOT BE BETWEEN CLOSE FAMILY RELATIONS

As an avid amateur genealogist, I discovered some time ago that one of my sets of second great-grandparents were brother and sister! I was shocked. After quite a bit of digging I was able to determine what had happened. Their widowed parents had married when they and their respective children were older. My second great-grandparents were not blood relatives and did not even grow up together. Old Testament law clearly forbade their marriage, but these German Catholic peasants did it anyway. Other digging into my ancestral past uncovered some first-cousin marriages as well. As we find in Jane Austen novels, people have not always considered these problematic, nor did God forbid Old Testament believers from marrying cousins.[42]

The church has generally insisted on restrictions based on bloodline and even in-law relationships, rooted in key passages such as Leviticus 18:6–18 and 20:11-12, 14, 17; Deuteronomy 22:30; 27:20, 22–23; and 1 Corinthians 5:1-5. Western countries have encoded many of these in their laws.

Hodge points out that if the Old Testament law is no longer binding, then we may turn to the law of nature, which generally agrees with it. Most Christian denominations have accepted these restrictions as still binding, but with some variation of specific rules and enforcement. The main reason, besides Paul's application of part of this in Corinth (1 Cor 5:1-5), is that these laws reflect permanent aspects of human relationships rather than matters specific to ancient Israel.[43] The laws of most American states

---

42. In modern times, people have based their objections more on genetics than on religion.
43. Hodge, *The Westminster Confession*, 306–7.

reflect these restrictions, as well as forbidding first-cousin marriage. My firm belief is that these Old Testament restrictions are still valid and that they are part of God's design for marriage, such that no incestuous marriage can be truly legitimate, whether or not the law allows it.

Will incest restrictions hold up in our new world of autonomous marital choice? Some legal professionals have wondered if establishing a "right" to same-sex marriage would logically extend not only to polygamy, but to incest as well. This is not far-fetched. Supreme Court Justice Sonia Sotomayor raised the question seriously to the lead attorney petitioning to overturn California's former ban on gay marriage,[44] and a Boston College Law School professor has indicated approvingly that he believes that legalizing gay marriage will ultimately lead to the same for incestuous ones.[45] We are seeing a tiny but growing movement to normalize incest using the same arguments used to legalize same-sex marriage. Activists are introducing terms like "Genetic Sexual Attraction" (GSA)[46] and "consanguinamory."[47] It is usually not a good thing when people replace moral terms for sinful activity with scientific-sounding, morally neutral jargon, especially when activists tie them to pro-normalization movements.[48] On the other hand, almost all Western nations consider incest a criminal offense. It appears unlikely that society will mainstream consensual incest any time soon, but long term this is certainly possible.

MARRIAGE IS FOR LIFE

In the Anglican wedding ceremony, the minister requires partners to each promise to be faithful to their spouse "so long as ye both shall live," and the bride and the groom each promise to honor their vows "till death us do part."[49] Jesus, drawing out the meaning of "one flesh," admonishes the

44. Fisher, "Does a Victory for Gay Marriage Lead to Polygamy? It Depends On Your Reasoning."

45. Owens, "Leftist Law Professor Says Gay Marriage Likely to Lead to Legalized Incest, Polygamy."

46. Siblings, or parent and child, separated at birth typically, who meet and develop a strong romantic and sexual attraction as adults.

47. This refers to any incestuous romantic and typically sexual attraction. If this leads to the formation of a consensual incestuous relationship, then, in this new terminology, one has a "consanguinamorous" relationship.

48. See, for example, the website *Full Marriage Equality* that exists for, among other things, pursuing the decriminalization of incest and a constitutional right to incestuous marriage.

49. Book of Common Prayer, 313.

Pharisees that "what therefore God has joined together, let not man separate" (Matt 19:6b). In God's design, a marriage should not end until one or
both partners has died. Through common grace, as Stephens has noted, the
concept that valid marriage involves at least the intention of permanence
at its beginning is almost a cultural universal.[50]

I will not get into different Christian positions about divorce here.[51]
Some orthodox believers have held that people can never truly dissolve
a valid marriage. This is the Roman Catholic view,[52] also held by some
Protestants. Others believe that we can only dissolve valid marriages in
cases of serious breach of the marital covenant, such as willful desertion
or adultery, as the *Westminster Confession of Faith* teaches.[53] There is nothing
godly about a society, or church, that effectively practices no-fault divorce,
allowing divorce based upon the demand of one partner, for myriad reasons. It should be rare or unknown, not the end of 40–50 percent of all
marriages.[54]

A clear commitment to marital permanence also helps us take mate
selection and marriage preparation seriously. If I know there is easy access
to an exit door, I am far more likely to be careless in entering the room.

We have to start where we are, including ministering to a lot of divorced
and often remarried people and their families. However, we should not
normalize this sad state of affairs. We need to restore the expectation of,
and commitment to, marital permanence.

The concept of *annulment*, which commonly confuses people, is relevant
here. Annulling a marriage does not dissolve a real one-flesh marital union.
In church and civil law, annulment is the recognition that a true marriage
never existed. Sometimes annulment involves finding fault in one partner
or both (as in cases of bigamy, marriage by force or fraud, or consensual
incest). Or there may be no fault, as when for example a couple discovers
only after marriage that they are half-siblings who have the same mother, a
scenario that appears in the life of *Moll Flanders* in Daniel Defoe's classic book
of that name. Annulment does not violate marital permanence. It rejects as

---

50. Stephens, *The Family in Cross-Cultural Perspective*, 6, 11.

51. Though I will be doing so in chapter 10.

52. *Catechism of the Catholic Church*, 409.

53. *Westminster Confession of Faith*, 82.

54. Some contest these percentages. I shall show in chapter 10 that they are generally accurate.

marriages unions that actually are not. Things like adultery are not grounds for annulment since this occurs after a valid marriage has taken place. In fact, only truly married people can commit, or be victims of, adultery.

Marital permanence does not mean beyond the grave. Despite the well-meaning sentiments on tombstones and eulogies that picture a loving couple united in wedded bliss into eternity, Scripture teaches otherwise. Jesus was direct about this in addressing another "gotcha" question, which confronted him with a hypothetical woman who in life had seven husbands as each had died. Whom would she be married to in heaven? Jesus answered, "in the resurrection they neither marry nor are given in marriage, but are like angels in heaven" (Matt 22:30). Marriage between man and woman is a sacred relationship that has eternal ramifications, but it is a provision he has made for this life, not the one to come.

MARRIAGE IS A SEXUAL UNION

The *Westminster Confession of Faith* and the Anglican matrimonial service both address the strong tie between sexual intercourse and marriage, in the context of describing the "purposes" of marriage, which we shall be addressing more in the next few chapters. These have to do with providing a legitimate sexual outlet and the procreation of children.[55] Vaginal sexual intercourse is in view here, not other forms of sexual expression. This is the sex act that procreates. The method by which a bride's virginity was proved in the Old Testament clearly shows that married couples were to have sexual intercourse following the ceremony (Deut 22:13–21), something called *consummation*.

Intercourse is also the only form of sexual expression that actually brings together the complementarity of male and female into one flesh, and as such is deeply spiritual as well as physical. As the Puritan Thomas Becon said, we can define marriage as "a coupling together of two persons into one flesh."[56] Although the one-flesh reality of marriage radiates through all aspects of the marital relation, it comes together powerfully and necessarily in sexual intercourse between husband and wife. Sherif Girgis and his coauthors have pointed out that the true "*comprehensive* union" of marriage logically "must include bodily union."[57] As René Gehring notes, biblical scholars have always

55. *Westminster Confession of Faith*, 80; Book of Common Prayer, 311–12.
56. Ryken, *Worldly Saints*, 44.
57. Girgis et al., *What Is Marriage?*, 24 (emphasis added).

understood the connection between sexual intercourse and the one-flesh marital bond. For example, the ancient Jewish historian Josephus discusses this.[58] Gehring quotes Loader's acknowledgment that "sexual intercourse was an essential element in creating a psychosomatic union."[59]

However, sexual intercourse alone does not marry a man and a woman. This is clear in Jesus' talk with the Samaritan woman recorded in John 4:18, where he tells her, "you have had five husbands, and the one you now have is not your husband." Living together in this manner involved sexual intercourse and yet Jesus did not treat her as married.

I have had countless well-meaning Christians tell me over the years that cohabitation is essentially marriage, and what cohabiting Christians need to do is simply regard themselves as married and remain that way for life. I understand that these situations can be complex, particularly when children are involved. However, a man and a woman are not married until they actually make those public vows and receive the recognition required that they have formally embraced the obligations of husband and wife.

Similarly, there is no requirement that, if an unmarried couple has had sexual intercourse, or even cohabited, they must then get married. Certainly, counseling such couples requires great pastoral wisdom, especially where the couple has had children. However, simply requiring marriage in cases of sexual activity and cohabitation has led to countless bad marriages. Biblically, unmarried people having sex is the sin of "fornication," and those engaged in it need to repent. Still, we should not punish believers falling into this sin by pressuring them into marrying someone whom they should not be marrying. This fallacy becomes even more obvious when considering unmarried believers who have had sexual relations with more than one person. Which one will we require them to wed?

On the other hand, until sexual intercourse takes place, there is no marriage.[60] The New England Puritan order for wedding days, which is not strange to us, made this clear. There was the public sharing of

---

58. Gehring, *The Biblical 'One Flesh' Theology as Constituted in Genesis 2:24*, 230.

59. Ibid.

60. Can we make exceptions to this requirement in rare situations where, due to age or infirmity, sexual intercourse is not physically possible but a couple wishes to marry anyway? I would agree with what Jim Newheiser asserts in *Marriage, Divorce, and Remarriage*, 23, that the church should accept this, including the couple still having physical intimacy as husband and wife, provided both partners agree. If conditions change, they should come together in sexual intercourse, however. Also contrary to Newheiser, I do not believe such a marriage would be fully complete. Sexual intercourse cannot be set aside so lightly.

vows and declaration of marriage by the officiating person, a celebration, and then the couple consummated their marriage through private sexual intercourse.[61] Said Morgan, "The final step in the marriage was sexual. Unless it were consummated in bodily union, no marriage was complete or valid."[62]

This does not mean that if a married couple at some point can no longer have sexual intercourse through some involuntary impediment that they are no longer married. To claim this would be to recognize grounds for dissolving marriage that are not found in the Bible, and jettison vows to remain faithful through all the terrible things life may bring. On the other hand, no married couple should ever voluntarily abandon sexual intercourse.

My mother raised me as a serious Roman Catholic and then I converted to evangelical Protestantism as a young man. I received a thorough Catholic education. Thus, I have often had occasion to consider the claim that Mary was a perpetual virgin. In this understanding, Mary and Joseph never had sexual intercourse, or children, after Jesus was born. However, the Scriptures only teach that Joseph "knew her not *until she had given birth to a son*" (Matt 1:25, emphasis added). If Joseph and Mary never had intercourse, then they never got married. At most, they lived out a lifetime engagement. This means that, in some senses, they brought up Jesus as an illegitimate son.

This teaching reflects the earlier Roman Catholic idea (now greatly modified[63]) that somehow virginity is superior to sexual marriage. Early church leaders like Augustine praised married couples who completely abstained from sex,[64] despite the apostle Paul's clear admonition that married couples should not do so except for brief periods devoted to prayer and fasting (1 Cor 7:5). It is certainly true that singleness and celibacy, whether a permanent or temporary calling, can be wonderful and of enormous benefit to the church (1 Cor 7:32–35). Many ministries, for example those associated with intense hardship and dangers, may even require singleness. However, God has only gifted some, but not most, people to live out their entire lives without marriage and sex (Matt 19:10–12). Married people should

---

61. Morgan, *The Puritan Family*, 31.
62. Ibid., 34.
63. *Catechism of the Catholic Church*, 404–5.

esteem and honor their faithful single brethren, never regarding them as inferiors. They should not regard them as spiritually superior either. As the writer of Hebrews (13:4) said, "Let marriage be held in honor among all."

In considering the place of sexual *intercourse* in God's definition of marriage, we find another reason why Christians should never view same-sex marriage as valid. It is physically impossible for man-man and woman-woman. To claim that same-sex couples can be truly married would regard other forms of sexual pleasuring as equivalent to sexual intercourse, but they are not. Same-sex couples cannot consummate marriage.

This point is not a side issue, and even secular legislators who support gay marriage have had to confront it. Many nations and states consider "failure to consummate" to be grounds for civil annulment,[65] and legal "consummation" means vaginal sexual intercourse. For example, when the British Parliament was debating their law legalizing same-sex marriage in England and Wales, the issue of existing provisions for annulment of unconsummated marriages became a real headache.[66] No one could identify any homosexual practice that was equivalent to intercourse, but lawmakers were also adamant that they needed to retain this protection, which was rooted in long-standing tradition, culture, and religious understanding. Their solution was to amend the act to exclude same-sex couples from obtaining annulment for non-consummation, while keeping that protection in force for heterosexuals.[67]

Sexual expression within marriage is a great gift. Through it, even couples unable to have children celebrate procreation, have their legitimate sexual desires satisfied, and acclaim the physical and supernatural reality of unity in one flesh. Christians should never be ashamed of marital sex, nor treat it with dishonor. It is not only a delight for them but also to our wise and loving God when married couples come together in love.

---

64. Ryken, *Worldly Saints*, 40.

65. Often with caveats, for example based on physical incapacity and/or hidden from partner until after marriage, but often without any.

66. Bowcott, "Gay Marriage: Some Legal Inequalities Will Remain."

67. The National Archives of the United Kingdom, "Marriage (Same-Sex Couples) Act 2013," and "Matrimonial Causes Act 1973." Interestingly, at this writing, same-sex married couples in England and Wales cannot legally commit "adultery" with someone of the same sex since it is defined as having sexual intercourse with someone other than one's spouse.

IS MARRIAGE A "SACRAMENT" FOR BELIEVERS?

Since the Council of Trent in 1545–63, the Roman Catholic Church has embraced as official dogma that marriages between baptized persons are sacramental. For Roman Catholics, this will require being married according to Catholic form, even when marrying someone who is not a Catholic, but this would not hold for baptized Protestants. Marriages among unbaptized persons are valid provided they meet the basic design set forth by God, but they are categorized as being natural only, not sacramental. Though Catholics must obtain special dispensations from the church to do so, they may marry someone who is not a baptized Christian, though this marriage would not be sacramental.[68]

Most Protestants, while holding that marriage is sacred and communicates profound spiritual truth, reject the idea that it is a sacrament, whether or not both partners have received baptism. With some exceptions (for example, foot washing among some groups), they usually believe that the Scriptures only give us two sacraments—baptism and the Lord's Supper.

We Protestants agree with Catholics that sacraments are "an outward and visible sign of inward grace." However, we have also asserted that they are rites that are exclusively attached to the church to be administered by its representatives, which have been instituted by Christ during his earthly ministry, apply and seal to *all* believers the benefits of being joined with Christ, visibly distinguish believers from unbelievers, and in which all Christians must partake.[69] This goes back to seminal works like Martin Luther's 1520 *Babylonian Captivity of the Church*.[70]

On this understanding, matrimony is clearly not a sacrament. A minister should be concerned if a church member does not wish to have his or her wedding conducted by an ordained pastor in the presence of believers absent some pressing reason. However, marriage does not *have* to be officiated by the church or its ministers in order to be legitimate and binding, as is true for sacraments. God instituted marriage in the garden. He does not require that all Christians get married, and indeed many should not

---

68. *Catechism of the Catholic Church*, 405–8. United States Conference of Catholic Bishops, *For Your Marriage*.

69. Hodge, *The Westminster Confession*, 327–32.

70. Moldenhauer, "The Babylonian Captivity of the Church."

be. Marriage does not visibly separate believers from unbelievers since all human beings may be legitimately married.

It is common for Roman Catholics (and Eastern Orthodox) to claim that Protestant rejection of marriage as a sacrament degraded the institution and helped lay the groundwork for its breakdown in the modern world. In fact, then-President of Duquesne University John Murray opened a conference I attended there in 1997 with pointed remarks stating precisely that. I respectfully and strongly disagree. By most measures, in the Reformation the quality of marriage, and honor that people gave to it, appeared to improve. Much fine social history attests to this.[71] Moreover, no one can read the Continental Reformers or Puritans without being deeply impressed with their high view of marriage.

MARRIAGE: A CONCISE CHRISTIAN DEFINITION

With great trepidation, I will now pull together all that I have covered so far into a unified, Christian definition of marriage. "Marriage is an irreplaceable and core institution of human society, created by God before the fall of Adam and Eve, which communicates deep spiritual truth, including speaking to the human race about the relationship of God to his people, pointing to the marriage between Christ and his church at the end of history. In it, one man and one woman, who are not restrained by conditions that would invalidate their union, and who are fully informed in all relevant matters, freely and publicly enter into the marital covenant, through solemn vows, to accept and fulfill all the obligations of marriage, including an exclusive sexual relationship, for all the days in which both live. They consummate these vows through sexual intercourse."

---

71. For example, Shorter, *The Making of the Modern Family*.

CHAPTER 2

MUTUAL HELP

How shall we call that a marriage where the husband and wife are still two persons, maintaining individuality as if it were a scrupulous condition of the contract? That is utterly foreign to the divine idea. In a true marriage, the husband and wife become one. Henceforth their joys and their cares, their hopes and their labors, their sorrows and their pleasures, rise and blend together in one stream.

Charles Haddon Spurgeon[1]

It is a mercy to have a faithful friend, that loveth you entirely, and is as true to you as yourself, to whom you may open your mind and communicate your affairs, and who would be ready to strengthen you, and divide the cares of your affairs and family with you, and help you to bear your burdens, and comfort you in your sorrows, and be the daily companion of your lives, and partaker of your joys and sorrow. And it is a mercy to have so near a friend to be a helper to your soul; to join with you in prayer and other holy exercises; to watch over you and tell you of your sins and dangers, and to stir up in you the grace of God, and remember you of the life to come, and cheerfully accompany you in the ways of holiness.

Richard Baxter[2]

---

1. Spurgeon, *Metropolitan Tabernacle Pulpit*, vol. 13, 415.
2. Baxter, *A Christian Directory*, 404.

MUTUAL SOCIETY, HELP, AND
COMFORT IN THE SCRIPTURES

OLD TESTAMENT

In the Old Testament, many passages point to the mutual help of husband and wife as a wonderful and God-ordained purpose for marriage. We can only delve into a subset, including the most important ones.

Old Testament writers usually specifically addressed male readers. For example, the opening chapter of the book of Proverbs is written to "my son" (1:8, 10, 15), followed by a lot of warning and advice directed at young men. This is true when it deals with marriage-related topics, as when King Lemuel relates his mother's oracle about how godly wives are a blessing to their husbands, and thus ought to be valued and praised by them (Prov 31:10–31). However, God clearly intended these for the instruction and edification of both men and women, as is true in the case of the latter passage.

As I did in the last chapter, let me begin at the beginning with what God sets forth in Genesis 2:18 in describing the creation of Eve and the first marriage. Recall that God declared, "It is not good that the man should be alone; I will make him a *helper* fit for him" (emphasis added). The account repeats this last, critical phrase, noting that among the animals that Adam named, "there was not found a helper fit for him" (v. 20). Creating Eve solved this problem, when God united the man and woman in mutual help as one flesh.

People often misread this passage as if Adam was "lonely" without Eve, that somehow, he was suffering psychologically in some way and that the woman was created to resolve this. This is not what the text says. Moreover, there was no sin and suffering in paradise, and Adam had perfect, direct communion with the Lord God. To be sure, God was anticipating the fall of humankind from grace, when marriage would help humans deal with loneliness and a host of other adversities and challenges, including death. However, in its initial creation, Adam needed a female partner with whom he could have children, take on the incredible work of ruling and subduing the earth, and who, like him, was an image-bearer of God (Gen 1:26–28).[3]

Throughout Proverbs, young men are reminded of the practical value of a good wife, someone who is wise, prudent, hard-working, compassionate, kind, loyal, and more (cf. 12:4; 18:22; 19:14; and especially 31:10ff). A

---

3. Wilson, *Reforming Marriage*, 17.

poorly chosen spouse will be a burden rather than a help (Prov 12:4; 19:13; 31:30), but a godly wife is a gift from God, greater than material inheritance (Prov 19:14). Ecclesiastes 9:9 connects marriage to a godly woman with both delightful companionship and fruitful labor, rooting both in a lifelong commitment of loyalty and love.

The Old Testament gives us many examples of mutual help from godly spouses. Much of it involves wives stopping their husbands from doing bad things, as when Rebekah stops Isaac from bestowing the vital messianic blessing on his unworthy and profane son Esau (Gen 27), or when Abigail prevents the churlish behavior of her husband Nabal from leading to the destruction of his household (1 Sam 25). But we also see positive tenderness. One of my favorites is the consistent care, devotion, and comfort Elkanah bestowed, for years, on his persecuted, barren wife Hannah (1 Sam 1:4–8):

> On the day when Elkanah sacrificed, he would give portions to Peninnah his wife and to all her sons and daughters. But to Hannah he gave a double portion, because he loved her, though the LORD had closed her womb. And her rival used to provoke her grievously to irritate her, because the LORD had closed her womb. So it went on year by year. As often as she went up to the house of the LORD, she used to provoke her. Therefore Hannah wept and would not eat. And Elkanah, her husband, said to her, "Hannah, why do you weep? And why do you not eat? And why is your heart sad? Am I not more to you than ten sons?"

NEW TESTAMENT

In his general instructions to married men and women, which are permeated with the assumption that they are to support and help each other, Peter informed Christian husbands that they are to understand and honor their wives as "heirs with you of the grace of life" (1 Pet 3:7). In declaring the advantages of being unmarried in service to God, Paul points out that married believers will need to care for and please their spouses and not solely focus on works of Christian service to those outside their families (1 Cor 7:32–34). Though stated negatively, he certainly was attesting to the kind of mutual attention and support that needed to mark Christian marriages. Paul did so knowing that most believers would marry, and even that most of the other apostles had wives to care for (1 Cor 9:5).[4] And in Ephesians 5:22–33, Paul admonishes husbands and wives to each give to the other all that is needful relative to their respective roles, including husbands caring for their wives as their own flesh. We can assume that for two who have become truly one, mutual help, support, and encouragement should be evident.

Perhaps the greatest example in the New Testament of spousal devotion is that of Joseph. Upon learning of Mary's pregnancy, knowing he was not the father, he first sought a way to deal with the situation to preserve Mary from the punishments associated with what he presumed were her sinful actions (Matt 1:18–19). Following the revelation of the angel that in fact the child was conceived by the Holy Spirit, he embraced her and the baby as his own, with all the shame and ridicule that would have certainly been unleashed on an orthodox Jewish working man in a small town (Matt 1:20–25). His care for her then included taking her safely, in advanced pregnancy, to Jerusalem, and then fleeing with his new family to Egypt (Luke 2:4–6; Matt 2:14–15). Joseph exhibits for us the tender, self-sacrificing love of an excellent husband.[5]

MARRIAGE AND FRIENDSHIP

All marriage ideally includes friendship. This is true even as, in everyday speech, people distinguish their spouse from their "best friend." Indeed, every married person should hold their spouse to be their best and dearest friend. Still, marriage goes well beyond friendship, and the two things are analytically distinct from each other. Modern Western people are often confused about this, because we lack a full understanding and appreciation of either.

First, marriage requires *sexual complementarity,* not only for the sake of procreation, but also for the particular kinds of mutual support and comfort husbands and wives provide for each other. This differentiates marriage not only from homosexual attachment, but also from friendship. I can and ought to have close friends who are males, but that would not fulfill the particular help I need from my wife. Douglas Wilson observes, "As a

---

4. Additionally, Luke 4:38–40 records the healing of Peter's mother-in-law.

5. An excellent film about the birth of Christ, *The Nativity Story* (New Line Cinema, 2007), captures all of this beautifully.

result of the creation order, men and women are oriented to one another *differently*. They need one another, but they need one another *differently*."[6]

Second, friendship relationships are not necessarily exclusive, two-person bonds. Friendship often accommodates the addition of a third party, or more, if the other conditions of friendships exist among these people.

Third, unlike marriages, friendships can end, or cool, for reasons that do not necessarily involve any animosity, sin, or wrongdoing. Geographic mobility, changing tastes, the commencement of new relationships, career restrictions, and more can lead us out of friendships.

Fourth, friendships tend to be heavily rooted in mutual *interests*. In *The Four Loves*, C. S. Lewis distinguishes *eros* and *philia* this way: "Lovers are normally face to face, absorbed in each other; Friends, side by side, absorbed in some common interest."[7] Thus, a man may have "guitar buddies," "hunting pals," and "football chums," none of whom is going to be jealous of the other as he moves from participating and talking about one interest or another. Other conversations then tend to flow from these common interests. For example, I had a close friend who shared a love for live blues-rock with me. We would often open up about other, more serious, matters as we drove to various venues, so over time we became very close.

My wife, meanwhile, sometimes enjoys going with me to musical performances such as this, but she does so very differently from my friend. They give her quality time with me and she likes seeing me relax and have fun, even if she does not "dig" the music the same way.

Yet take even a casual look at personal ads, even those for Christians, and you will see how often mutual interests, hobbies, and activities take center stage. I might not have married my wife of thirty-six years based on the mutual interests we had when we met. Many of the things both she and I enjoyed then are no longer that important to us. Moreover, some of our major hobbies today are not interests we share, nor are they things we cared about when we were young (for example, archery hunting for me, quilting for her).

Certainly, we should take enough notice of the things our spouses enjoy to be able to support, understand, and communicate with them. We should

---

6. Wilson, *Reforming Marriage*, 17 (emphasis in original).

7. Lewis, *The Four Loves*, 61, 65.

also create reasonable space for them to engage in these pursuits. Yet while healthy marriages normally involve and need some shared interests, the latter are not foundational or central to them.

Where there are friendships based on mutual interests between members of the opposite sex, this easily transforms into erotic or romantic attachment.[8] As C. S. Lewis correctly points out, when this happens between two singles, the relationship may change into something beyond friendship, including taking on the more exclusive character required of godly lovers.[9] There is an implicit warning for married people in this. They should be extremely careful in their friendships with the opposite sex. Certainly, these friendships should be lived out within larger groups and almost never be exclusive. Usually, they should not be unusually close. For example, it would have been inappropriate and potentially injurious to my marriage if my blues-rock friendship, with all those trips and alone time, had been with a female.

Finally, marriage ought always to represent friendship in its *greatest, best, and loveliest form*.[10] That means, as Aristotle taught us, a partnership in which each person values moral goodness in the other and is passionate to see the other advance in it.[11] This is, as he observed, "The friendship of good people alike in virtue" who "similarly wish good things to each other as good."[12] As Christians, we should understand this as people anxious to see each other grow in "godliness," to become more like Christ. Husband and wife should never allow their relationship to remain at any lower order of comradery than this.

Aristotle notes that we can have friends who are merely useful to us, or those whose companionship we find pleasurable. Such relationships can be mutually satisfying and legitimate, even though they are more about what others do for us, rather than what they are, or can become, as persons. Friendships of usefulness or pleasure are inherently impermanent. They are as fickle as the emotions or goods each person can deliver to the

---

8. Ibid., 67.

9. Ibid.

10. I am deeply grateful to Rev. Nathanael Devlin, associate pastor of Beverly Heights Presbyterian Church (EPC) in Pittsburgh, who directed and encouraged me to include and build on these powerful insights on friendship from Aristotle, applying them to Christian marriage.

11. *Nicomachean Ethics*, vols. VIII and IX, 4–5.

12. Ibid., 4.

other.[13] However, the highest form of friendship is as enduring as the moral excellence that each person enjoys and nurtures in the other,[14] especially when both rely on Christ, rather than themselves, to grow in godliness and anchor their relationship.

Moreover, in friendship the higher forms subsume the lower ones. If we are attracted to people because they are growing in godliness and wish the same for us, we will find them both useful and pleasant.[15] Again, this is especially true if both look beyond each other, to Christ, as their ultimate provider and delight.

Friendships like this can exist outside marriage, and I have had the honor of being part of such relationships. However, those joined as husband and wife in God's covenant should certainly be, in ever-growing measure, the very best of friends, in this finest form.

ADDITIONAL THOUGHTS ON MUTUAL HELP

The fact that God designed marriage to provide mutual help, support, and relationships in good times and bad for us as we fulfill our callings in this world opens up some other important considerations. I would like to address some of these here.

First, really meeting our spouse's needs in all seasons of life requires the kind of radical commitment to lifelong monogamy that Christianity teaches. How can my spouse supply me with "mutual society, help, and comfort . . . both in prosperity and adversity"[16] if he or she can divorce me for trivial reasons, or will not be there as I experience the bodily deterioration of age? My children count on me loving them and being loyal to them no matter what, even if I need to rebuke or disagree with them at times. My spouse should be able to count on no less.

In the introduction to this book, I critically mentioned the tortured claim of Christian Broadcasting Network (CBN) founder Pat Robertson that a Christian husband would be justified divorcing his wife if she had Alzheimer's disease.[17] In lovely contrast to this, when I interned at

---

13. Ibid., 4–5.
14. Ibid.
15. Ibid., 6.
16. Book of Common Prayer, 312.
17. Moisse and Hooper, "Pat Robertson Says Alzheimer's Makes Divorce OK."

a state psychiatric hospital many years ago, I watched the spouse of an Alzheimer's sufferer weep over and visit her husband, never abandoning him even as she had to relinquish him to residential care. A dear elderly man my wife and I know recently buried his wife after caring for her for years through senile dementia. I hope that is true for any of us who face such difficulties.

My marriage is something I lean on every day, and I can do this confidently, because it can bear the weight I need to put on it. To do this, our marriage itself needs support—from our larger extended family, church, friends, and most of all, God. Neither my wife nor I can or should be *all* the other one needs. To claim or live otherwise is to make an idol of marriage and to deny the larger network of people who love and care for us. Still, for marriage to "deliver the goods," we have to be able to *count on* our covenant—meaning our spouse—through thick and thin, even if that includes sin, physical deterioration or sickness, natural calamity, the death of a child, or anything else.

Here, let's consider more deeply the word "mutual" that we have been using so much in talking about "support," and look at some of its implications. I would like to do so by diving into two simple but powerful sociological concepts: *reciprocity* and *role*.

"Reciprocity" means that what each person gives and takes in a relationship roughly balances out over time. What we expect from the other is not more than what they can confidently expect from us. This is true in all healthy relationships except where some extraordinary distress intrudes, such as mental illness or physical disability.

"Roles" are simply the rights, duties, and expectations that we attach to social positions. As with stage actors, we perform our roles toward others, who also have roles to play toward us. People playing roles together create "role sets," such as "teacher-student," "audience-listener," "parent-child," and yes, "husband-wife." Rights, duties, and expectations are mutual. A wife's rights are her husband's duties, and vice versa.

Many different factors influence role expectations in marriage. These include our culture and family background. What she grew up with shaped what my wife expected when we got married, and the same was true for me. For some people, there are biological limitations that legitimately influence specific expectations. And these will be negotiated across the life span, changing with time and circumstances. Many couples, for example, take turns financially supporting each other at different points in life.

Across all or most marriages, there will be things that apply equally to husbands and wives. For example, both husbands and wives should be honest and sexually faithful. There are also things that are specific to males or females, such as breastfeeding versus inseminating. There will also be things that vary quite a bit by sex, often for highly personal and idiosyncratic reasons. Where there are legitimate choices, they do not need to be mechanical or bound by artificial rules, nor should we judge the choices that other married couples make. For example, Edmund Morgan relays the story of one Puritan captain who happily lived on a financial allowance from his wife—she handled all the money simply because she was much better at it. Two other Puritan ministers handed over the complete secular management of their households to their wives so they could focus on their ministerial duties.[18] Many evangelical traditionalists would denounce this, even as they might a household where the woman is "handy" while her husband does the laundry. They would be wrong.

One indispensable "expectation" for husbands and wives toward each other, as well as toward their children if God so ordains, is *self-sacrifice*. In marriage, self-sacrifice should be reciprocal to the extent it is possible. How equally each partner sacrifices for the other will change in nature, degree, and direction across life in ways few couples could imagine when they first took their oath of marriage, but it should normally equalize over time. I have now seen a beloved father, and mother-in-law, care for their spouse through prolonged, terminal cancer. This was very hard, even with the support of other caregivers. It *was* in fulfillment of vows each had made on their wedding day over half a century earlier. Each could identify ways that their cancer-stricken spouse had carried *them* through adversity as well.

This was beautiful. Conversely, a partner who is disinterested or ungrateful in response to the self-sacrifice of a devoted lover is shameful. We need to call on the guilty parties in such marriages to unreserved repentance, for their sake, as much as for the welfare of their spouse.

However, a couple of words of caution. We all know of situations in which a married person finds that the other is literally unable to reciprocate

18. Morgan, *The Puritan Family*, 43.

their sacrifice fully or even very much. Life can throw us some terrible curves, such as long-term crippling illnesses that strike young. Even in a godly marriage, circumstances may mean that marital sacrifice is one-sided. Here, God calls us to be faithful toward our vows and live out that sacrifice, by his grace and hopefully with the support of fellow believers.

Moreover, there are too many situations where believers must bear, year after year, the sin of a selfish spouse. God calls them to carry on in loving service and prayer anyway, just as in any other situation where they suffer from the sin of others (Matt 5:44–48; Luke 6:27–36). There are obvious exceptions, such as when their spouse is abusive, forcing them to sin, putting them or their children in danger, or other such serious situations.[19] If situations like this are not clearly resolved, then the innocent parties should leave for a safe place. But spousal selfishness, in itself, is not legitimate grounds for divorce.

The mutual support Christianity has in view is far different from the kind of need fulfillment seen in the modern "therapeutic marriage" perspective we discussed in the last chapter. In the Christian understanding, spouses help each other as they face, together, the difficulties and joys of life, and try to accomplish God's purposes for them in this world. This is nothing like relationships based on psychological gratification, personal fulfillment, spontaneity, and self-realization, where the people think it is acceptable to discard or avoid their commitment when such emotional rewards are not forthcoming. The latter undermines marital happiness and ultimately stability, while the former strengthens both. Here is how sociologist Robert Bellah and his coauthors described the tortured mind-set of those who embrace this "therapeutic" orientation, while still trying to live out and enjoy the benefits of a traditional approach to marriage.

> On the whole, even the most secure, happily-married of our respondents had difficulty when they sought a language in which to articulate their reasons for commitments that went beyond the self. These confusions were particularly clear when they discussed problems of sacrifice and obligation. While they wanted to maintain enduring relationships, they resisted the notion that

---

19. I address abuse as a possible ground for divorce in chapter 10.

such relationships might involve obligations that went beyond the wishes of the partners. . . . They had few ideas of the substantive obligations partners in a relationship might develop. . . . It was not that they were unwilling to make compromises or sacrifices for their spouses, but they were troubled by the ideal of self-denial the term "sacrifice" implied. If you really wanted to do something good for the one you loved, they said, it would not be a sacrifice. Since the only measure of the good is what is good for the self, something that is really a burden to the self cannot be part of love. Rather, if one is really in touch with one's feelings, one will do something for one's beloved only if one really wants to, and then, by definition, it cannot be a sacrifice. Without a wider set of cultural traditions, then, it is hard for people to find a way to say why genuine attachment to others might require the risk of hurt, loss, or sacrifice. They clung to an optimistic view in which love might require hard work, but could never create real costs to the self.[20]

It is hard to imagine how this approach can realistically handle the worst that life can throw at a marriage. Certainly, it does not encourage marriages where we "walk in love, as Christ loved us and gave himself up for us, a fragrant offering and sacrifice" (Eph 5:2).

MEASURABLE BENEFITS OF
MARITAL MUTUAL SUPPORT

Statistics clearly attest to the benefits of marriage. As University of Chicago sociologist Linda Waite and National Organization of Marriage founder Maggie Gallagher put it in the subtitle of their highly influential book *The Case for Marriage*, "married people are *happier, healthier,* and *better off financially*" compared to those who are single or divorced.[21] It is disappointing that a 2010 Pew Research Center survey revealed that from half to a large majority of Americans think that married people are no better off than singles in these three areas.[22] They are badly misinformed. An overwhelming body of evidence supports Waite and Gallagher's

---

20. Bellah et al., *Habits of the Heart*, 109–110.
21. New York: Broadway Books, 2000 (emphasis added).
22. Pew Research Center, "The Decline of Marriage and Rise of New Families," 24.

claim.[23] Nor are these differences merely the result of "selection effects," namely, that people who are, or are more likely to be, healthy, happy, and prosperous are simply more likely to get or stay married. While such effects explain *part* of the gap between married people and others in these critical areas, most studies that control for selection effects find that marriage itself also fosters these positive results.[24]

Consider the issue of *happiness*. To be sure, some aspects of married life, especially having and raising children, but also events such as the inevitable interpersonal difficulties and health issues faced by spouses, can be associated with stressors such as anxiety and insomnia.[25] However, overwhelmingly, compared to the unmarried, married men and women have lower levels of psychological distress, less abuse of alcohol and drugs, and better overall mental health.[26] A ten-year study involving about fourteen thousand adults found that "marital status was one of the most important predictors of happiness."[27] Following up on research like this, I looked at the "happiness" item in the highly regarded General Social Survey.[28] Compared to the divorced, separated, widowed, and never married, those who were married were between 1.8 to 2.45 times more likely to describe themselves as "very happy." They were 2.4 times less likely than never married, and 2.7 times less likely than divorced respondents, to describe themselves as "not too happy." There were huge gaps in happiness between the married and others among blacks and whites, at every different educational level, among those who grew up in the poorest to the wealthiest homes, at each age category, and for those who placed themselves in any social class.

Married people, especially men, are also a lot less likely to commit suicide.[29] Waite and Gallagher make the staggering observation that "Married

---

23. See, for example, an excellent rebuttal to a short piece, based on a questionably accurate summary of a single Swiss study that appeared in the *New York Times* denying these benefits. VanderWeele, "What *The New York Times* Gets Wrong About Marriage, Health and Well-Being."

24. Waite and Gallagher, *The Case for Marriage*, 51–52, 68, 110–23. See also Starbuck and Lundy, *Families in Context*, 248, and Cherlin, *Public and Private Families*, 203, 206–7; and Wilson, *The Marriage Problem*, 17.

25. See, for example, Starbuck and Lundy, *Families in Context*, 248.

26. Waite and Gallagher, *The Case for Marriage*, 66, 71; Cherlin, *Public and Private Families*, 206–7.

27. Waite and Gallagher, *The Case for Marriage*, 67.

28. Smith et al., *General Social Surveys, 2000–2016*. I combined years 2000 through 2016, which included almost twenty thousand respondents who answered that question and gave their marital status. This is a huge sample.

29. Waite and Gallagher, *The Case for Marriage*, 48, 52, 67.

men are only half as likely as bachelors, and about one-third as likely as divorced guys, to take their own life."[30] In one study examining about eighty thousand suicides in the United States between 1979 and 1981, "widowed and divorced persons were about three times more likely to commit suicide than the married were."[31] Another study looked at suicides between 1991 and 1996, comparing blacks and whites, males and females. The suicide rate for married people was lower. Studies showing that married people commit suicide less have appeared consistently for about one hundred years.[32]

Moving on to *physical health,* we again see a big marriage advantage. Andrew Cherlin, a highly respected Johns Hopkins University sociologist, points out that married people have lower death rates and longer life expectancies, and rate their own health higher.[33] This mirrors claims made by Waite and Gallagher[34] and Harvard epidemiologist Tyler VanderWeele,[35] and is true for all leading causes of death, especially illnesses caused by sinful or dangerous behavior.[36] Other researchers agree: "Literature on health and mortality by marital status has consistently identified that unmarried individuals generally report poorer health and have a higher mortality risk than their married counterparts, with men being particularly affected in this respect."[37]

One of the most direct ways that marriage helps folks, particularly men, maintain healthy habits and resist destructive ones is through what Waite and Gallagher called "the virtues of nagging."[38] What they mean by "nagging" is monitoring and correcting negative behavior, while encouraging and praising positive practices,[39] not the negative, tearing down we often

---

30. Ibid., 52.

31. Ibid., 67.

32. Luoma and Pearson, "Suicide and Marital Status in the United States, 1991–1996." Black females have very low rates of suicide and so could not be validly included in the study, see page 1519. The only exception was black males under twenty-five years of age, where married had *slightly* higher suicide than singles.

33. Cherlin, *Public and Private Families,* 206.

34. Waite and Gallagher, *The Case for Marriage,* 47–51.

35. "What *The New York Times* Gets Wrong About Marriage, Health and Well-Being." VanderWeele notes that one Swiss study did not replicate the finding about "self-rated" health, but he noted problems with that measure over objective health indices.

36. Ibid., 48.

37. Robards et al., "Marital Status, Health, and Mortality," 295. See also: Stewart, "Does a Better Relationship Mean Better Health?"; and Emling, "A Happy Marriage Leads to Better Health, Study Finds."

38. Waite and Gallagher, *The Case for Marriage,* 55.

39. Ibid., 55–57.

think of when we hear that word. Their claim is accurate, powerful, and scriptural (cf. Prov 25:11; 27:6; Luke 17:3; Gal 6:1–2). Research consistently supports their claim that "a spouse's nagging can have a powerful impact on one's health for both men and women," and that emotional support "can have profound effects on physical well-being."[40] Documented areas include smoking, exercise, sleep, risky behavior, alcohol and drug abuse, management of chronic disease, immune system, depression, obesity, blood pressure, stroke, life expectancy, and dementia, survival following cardiac surgery, heart attacks, and cancer diagnoses.[41]

In managing my own heart disease, I have benefited enormously from the admonitions and encouragement of my wife in areas such as attitude, stress, diet, and destructive habits. Without being dramatic, this is one reason that I am alive and in relatively good health fifteen years from being diagnosed with a coronary artery blockage.

However, it is not just marriage, but *good* marriage, which leads to these positive psychological and physical effects. Waite and Gallagher caution that "the quality of the relationship between spouses makes a difference: As a marriage improves over time, so does the reported health of husband and wife."[42] Adds Rebecca Stewart, "the flip side is also true. Being in an unhappy marriage can be unhealthy."[43] As we have seen, Scriptures teach the same.

The *financial benefits* of marriage are obvious and do not exist only because people who are better off are more likely to get married. This includes growth in accumulated wealth over time, savings and investments, access to combined incomes and inheritances (as in insurance policies, social security and pension benefits, other assets), support of expanded family networks (that is, in-laws), and the ability for husbands and wives to specialize more in particular areas.[44] A great deal of research also documents the degree to which men become more productive when they marry, even when

---

40. Ibid., 56.

41. Ibid., 55–57; Wells, "The Eight Surprising Health Benefits of Getting Married"; "Does a Better Relationship Mean Better Health?" Note that the latter source is from WebMD, a website that requires that all articles be reviewed for accuracy by medical doctors.

42. Waite and Gallagher, *The Case for Marriage*, 56.

43. "Does a Better Relationship Mean Better Health?" See also "A Happy Marriage Leads to Better Health, Study Finds."

44. Waite and Gallagher, *The Case for Marriage*, 110–18.

relevant demographic variables are controlled to obtain "apples to apples" comparisons.[45] W. Bradford Wilcox is associate professor of sociology at the University of Virginia, director of the National Marriage Project, and a fellow with the Institute of Family Studies. What he has found in extensive research is that "men who get married work harder and more strategically and earn more money than their single peers from similar backgrounds. Marriage also transforms men's social worlds; they spend less time with friends and more time with family; they also go to bars less and to church more."[46]

Married people also share both risks and resources. Jonathan Clements makes this common-sense observation: "It's cheaper for two people to live together than live apart. Getting married also allows you to pool risk. For instance, if you lose your job but your spouse is still working, it will likely be easier to cope financially than if you were single."[47]

Finally, anything that improves people's psychological and physical health is also going to enable them to be more productive. For example, if the "nagging" of a man's wife prevents him from over-drinking, he won't be starting any workdays with a hangover, and will be less likely to develop chronic problems such as diabetes that will undermine productivity. In fact, we could say that all three of these areas (happiness, health, and prosperity) positively influence each other.

WHAT ABOUT COHABITATION?

It is mutual help within stable, covenant relationships demanding significant investment and sacrifice, with clear structure and boundaries, that yields these remarkable benefits of marriage. So far, most research shows that cohabitation does not match the beneficial effects of marriage in any major area.[48] That is not surprising, since many folks consciously avoid or

---

45. Ibid., 100–101; Wilcox, "Don't Be a Bachelor: Why Married Men Work Harder, Smarter, and Make More Money."

46. Ibid.

47. "Getting Married Has Its Financial Benefits."

48. "Does a Better Relationship Mean Better Health?"; Starbuck and Lundy, *Families in Context*, 249; Popenoe and Whitehead, *Should We Live Together?*, 7; Waite and Gallagher, *The Case for Marriage*, 63–64, 67–68, 73–74, 111, 113–14, 116–18. The possible exceptions are those who are engaged with definite plans to marry. However, there is still good evidence that engaged couples are better off waiting until marriage both to have sex and to cohabit, as the Bible clearly instructs. Regardless, most cohabitation is not between formally engaged couples with explicit wedding plans. I will explore this further in chapter 9.

at best forestall the formal commitments and obligations of marriage by cohabiting, making it easier legally, practically, and emotionally to walk away.[49] As opposed to the clarity of marital expectations, cohabitation is marked by high levels of ambiguity and uncertainty.[50]

People in cohabiting relationships tend to maintain separate finances,[51] even though they are able to cut cost-of-living and share housework.[52] Cohabiters are also not as invested, emotionally or practically, in their partner.[53] This is logical given that, by design, neither person has made a lifelong commitment to the other, and because these arrangements tend to be unstable. In the United States, most cohabiting unions break up or shift to marriage within a few years,[54] and when they move on to getting married, roughly two-thirds eventually divorce.[55] The fact that cohabiters are more likely to be sexually unfaithful to their partners than are married people certainly does not help.[56]

Cohabiters tend to spend less time with their partners than those connected by marriage. In fact, the more that young people value individual autonomy, the more likely they are to cohabit rather than marry.[57] This independence undermines the "social insurance" aspect of their relationships. Being able to count on one's partner in times of sickness, loss of employment, or other adversity is much less a feature of cohabitation than of marriage.[58] As one woman candidly told her cohabiting partner, "If you ever need me, we're going to be in trouble."[59]

---

49. Waite and Gallagher, *The Case for Marriage*, 38.

50. Stanley et al., "Sliding Versus Deciding," 503–4.

51. Waite and Gallagher, *The Case for Marriage*, 39–41, 116–17.

52. Ibid., 42–43.

53. Ibid., 63, 73. Wilson, *The Marriage Problem*, 39; Popenoe, *Cohabitation, Marriage, and Child Well-Being: A Cross-National Perspective*, 13.

54. Copen et al., "First Premarital Cohabitation in the United States," 1, 5; Popenoe and Whitehead, 6–7; Waite and Gallagher, *The Case for Marriage*, 38; Binstock and Thornton, "Separations, Reconciliations, and Living Apart in Cohabiting and Marital Unions," 436.

55. Ibid., 441. This relationship between cohabiting and higher divorce risk is complex. We will address it in greater detail in chapter 9.

56. Cherlin, *Public and Private Families*, 170; Waite and Gallagher, *The Case for Marriage*, 39, 91, 93.

57. Ibid., 44–45, 73.

58. Ibid., 46.

59. This quote is taken from the classic book *American Couples: Money, Work, Sex* by sociologists Philip Blumstein and Pepper Schwartz (New York: William Morrow, 1983) as cited in Waite and Gallagher, *The Case for Marriage*, 46.

Not surprisingly, cohabiters enjoy less support from their lovers' families than married people do,[60] which further reduces the social buffers protecting them through the inevitable vicissitudes of life. People who intend on remaining in cohabiting relationships cut themselves off from the teaching, social, and spiritual support of active membership in churches that hold to biblical theology and practice. A church that will not call on them to repent is not one that is teaching the whole counsel of God, and they separate themselves from God by embracing ongoing sexual sin (fornication). Also, like it or not, cohabiting offers far fewer legal protections and benefits than marriage does, though this is changing.[61]

WHAT ABOUT SAME-SEX MARRIAGE?

It is not easy to use empirical evidence to determine if same-sex marriage delivers the same benefits to the same degree as heterosexual marriage, beyond noting the obvious advantages (various legal protections, ability to share resources and labor, and so on). At this time, social scientists face four key problems in addressing this important question.

First, same-sex marriage is a recent phenomenon.[62] The Massachusetts Supreme Court imposed the first legal same-sex marriages in the United States in 2004, and this only applied to that state. At that time, worldwide there were only five other jurisdictions that allowed it. Other jurisdictions trickled in over the next decade or so, but it was not until the famous *Obergefell v. Hodges* decision of June 26, 2015, that the Supreme Court required all American states and territories to recognize same-sex marriage. Thus, it simply has not been around long enough to study its effects on the areas discussed above. We do not know what a representative cross-section of same-sex couples will look like ten or fifteen years into marriage.

Second, as of the beginning of 2016 no more than about 4 percent of the American population identified as gay, lesbian, bisexual, or transgender (LGBT).[63] In 2011, about 1.7 percent identified as exclusively

---

60. Ibid., 117–18.

61. Cherlin, *Public and Private Families*, 189–90; Kennedy and Bumpass, "Cohabitation and Children's Living Arrangements," 1665–66.

62. Despite claims by some gay activists, practices in some cultures documented by anthropologists, such as berdache relationships, are not comparable to modern same-sex marriage.

63. Gates, "In U.S., More Adults Identifying as LGBT."

homosexual.[64] According to General Social Survey data, only 2.2 percent of adults identified as homosexual in the years 2014 and 2016 combined.[65] The 2010 Census documented about 650,000 same-sex couple households, of which only one in five (about 130,000) were "married." Later, the Census Bureau had to revise even these figures downward after the Census Bureau discovered that 73 percent of "same-sex couples" were actually opposite-sex. According to Gallup polling, as of June 2017, only 10.2 percent out of that already small percentage who identified as LGBT were married to a same-sex partner, while 13.1 percent were in opposite-sex marriages.[66] As of March 2018, the US Census Bureau admitted that they did not yet know the number of same-sex marriages in the United States, and as of 2015 tax records showed less than one-half of 1 percent of married filers were in same-sex marriages.[67] All of this means that social scientists studying same-sex marriage must cope with small samples and confusing, dynamic realities, which makes good research difficult.

Third, rampant political correctness in the social sciences and academia discourages qualified researchers from publishing findings that question how well same-sex coupling works.[68] Fourth, with the support of media and many so-called experts, activists blame negative outcomes associated with homosexuality on the direct or indirect effects of discrimination, whether or not there is direct evidence that bigotry explains these differences. Progressives accuse people who do not accept homosexuality, especially the seriously religious, of causing their problems.[69]

---

64. Gates, "How Many People are Lesbian, Gay, Bisexual and Transgender?"

65. Percentages have risen as more people, especially younger cohorts, are comfortable identifying as homosexual.

66. Jones, "In U.S., 10.2% of LGBT Adults Now Married to Same-Sex Spouse."

67. Jao, "U.S. Cities With the Highest Rate of Same-Sex Married Couples."

68. See, for example, the shocking treatment of University of Texas–Austin sociologist Mark Regnerus following publication of his findings suggesting outcomes from same-sex parenting may not be as good as those from heterosexual parents. This is discussed at length in Redding, "Politicized Science."

69. See, for example, the American Psychological Association pamphlet *Answers to Your Questions: For a Better Understanding of Sexual Orientation and Homosexuality*; or the quick shift to blaming discrimination for many health problems of gay men in Centers for Disease Control sites for Gay and Bisexual Men, "For Your Health: Recommendations for A Healthier You" and "Mental Health." Also, National Institutes of Health, "Director's Message," declares "sexual and gender minorities" to be a "health disparity population" and blames many of these health problems on discrimination.

What we do know gives us sound reasons to doubt that solid research over time will show homosexual couples to be comparable to heterosexual ones in mental and physical health and prosperity. Why?

Let us start with the issues of sexual exclusivity. Many homosexual people reject heterosexual norms for marital faithfulness.[70] The overwhelming majority of gay men, for example, have sex with someone other than their partner much more than among heterosexuals. Gay activists are now openly admitting that they do not see monogamy as a feature of their marriages, and some have even substituted the term "monogamish"—meaning open to outside relationships but not actively looking for them—to describe the new sexual ethic for gay marriages. Says pro-gay journalist Nico Lang, "What makes these newly married couples unique is more than their gender. Surveys indicate that a high percentage of same-sex relationships—particularly among queer men—are non-monogamous, and often even after marriage."[71] It is interesting that pop star Elton John said that his partner David Furnish's affairs with numerous other men were not true "unfaithfulness" because Mr. John knew about and accepted them.[72] The problem is greater for gay men. It is hard to believe that such relationships can create the mutual support or stability of heterosexual marriage, not to mention the protection against sexually transmitted diseases (STDs) that traditional married couples enjoy.

In addition, although the issue is overstated at times, even progressive activists admit[73] that homosexual households are marked by generally higher levels of domestic violence than those of heterosexual married or cohabiting couples.[74] This is true for males and females. We do not know whether same-sex marriage will lower this to the level of traditional married couples. I expect that problems with fidelity will almost certainly continue to aggravate this problem.

Next, the gap between heterosexuals and homosexuals in both physical and mental health is huge, much of it tied to behavior that same-sex

---

70. American College of Pediatricians, "Promiscuity," and "Mental Health."

71. "Gay Open Marriages Need To Come Out Of The Closet." See also American College of Pediatricians, "Promiscuity," and Reilly, *Making Gay Okay*, 234.

72. JRKM, "Elton John's Canadian husband David Furnish in tabloid sex tale."

73. Glass, "2 Studies That Prove Domestic Violence is an LGBT Issue."

74. See, for example, Tjaden and Thoennes, *Extent, Nature, and Consequences of Intimate Partner Violence*; Walters et al., "The National Intimate Partner and Sexual Violence Survey (NISVS)."

married couples do not seem to be fully abandoning. These include staggering rates of a range of STDs, bowel and other digestive disorders, risky behaviors, smoking, alcohol and drug abuse, depression, suicide, bipolar and anxiety disorders, asthma, diabetes, and more. These problems lead to higher rates of heart disease, stroke, diabetes, and a host of cancers.[75] Not surprisingly, compared to heterosexuals, homosexual life expectancies are much lower. Even in countries like Norway and Sweden with long-established acceptance of homosexuality, estimates are an average of twenty years shorter life span for gay men,[76] making their lifestyle more dangerous than smoking. An article authored by a gay writer almost two years after the 2015 *Obergefell* decision, entitled "Together Alone: The Epidemic of Gay Loneliness," cites these types of statistics, as well as extensive personal experience in the gay community, to point out that legal same-sex marriage has not helped as much as advocates claimed it would. He approvingly quotes a top expert to point out that even among the legally married in very liberal places, heterosexual men are doing much better. For example, "In Sweden, which has had civil unions since 1995 and full marriage since 2009, men married to men have triple the suicide rate of men married to women."[77]

I would not be surprised to find out that in many ways, those in same-sex marriages will be healthier than those who are not. However, particularly for males, I do not expect they will be nearly as healthy, on average, as heterosexual singles or cohabiters, much less married heterosexuals. They would have to travel a greater distance to get there, and they would need to make bigger changes in their lifestyles when they get married than we are currently seeing.

Hope for gays and lesbians does not lie in marriage to a same-sex partner. Rather, it rests in turning from these dead works to Christ in repentance and faith, even as he lovingly requires from the rest of us sinners (Heb 6:1).

---

75. Here are references that document hard evidence of disturbing health deficits among the homosexual population: Ibid; Centers for Disease Prevention and Control, "Mental Health"; Ward et al., "Sexual Orientation and Health Among U.S. Adults"; American College of Pediatricians, "Physical Health" and "Mental Health"; Reilly, *Making Gay Okay*, 233–36.

76. Ibid., 234–35.

77. Michael Hobbes, March 2, 2017.

NO HOPE FOR THE UNMARRIED?

The blessings of mutual support in good marriages are indeed wonderful, an evidence of God's gracious provision for the human race, and the degree to which his blessings fall on the just and unjust alike when they live in even rough accord with the scriptural pattern. Does this leave the single person outside of God's blessings? What about those who are called to a life of holy, committed celibacy, including our same-sex-attracted brothers and sisters who are committed to walking out their Christian life in this way?

Let us not forget that whatever God calls us to do, he equips us to perform and blesses us in the doing of it (Heb 13:21; Eph 5:23–24). It is also good to keep in mind that rushing into marriage to enjoy its benefits is foolish— not being married is preferable to being in a bad marriage. Moreover, for the believer, in a healthy church there will be strong supportive ties to others, protective leadership, meaningful work beyond simply satisfying one's own desires, and connection to families through worship, fellowship, and service. As the apostle Paul stated, singleness frees believers up for service that would be difficult for those who have spouses and children to be concerned about (1 Cor 7:7–8, 26, 32–34). Even from a secular viewpoint, here is what two sociologists say after detailing the benefits of marriage: "Marriage alone does not guarantee happiness."[78] If people are able to have social ties and support similar to married people through other means, they will be just as happy as the latter. If they are married but their lives are not characterized by healthy social relationships, they will not be happy.[79]

Regardless, we can say this: It is not good for humans to be alone (Gen 2:18).

---

78. Starbuck and Lundy, *Families in Context*, 248.

79. Ibid.

CHAPTER 3

SEXUAL FULFILLMENT

Therefore all immoderation of the flesh is wrong, but insofar as our Lord supports us, he has ordained such a means whereby this weakness will not be imputed as a vice. . . . The mantle of marriage exists to sanctify what is defiled and profane; it serves to cleanse what used to be soiled and dirty in itself. Therefore when we see that our Lord is that benign and has ordained such a remedy, are we not that much more malicious and ungrateful if we do not use it and if all the excuses that men put forth are not rejected? . . . Now with respect to this subject, let us carefully note what the apostle says about the marriage bed, for when men and women keep themselves within the bounds of the fear of God and complete modesty, the bed is honorable.

John Calvin[1]

Wherefore lest we should be too timorous, in the awe that our flat sages would form us and dress us, wisest Solomon among his gravest Proverbs countenances a kind of ravishment and erring fondness in the entertainment of wedded leisures; and in the Song of Songs, which is generally believed, even in the jolliest expressions, to figure the spousals of the church with Christ, sings of a thousand raptures between those two lovely ones far on the hither side of carnal enjoyment. By these instances, and more which might be brought, we may imagine how indulgently God provided against man's loneliness.

John Milton[2]

---

1. Translation by Benjamin Farley in *John Calvin's Sermons on the Ten Commandments*, 179–80.

2. Milton, *The Prose Works of John Milton*, vol. 1, 293. I am grateful for Leland Ryken's *Worldly Saints* directing me to this quote.

When engaged in lawfully within the context of healthy relationships, sex within marriage is a lovely, healthy, and essential celebration and realization of the one-flesh union that in itself points forward to the mystery of Christ and his bride. All married couples who are able to ought to enjoy it regularly and without shame. Indeed, willfully neglecting these nuptial delights hollows out the marital bond.

On the other hand, all forms of sexual activity outside of marriage are sinful and harmful, properly earning stern biblical labels such as fornication, adultery, harlotry, or worse. They all lead to destructive physical, emotional, social, and spiritual consequences, and display contempt for the provision God has made for humankind in either marriage or sanctified celibacy.

In Scripture, both of these sides of the coin of sexual activity are strongly, clearly, and abundantly declared. Yet God's people struggle to get the balance right. Throughout history, in one direction or the other, the church has erred. From the early church fathers through medieval times, virginity and celibacy were extolled as morally superior to sexually active married life. Prior to the Reformation, much of the Western church looked upon even marital sex as inherently lustful and even dirty, only justifiable by the possibility of procreation, which those faithful who are more anxious for holiness should severely limit or even abandon. That view did not die easily and still holds some sway in the official dogma of the Roman Catholic Church, though it appears to have little currency among rank-and-file Catholics. Dwelling uneasily alongside of the minimal remaining vestiges of this hyper-prudism, errant believers today are mostly harming the contemporary church by unprecedented tolerance or even whole-hearted acceptance of premarital sex, cohabitation, and other forms of sexual activity outside marriage. Many modern evangelicals who continue to restrict sex to marriage have unwittingly turned marital sex into a kind of idol, focusing on individual gratification and heightened sexual experiences over the mutual love, care, and respect within which husbands and wives should live out their sexual relationships. Either way, much of the contemporary evangelical world has lost sight of the essence of the wholeness, beauty, meaning, and holiness of marital erotic love.

I will focus mostly on the positive benefits and moral goodness of marital sex in this chapter, exploring God's plan that, in marriage, people can satisfy their natural desire for sexual fulfillment while avoiding fornication, idolatry, and other forms of sexual uncleanness. After this, I will look at the mutually beneficial relationship of sex and marriage. Finally, I present some balanced, common-sense principles and ideas that churches can communicate in order to help Christians develop a healthy outlook on sex within marriage. However, first, I must spend some time on what God wants people to avoid—sexual activity outside of marriage.

THE SINFULNESS OF SEX
OUTSIDE OF MARRIAGE

WHAT THE SCRIPTURES TEACH

The Scriptures strongly, consistently, and clearly condemn all sex outside of marriage. In spite of the disagreements between Roman Catholics and Protestants on the relative goodness of celibacy or the purposes of sex within marriage, there is no argument between Rome, Geneva, or Wittenberg on this point.

Adultery is a violation of the Ten Commandments (Exod 20:14) and carried the death penalty in the Old Testament (Lev 20:10; Deut 22:22), which also regularly denounced it and tied it to a host of calamitous consequences (cf. key portions of Prov 5–7 and Hos 4). While in the New Testament adultery ceased to be punishable by execution, it remained a terrible offense (cf. Matt 5:32; 19:9; 1 Cor 7:2; Heb 13:4). In fact, Jesus extended his condemnation of it to harboring sexual lust in our hearts (Matt 5:27–30). Adulterers can receive forgiveness and restoration if they repent of it before God (1 Cor 6:9–11; 1 John 1:9).[3] Yet even so, it constitutes a grave violation of the marital covenant.

Moreover, it is no accident that the Bible so often depicts apostasy and idolatry as adultery (cf. Jer 3:1–14, 20; 13:27; Ezek 16:15–43; Jas 4:4). Since—as we have already emphasized drawing on the Anglican *Book of Common Prayer*—marriage symbolizes "the mystical union that is betwixt Christ and his church,"[4] this is hardly surprising. In fact, as Francis Schaeffer observed in a discussion of adultery and sexual sin generally, "God never allows us to tone down on the condemnation of sexual sin. Sexual sin shatters the

---

3. I am grateful for R. C. Sproul's brief but potent discussion of the above points in *The Intimate Marriage*, 116.

4. 311.

illustration of the relationship of God and his people, of Christ and his church."[5]

Though Scripture does not denounce fornication as strongly or punish it as severely as adultery, it does reject it as both sinful and unwise. In the Old Testament, Hebrew brides were required to be virgins (Deut 22:13–21). The sexual restrictions upon unmarried males in the Old Testament were looser. For example, single males who engaged in activities such as visiting prostitutes did not face legal punishment, though such practices were not approved of (cf. Gen 38:15–26). The Law did not punish Hebrew men who were not virgins at marriage, but we do find that if they seduced a virgin they had to marry her or pay her bride-price (Exod 22:16–17).

Men under the Old Testament law could have more than one wife as well as concubines. However, polygamy was a man-made practice that God controlled (cf. Exod 21:20) and at times directed toward positive ends in a fallen and broken world.[6] We see Jesus making a similar point about "easy divorce" regulations in the Old Testament, that this was allowed as a concession and not part of his original design for marriage (Matt 19:3–9). The New Testament teaching voided polygamy. For example, though 1 Timothy 3:2 and Titus 1:6 were not explicitly focused on polygamy,[7] they plainly declare that Christian males should be "one-woman men."[8]

Going beyond the Old Testament and returning to God's creational intentions for sex and marriage, the New Testament clearly prohibits premarital sex for men and women alike. Paul states that if people are to have sexual relations, they should do so within marriage only. To do otherwise is to engage in *porneia* (1 Cor 7:1–2, 8–9). The best translation of this Greek word is "fornication"[9] but in various versions of the Bible it is also assigned softer terms such as immorality, sexual immorality, and "unchastity." In three places, *porneia* appears on lists of grave sins along with adultery, which is listed separately (Matt 15:19; Mark 7:21; 1 Cor 6:9).

---

5. *The Church Before the Watching World*, 45. I am also grateful for the excellent list of biblical references on spiritual adultery and "whoredom" provided here, 47–50.

6. For example, Levirate marriage, which provided for the lineage and widows of deceased brothers or other near-kin, was not exempted if the brother or other kin in line to marry the widow was already married (Gen 38:6–10; Deut 25:5–10).

7. This is because those to whom Paul addressed these letters were already monogamous.

8. Towner, *1–2 Timothy & Titus*, 84, 225.

9. As, for example, R. C. Sproul does in *The Intimate Marriage*, 116.

Porneia encompasses a range of types of illicit sexual misconduct, which can include adultery,[10] unless restricted by context.[11] Therefore, the use of this term in the Bible is not tolerant of hair-splitting by claiming that forms of sexual activity between unmarried persons other than intercourse are not "sin." *All* sexual activity is restricted to marriage. Fornication is condemned often in the New Testament.[12]

In both testaments, God enjoins his people to sexual exclusivity with their marriage partner. This means no other partners before marriage. Everything we see the Scriptures teaching about marriage casts aspersions on sex outside of it. As the *Catechism of the Catholic Church* states: "Fornication is carnal union between an unmarried man and an unmarried woman. It is gravely contrary to the dignities of persons and of human sexuality which is naturally ordered to the good of spouses and the generation and education of children."[13]

WHAT PROFESSING CHRISTIANS BELIEVE

I combined the General Social Surveys conducted between 2010 and 2016[14] to look at over 1,400 Protestants tied to conservative denominations, comparing them to over 4,000 who identified as affiliated with moderate or liberal Protestants, Roman Catholics, Jews, and "none-of-the-above."[15] Let's see what they thought about the morality of adultery and pre-marital sex.

As table 3.1 shows, conservative Protestants were more likely to hold biblical beliefs about adultery than were others. Still, how one out of every ten of them could think that adultery is *not* always wrong is puzzling, even shocking.

Table 3.2, however, is heartbreaking. Even though Protestants in conservative churches are more likely to hold biblical views on premarital sex than others are, only a little over one-third agree with the clear teaching of Scripture that it is *always* wrong. In fact, just as many of them said

---

10. As it does in Matthew 19:9; see Keener, *Matthew*, 297–98.

11. Ibid., 298.

12. Specific texts include: Acts 15:20, 29; 21:25; 1 Cor 5:1; 6:13, 18; 2 Cor 12:21; Gal 5:19; Eph 5:3; Col 3:5; 1 Thess 4:3.

13. *Catechism of the Catholic Church*, 565.

14. Smith et al.

15. There were small numbers of others as well (Muslims, Buddhists, etc.), but I did not include those in this discussion here.

Table 3.1: "What is your opinion about a married person having sexual relations with someone other than the marriage partner ... is it always wrong, almost always wrong, wrong only sometimes, or not wrong at all?" (GSS 2010–2016)

Religious Affiliation	Always Wrong	Almost Always Wrong	Wrong Only Sometimes	Not Wrong At All
Conservative Protestant:	89%	6%	4%	1%
Moderate Protestant:	85%	11%	3%	1%
Liberal Protestant:	73%	19%	6%	2%
Roman Catholic:	81%	12%	6%	2%
Jewish:	56%	30%	13%	1%
None:	61%	20%	15%	4%

premarital sex is *not* wrong *at all*. This is staggering—the majority of conservative Protestants now believe that fornication can be morally acceptable. In fact, in the same years and survey, over half of those Protestants who claimed to believe that the Bible was the inerrant word of God, to be read literally and word-for-word, did not believe that premarital sex was always wrong, and close to a third of these said that it was not wrong at all. We are living through a massive breakdown in faithfulness among professing Protestant believers to a fundamental, clear, core, historical teaching of the Christian faith.

Two other facts are also disheartening. First, the percentage of those associated with conservative Protestant churches who reject premarital sex has gone down sharply in recent years. From 2000 to 2006, the percentage saying it is "always wrong" was about half, but then dropped steadily down to only a little over one-third by 2016. Thus, in a period of only ten years we have seen a very sharp decline in faithfulness to biblical teaching about premarital sex. Second, younger people attached to conservative Protestant churches are overwhelmingly morally comfortable with premarital sex. For the years 2010 through 2016, among those eighteen to twenty-nine years of age, only 28 percent believed that premarital sex was always wrong, while about half said it was not wrong at all. Among those

Table 3.2: "If a man and woman have sexual relations before marriage, do you think that it is always wrong, almost always wrong, wrong only sometimes, or not wrong at all?" (GSS 2010–2014)

Religious Affiliation	Always Wrong	Almost Always Wrong	Wrong Only Sometimes	Not Wrong At All
Conservative Protestant:	38%	9%	14%	39%
Moderate Protestant:	30%	8%	16%	46%
Liberal Protestant:	17%	8%	22%	53%
Roman Catholic:	14%	7%	19%	60%
Jewish:	5%	2%	15%	78%
None:	4%	2%	12%	82%

ages thirty to forty-nine it was not much better, with only about one-third saying fornication is always wrong and 44 percent saying it is not wrong at all. Things do not bode well for the future church standing firm for biblical sexual morality. We are getting worse, and the decline is accelerating.

Those who attend church regularly are far more likely to hold to biblical views on premarital sex. For 2010 through 2016, 58 percent of conservative Protestant respondents who said they attended religious services about weekly or more thought that premarital sex is always wrong. For those weekly attenders ages eighteen to twenty-nine this figure was 51 percent, and for those ages thirty to forty-nine it was 57 percent. Regular participation in the life of the church makes a positive difference in beliefs about premarital sex, though even among regular churchgoers the numbers are depressing.

Therefore, it is sad that the same 2010 to 2016 GSS shows that less than half of conservative Protestants say that they attend religious services about weekly or more. It is worse among the young, where only about one-third of conservative Protestant adults under the age of thirty attend church about weekly. We also know that people overestimate their church attendance on surveys,[16] so the situation is actually worse than the polls

---

16. Johnstone, *Religion in Society*, 106.

indicate. The same Scriptures that teach us to "flee from sexual immorality" (1 Cor 6:18) also admonish us not to neglect the weekly gathering of the saints (Heb 10:25; cf. Acts 20:7). Sadly, many modern professing believers reject both.

Regardless, being in church regularly exposes people to church teaching, fellowship, hymns, social support, and so on that reinforce fidelity to truth while catching and addressing error. Churches have a lot of work to do to bring professed believers, even those who are regularly in church, on board with a biblical sexual ethic, but they should be encouraged that their efforts can make a big difference. Professing believers who withdraw from the flock become lost, prey for wolves, because their shepherds cannot properly care for them. Church leaders need to encourage their members to be consistent in worship, instruction, and fellowship, and then make sure to communicate a biblical sexual ethic and worldview during these times.

WHAT PROFESSING CHRISTIANS PRACTICE

Sticking with the 2010 through 2016 GSS, look at the abysmal reality shown in table 3.3. Respondents who had ever been married indicated if they had ever committed adultery. Like other sensitive questions about sexual behavior, here the GSS used "secret ballot" techniques to encourage a maximum level of honesty.[17] The bottom line is that those affiliated with conservative Protestant churches, male or female, were at least just as likely to have committed adultery as others were. This was true overall, and for those forty to sixty-five years of age (when they had been married longer and thus had more time to cheat on their spouses). Sadly, none of these percentages for conservative Protestants was significantly lower among those who attended church weekly or more often, either. Professing evangelicals, even regular churchgoers, cheat on their spouses at least as much as everyone else. This is scandalous.

The picture with premarital sexual activity is just as troubling. In a way, that should not be surprising, as at least 95 percent of today's Americans

---

17. Respondents complete the answers privately and anonymously. For items asking about illicit sexual behavior, many "guilty parties" will not admit the behavior even here. However, by giving them total anonymity the surveyors get what is probably the most honest answers one could hope for, and these can still be used to compare groups, since there is no reason to believe that the conservative Protestants, for example, will be more honest here than the others if they have committed adultery. In fact, we could argue the opposite.

Table 3.3: "Have you ever had sex with someone other than your husband or wife while you were married?" Percent of Ever-Married Respondents Answering "Yes," Overall, and Over 40–65 Years Old (GSS 2010–2016)

Religious Affiliation	Males	Females	Males 40–65	Females 40–65
Conservative Protestant:	23%	14%	25%	16%
Moderate Protestant:	21%	14%	21%	20%
Liberal Protestant:	23%	12%	26%	15%
Roman Catholic:	20%	12%	21%	14%
Jewish:	14%	18%	17%	17%
None:	25%	20%	24.5%	22%

have sex before marriage, and these types of high percentages have been around for decades.[18] It was not always so. Although premarital sex was more common in the previous couple of centuries than we like to think (depending on the era), it was less common. Moreover, through the 1950s it generally occurred more in the context of relationships that were serious and headed for marriage, with far less recreational sex, partners, "experimentation," and the like than we see today.[19]

As table 3.4 shows, among never-married respondents affiliated with conservative Protestant churches ages twenty-three to thirty-nine, the percentages are not much better than the population as a whole.[20] The table also shows that, thankfully, those who are regular church attenders do a *lot* better, but even there the results are distressing. Is it any wonder that non-Christians so often accuse the professing church of sexual hypocrisy?

I believe that God does not call us to be satisfied with awful numbers like this, but he also does not want us to despair. We need to instruct, encourage, and call on believers who have failed in these areas to embrace

18. Finer, "Trends in Premarital Sex in the United States, 1954–2003," 73.

19. Elliot, *Not My Kid*, 14; Wiederman, 664–65; Cherlin, *Public and Private Families*, 166, 210. Edmund Morgan (*The Puritan Family*, 33) notes that among the New England Puritans, sex between engaged couples was quite common and they treated it more indulgently than other forms of premarital sex, though still regarding it as sin to be confessed and forsaken.

20. I included 2004 through 2014 to have sufficient numbers in the smaller categories of respondents here.

Table 3.4: "Now, think about the past five years—the time since and including the past 12 months, how many sex partners have you had in that five-year period?" Never-Married Respondents 25–40 Years Old Who Are Affiliated with Conservative Protestant Denominations Only (GSS 2000–2016)

	Male	Male Weekly Church Attender	Female	Female Weekly Church Attender
None:	11%	32%	8%	19%
One:	15%	14%	31%	32%
Two:	11%	11%	24%	22%
3 or More:	63.5%	43%	37%	26%

repentance and renewal, and then press forward in Christ. We must also equip and strengthen our single brothers and sisters who are striving to maintain their virginity until marriage. However, we need to face reality squarely to do this, rather than pretend things are better than they are.

In the next and seventh chapter, I will lay out some of the negative fallout of sexual promiscuity generally and in the churches. In chapter 7, I will also consider practical steps parents can take to help singles maintain or regain sexual integrity. Generally, when we look at the teachings of Scripture versus the beliefs and practices within the modern professing church, it is easy for us to err toward much of what the church has done in the past—denounce sex and warn about its dangers. This focus on sex as something inherently "bad" has a long history in Christianity (and has thankfully changed), and it has been a major reason why things are such a mess today. Instead, like the Puritans and the Scriptures they appealed to, we need to set forth the beauty, goodness, delight, legitimate sensual pleasures, and godliness of sex within marriage and encourage believers to strive for that rather than settle for something less.[21] We must do that even while assuring our brethren who may remain celibate over the long term that God has measureless glories in store for them as well. C. S. Lewis captured well the general approach we need to have when talking to believers about sex and sexual purity, namely, that in spurning God's way we are

---

21. Cf. Sproul, *The Intimate Marriage*, 117–20; and Ryken, *Worldly Saints*, 43–51.

settling for too little rather than demanding too much. "It would seem that Our Lord finds our desires, not too strong, but too weak. We are . . . like an ignorant child who wants to go on making mud pies in a slum because he cannot imagine what is meant by the offer of a holiday at the sea. We are far too easily pleased."[22]

SEX WITHIN MARRIAGE: LOVELY, HEALTHY, AND MORALLY PURE

WHAT THE SCRIPTURES TEACH

In both the Old and New Testaments, God not only directs us to find our sexual fulfillment only within marriage—he encourages us to delight in it with all the senses and without shame. It is an expression of the one-flesh reality of marriage and the beauty of Christ's relationship with his bride, the church. Scripture asserts that regular sexual activity is necessary for healthy marriage under normal circumstances and refraining from it is harmful. God tells us that marital sex is holy and good by both example and precept, as opposed to the extreme condemnation he declares for all sex outside of marriage.

Adam "knowing" Eve is the first human action we read about following man's expulsion from paradise (Gen 4:1). Here we find the beautiful reality Noel Paul Stookey mentions in part of the song I quoted to start the introduction of this book: "Woman draws her life from man, and gives it back again."[23] In one of the great love stories in the Bible, Isaac falls head over heels for Rebekah at first sight, brings her into his mother Sarah's tent on their wedding night, loves her, and so finds comfort after his mother's death (Gen 24:67). Later, we find them having sexual relations in the great outdoors, with the Hebrew terms used to describe it suggesting light-heartedness, play, laughter, sport, and merriment (Gen 26:8–9). Interestingly, the term used to describe their intimacy is the same as that used for Isaac's name.[24]

Solomon recommends a whole-hearted immersion in sex within marriage, involving all the senses and the entire body, which husband and wife are to enjoy completely like the finest food and drink. Consider this

---

22. "The Weight of Glory," 263.
23. "Wedding Song (There Is Love)."
24. *New Geneva Study Bible*, 52.

amazing passage from the Song of Songs (7:1–13), in which the groom sets forth the beauty of his bride and his intimate longing to enjoy all of her, and she responds in kind:

HE:
How beautiful are your feet in sandals, O noble daughter! Your rounded thighs are like jewels, the work of a master hand. Your navel is a rounded bowl that never lacks mixed wine. Your belly is a heap of wheat, encircled with lilies. Your two breasts are like two fawns, twins of a gazelle. Your neck is like an ivory tower. Your eyes are pools in Heshbon, by the gate of Bath-rabbim. Your nose is like a tower of Lebanon, which looks toward Damascus. Your head crowns you like Carmel, and your flowing locks are like purple; a king is held captive in the tresses. How beautiful and pleasant you are, O loved one, with all your delights! Your stature is like a palm tree, and your breasts are like its clusters. I say I will climb the palm tree and lay hold of its fruit. Oh may your breasts be like clusters of the vine, and the scent of your breath like apples, and your mouth like the best wine.

SHE:
It goes down smoothly for my beloved, gliding over lips and teeth. I am my beloved's, and his desire is for me.

THE BRIDE GIVES HER LOVE:
Come, my beloved, let us go out into the fields and lodge in the villages; let us go out early to the vineyards and see whether the vines have budded, whether the grape blossoms have opened and the pomegranates are in bloom. There I will give you my love. The mandrakes give forth fragrance, and beside our doors are all choice fruits, new as well as old, which I have laid up for you, O my beloved.

We also see similar language used when Solomon gives wise advice to young men about how to avoid sexual sin and its destructive results. He certainly does not give us a stark choice between abstinence and lust, nor play the role of a dour killjoy. "Drink water from your own cistern, flowing water from your own well. Should your springs be scattered abroad, streams of water in the streets? . . . Let your fountain be blessed, and rejoice in the wife of your youth, a lovely deer, a graceful doe. Let her breasts fill you at all times with delight; be intoxicated always in her love" (Prov 5:15-16, 18-19).

The apostle Paul gives similar advice that marital sex is God's solution for sexual sin for most people, although with less embellishment and lyrical language. In 1 Corinthians we have this well-known passage (7:2-5):

> But because of the temptation to sexual immorality, each man should have his own wife and each woman her own husband. The husband should give to his wife her conjugal rights, and likewise the wife to her husband. For the wife does not have authority over her own body, but the husband does. Likewise the husband does not have authority over his own body, but the wife does. Do not deprive one another, except perhaps by agreement for a limited time, that you may devote yourselves to prayer; but then come together again, so that Satan may not tempt you because of your lack of self-control.

Later in that chapter (7:36b), Paul declares simply, "If his passions are strong, and it has to be, let him do as he wishes: let them marry—it is no sin." The writer of Hebrews advances a similar prescription (13:4): "Let marriage be held in honor among all, and let the marriage bed be undefiled, for God will judge the sexually immoral and adulterous."

PROTESTANT RECLAMATION OF BALANCED BIBLICAL TEACHING ON MARITAL SEX

When the Reformers arrived on the scene, for many centuries Western Christianity had viewed sex of any kind negatively, marital or not. The medieval Roman Catholic Church held that sex was justified only by the possibility of procreation, and that it always involved some degree of sinful lust. They limited sex for married people in many ways. Medieval teaching echoed many of the church fathers—such as Ambrose, Augustine, Jerome, Origen, and Tertullian—who elevated celibacy and virginity above marriage. Many of these teachers even praised married couples who abandoned sex, in contradiction to the apostle Paul's clear instructions that spouses should only do so for brief periods of prayer and fasting (1 Cor 7:3-5). Arguing from silence, many even claimed that Adam and Eve did not have sexual desire in paradise, and had they never sinned God would have provided other means for the procreation of the human race.[25]

Modern people often depict our early Protestant brethren as sexual prudes. This is clearly false. In fact, at the dawn of the Reformation, Catholic critics such as Thomas More accused them of sensuality and lust, partly for their strong defense of marriage and of the marriage bed.[26]

Paul's extended recommendation of celibacy and refraining from marriage in 1 Corinthians 7, perhaps his most important teaching on sex in marriage, has contributed to this denigration of marital sex by sincere Christians over the centuries. It is true that believers should not despise celibacy. We ought to instead highly value those among us who choose to remain single as part of their particular callings before God. However, as R. C. Sproul points out, "Paul's comparison between marriage and celibacy is not a contrast between good and bad but between good and better."[27] A. A. Hodge reminded his readers that the union of marriage is highly honored by God signifying by it his relationship with his church. He went on to note that God himself married Adam to Eve in a pure world, that godly marriage calls forth and develops "the noblest moral instincts and faculties," while imposing celibacy on all men and women who would be seriously devoted to God has produced many evils throughout church history.[28] Jesus clearly stated that God has only given the gift of celibacy to some (Matt 19:11–12). Common-sense observation tells us that this is not the majority of people. Besides, Paul tied his recommendation of celibacy to particular kinds of Christian service in a time of severe challenge and persecution. A. A. Hodge agrees that "the unmarried are exposed to less worldly care than the married; therefore . . . in times of persecution and public danger, and with reference to some special kind of service to which God providentially calls a man, it may be both his interest and his duty not to marry."[29] This is certainly true for many kinds of missionary service.[30]

---

25. See Packer, *A Quest for Godliness*, 261; Sproul, *The Intimate Marriage*, 117–18; Ryken, *Worldly Saints*, 40–42.

26. Packer, *A Quest for Godliness*, 41.

27. Sproul, *The Intimate Marriage*, 120.

28. Hodge, *The Westminster Confession*, 304.

29. Ibid.

30. Ibid.

Among the earlier Protestants, like John Calvin,[31] the Puritans were forthright in refuting the Roman Catholic view of marital sex, and indeed praising the latter. John Milton claimed that the "one flesh" passage in Genesis 2:24 was given to us "to justify and make legitimate the rites of the marriage bed; which was not unneedful, if for all this warrant they were suspected of pollution by some sects of philosophy and religion of old, and latelier among the Papists."[32] Married saints were encouraged to embrace sex with exuberance and not just out of duty. One Puritan writer encouraged spouses to "joyfully give due benevolence one to another; as two musical instruments rightly fitted do make a most pleasant and sweet harmony in a well-tuned consort."[33] William Gouge encouraged married couples to "engage in sex 'with good will and delight, willingly, readily, and cheerfully.'"[34]

Puritans also believed that sex should be regular. One Puritan man even lodged a formal complaint against another for slandering him with the charge that he would go for weeks at a time without having sex with his wife.[35]

R. C. Sproul assures us that, outside of those things that Scripture clearly forbids, in marriage there is considerable freedom in the type of sexual acts a couple may choose to enjoy.[36] However, since he wrote that in 1975, the landscape has changed enormously, and married couples need more guidance than this. Much of this is due to pressures and expectations fueled by pornography, sex manuals and advice, and the like. Increasingly, husbands particularly are demanding acts from their wives that, even if not forbidden by Scripture, are potentially degrading, dehumanizing, and objectifying. Fallen human beings are capable of abusing every legitimate freedom, fashioning their spouses' bodies into idols or selfish instruments used merely to feed their own pleasures.

The Puritan answer was a good one: the pleasures of the marriage bed should take place under a canopy of sacrificial love and mutual affection.

---

31. Witte, "Marriage and Family Life," 463; see also Calvin's *Sermons on the Ten Commandments*, 178–83.
32. Quoted in *Worldly Saints*, 43.
33. Quoted in ibid., 44.
34. Ibid., 44, 46.
35. Morgan, *The Puritan Family*, 63.
36. Sproul, *The Intimate Marriage*, 133.

Said Francis Bremer: "Love was the cement of the Puritan family and sex was viewed as one of the means of expressing that love."[37]

We can also apply what we touched on in chapter 2 about marriage reflecting the highest form of friendship, one in which each partner seeks always and in everything to nurture goodness, nobility, and virtue in the other. Without spinning extrabiblical rules, we can honestly consider whether a particular act exemplifies moral excellence, bonds the couple together in warm affection, and is mutually ennobling. In this, as in all other things, is this sexual act something that is a means to honor and enjoy God in our relationship with our spouse? Looked at this way, many of the pleasure techniques pushed by so-called sexual experts fall dreadfully short.

Another Puritan antidote to modern excess, even among married believers, is their insistence that sex lives should be private. The Puritans were quite definite about this. As Ryken points out, they believed this is "not because [sex] is bad, but because of its inherent nature as a total union between two people who commit themselves to each other permanently."[38] We live in an age of unseemly public displays of affection and lack of modesty. Ryken remarks approvingly that, by contrast, "The Puritans had an abhorrence of erotic displays in public. . . . But this negative attitude toward public dalliance did not extend to private love."[39]

Our forebears were not perfect, but we can learn a lot from them. Following their historical example can help us to embrace sexual fulfillment as a legitimate and beautiful purpose of marriage, without going so far that we fall headlong into sex-crazed modernity.

MARRIAGE AND SEX ENRICH EACH OTHER

Good sexual relationship and marital happiness are mutually enhancing. This should not surprise us since, as I have been underscoring, the two are designed by God to go together.

In 2010, about half of Americans polled by the Pew Research Center said that marriage made no difference in how easy it is to have a fulfilling sex life.[40] This fits popular misconceptions about the carefree sex lives of

---

37. Quoted in Ryken, *Worldly Saints*, 51.
38. Ryken, *Worldly Saints*, 46.
39. Ibid.
40. Pew Research Center, "The Decline of Marriage and Rise of New Families," 24.

singles and divorcees, and the notion that marriage dulls and stifles sex. However, social research strongly suggests otherwise.

Waite and Gallagher draw on a great deal of research to show that compared to others, married people are better off sexually. "Married people have both more and better sex . . . [and] enjoy it more, both physically and emotionally. . . . Cohabitors have more sex than married couples, but they don't necessarily enjoy it as much. Marriage, it turns out . . . is good for your libido."[41] Why? Besides the fact that a husband and wife live together and thus are readily and mutually accessible (also true for cohabitors), the key is that "committed sex is better sex."[42] Commitment enriches emotional depth and, for women especially, creates a sense of security, especially where pregnancy is a real possibility. Married people also have a lifetime to practice, learn, grow, and adjust across the seasons of life. Thus, their sex lives improve over time.[43] Finally, the exclusive nature of marriage means that married couples not only feel more secure with one another, but also put more effort into making their sex lives more enjoyable and fulfilling.[44]

It is a good thing that faithfully married people do tend to prioritize having a quality sex life, because this is also critical to the health and happiness of their marriages. For example, married couples who have sex more frequently are much more likely to say that their marriage is very happy, as we can see in the General Social Survey.[45] The Survey of Marital Generosity found that married parents with "above-average levels of sexual satisfaction" were much more likely to be happy in their marriages, and much less likely to be prone to separation or divorce. Thus, "sexual satisfaction

---

41. Waite and Gallagher, *The Case for Marriage*, 79. In the General Social Survey years 2006–2016, in every major age group including those less than thirty, with a very slight exception for divorced person ages seventy to seventy-nine, married people were far more likely to be having sex weekly or more often than singles, divorced or separated, for example. (Though for those ages eighteen to thirty, married versus divorced was only a slight difference. The rest were quite large.)

42. Ibid., 83, see also 85.

43. Ibid., 88–89.

44. Ibid., 96.

45. Among married respondents from 2000 through 2016, 68 percent of those who had sex weekly or more said their marriages were "very happy," versus 59 percent of those who had sex one to three times a month, and 52 percent if they had sex less than that. With age, sexual frequency naturally drops off as couples get older, and in some cases experience health issues that diminish or end their sexual activity. Yet even among married respondents seventy and older, more sex is associated with higher marital happiness.

emerges as one of the top five predictors of marital quality and stability for both mothers and fathers in today's families."[46]

From the very beginning, God designed marriage and sex to go together. Marriage is the garden he created within which sex, cultivated properly and for the right reasons, with regular attention and care, could best thrive and produce pleasing, delightful, positive fruit. One major consequence of the explosion of sex outside marriage in modern societies has been decreased commitment to marriage itself and less willingness to marry, to the detriment of all of us.[47]

CONSTRUCTIVE AND BALANCED
APPROACHES FOR THE CHURCH

Given that sexual fulfillment is one of God's basic purposes for marriage, helping God's people to understand that within a balanced framework is vital. What are some of the basic, core principles the church can communicate to help members approach marital sex in a balanced, godly, common-sense way that helps their marriages to be more successful?

First, our appreciation for how marital sex changes as life unfolds, combined with what we know about how true sexual fulfillment flows naturally out of godly marital life and the challenges that typical married couples face, can help us to provide wise, balanced, mature counsel to our youth. For example, I often advise young people against the "try before you buy" lie, the fiction that singles must have sex with prospective marital partners in order to ensure that they will be sexually compatible. In fact, recent data from the University of Denver's Relationship Development Study shows that having multiple sex partners prior to marriage reduces marital quality,[48] which as we have seen decreases sexual fulfillment in marriage. Regardless, the sexual experience of unmarried, twenty-something couples tells us nothing about what their sex lives will be like across the span of their lives. I have marveled at how quickly younger folks grasp this when I lay it out logically and honestly.

---

46. *When Baby Makes Three*, 36.

47. This is a key argument in Mark Regnerus's book *Cheap Sex*. See, for example, his chapter "Cheap Sex and the Modern Mating Market," pages 22–61.

48. Rhoades and Stanley, *Before "I Do,"* 6, 8.

Second, it is critical to point out that sexual fulfillment flows from the overall quality of the lives that married people build together, of their love for and commitments to each other and to God. For example, social scientists analyzed factors associated with sexual fulfillment in married persons. One of the key elements connected to fulfilling sex was something called "marital generosity."[49] This means simply doing nice things for each other out of love and consideration of the needs of the other, such as showing respect, extending forgiveness, making coffee or toast for one's husband or wife in the morning, warming up the car when it is cold, that kind of thing.[50] Other features of marriages with the most fulfilling sex lives included mutual commitment, "religious faith," "couple-centered quality time" and, for women, husbands helping them with the housework.[51] Married people of faith who love and prioritize each other in simple, consistent ways are the most satisfied sexually.

Third, Christians need to understand that, in the normal course of married life, they will face realities that significantly interrupt or diminish sex. Sometimes these down periods will last for a long time. One of the first such periods that most young married people encounter is having a baby. As social scientists at the National Marriage Project and Institute for American Values note, citing solid research: "After a baby comes along, most couples see their sexual activity and satisfaction drop, at least for a time."[52] With pregnancy, childbirth, sleepless nights, and all the adjustments that come with babies and then toddlers, this is hardly surprising.

Given the role that God has assigned sex in marriage, and its many benefits for married persons, the follow-up advice of these researchers is also sound: "Our findings suggest that it is important for couples to renew the sexual dimension of their relationship as quickly as possible."[53] They could have made the same recommendation for renewing regular sex, whenever possible, after all of life's inevitable interruptions, and its disasters, trials, and sorrows, too—surgery, extreme grief or stress, prolonged separation, chronic illness, and more. We need to teach married saints to gracefully

---

49. *When Baby Makes Three*, 36.
50. Ibid., 38.
51. Ibid., 36.
52. Ibid., 35.
53. Ibid., 36.

accept the difficulties but also to, as the apostle Paul admonished (1 Cor 7:5), "come together again" when they are able.

Following on this point, churches need to be places where married couples can come for help with sexual difficulties in their marriage. Church leaders should view these matters as part of the array of issues that pastors, elders, and Christian counselors will need to tackle in marital, and also premarital, counseling. Many couples will experience disagreement and even conflict related to their sex lives and benefit from pastoral insight, help, and encouragement in resolving those. Increasingly, too, people in our churches are dealing with various kinds of damaging ideas and experiences that affect their marital sex lives, such as exposure to pornography, sexual assault, incest, abortions, sexual memories and other residual effects of past relationships, and more. To the extent that couples are referred to outside counsel, programs, videos, and reading materials, it is critical that these be carefully vetted by church leaders and, ideally, explicitly Christian. Worldly "sex help" is increasingly amoral, nonjudgmental, and even may offer advice (such as the "positive use of erotica") or training that is clearly sinful. There are excellent Christian alternatives that honor marriage and God's design for sex, and we should use them.

However, a lot of sexual advice for married couples from Christian counselors and authors is not balanced or sound. Too much of it bombards married couples with unrealistic expectations of continuous, spectacular lovemaking, encouraging them to fill their lives with spicy, almost daily, sexual activity, sensualizing almost everything, and instructing them how to do so. It is almost as if many evangelicals use the promise of constant and exciting marital sex to offset the rigors of premarital chastity. This kind of teaching is bound to leave thousands of couples who have perfectly normal sex lives feeling as if their love life does not measure up. Christian counselors and women's leaders often admonish believing wives to meet the "sexual needs" of their husbands continuously—dressing seductively, mastering exotic sexual techniques, and never saying "no" to sex or to particular sexual activities their partners desire unless prevented by illness or some other inescapable barrier. Explicitly or implicitly, many Christian women are being taught that they must make sure that their spouses are always sexually satisfied in order to make sure that their husbands won't be overcome with sexual temptation or frustration.[54]

---

54. See, for example, Leman, *Sheet Music*, 46–54.

One popular Christian author even encourages married people to masturbate when regular intercourse alone is not enough or for some reason is unavailable.[55] He seems to focus particularly on men doing this, and their wives tolerating it.[56] Another author, widely read for her sexual advice to Christian women, suggests that masturbation can be a legitimate part of the marital repertoire if it involves fantasizing sexually about one's spouse, or is part of sexual therapy.[57] She even suggests it may be a valuable means for singles to maintain their sexual purity and learn to exercise self-control.[58] My point here is not to denounce masturbation so much as to question the whole focus on seeing marital sex as heavily or even primarily a self-seeking means for meeting individual "needs" for sexual release rather than a powerful means for expressing love, and fostering intimacy, between husband and wife.[59]

It is hard to square some modern Christian sexual advice for married people with upholding mutual love and respect, maintaining our bodies in "holiness and honor, not in the passion of lust like the Gentiles who do not know God" (1 Thess 4:4–5), or with nurturing fruits of the Spirit such as patience and self-control (Gal 5:22–23). This kind of teaching unwittingly encourages spouses (usually husbands) to make their individual, sensual needs a higher priority than their partner's preferences and welfare. Teaching like this can subtly transform spouses from lovers and life partners into dispensers of sexual gratification. In healthy marriages, each spouse at times will yield to the other, and this is as true in engaging in lovemaking as anything else. There is nothing wrong with learning new ways to enhance marital sex. However, the unbalanced pursuit of sexual excitement can push couples into destructive and degrading experimentation and obsession, leaving them unable to find satisfaction in what is normal, sufficient, and realistic across the life span.

We must never forget that sex is the representation and realization of the one-flesh reality of marriage. Thus, like marriage, it integrates the spiritually sublime and mysterious with the physical and the sensual.[60] When

---

55. See, for example, ibid., 252–53.
56. Ibid.
57. Slattery, "Masturbation: Is It Wrong?"
58. Ibid.
59. DeRouchie, "If Your Right Hand Causes You To Sin: Ten Biblical Reflections on Masturbation."
60. Ryken, *Worldly Saints*, 49.

the Scriptures tell us that the husband is to love his wife as his own flesh, and that the wife is to respect her husband (Eph 5:28, 33), this includes how they approach and enjoy each other sexually. Because we are human, and sexual desire is such a powerful natural force, it is too easy for us to forget this. When we think about our spouses sexually, we must never look on them merely as a physical source of carnal pleasure. They are for us to *love*.

CHAPTER 4

PROCREATION OF CHILDREN

This blessing of God may be regarded as the source from which the human race has flowed. And we must so consider it not only with reference to the whole, but also, as they say, in every particular instance. For we are fruitful or barren in respect of offspring, as God imparts his power to some and withholds it from others. . . . Now, what I have said concerning marriage must be kept in mind; that God intends the human race to be multiplied by generation indeed, but not, as in brute animals, by promiscuous intercourse. For he has joined the man to his wife, that they might produce a divine, that is, a legitimate seed. Let us then mark whom God here addresses when he commands them to increase, and to whom he limits his benediction. Certainly he does not give the reins to human passions, but, beginning at holy and chaste marriage, he proceeds to speak of the production of offspring. . . . Still that pure and lawful method of increase, which God ordained from the beginning, remains firm; this is that law of nature which common sense declares to be inviolable.

John Calvin[1]

Raising children is probably the most effective form of social action in which most of us will ever engage. . . . Very little that most men and women do . . . is as satisfying or makes as much difference.

Rita Kramer[2]

---

1. Calvin, *Commentary on the First Book of Moses Called Genesis*, vol. 1, 98–99.
2. Kramer, *In Defense of the Family*, 42.

In reading the opening chapters of Genesis, it is easy to miss the fact that, though God commanded and empowered all living creatures to multiply (Gen 1:20–28), as John Calvin reminds us,[3] he made a critical distinction between humans and the "brute animals." God's marvelous design was that for humankind, unlike all other living creatures, procreation was to take place within and under the protection of the marriage covenant, which we find him sealing in Genesis 2:22–24. Unlike animals, human children were to be a product of volitional, covenantal lovemaking, not copulation directed by instinct, sex drives, or uncontrolled lust. As Calvin also noted in the above quote, God made it physically possible for humans to sire children outside of marriage and even apart from any real love or commitment, but it is not right or good for them to do so. As much as we ought to love and care for every human regardless of how he or she came into this world, the consequences of separating childbearing from marriage have been consistently tragic. That infants and children need married parents, mother and father, is something that God in his wisdom built into the natural order, and something on which social health and stability depend.

As an avid deer hunter, I notice rough similarities between the relationship of a doe and her fawn and that of a mother and child, but there ought to be little in common between whitetail rutting and fawning and the ways that human beings court, marry, and have children. It is one of the vulgarities of modernity that, having substantially abandoned the idea that humankind should strive to discover and comply with the dictates of a created order, we increasingly see both human sexuality and procreation in the animalistic terms of evolutionary materialism. To a rising proportion of modern people, both sex and children are more about self-realization, psychological needs, and biological drives than about love, self-sacrifice, lifelong commitment, self-control, and intentionality. We seem to think that we can simply bring children into any of a variety of arrangements that we choose and they will grow up healthy so long as we are happy. Yet reality keeps punching back. Fawns do not need committed fathers to thrive, but children do. We ought to help children overcome the gaps left by absent parents, but we can only do so once we accept the fact

---

3. Calvin, *Genesis*, 98–99.

that some critical things really *are* missing for them. In healthy human societies, procreation and marriage go together.

In this chapter, I will first look at how the Scriptures connect procreation and marriage, and what they teach us about the intrinsic value of children. I will then consider the beliefs and practices of the earlier Protestants in both of these areas, and the impact they had. Following this, I will analyze the practices and beliefs of modern culture, and the American professing evangelical church in particular, concerning procreation and children. Next, I will consider how social science clearly and abundantly affirms the idea that children are best cared for by married parents, a mother and a father. Society also benefits when this is the norm. Finally, I will touch on the difficult subject of infertility.

PROCREATION AND CHILDREN IN THE SCRIPTURES

CONNECTING CHILDBEARING AND MARRIAGE

The most obvious way that the Scriptures teach that procreation should take place within marriage is what I considered at length in the last chapter, namely, that God teaches us that sexual intercourse is for marriage only. Since sex has been the means by which women have become pregnant from the beginning of time,[4] this logically and morally ties procreation to marriage. When a woman becomes pregnant outside marriage, it is always a result of sexual sin, usually of both the man and the woman and always of at least one of them.[5]

In the Old Testament, Israelites were required to exclude from the congregation those who were born of "forbidden unions," and thus outside of legitimate marriages (Deut 23:2). Though this appears harsh, this applied to periods of formal worship only, not membership in the overall faith community, and it served to exclude obvious representation of "violations of the principle of holiness and purity that must characterize Israel in its

---

4. As it is even today, except as modern technologies such as in vitro fertilization (IVF) are used to conceive outside of normal sexual intercourse.

5. Some readers might wish to make an exception for surrogacy, which they think might be biblically justified in cases where both the egg and the sperm come from a married couple who then raise their child. I will discuss this later. In fornication and adultery both partners have sinned; in pregnancy caused by rape a heinous offense has been committed by the male.

status as a chosen people."[6] Moreover, this law almost certainly discouraged sex outside marriage and encouraged men, in many cases, to marry women they had impregnated.[7] This protected children and society in many ways. In the New Testament, the writer of Hebrews describes illegitimacy as an undesirable state, putting the child outside the discipline and care of a loving father (12:8). Nowhere in Scripture is having children out of wedlock described in positive terms.[8] It is telling to consider that God even provided a married father and mother for his Son Jesus, ensuring that he was raised as the legitimate son of Mary and Joseph (Luke 3:23).

It is also difficult to reconcile a married couple's choice not to have any children—apart from physical infirmities or other unusual contingencies— with what the Scriptures teach. The Genesis commandment for men and women to multiply is straightforward, and there is no reason to believe this has changed. Furthermore, the fruit of marriage generating from the love between two persons united by God is like the Trinity itself in begetting life. As Pope Benedict XVI said, and Protestants should have no problem affirming, "In marriage the man and the woman, created in God's image, become 'one flesh' (Gen 2:24), that is, a communion of love that generates new life. The human family, in a certain sense, is an icon of the Trinity because of its interpersonal love and the fruitfulness of this love."[9] We must recall that Jesus was born into a human family,[10] to a mother who willingly accepted him into her body and her life knowing the difficulties and sorrow that he would bring for her and her betrothed, Joseph.

Moreover, the Scriptures frequently describe barrenness as something negative. Married women in the Bible typically sought deliverance from, and comfort through, infertility, responding with great joy when and if the Lord gave them children. In fact, this theme figures prominently in some of the most famous episodes in Bible history: Abraham and Sarah, the struggles between Rachel and her sister Leah, Samuel's mother Hannah,

---

6. Merrill, *The New American Commentary: Deuteronomy*, 308.

7. See liner note in *The Geneva Bible*, 90, and John Gill's notes on this verse in *Exposition of the Old and New Testament*.

8. See, for example, Genesis 19:36–38, Judges 11:1, and perhaps Zechariah 9:6.

9. "Angelus." I am grateful to Nathaniel Devlin, associate pastor of Beverly Heights Presbyterian Church (Pittsburgh, PA), for encouraging me to draw on the Trinity in showing why Christian spouses should welcome children.

10. Ibid.

and Mary's cousin Elizabeth, to name just some of the more obvious and memorable occasions.[11]

This does not mean that the Scriptures teach that it is wrong to marry if infertility, age, or some other condition makes procreation unlikely or unwise. Nor does it mean that married people cannot take reasonable steps, including using contraception, to limit the number of children that they have— for example, to what they can realistically care for. Delaying childbearing is also not, in and of itself, necessarily sinful.[12] However, I agree with Christian teachers such as Al Mohler,[13] Francis Schaeffer,[14] and Jim Daly[15] that married believers should not choose to remain childless deliberately and permanently unless some clear infirmity or unusual circumstance precludes having or raising children.[16] To do so is to reject something that God clearly wants from marriage (cf. Gen 1:28; Mal 2:15), and that all branches of orthodox Christianity have always treated as a, if not the, central purpose of marriage. The *Catechism of the Catholic Church* states this beautifully: "By its very nature the institution of marriage and married love is ordered to the procreation and education of the offspring and it is in them that it finds its crowning glory."[17]

---

11. For Abraham and Sarah, there is Genesis 15:1–6, 17:15–21, 18:9–15, and 21:1–7. For Leah and Rachel (the latter being the one who struggled with infertility), look especially at Genesis 29:31–30:24. For Samuel's mother, Hannah, the relevant passages are in 1 Samuel 1:1–19. On Elizabeth, we have Luke 1:5–24.

12. See Albert Mohler's thoughtful and balanced piece on this, "Can Christians Use Birth Control?" It captures my views on this almost exactly.

13. Ibid. See also "Deliberate Childlessness: Moral Rebellion With a New Face" and "Deliberate Childlessness Revisited."

14. *Letters of Francis A. Schaeffer*, 251.

15. "Is Intentional Childlessness Biblical?"

16. For a contrasting view, see James V. Brownson's *Bible, Gender, Sexuality*, 115–19. His analysis, set within a larger context defending gay marriage, seems to make numerous logical errors. For example, the fact that animals are also told to multiply, but without marriage, says nothing about whether married humans who can have children should refuse to do so, since marriage is the appropriate context for childbearing given to humans but not animals (as I have already discussed). He asserts that having children is a "blessing" rather than a "command" (115), but it is a command; and besides, since when is rejecting God's blessing, particularly one so central to his plan for the human race, appropriate? The fact that infertility does not negate marriage hardly speaks to whether voluntary refusal of procreation by married couples is morally right. New Testament discussions of marriage that don't mention procreation prove nothing. Marriage is a sexual relationship, and that this would lead to pregnancy for all but the infertile did not need elaboration. It is hardly surprising that the writers did not explicitly discuss what they knew their readers widely and obviously assumed. Brownson appears to want us to alter the obvious results of sound biblical exegesis and historic teaching based on little more than the modern availability of contraception (118).

17. 412.

Where fulfilling one's Christian calling makes it dangerous or impossible to have and raise children, the apostle Paul recommended celibacy (1 Cor 7:7–8, 32–35). Certainly, being married, including fulfilling one's conjugal duties (1 Cor 7:2–5), while deliberately remaining childless, was not an option for most of human history and for the biblical writers. To be married was by definition to be open to having children. This has not changed.

INTRINSIC VALUE OF CHILDREN

God made procreation fundamental to his first blessing of humankind (Gen 1:28). From beginning to end, the Scriptures portray children as a positive good, of inherent and intrinsic value, requiring no justification beyond their own existence. I heartily agree with Al Mohler that "we are commanded to receive children with joy as God's gifts, and to raise them in the nurture and admonition of the Lord. We are to find many of our deepest joys and satisfactions in the raising of children within the context of the family."[18] It is hard to imagine that Jesus, who said, "Let the little children come to me, and do not hinder them, for to such belongs the kingdom of heaven" (Matt 19:14), would disagree. Consider this amazing incident recorded by Matthew (18:1–6):

> At that time the disciples came to Jesus, saying, "Who is the greatest in the kingdom of heaven?" And calling to him a child, he put him in the midst of them and said, "Truly, I say to you, unless you turn and become like children, you will never enter the kingdom of heaven. Whoever humbles himself like this child is the greatest in the kingdom of heaven. Whoever receives one such child in my name receives me, but whoever causes one of these little ones who believe in me to sin, it would be better for him to have a great millstone fastened around his neck and to be drowned in the depth of the sea."

Psalms 127 and 128 beautifully identify godly procreation as a blessing from God. "Behold, children are a heritage from the LORD, and the fruit of the womb a reward. Like arrows in the hand of a warrior are the children of one's youth. Blessed is the man who fills his quiver with them!"

---

18. "Deliberate Childlessness."

(127:3–5a). "Blessed is everyone who fears the LORD, who walks in his ways! You shall eat the fruit of the labor of your hands; you shall be blessed, and it shall be well with you. Your wife will be like a fruitful vine within your house; your children will be like olive shoots around your table. . . . May you see your children's children! Peace be upon Israel!" (128:1–4, 6).

Psalm 139 uses magnificent, powerful language to remind us that God knows each human child from the moment of conception. "For you formed my inward parts; you knitted me together in my mother's womb. I praise you, for I am fearfully and wonderfully made. Wonderful are your works; my soul knows it very well. My frame was not hidden from you, when I was being made in secret, intricately woven in the depths of the earth. Your eyes saw my unformed substance; in your book were written, every one of them, the days that were formed for me, when as yet there was none of them" (139:13–16). I would urge anyone to read this psalm who is ever feeling insignificant, or who thinks that there is any human person, in any condition, anywhere on the earth, whose life has no meaning or value.

Numerous Scriptures attest that children, as with other divine blessings, will only delight us if we receive and fulfill our duties toward them according to God's design. Children require years of self-sacrificial attention from parents. As mothers and fathers working together, parents need to provide children with instruction, oversight, discipline, encouragement, and nurture if they are to grow up to be adults who will bring joy to their parents (Deut 6:7; Prov 1:8; 22:6, 15; Eph 6:4). Neglecting these things can mean that children God intended as a blessing and comfort to their parents instead become a source of grief and shame (Prov 10:1; 17:25; 29:15). After all, every child is a born sinner, just like his or her parents (Ps 51:5; Rom 3:9–10; 5:12, 18–19). When children stray—whether because of parental failings or their own sin and folly—the patient prayers, admonitions, and steadfast love of godly parents can avail much, and they can be there with open arms if their children repent (Luke 15:11–32).

Children may also come along at especially difficult times in our lives or bring with them unusually tough challenges such as serious birth defects. This makes them no less of a blessing. We can consider here the birth of Benjamin to Jacob (Gen 35:16–18). Though his beloved Rachel died during his birth, Jacob still considered him a gift from God (cf. Gen 42:33–38). A little-known fact about the great twentieth-century French leader Charles de Gaulle is the deep love and devotion he had for his daughter Anne, who had Down syndrome. In an era when such children were typically viewed as shameful and were institutionalized, Charles and his wife, Yvonne, embraced and sacrificially cared for Anne until she died in her father's arms at twenty years of age. Said de Gaulle to a priest, "For me, this child is a grace, she is my joy, she helps me to look beyond all the failures and honors, and always to look higher."[19]

As much as possible the church needs to come alongside to encourage and help parents who face these kinds of hard providences. Embracing and raising these children is worth it, but taking on challenges like this can be tough on marriages and families.

Indeed, the practical demands, disappointment, and even heartbreak tied to having and raising children are a main part of the reasons why God designed procreation and childrearing to take place within and under the protection of covenant marriage, which also makes great demands on us. Good marriages provide the structure, stability, warmth, love, and commitment within which spouses care for each other and their children, mutually and as a team. This is one of the greatest areas in which, as we saw in chapter 2, parents are to be helpmates, mutually encouraging each other and sharing the load.

Scripture clearly teaches that children have inestimable, intrinsic value—after all, each is essentially an immortal, as C. S. Lewis so beautifully stated.[20] As with so many other gifts God may bestow upon us, when we gratefully accept them along with all the duties and demands that come with them, they are more likely to be to us, society, and God's kingdom, all the blessings they are capable, by God's grace, of being.

CHILDREN AND THE PURITAN, REFORMATION HERITAGE

In ancient Rome, parents often abandoned unwanted infants, leaving them exposed to the elements. Of course, many died. Third parties could take them but, sadly, often did so only to sell them into slavery and even prostitution.[21] Early Christians vigorously denounced this practice, often

---

19. Gregg, "A Father's Love: The Story of Charles and Anne."
20. Lewis, "The Weight of Glory," 273–74.
21. Judith Evans Grubbs, "Infant Exposure and Infanticide," 83–84, 93–95.

rescuing and adopting these *"expositi."*[22] Their love and acceptance of the "least of these" against the cruelty of the pagan world stands as a wonderful testament to our ancient faith and remains an inspiration for today's pro-life movement.

Unfortunately, as eminent family historian Edward Shorter has documented, in Western society of the Middle Ages, things had gone downhill. Infants "were seen . . . as creatures apart from people. Barely possessing souls of their own, they came at the Will of God, departed at his behest, and in their brief mortal sojourn deserved little adult sympathy or compassion."[23] The "indifference" with which babies were treated led to an extraordinarily high number of infant deaths from things such as filth, neglect, malnutrition, and lack of human contact—practices that even most peasants could have typically avoided.[24]

Shorter credits the rise of industrial capitalism with making "good mothering" and many other dramatic improvements in marriage and family normal and expected.[25] However, there is powerful evidence that Protestantism, especially Calvinism, played a major and direct role in these wonderful changes,[26] including in the ways parents welcomed, viewed, and treated children, and organized households around their care.[27] For example, Puritan communities quickly became notably different from others in how they treated children,[28] changes that eventually influenced everyone for the better, Protestant and Catholic alike.

MODERN PRACTICES AND BELIEFS ON PROCREATION AND CHILDREN

In light of the biblical norm of procreation within marriage, things do not look good in the United States. We see that increasingly, people have become almost indifferent to providing children the gift of two married parents, and value having children less overall. This is clear in concrete outcomes and attitudes. Professing believers—especially those who faithfully

---

22. Ibid., 97, 99.
23. Shorter, *The Making of the Modern Family*, 169.
24. Ibid., 170–81, 203–4.
25. Ibid., 255–58.
26. Garrett, "The Protestant Ethic and the Spirit of the Modern Family," 222.
27. Cf. ibid., 229–30.
28. Ibid.

participate in the life of the local church—are doing better in having children within marriage and valuing them overall, but there is a lot of room for improvement.

REALITY OF BEARING AND REARING CHILDREN
APART FROM MARRIAGE

First, consider out-of-wedlock births. The increase and current percentages here are staggering and have a negative impact upon all of us. The picture among evangelicals is not very bright, except that things are better for those who regularly attend church.

As of 2016, over half of all Hispanic births, and 70 percent of all black births, in the United States were out of wedlock, with the overall percentage being 40 percent and the white and Asian/Pacific Islander figures being 28.5 percent and 13 percent, respectively. And this represents a slight decline from the year before. In 1980, the overall percentage was less than half that, and the white percentage was three times less. Going further back is even more startling—in 1960, just a little over one of five black children were born out of wedlock, while less than 5 percent of white and only about 5 percent overall were. In 1940 and 1950 percentages

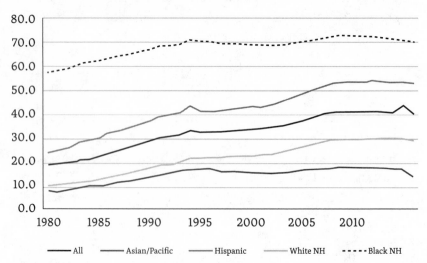

Figure 4.1: Percentage of Births Out of Wedlock 1980–2016[29]

---

29. *Health United States, 2015,* 73; supplemented by Martin et al., "Births: Final Data for 2015," 46, and "Births: Final Data for 2016," 31.

were even lower.[30] Yet by 2009, over 50 percent of *all* births to women under the age of thirty were out of wedlock, as well as most births to white women without a college education.[31] This massive increase in non-marital child-bearing is a national tragedy.

Among never-married women between the ages of thirty and forty-five in the period 2006 through 2016, 59 percent had borne a child; 40 percent had two or more. Among African-Americans 74.5 percent had, with 51 percent having two or more, while for whites those percentages were 43 percent and 27.5 percent. Percentages were worse among those who had not gone to college. Among African-Americans, 82 percent had at least one child and 60 percent had two or more; for whites these percentages were 67 percent and 45 percent.[32]

Analyzing a large national data set, sociologist W. Bradford Wilcox discovered that 24 percent of children born to evangelical Protestant women were out of wedlock at a time when the percentage overall was 33 percent. However, when he separated evangelicals who were regular churchgoers from what he called "nominal" evangelicals, the results were startling. Only 12 percent of the babies born to churchgoing evangelical Protestant women were out of wedlock, which was almost three times lower than the national percentage. By contrast, 33 percent of births to "nominal" evangelical women were non-marital, which was identical to women overall.[33]

Wilcox and Nicholas Wolfinger also explored the effects of church attendance and belief on women who had conceived out of wedlock, focusing on urban Christians. They discovered that those who attended church regularly were 63 percent more likely to marry within a year of giving birth. This relationship applied to all racial and ethnic groups and was even stronger if the father also attended church. However, the longer women delayed getting married, the less likely they were to do so. In addition, regular church-attending fathers were 95 percent more likely to get married before the baby was born, while church-attending women were 40 percent more likely to do so.[34] Interestingly, while pro-marriage beliefs made

---

30. Heritage Foundation, "Four in Ten Children Are Born to Unwed Mothers." Also, *Report to Congress on Out-of-Wedlock Childbearing*, vi.

31. DeParle and Tavernise, "For Women Under 30, Most Births Occur Outside Marriage."

32. General Social Survey 2006–2016.

33. Wilcox, "How Focused on the Family?", 265–66.

34. Wilcox and Wolfinger, "Then Comes Marriage," 578–79, 582–83.

a positive difference, the type of church attended did not appear to matter. Those in evangelical churches who did not hold such beliefs, or who did not attend services regularly, were no better off.[35]

Putting both of these studies together, we can see that evangelical women who regularly attend church are less likely to have out-of-wedlock babies, and more likely to get married to the father if they do so. Once again, the facts confirm the wisdom of Hebrews 10:24–25.

Second, a growing reality that many people are not aware of is the extent to which having and raising children outside of marriage is associated with cohabitation. Representing a growing trend, in 2016 about 4 percent, or over 2,900,000, American children were living with two biological parents who were cohabiting, not married.[36] Over 2,400,000 more lived with one parent living with an unmarried partner who was not their parent.[37] This combines to over 5,300,000 children, or over 7 percent, living with cohabiting couples. About 39 percent of American children will live in a household headed by a cohabiting couple by age twelve, and 46 percent by age sixteen.[38] The number of American children in cohabiting households has increased by over 60 percent since 1996.[39] As of 2017, 37 percent of cohabiting heterosexual couples were living with at least one biological child of either partner,[40] almost the same as the 39 percent of households headed by married couples who do.[41]

How do evangelicals compare here? Starting in 2012, the General Social Survey began asking respondents to indicate if they were cohabiting. Among those twenty-two to forty years of age, 15 percent were in a cohabiting relationship, and 61 percent of these had children. Among self-identified conservative Protestants in that age group, 10 percent were

35. Ibid., 580–81, 583.

36. US Census Bureau, "Living Arrangements of Children Under 18."

37. Ibid.

38. Pew Research Center, "Parenting In America," 18.

39. In 1996, about 3,285,000 children lived in a household headed by cohabiting partners, either both biological parents or only one a biological parent. Fields, *Living Arrangements of Children*, 1996.

40. US Census Bureau, Table UC3, "Opposite Sex Unmarried Couples By Presence Of Biological Children Under 18, And Age, Earnings, Education, And Race And Hispanic Origin Of Both Partners: 2017," *America's Families and Living Arrangements: 2017.*

41. Calculated by me from the data in US Census Bureau, "Table FG3. Married Couple Family Groups, by Presence of Own Children Under 18, and Age, Earnings, Education, and Race and Hispanic Origin of Both Spouses: 2017."

currently cohabiting, 74 percent of whom had children. Meanwhile, for evangelicals in that age group who attended church at least weekly, the picture was a lot better—only 5 percent were cohabiting, though over 90 percent of these were raising children.[42] So overall, evangelicals, especially those who attend church regularly, are less likely to cohabit, but are more likely to have children if they do.

Third, remember that divorce, and to a much lower extent death, of parents further separate American children from married parents. For those who understand how important living with two biological or adoptive parents who are married to each other is to the welfare of children, the composite picture is depressing. In 2017, only 65 percent of American children under 18 were living with two, married parents.[43] However, in many of these households, at least one of those parents was a stepparent.[44] In 2017, 26 percent of children were living with a single parent. About 12 percent were living with a single parent who was divorced or separated (not necessarily from the child's biological parent), 13 percent with a single parent who had never married, and only about 1 percent with a widowed parent. About 4 percent lived with neither parent.[45]

Consider also that many children who are currently living with both parents will see that arrangement end before they reach adulthood. The degree of instability is shocking. One study by the US Census found that, between 2008 and 2011, 31 percent of children under the age of 6 had a parent or parental partner enter or leave their household.[46]

Sadly, but not surprisingly, evangelicals overall are not doing better, though again those who attend church regularly are generally better off. Table 4.1 shows that conservative Protestant households with children were not different from households overall in the percentages headed by married couples, widows, divorced and separated, and never-married

---

42. We have to approach these last numbers cautiously—there were only eleven cohabiting couples who were both conservative Protestants and attended church at least once per week.

43. US Census Bureau, "Living Arrangements of Children Under 18."

44. For example, in 2009, about 8 percent of children lived with a stepparent. See Pew Research Center, "Parenting In America," 19. The way the US Census Bureau collects data makes it difficult to determine exactly how many children living with "two married parents" are in situations where one of those parents is a stepparent.

45. Calculated by me from US Census Bureau, "Living Arrangements of Children Under 18."

46. Laughlin, "A Child's Day: Living Arrangements, Nativity, and Family Transitions: 2011," 12.

Table 4.1: Households with Children by Marital Status (GSS 2006–2016)

	Overall	Conservative Protestant	Conservative Protestant and Weekly Attender
Married:	54.5%	52%	60%
Widowed:	10.5%	12%	13%
Divorced/ Separated:	23%	24.5%	18.5%
Never-Married:	12%	12%	8.5%

parents. However, those in which parents attended church services at least weekly were more likely to be headed by a married couple.

BEARING CHILDREN

Americans are also having fewer children. For a modern population to replace itself, each woman needs to have a little less than 2.1 children in her lifetime. As of 2017, that number was 1.87.[47] It had only been at or above replacement levels in five or six years since 1970.[48] These low fertility rates are evident across the world, especially in wealthier nations. The only European country even close to replacement level is France, and virtually all modern Asian countries are well below the United States.[49] Between 1976 and 2014, the percentage of women between the ages of forty and forty-four who had given birth to only one child increased from 11 percent to 22 percent, and those who had two children from 24 percent to 41 percent. Those with three children remained about the same at about one-quarter, while those with four or more children dropped from 40 percent to 14 percent.[50]

As of 2014, about one in five pregnancies in the United States ended in legal abortion. Thankfully, this was down from about three in ten in the early 1980s, and raw numbers have been dropping steadily since 1990.[51] Still, there were well over 900,000 abortions in 2014.[52] As of 2015, we had

---

47. CIA, "Country Comparison: Total Fertility Rate."
48. Martin et al., "Births: Final Data for 2015," 20.
49. CIA, "Country Comparison: Total Fertility Rate."
50. Pew Research Center, "Parenting in America," 20.
51. National Right to Life, "Abortion Statistics: United States Data and Trends."
52. Guttmacher Institute, "Induced Abortion in the United States."

endured close to fifty-nine million abortions since the *Roe v. Wade* Supreme Court decision legalized them nationwide in 1973.[53] This number is almost four times the combined populations of New York City, Chicago, and Los Angeles.

So how are professing evangelical Protestants doing in these areas? In abortions and total fertility, evangelicals do better than the overall norms. Those who maintain regular participation in a local church tend to have more children and fewer abortions.

According to the Pew Research Center, as of 2014 the average evangelical Protestant between the ages of forty and fifty-nine had 2.3 children born to them. This fertility rate was higher than the national average and for any religious group except Mormons and members of historically black denominations.[54] Although this study did not address church attendance, the General Social Survey for 2006 through 2016 makes it clear that, among conservative Protestants, weekly church attenders have more children. Weekly attenders who were ever married and ages forty to fifty-nine averaged about 2.6 children apiece, compared to 2.2 who attended rarely or never.

Out of over 8,300 women obtaining abortions at eighty-seven facilities in 2014 and 2015, 13 percent indicated their religion as "evangelical Protestant." Happily, analysis showed that this percentage was much lower than evangelical women's share of the population, and that their rate of abortions had dropped significantly since 2008, when they were 15 percent of all sampled abortion patients.[55] However, this still comes out to over 111,000 evangelical women obtaining abortions in 2014,[56] and even more in years with both higher numbers of abortion and greater percentages of evangelical Protestants obtaining them.

---

53. National Right to Life, "Abortion Statistics: United States Data and Trends."

54. Pew Research Center, "America's Changing Religious Landscape," 64.

55. Jerman et al., *Characteristics of U.S. Abortion Patients in 2014 and Changes Since 2008*, 5–6. In 2014, evangelical Protestant women were 26 percent of the population of women ages fifteen to forty-four, but 13 percent of those obtaining abortions. By contrast, Mainline Protestant women were 17 percent of those obtaining abortions and 22 percent of the population. For Catholics these percentages were 24 percent and 22 percent respectively, and those of "no religious affiliation" were 38 percent of those obtaining abortions but only 21 percent of women fifteen to forty-four.

56. Based on exact 2014 totals in Guttmacher Institute, "Induced Abortion in the United States."

Again, there is evidence that church attendance matters. An earlier 2008 report on women obtaining abortions, by the same organization, found that 15 percent of those who obtained abortions attended church weekly, and 13 percent attended one to three times per month, while more than twice as many—32 percent—attended church less frequently than that.[57]

Regardless, it is clear that *abortions are far too common in evangelical Protestant churches*, more than many in the pews or pulpits want to admit. These churches need to teach, minister to, and support post-abortive women, as well as those considering abortions, along with the biological fathers, families, and others affected.

VALUING CHILDREN

In several survey years between 1988 and 2012, the General Social Survey had respondents react to items about children, including those summarized in tables 4.2 and 4.3. Results are encouraging. For example, about 90 percent of conservative Protestants and weekly church attenders believe that watching children grow up is life's greatest joy, and the overwhelming majority in both groups support waiting until marriage to have them. However, one in four conservative Protestants, and two in ten weekly church attenders, do *not* agree that it is best to be married before having children. Many view children as infringing on their freedom "too much."

Other items about children included in the General Social Survey deal with the issue of single parenting. Between 1994 and 2012, Americans moved in a decidedly liberal direction on this issue. Though they were *slightly* less enthusiastic about this, conservative Protestants and weekly church attenders showed a similar shift. Many Americans, and professing believers, hold views that certainly conflict with abundant social-science research, as we shall see.

In 2012, the General Social Survey asked about homosexual parenting, breaking this separately between gay males and lesbians. The results may surprise those who see evangelicals as uniformly opposed to gay parenting. It is almost certain that views have continued to move in a more liberal direction in the years since 2012. Conservative Protestants and regular

---

57. *Characteristics of U.S. Abortion Patients, 2008*, 10. This did not distinguish evangelical Protestants from others in the church-attendance figures.

Table 4.2: Percent Agreeing or Disagreeing on Children Items by Religion (GSS 1988, 1994, 2002, and 2012)

Survey Item	Conservative Protestant	Moderate Protestant	Liberal Protestant	Catholic	Jew	None
AGREE						
"Watching children grow up is life's greatest joy"	89%	88%	84%	88%	75%	72%
"People who want children ought to get married"	75%	72%	75%	67%	74%	51%
DISAGREE						
"Having children interferes too much with the freedom of the parent"*	79%	74%	78%	74%	78%	61%

* 2002 not included.

Table 4.3: Percent Agreeing or Disagreeing on Children Items by Church Attendance (GSS 1988, 1994, 2002, and 2012)

Survey Item	Attend Never/Rarely	Attend about Monthly	Attend Weekly or More
AGREE			
"Watching children grow up is life's greatest joy"	82%	88%	90%
"People who want children ought to get married"	61%	67%	81.5%
DISAGREE			
"Having children interferes too much with the freedom of the parent"*	70%	68%	82%

* 2002 not included.

Table 4.4: Percent Agreeing that "One Parent Can Bring Up a Child as Well as Two Parents Together" (GSS)

	1994	2002	2012
Overall:	36%	42%	49%
Conservative Protestants:	33%	41%	42%
Weekly Church Attenders:	30%	33%	40%

church attenders were definitely much less accepting of homosexual parenting than others. Interestingly, folks were a bit less likely to accept gay male, than lesbian, parenting. Yet sadly, three of ten evangelicals, and one of four weekly church attenders, thought that lesbians could bring up children as well as heterosexual couples.

Overall, once again it is clear that the percentages of those who no longer agree with what the Bible teaches, and what church leaders throughout history have taught and continue to teach, are higher than many of us suspect.

Recent trends suggest that things will get worse before they get better. Progressives are advancing within the ranks of self-identified evangelicals. For the sake of God's kingdom, and of the children who are being subjected to these beliefs and practices but who are not free to choose the circumstances they will be raised in, we must—with compassion and grace—turn the tide toward gracious faithfulness among professing conservative Christians.

DO CHILDREN NEED MARRIED MOTHERS AND FATHERS?

The entire biblical teaching on what marriage is, the procreative character of sex, the degree to which divorce and sex outside wedlock are discouraged— all point to the fact that, ideally, children should be born to and raised by a married father and mother. Proverbs 1:8 assumes this: "Hear, my son, your father's instruction, and forsake not your mother's teaching." The fifth commandment clearly reflects the normative structure of parenting: "Honor your father and your mother" (Exod 20:12a).[58] Just after laying out respective

---

58. This is the fourth commandment in the Catholic numbering system.

Table 4.5: Percent Agreeing that "A Same-Sex Couple [Male-Male or Female-Female] Can Bring Up a Child as Well as a Male-Female Couple," by Religion (GSS 2012)

Referring To	Conservative Protestant	Moderate Protestant	Liberal Protestant	Catholic	Jew	None
Lesbian Couple:	29%	41%	50%	52%	55.5%	66%
Gay Male Couple:	26.5%	34%	47%	47%	44%	62%

Table 4.6: Percent Agreeing that "A Same-Sex Couple [Male-Male or Female-Female] Can Bring Up a Child as Well as a Male-Female Couple," by Church Attendance (GSS 2012)

Referring To	Attend Never/ Rarely	Attend About Monthly	Attend Weekly or More
Lesbian Couple:	61%	40%	25%
Gay Male Couple:	57%	36%	21%

admonitions for husbands and wives, Paul refers to this commandment directly, to fathers and mothers, in urging children to "obey your parents in the Lord" (Eph 6:1–2). The Bible does not picture being born out of wedlock as an ideal state (Heb 12:8). God hates divorce at least partly because of its impact on children, since producing "godly offspring" is a major reason he makes the man and woman "one" and binds them by a solemn, permanent marital covenant (Mal 2:15).

We have always understood that, in this broken world, children will often not have ideal parenting situations. One or both parents might die, or be separated from their children by divorce, imprisonment, or in many other ways, not all of which involve parental sin. Some children will be born out of wedlock in situations that the biological parents can or should not remedy by marriage, including lamentable circumstances such as pregnancy caused by rape. Having decided against abortion, a pregnant girl may not feel able to give up her child. We know, too, that having married parents is no guarantee of good parenting. Many single parents do a fine job raising their children, though it is much harder to do so without a spouse.

We ought to help children and parents in these situations by attempting to correct what is damaged or lacking, because we know that such situations are not ideal. If we embrace the fiction that all "alternative" family structures are equal when it comes to raising children, then we will not privilege and promote procreation and parenting by married mothers and fathers. We will not have logical reasons to assist parents or children in homes lacking them, nor have a clear understanding of exactly what they need. Our politically correct myopia will hurt, rather than help, both parents and children.

THE SINGLE-PARENTING DISADVANTAGE
AND ITS EFFECTS ON CHILDREN

Social science research overwhelmingly supports the claim that, on average, children do much better raised in households with married mothers and fathers. Detailing the various ways this is true, and evidence for it, can easily encompass entire chapters,[59] lengthy articles,[60] or even books.[61] That will be not be possible here, but an accurate summary certainly is.[62]

As compared to children raised in dual-parent homes, those in single-parent homes face significant disadvantages. We cannot explain these away as "selection effects" (that is, that single parents just happen to be different, on average, in other ways that effect child outcomes). Differences between children raised in single- versus dual-parent households show up in innumerable studies that "control" for such factors. In 2000, Waite and Gallagher summarized this well: "Children raised in single-parent households are, on average, more likely to be poor, to have health problems and psychological disorders, to commit crimes and exhibit other conduct disorders, have somewhat poorer relationships with both family and peers, and as adults, eventually get fewer years of education and enjoy less stable

---

59. See, for example, chapter 9 in Waite and Gallagher, *The Case for Marriage*.

60. See, for example, the award-winning 1993 article by Barbara Dafoe Whitehead, "Dan Quayle Was Right."

61. See, for example, well-known volumes such as David Blankenhorn's 1995 book *Fatherless America*, or David Popenoe's ground-breaking 1996 book *Life Without Father*.

62. Note that I will go into more detail on these matters, especially on the particular impacts of divorce upon children, in chapter 12.

marriages and lower occupational statuses than children whose parents got and stayed married. This 'marriage gap' in children's well-being remains true even after researchers control for important family characteristics, including parents' race, income, and socioeconomic status."[63] Research supports the almost universal preference among societies for children to be born into marriages.[64]

However, Waite and Gallagher made this statement almost two decades ago, a long time in the world of social science. Has anything changed since then? Here is Isabel Sawhill, a senior fellow at the liberal Brookings Institution, in 2012: "A wealth of research strongly suggests that marriage is good for children. Those who live with their biological parents do better in school and are less likely to get pregnant or arrested. They have lower rates of suicide, achieve higher levels of education and earn more as adults. Meanwhile, children who spend time in single-parent families are more likely to misbehave, get sick, drop out of high school and be unemployed."[65] These deficits have remained no matter what other factors researchers have statistically accounted for.[66]

Starbuck and Lundy, writing in 2015, repeat every point noted by Sawhill, Waite and Gallagher, and numerous other social scientists, noting additionally greater risk of substance abuse, leaving home early for reasons other than going to college, diminished parent-child relationship, and self-concept issues in children raised in single-parent homes.[67] They conclude: "Virtually every study on the matter . . . indicates that children are generally better off being raised by two loving parents rather than one."[68]

On average, married parenting simply works better, and makes a hard, time-consuming task that stretches over many years, easier. Sawhill states the obvious: "raising children is a daunting responsibility. Two committed parents typically have more time and resources to do it well."[69] Contrary to what some think, children raised by their mothers alone actually have

---

63. Waite and Gallagher, *The Case for Marriage*, 125.

64. Ibid., 126.

65. Sawhill, "Twenty Years Later, It Turns Out Dan Quayle Was Right About Murphy Brown and Unmarried Moms," 2012.

66. Ibid.

67. Starbuck and Lundy, *Families in Context*, 368–69.

68. Ibid.

69. Sawhill, "Twenty Years Later."

less time with them than if there is a father in the home, due to the oner-ous time demands upon her.[70] "Two parents," note Waite and Gallagher,

> can divide pay and work in the home between them, while single parents must do it all themselves. Two-job couples can divide child care between them by working different shifts or coordinating their hours to arrange more parental time with their kids. Having Mom and Dad in the same home means more parental supervision, more help with homework, another shoulder to cry on after a hard day. Two parents make it twice as likely that a child will find a good math tutor in his home, as well as someone who can help out with the art projects, than a child with only one parent to turn to.[71]

On the money side, we again see in research what common sense should tell us. Here is Sawhill again: "Marriage brings economic bene-fits. It usually means two breadwinners, or one breadwinner and a full-time, stay-at-home parent with no significant child-care expenses. . . . And it's not just a cliché that two can live more cheaply than one; a single set of bills for rent, utilities and other household expenses makes a differ-ence."[72] According to the US Census, in 2016, while 8.4 percent of children in married-couple households were living in poverty, the percentage was 19.9 percent for those living with a single father, and a whopping 42.1 per-cent for those living with a single mother. Among children under the age of six, 49.1 percent of those living with a single mother were poor, com-pared to 9.5 percent of those living with married parents.[73] This means that young children living in female-headed homes were more than *five times* more likely to be poor.

COHABITATION AND CHILDREN

What about children raised by two *unmarried* parents? Certainly, the advan-tages of shared parenting and income advantages are at least potentially present to cohabiting couples in ways that are not the case for single par-ents. However, children in such environments continue to fare worse than

---

70. Waite and Gallagher, *The Case for Marriage*, 128.

71. Ibid., 127.

72. Sawhill, "Twenty Years Later."

73. Semega et al., "Income and Poverty in the United States: 2016" (2017), 14.

in households headed by married parents. Much of this has to do with lower average levels of commitment and stability in cohabiting unions. Here is what Sawhill says about this: "Marriage is a commitment that cohabitation is not. Taking a vow before friends and family to support another person 'until death do us part' signals a mutual sense of shared responsibility that we cannot lightly dismiss. Cohabitation is more fragile—cohabiting parents split up before their fifth anniversary at about twice the rate of married parents. Often, this is because the father moves on, leaving the mother not just with less support but with fewer marriage prospects. For her, marriage requires finding a partner willing to take responsibility for someone else's kids."[74]

In 2017, the Social Trends Institute released a major international study of the impact of cohabitation on family stability in sixteen European countries and the United States.[75] This addressed the assertion that as cohabitation becomes more common, accepted, and practiced among more people of higher socioeconomic status, the differences between children in cohabiting versus married households will disappear. Instead, researchers found that children suffered from the effects of higher levels of instability in cohabiting unions, across nations and socioeconomic status. As the authors noted, "Family instability is associated with a host of negative outcomes for children even among children in higher income households. . . . Union transitions appear to present children with more challenges than merely being reared by a lone parent. . . . Cohabitation is less stable than marriage, even when children are present."[76] One of the authors later highlighted their stunning finding that "the least educated married families in Europe enjoy more stability than the most educated cohabiting families."[77]

Moreover, it is becoming clear that many of the problems noted with single-parent families generally are exacerbated by the fact that increasingly, children in these situations experience numerous transitions in and out of the marriages, divorces, and cohabitations their mothers subsequently enter into.[78] Sociologist Andrew Cherlin has called this tendency

---

74. Sawhill, "Twenty Years Later."
75. DeRose et al., "The Cohabitation Go-Round."
76. Ibid., 6–7.
77. Veith, "Exploding Myths About Cohabitation," 2017.
78. DeRose et al., "The Cohabitation Go-Round," 6.

to move in and out of marriage, divorce, and cohabitation "the marriage go-round."[79] Increasing numbers of children are experiencing radically different household types, and even a revolving number of parental partners, during their growing-up years, as we alluded to earlier.

WHAT ABOUT SAME-SEX PARENTS?

Major professional associations such as the American Psychological Association have concluded for years that research clearly shows "no difference" between children raised by homosexual versus heterosexual couples.[80] Courts all the way through the US Supreme Court's famous *Obergefell* decision of June 2015 have mostly favored this interpretation. However, reality is far messier than that, and these organizations are basing many or all of their certainties upon research that is embarrassingly deficient.

Most research on same-sex parenting has used small samples drawn from volunteers solicited through newspaper ads, political rallies, personal contacts, bookstores, medical clinics, and the like.[81] The homosexual parents studied have been disproportionately white, well off, highly educated, and living in liberal urban or university settings.[82] Even large differences may not be "statistically significant" where the samples are small. Meanwhile, the percentages of children raised by homosexual couples have been so tiny, and subjects so hard to locate, that it has been difficult for researchers to pull together large random samples. Thus, most of this research probably does not accurately represent the homosexual parenting population.

To make matters worse, pro-gay advocacy groups have done much of this research,[83] raising legitimate concerns about bias. In addition, many children in households headed by homosexual couples have also gone through numerous difficult transitions, including being part of heterosexual

---

79. Cherlin, *The Marriage-Go-Round*, 2009.

80. *APA On Children Raised by Gay and Lesbian Parents*, 2012. Interestingly, the APA was concluding in 2004 that same-sex parenting posed no risks, despite (as we see below) the lack of good research to base such important claims upon.

81. Sullins, "Emotional Problems among Children with Same-Sex Parents: Difference by Definition," 100. Manning, Fettro, and Lamidi, "Child Well-Being in Same-Sex Parent Families: Review of Research Prepared for American Sociological Association Amicus Brief."

82. Ibid., 371.

83. Starbuck and Lundy, *Families in Context*, 371.

married, divorced, and cohabiting households. It is difficult to disentangle the impact of all these living situations and changes upon them.[84]

A comprehensive review in 2014 of forty-eight studies done on United States populations since 2002 was very revealing. Only ten had samples of over one hundred same-sex families, and only six were over 160.[85] Of these six larger studies, one was done for a gay advocacy group and focused solely on self-reported school experiences.[86] Another three looked only at grade retention,[87] one arguing that kids in same-sex homes had significantly slower progress in school,[88] the other two, both by the same author, arguing the opposite. Only the remaining two, both by Mark Regnerus, looked at a spectrum of relevant emotional, social, and interpersonal outcomes. Both still had relatively small samples of respondents exposed to same-sex parenting (236 and 248), and these were all adults at the time they were surveyed.[89] While Regnerus's research uncovered deficits in adult children who had experienced same-sex parenting, the limitations of his research make this far from conclusive.

There are also enormous pressures on academicians in the social sciences to stay clear of publishing negative assessments of same-sex parenting. For example, there was an explosion of professional threats and criticisms directed against Regnerus, including impugning the motives of him, his reviewers, and the journal that published his studies, charges of conspiracy, conflict of interest, doing "pseudo-science," and scientific misconduct.[90] His university's advisory panel could not find evidence to

---

84. Ibid.

85. Manning, Fettro, and Lamidi, "Child Well-Being in Same-Sex Parent Families: Review of Research Prepared for American Sociological Association Amicus Brief," summarized in table on pages 488–90.

86. Kosciw and Diaz, *Involved, Invisible, Ignored: The Experiences of Lesbian, Gay, Bisexual and Transgender Parents and Their Children in Our Nation's K–12 Schools*, 2008.

87. That is, the percentage of children from different types of families who are kept in the same grade for more than one academic year. Rosenfeld, "Nontraditional Families and Childhood Progress Through School," 2010; Allen, Pakaluc, and Price, "Nontraditional Families and Childhood Progress Through School: a Comment on Rosenfeld," 2013; Rosenfeld, "Reply to Allen et al.," 2013.

88. That is, the one by Allen et al., above.

89. "How Different Are the Adult Children of Parents Who Have Same-Sex Relationships? Findings From the New Family Structures Study," and "Parental Same-Sex Relationships, Family Instability, and Subsequent Life Outcomes For Adult Children: Answering Critics of the New Family Structures Study with Additional Analyses." Both are from 2012.

90. Redding, "Politicized Science," 439.

support any of these charges.[91] Meanwhile, social scientists have consistently accepted much weaker research that has affirmed homosexual parenting.[92]

Moreover, as I noted in chapter 2, there were no married same-sex couples in the United States until the Massachusetts Supreme Court imposed same-sex marriage in that state in 2004, and as of 2009 there were only a handful of states that allowed it. Other nations that have legalized it have also only done so fairly recently. As of mid-2014, only eleven states and the District of Columbia offered same-sex marriage. Thus, absolute numbers of same-sex *married* couples who have been parenting for any length of time are very small. We simply do not have large numbers of people adopted by or born to married same-sex couples who have now gone through childhood, adolescence, into adulthood, to study.

Even setting aside the unfairly maligned Regnerus studies, the research we do have from larger studies of children who have been at least partially raised by same-sex couples suggests that they will have more problems than those raised by married, biological parents. This should not be surprising, since such children are only attached biologically to, at most, one of their parents. Besides, either a male or a female parenting figure is always absent. We also have the problem of greater risk of exposure to the kinds of negative realities associated with gay and lesbian lifestyle and relationships discussed in chapter 2.

One study of 512 children of same-sex parents drawn from a sample of over 207,000 found that, compared to those of opposite-sex parents, they were at least twice as likely to suffer from serious emotional problems. These included higher incidence of learning disabilities, Attention Deficit Disorder, and using mental health services.[93] Same-sex couples with children are about two times more likely to break up than heterosexual ones.[94] In fact, one study of 158 five- to ten-year-olds found that poorer outcomes for children of same-sex parents were due mainly to the greater

---

91. "University of Texas at Austin Completes Inquiry into Allegations of Scientific Misconduct," August 29, 2012.

92. "Politicized Science," 440.

93. "Emotional Problems among Children with Same-Sex Parents: Difference by Definition," 99, 105.

94. Regnerus, "New Research on Same-Sex Households Reveals Kids Do Best With Mom and Dad," 2015.

number of transitions they experience.[95] However, again, we need much more research, of much higher quality, before we can draw *any* social-scientific conclusions about the effects of same-sex parenting.

Regardless, the goal of Christian parents should be to raise children who serve and honor God, keep his commandments, and stand for the same against contrary cultural pressures. Given what Scripture teaches us about marriage and sexuality, by definition, parenting by same-sex married couples will not do this. No matter how skilled, loving, well intentioned, or even religious such parents are, they are modeling and promoting destructive lies to their children that will move them away from, rather than toward, true saving faith.

DEALING WITH INFERTILITY

One danger of emphasizing the value and joy of fertility within marriage is increasing the pain of married couples who want children but cannot have them. With this, it is too easy to increase pressure on a married couple to do almost anything legally to have children. It is important for those dealing with this to remember that infertility does not damage the beauty or validity of their marriage, God is sovereign, and adoption is usually an option and a profoundly good one. After all, God sent his Son into the world so that we might be adopted as his sons and daughters and, having been received into his family, enjoy all the privileges of being heirs of the kingdom (Gal 4:4–7).

Infertility can be a heartbreaking issue for married couples to face, and it is not hard to understand that they may want to have their own biological children, turning to modern medical technologies to make this happen. However, modern fertility treatments include many morally problematic options. I would encourage couples struggling to get pregnant to learn as much as they can about the choices that physicians present them with, to think them through biblically and carefully, and where necessary, to get sound and honest advice from a knowledgeable pastor or other Christian counselor. No matter how much anguish they face, which I know can be considerable, they must not pursue sinful avenues to conception that will, in the end, always lead to more harm, and guilt, than good.

---

95. Potter, "Same-Sex Parent Families and Children's Academic Achievement," 567.

It is my considered view that the clearest possible teaching we have from the Scriptures is that married couples should seek procreation within marital lovemaking. Medical fertility treatments, including surgery, that help a couple do so are fine. Interventions that involve fertilizing an egg with the husband's sperm within his wife's body, such as artificial insemination, may also be defensible where other interventions do not work.

We have seen many heart-breaking things flowing from "whatever works" approaches to helping couples have biological babies apart from intercourse. For example, various types of assisted reproductive technology (ART),[96] where physicians unite egg and sperm outside the woman's body and then implant fertilized eggs into her, carry a risk of multiple-child pregnancy. In such cases, doctors may recommend "pregnancy reduction"—that is, aborting the "excess" fetuses. As I have written elsewhere, this is morally reprehensible.[97] Beyond this, we have technicians fertilizing human eggs and then freezing or destroying them. There is even pressure to use them in medical research and treatment. Life begins at conception, and to treat a human being created in the image of God in this fashion is morally repugnant. The use of donor eggs, sperm, and surrogates involves third parties in the process of insemination and gestation, upending the biblical ideal of children generated through the one-flesh unions of their parents.

Where technicians must collect sperm from the husband, doing so through masturbation apart from marital lovemaking is clearly sinful, but there are ways to avoid it. For example, the Catholic Church recommends that a couple use a condom and intercourse to do this.[98]

What about implanting women with frozen embryos obtained from biological parents? This "embryo adoption" has become increasingly popular with Christian couples. It really is a form of legal adoption. Here, I would agree with Russell Moore, president of the Southern Baptist Convention's

---

96. These include in vitro fertilization (IVF), intracytoplasmic sperm injection (ICSI), gamete intrafallopian transfer (GIFT), and zygote intrafallopian transfer (ZIFT). See Healthwise Staff, "Assisted Reproductive Technology," 2015.

97. Ayers, "Abortion's Slippery Slope: The 'Two-Minus-One Pregnancy'," 2011.

98. Klaus, "Reproductive Technology (Evaluation & Treatment of Infertility): Guidelines for Catholic Couples." They require that the condom be perforated, to at least allow a chance for procreation during intercourse, in keeping with Catholic theology. I do not think that this is biblically necessary, as I am not opposed to contraception.

Ethics and Religious Liberty Commission, that this is morally acceptable, as it is very different from various forms of ART, sperm or egg donation, or surrogacy.[99]

First of all, these embryos "already exist, and they already exist as persons created in the image of God."[100] To adopt them, and provide them with a loving family, is a good thing, as is any other adoption of a child in need of parents and a home. Second, the adoptive parents were not party to "creating" or freezing these embryos. That moral blame falls on their biological parents, and their children should not suffer for it. Third, embryo adoption does not violate or denigrate the one-flesh union of husband and wife any more than any other adoption. I like Moore's final point: "These aren't 'unused embryos' as though they were things or tools. These are image-bearing persons who their Creator, not their 'usefulness,' endowed with certain inalienable rights. Opening our hearts, and our homes, and our wombs, to the least of these is a Christ-like thing to do."[101]

In fact, I would liken embryo adoption by married Christian couples to the early church's practice of rescuing the abandoned infants of ancient Rome. It affirms the beauty and safety of having and raising children within the protective, loving embrace of a married mother and father, and brings them into the protection and teaching of Christian parents and churches.

God loves children and wants them, and so should we. He bases his love for them on nothing more than their humanity, apart from any qualities they do or do not possess. We should be thankful for that, for that is how he receives us as his sons and daughters. He has designed the human race so that we are physically able to conceive children outside of marriage but should never willingly do so. We should seek to provide every human child with married parents, and welcome each into this world with open arms and full hearts. Evangelicals are sliding away from upholding God's creational design for children in belief and practice, dishonoring him, harming ourselves, and undermining our witness to the world. It is time for us to repent of this and turn to him for forgiveness for our failures

---

99. "Should Christians Adopt Embryos?"
100. Ibid.
101. Ibid.

and the grace to change, recommitting ourselves to living in accordance to his design and heart for bearing and raising children. Only then are we going to fully experience the blessings he wants for us in that and be a model for a nation and larger Western world that has increasingly abandoned the structures and beliefs needed for families and children to thrive.

PART 2

BEFORE MARRIAGE—
MATE SELECTION AND
PREPARATION FOR
MATRIMONY

INTRODUCTION TO PART 2

*Three things are too wonderful for me; four I do not understand: the
way of an eagle in the sky, the way of a serpent on a rock, the way of a
ship on the high seas, and the way of a man with a virgin.*

Proverbs 30:18–19

F inding the right partner and then pursuing marriage with him or her
is typically delightful, exhilarating, agonizing, and perilous—often
all at the same time. The decisions that people make during these seasons
are of inestimable consequence for them, the cause of Christ, the children
they may have and raise together, and numerous other people. Both the
Scriptures and human experience attest to the value of that grave, ecclesi-
astical admonition in the *Book of Common Prayer* that marriage should not
"be enterprised, nor taken in hand, unadvisedly, lightly, or wantonly . . . but
reverently, discreetly, advisedly, soberly, and in the fear of God."[1]

The months or years people spend meeting and considering potential
partners, falling in love, courting, becoming engaged, and preparing for
marriage are difficult to navigate. In the many assessments and delib-
erations involved, folks often find it difficult to distinguish the trivial
and irrelevant from the significant and relevant, accurate from false
impressions, and so on. Confusing signals and contradictory counsel
abound. Lovers headed toward marriage also typically, and rightly, experience powerful longing, and strong, often conflicting, emotions. Many
young lovers can sympathize with the betrothed woman in the Song of
Songs, "Sustain me with raisins; refresh me with apples, for I am sick
with love" (2:5).

---

1. Book of Common Prayer, 311.

People should certainly relish those "happy golden years" to the fullest and remember them fondly into old age. Yet as they travel the road to marriage, they should never neglect biblical principles, sober and prayerful reflection, wise counsel, and sound practical wisdom. Like the idealized John Alden of the famous Longfellow poem excerpted at the beginning of chapter 5, they should welcome blissfully falling "head over heels," but only with a godly person who is also particularly suited to them. Henry Smith aptly summarized this: "To direct thee to a right choice therein, the Holy Ghost gives thee two rules in the choice of a wife, godliness and fitness." They must also proceed guided by practical wisdom and godly principles.

In this section of this book, I will deal with mate selection and preparation for marriage in depth. In the current chapter, we will look at general biblical principles for choosing a spouse, rooted in an explicit, grounded understanding of God's definition of, and purposes for, marriage. Chapter 6 will provide more practical advice in areas where the Scriptures do not provide clear "yes" or "no" answers, but in which God does not leave us blind. Chapter 7 is a call to premarital sexual integrity, including reality versus myth, the consequences of sex outside marriage, and God's gracious provision for those who have failed in these areas. Chapter 8 will look at modern dating practices and their often-negative consequences, along with better, biblical principles and alternatives. Finally, chapter 9 will look at common misperceptions about cohabitation, particularly as a flawed strategy for mate selection and premarital preparation, over against sound, proven strategies couples can use, and churches can sponsor, that actually do successfully prepare couples for marriage.

CHAPTER 5

CHOOSING A PARTNER IN THE LORD

Oft when his labor was finished, with eager feet would the dreamer
Follow the pathway that ran through the woods to the house of Priscilla,
Led by illusions romantic and subtile deceptions of fancy,
Pleasure disguised as duty, and love in the semblance of friendship.
Ever of her he thought, when he fashioned the walls of his dwelling;
Ever of her he thought, when he delved in the soil of his garden;
Ever of her he thought, when he read in his Bible on Sunday
Praise of the virtuous woman, as she is described in the Proverbs, —
How the heart of her husband doth safely trust in her always,
How all the days of her life she will do him good, and not evil,
How she seeketh the wool and the flax and worketh with gladness,
How she layeth her hand to the spindle and holdeth the distaff,
How she is not afraid of the snow for herself or her household,
Knowing her household are clothed with the scarlet cloth of her weaving!
Henry Wadsworth Longfellow[1]

Beauty recommends none to God, nor is it any certain indication of
wisdom and goodness, but it has deceived many a man who has made his
choice of a wife by it. There may be an impure deformed soul lodged in a
comely and beautiful body. . . . It is a fading thing at the best. . . . But the
fear of God reigning in the heart is the beauty of the soul; it recommends
those that have it to the favour of God, and is, in his sight, of great price;
it will last forever, and bid defiance to death itself, which consumes the
beauty of the body, but consummates the beauty of the soul.
Matthew Henry[2]

---

1. Longfellow, *The Courtship of Miles Standish*, 98–99.
2. Henry, *Commentary on the Whole Bible: Volume 3*, 804.

O utside of embracing Jesus Christ in faith and repentance, the most important decision most of us will ever make is choosing our husband or wife. As Scripture abundantly attests, this will radically shape the course and quality of our lives for good or ill. Proverbs, for example, teaches men that finding a superb wife is an incomparable blessing (cf. 18:22; 19:14; 31:10), while marrying the wrong woman will bring unrelenting misery (cf. 19:13b; 21:9, 19; 27:15-16). "An excellent wife is the crown of her husband, but she who brings shame is like rottenness in his bones" (Prov 12:4). These passages are equally valid for women seeking husbands.

In this chapter, I will first consider that, in selecting their mates, Christians should not merely seek personal ends such as sexual fulfillment or individual happiness, though these things are certainly lawful and good. Rather, they ought to find someone with whom they can live out covenant marriage as God has defined it, for the purposes he has given it. I will then go on to examine character traits that one ought to look for in a prospective marriage partner. Finally, I will address the issue of "equal yoking"—the principle that believers ought not to marry unbelievers, including God's reasons for this restriction, and what this *does* and *does not* require.

SUITABLE SPOUSES FOR
GOD-ORIENTED MARRIAGES
CHOOSING A MARRIAGE PARTNER IN LIGHT OF WHAT
MARRIAGE TRULY "IS" AND IS TRULY "FOR"

In warning Christians against entering marriage carelessly and without proper regard for God's expectations, the *Book of Common Prayer* reminds them to do so, instead, "duly considering the *causes* for which Matrimony was ordained."[3] We have now considered these three ends at length, which bear repeating here: "the procreation of children, to be brought up in the fear and nurture of the Lord . . . to avoid fornication . . . mutual society, help, and comfort, that the one ought to have of the other, both in prosperity and adversity."[4]

Christians should marry someone with whom they are willing and able to *do* important things. To have sex together, delighting in it, while

---

3. Ibid. (emphasis added).
4. Ibid., 311–12.

encouraging sexual fidelity and purity of mind, body, and heart in each other. To assist, care for, and support each other, in hundreds or even thousands of ways, as they tackle their mostly mundane and everyday tasks, responsibilities, and plans, from young adulthood through old age and infirmity, in good times and bad, "in sickness and in health."[5] To comfort, encourage, and provide company for each other, as a bulwark against isolation, loneliness, and despair. Normally, to have and care for children together, as a team, and modeling godly marriage to them, with all the challenges and delights, disappointments and accomplishments, joy and grief, that brings. To do all of this one day at a time (Matt 6:34), by the grace of God, under his lordship, and in his service (cf. Matt 6:33; Phil 2:13; 4:13; Col 3:23–24). In other words, to serve God together.

All of this assumes that believers should have found someone they are willing to be joined to "so long as [they] both shall live."[6] No holding back, no exit strategies, on honest, informed exploration and reflection, appreciating that there are flaws, known and unknown, in every potential partner and that God's grace and assistance will be needed from beginning to end (cf. Rom 3:23). Someone with whom they are willing to be joined, as one flesh, by God himself (Gen 2:24; Matt 19:4–6; Mark 10:7–9; Eph 5:31). Someone they are prepared to give complete ownership of their bodies (1 Cor 7:4) and earthly property.[7] Someone with whom they can form a marriage symbolizing "the mystical union betwixt Christ and his Church"[8] (Eph 5:32) to a watching, needy, increasingly confused world.

This is quite different from the ways that many people today, especially those who are younger, think about getting married and what they want from their mates. The radical disjuncture between today's prevailing approach and a biblical one may not be obvious on the surface, in such things as listing preferred personal traits in prospective partners. After all, who would *not* want a spouse who is a good parent, puts his or her family first, is caring and compassionate,[9] and so on? Rather, the difference lies at the level of the presuppositions and worldviews that rest below the surface.

---

5. Ibid., 313.

6. Ibid.

7. Ibid., 314.

8. Ibid., 311.

9. Wang and Taylor, *For Millennials, Parenthood Trumps Marriage*, 10.

These are clear in the ultimate reasons most aspiring to marriage today give for choosing to be married at all, in the relative importance and place of matrimony in their lives, in the kinds of demands they believe marriage and their spouses can legitimately make upon them, and what they can therefore expect from their partner.

As I touched on in chapters 1 and 2, most Americans today see marriage as a way to meet their personal needs.[10] Sociologists talk about a shift from institutional to companionate to individualistic marriage that has taken place since the end of the nineteenth century.[11] This emphasis on the self has accelerated and deepened over the past several decades. Andrew Cherlin bluntly states that, for contemporary Americans considering marriage, "Feeling that you [are] meeting your obligations to others [is] less central; feeling that you [have] opportunities to grow as a person [is] more central."[12] This agrees with the earlier assessment of Robert Bellah and his *Habits of the Heart* coauthors that, for most Americans, marriage has become a vehicle for "finding oneself," experiencing "psychological gratification," "spontaneous interpersonal intimacy," and "personal growth and self-fulfillment." Thus, in contrast to earlier generations, it is "less firmly anchored . . . in an objective pattern of roles and institutions."[13]

This is bound to affect, down deep, what people look for in and from a partner. Contrast that with the very different views of love and marriage that Bellah and company found among their committed evangelical interviewees in the early 1980s:

> These Christians stress that, at least in modern society, there is no basis for permanent commitment in marriage apart from Christian faith itself. . . . The other values on which people try to build marriage are fragile. . . . Christian love is . . . built of solider stuff than personal happiness and enjoyment. It is, first, a commitment, a form of obedience to God's word. In addition, love rests less on feeling than on decision and action. Real love may even, at times,

---

10. See Bellah et al., *Habits of the Heart*, 85, 90–93, 109–110; also Coontz, *Marriage, a History*, 23; Starbuck and Lundy, *Families in Context*, 230.

11. Cherlin, *Public and Private Families*, 196–99.

12. Ibid., 198.

13. Bellah et al., *Habits of the Heart*, 85.

require emotional self-denial, pushing feelings to the back in order to live up to one's commitments. Most critical in love are a firm decision about where one's obligations lie and a willingness to fulfill those obligations in action, independent of the ups and downs of one's feelings. Of course, these Christians seek some of the same qualities of sharing, communication, and intimacy in marriage that define love for most Americans. But they are determined that these are goods to be sought within a framework of binding commitments, not the reasons for adhering to a commitment. *Only by having an obligation to something higher than one's own preferences or one's own fulfillment, they insist, can one achieve a permanent love relationship.*[14]

For the Christian with a biblical worldview, marriage is the best, most legitimate and desirable means for achieving the basic purposes God has given it. Unfortunately, as we have already seen—most people today, especially young adults, do not view marriage as a necessary precondition for sex, parenting, or securing a live-in partner, and their actions reflect this.

A 2010 Pew Research Center survey of attitudes toward marriage and mate selection underscores a lot of this. Among eighteen- to twenty-nine-year-olds, only 30 percent rated having a successful marriage as "one of the most important things," while 52 percent said this about being a good parent.[15] Only 49 percent thought that having children was a very important reason to be married.[16] The majority of births in this age group were out of wedlock.[17] All of this showed that parenting and marriage had become "delinked" in the minds of millennials.[18] Marriage is just one way to do parenting. Thus, the fact that most believed that being a good parent (91 percent for men, 93 percent for women) and putting family first (74 percent for men, 88 percent for women) were "very important" qualities in a marital partner did *not* mean they tied marriage to parenting.[19]

---

14. Ibid., 96–97 (emphasis added).
15. *For Millennials*, 1.
16. Ibid., 12.
17. Ibid., 6.
18. Ibid., 1.
19. Ibid., 10.

Similarly, while 57 percent of men, and 42 percent of women, wanted a spouse who was a "good sex partner,"[20] only 28 percent thought that sexual fulfillment was easier in marriage, and 11 percent thought it was harder.[21] As for needing marriage for mutual help and support, only 26 percent thought marriage was important for happiness. Only 8 percent believed it fostered career success, while 34 percent thought it undermined it, and just 37 percent of millennials thought it improved financial security. Only 16 percent said marriage improved social status, while 21 percent thought it hurt this.[22] Most did feel that love (88 percent), companionship (71 percent), and lifelong commitment (76 percent) were important reasons to marry, but if you will recall, this is tied to self-gratification and believing that these needs could be met in a romantic partnership other than covenant marriage. In fact, 44 percent said marriage was obsolete, and 46 percent applauded the ever-expanding variety of familial options.[23]

As we have seen, in spite of all of this, marriage continues to deliver huge benefits to spouses, children, and society. That is good news. However, increasingly, people do not view marriage as something that has specific contours and requirements external to their own desires, which is essential to social health, children, safe and fulfilling sexual lives, and lifelong companionship for most people. They are even less prone to view marriage, or singleness for that matter, as a vehicle of service to God and others. However, by the guidance of the Holy Spirit and the Word of God, Christians can live and model a radically different, covenantal approach to marriage rooted in creation itself. As we saw above, many do, or at least try to do so, meaning godly priorities must direct their mate selection.

SCRIPTURAL CHARACTER TRAITS FOR PROSPECTIVE MARRIAGE PARTNERS
Caveats and Qualifications

Choosing the kind of partners extolled in the Bible is essential to doing marriage God's way. There are certain character traits that persons who follow Scripture should seek in their prospective marital partners. Having said this, let me underscore several important caveats and qualifications.

---

20. Ibid.
21. Ibid., 11.
22. Ibid.
23. Ibid., 3.

First, we must not forget that *both* partners should have these qualities. Any Christian who is serious about marriage should possess and be cultivating these virtues in themselves. An old friend of mine used to like to say, "Try to be what you want others to be." Adopting this stance keeps us humble and teachable, and undermines a critical spirit (Matt 7:3-5).

Second, no human being is going to, even remotely, approach perfection on any of these qualities. Many of us have failed miserably in the past in some or all of these areas. In the future, some of us will struggle with things that were not problems at the time we married. There is also no clear way of knowing exactly "how much is enough" of any of these qualities, and this includes just how stable or consistent we need to be in living them out. Moreover, spouses are supposed to help each other in their weaknesses and sins. This is part of what God designed marriage to do. No principles can give us a set of clunky rules that will relieve us of the need for wisdom, discretion, charity, and counsel in evaluating the suitability of ourselves or anyone else for something as hard, important, or with as many future unknowns, as godly marriage.

Therefore, the questions people should be asking about their potential spouse (and themselves) should be those such as, "Is this quality rooted and growing in this person?" and "Does he or she take this seriously?" Before and after marriage, for any believer and his or her spouse, here is a word from the apostle Paul that we should never forget: "Not that I have already obtained this or am already perfect, but I press on to make it my own, because Christ Jesus has made me his own. Brothers, I do not consider that I have made it my own. But one thing I do: forgetting what lies behind and straining forward to what lies ahead, I press on toward the goal for the prize of the upward call of God in Christ Jesus" (Phil 3:12-14).

Third, while it is certainly noble for someone to try to be a person whom a godly partner would want to marry, our fundamental aim should always be integrity and holiness before God as a grateful response to the love he has shown us. The Christian life is not about earning love from, or impressing, anyone. "Being a good person" just to please someone we hope to marry is not real sanctification and Christian growth. How long is change like that going to last?

Fourth, all these character traits will not be present in equal amounts in anyone. Again, that is one of the wonderful things about the marital team, namely that one will often be stronger precisely where the other is weak. After marriage, the two will be one flesh, and each person's weaknesses, and strengths, will be fully "owned" by their spouse. Moreover, no one ever outgrows the need for God's grace. What is key is the extent to which people are honest about their weaknesses and rely upon God in them. Here is the apostle Paul again: "But he said to me, 'My grace is sufficient for you, for my power is made perfect in weakness.' Therefore I will boast all the more gladly of my weaknesses, so that the power of Christ may rest upon me. For the sake of Christ, then, I am content with weaknesses. . . . For when I am weak, then I am strong" (2 Cor 12:9–10).

Fifth, any quality will appear in a huge variety of forms and actions, across individuals, personality types, situations, times, places, cultures, and so on. Compassion, integrity, perseverance, forbearance, generosity, honesty, and everything else does not always look the same. For example, sometimes courage is speaking up, but other times it is staying silent. Sometimes love means saying "yes" or "no" to the same request, depending on circumstance and need. We so often miss virtues in others when we have static and limited expectations of how people are supposed to express them.

Sixth, godly character traits reinforce and build on each other, and these characteristics are not typically present alone (cf. 2 Pet 1:5–9). Growth in one virtually always leads to improvement in others. For example, someone who is wise will also have self-control (cf. Prov 29:11), the fear of God leads to wisdom (Prov 1:7; 9:10), being compassionate and forgiving are linked (Ps 51:1), and so on.

With all these qualifications and considerations, let us look now at the qualities that the Scriptures indicate should be present in any truly godly partner. Each of these is relevant for prospective husbands *and* wives. While men and women will often express and apply these traits very differently, they are important in both. The astute reader will also notice that these character traits should be present and growing in *all* Christians. However, here I focus on those that the Scriptures directly identify as necessary in potential spouses, as partners and as future parents, which experience and logic have shown are especially relevant to establishing a happy, godly, productive marriage and family.

Qualities for Prospective Husbands and Wives

First, the person should be actively pursuing *wisdom*.[24] To summarize a complex topic, being wise means having sound judgment, knowing how to apply experience and knowledge to achieve desirable, and morally good, ends. It also means having common sense, including being able to perceive and avoid danger (cf. Prov 22:3; 27:12). J. I. Packer defines it this way: "Wisdom is the power to see, and the inclination to choose, the best and highest goal, together with the surest means of attaining it. Wisdom is, in fact, the practical side of moral goodness. As such, it is found in its fullness only in God."[25] Thus, someone intent on becoming wise will follow hard after God, including diligently studying the Scriptures (Ps 119:97–100). Being foolish is the opposite of being wise.

Wisdom is not the same as thing as "intelligence," especially as we tend to define the latter today. In fact, many "smart" people are quite foolish, while there are numerous wise folks of average or sub-average IQ.

Discretion is inseparable from wisdom and overlaps with it in many ways. The two qualities are constantly discussed together in the Scriptures (cf. Prov 2:10–11). Common synonyms for discretion include "carefulness," "prudence," "caution," "moderation," "foresight," "tact," "discrimination," and "diplomacy." It includes being careful and appropriately guarded in speech or action, not being rash or gullible (Prov 14:15–16). Discretion is part of being mature and responsible, as opposed to being immature and irresponsible.

It is hard to imagine why anyone would want to marry a fool—a rash and reckless person who lacks common sense—rather than someone who is wise and discrete. Abigail was a wise woman married to a fool named Nabal,[26] and the Scriptures do not describe it as a happy situation for her or her family (1 Sam 25). The warnings in Scripture about foolish men and women and what happens to those who are tied to, and dependent upon, them are too numerous to recount here. We have the constant scriptural admonitions that any man entrusted with any responsibility ought to be wise and discrete (cf. Matt 24:45–46). Surely this includes a wife and a

---

24. Deffinbaugh, "The Way of the Wise."

25. Packer, *Knowing God*, 80.

26. Given her culture, Abigail probably did not freely choose to marry Nabal. The point is not that she made a poor choice, but that being married to a fool, however it happens, is not a good thing.

family. Men are encouraged directly to look for wisdom and discretion in those with whom they would build a home and raise a family. "The wisest of women builds her house" (Prov 14:1a). "House and wealth are inherited from fathers, but a prudent wife is from the LORD" (Prov 19:14). The excellent wife of Proverbs 31 "opens her mouth with wisdom" (v. 26).

Second, a future husband or wife should be someone who *fears the Lord*. King Lemuel's mother told him directly to seek such a woman: "Charm is deceitful, and beauty is vain, but a woman who fears the LORD is to be praised" (Prov 31:30). It is hard to imagine why this would not be equally important to a woman seeking a *godly* husband. Consider just the rudiments of fearing God: seeking to obey his commandments, including the moral law as laid out in the Decalogue (Exod 20:3–17), not just in external behavior but in what he or she strives to be conformed to in heart, mind, and will (Deut 6:5; Matt 22:36–37). Shunning evil (Prov 16:6b). Eschewing adulterous behavior, thought, and affection (Matt 5:27–28). Avoiding covetousness, envy, theft, and dishonesty. Honoring parents, and indeed all who hold legitimate authority.[27] Remaining faithful to God, not being an idolater or blasphemer. Not only not murdering, but also refusing to harbor violence and anger (Matt 5:21–22). Honoring the Sabbath, including being intent on attendance at public worship, being connected to a local church (Heb 10:24–25). Marriages in which both husband and wife fear the Lord, and lead their households in doing so, will be blessed by God, and be a blessing to others. Why would anyone seeking a mate want anything less than someone who fears the Lord? "Fear God and keep his commandments, for this is the whole duty of man" (Eccl 12:13b).

Third, acceptable prospective mates will have a *good work ethic*—they will be *diligent*. Once again, King Lemuel's mother was blunt about this with regard to the excellent wife. After providing numerous details about her industrious ways from morning to late at night, she points out, "She looks well to the ways of her household and does not eat the bread of idleness" (Prov 31:27). Condemnations of slothful people, and praise for those who work hard with great attention and care, appear throughout the Bible. "The hand of the diligent will rule, while the slothful will be put to forced labor" (Prov 12:24). "The soul of the sluggard craves and gets nothing, while

---

27. Cf. Q. 124 of the Westminster Larger Catechism, in the *Westminster Confession of Faith*, page 81 of the Larger Catechism section.

the soul of the diligent is richly supplied" (Prov 13:4). "Whatever your hand finds to do, do it with your might" (Eccl 9:10a). "Whatever you do, work heartily, as for the Lord and not for men" (Col 3:23). A lengthy section of 2 Thessalonians repeatedly condemns idleness and encourages believers to work hard (3:6–15). Building, providing, and caring for a family is difficult, at times exhausting. There are many things, most quite mundane, that we must diligently pursue day and year, in and out, in order to succeed and be a good witness for Christ. A life partner with a good work ethic is essential. After all, "if anyone does not provide for his relatives, and especially for members of his household, he has denied the faith and is worse than an unbeliever" (1 Tim 5:8).

The Scriptures closely link *compassion* to diligence. This is not surprising, since we are to "not grow weary in doing good" (2 Thess 3:13b). In turn, compassion leads to and overlaps other qualities essential to godliness in general, and to being a good husband or wife, father or mother, specifically: *kindness, forgiveness, generosity, charity,* and *hospitality.* The Proverbs 31 woman "opens her hand to the poor and reaches out her hands to the needy" (v. 20). "The teaching of kindness is on her tongue" (v. 26b). Luke tells us about a miracle involving Tabitha, an early Christian who "was full of good works and acts of charity" (Acts 9:36b). Paul talks about worthy widows "having a reputation for good works: if she has brought up children, has shown hospitality, has washed the feet of the saints, has cared for the afflicted, and has devoted herself to every good work" (1 Tim 5:10). God is compassionate (cf. Lam 3:22–23), and those who want to be like him will be as well. The apostle Paul urged the Ephesians, "Be kind to one another, tenderhearted, forgiving one another" (Eph 4:32a), and the Colossians, "Put on then . . . compassionate hearts, kindness, humility, meekness, and patience, bearing with one another . . . forgiving each other" (Col 3:12–13). A godly man who is supervising his household well must be "hospitable" (1 Tim 3:2; Titus 1:8), and also "gentle" (1 Tim 3:3).

All of these are practical manifestations of *love* without which, said Paul, we are just "a noisy gong or a clanging cymbal" (1 Cor 13:1b). Love is the master virtue; it "binds everything together in perfect harmony" (Col 3:14b). It is important that someone's prospective mate truly love him or her. This means treating the other in a loving manner, and thus with kindness, being forgiving rather than holding grudges, being generous with their time and property, and so on. It is not primarily about feelings, as wonderful as these can be, but about actions.

However, it is critical to see that the ideal mate should be a loving person *generally*. Building a godly marriage is not only about the husband and the wife loving each other. Together they must build a family and a home that glorifies God and serves others. For this to happen, the love of each spouse has to extend to children, neighbors, other family members, coworkers, fellow believers, and even to enemies (Luke 6:35a).

Fourth, Christians should consider how *prayerful* their intended partner is, including whether or not they are intent on growing in this area of their lives. We often miss the prayerfulness, for example, of godly women of the Bible such as Isaac's wife, Rebekah (Gen 25:22–23), or Samuel's mother, Hannah (1 Sam 1:10–17). Notice in this record about Rebekah that she was pregnant in answer to Isaac's prior prayer for her (Gen 25:21). They were both praying people. It is almost impossible to overstate the importance of prayer in the Christian life, or the degree to which the Bible admonishes and encourages it in us. The apostle Paul went so far as to call us to "pray without ceasing" (1 Thess 5:17).

Building a godly marriage and family will mean prayer of all types in all seasons and for all sorts of reasons. The longer folks are married, the more reasons they have to pray. Moreover, to be in relationship with Jesus and to have real, vital Christian life is to be connected to him as branches are to a vine (John 15:5), and prayer is necessary for this. No one wanting a Christ-centered marriage can neglect prayer. Moreover, every marriage can tap into the power of "two or more agreeing" in prayer (Matt 18:19–20). Therefore, it is critical to have a partner who prioritizes and practices prayer and wants to grow in that with his or her spouse, and that both partners saturate the process of mate selection and marital preparation in prayer.

Fifth, as I noted in chapter 2, a prospective marital partner should be your best and dearest friend. Thus, as Deffinbaugh aptly points out, "the traits of a good friend relate to the character of one's mate," yet "some have foolishly chosen to marry one who fails to qualify even as a friend."[28] If you and your intended do not share a close and warm friendship and all that this entails, why would you consider marrying him or her? Moreover, if your

JOHN 15:5

---

28. Deffinbaugh, "The Way of the Wise."

friendship does not have the pursuit of godliness at its center, as opposed to a relationship based on utility or pleasure,[29] you are not making a good marital choice.

Drawing liberally on the book of Proverbs, Deffinbaugh skillfully specifies what friendship means,[30] which also makes the benefits of marrying a true friend, and the ties of friendship to biblical marriage, abundantly clear. Friends are *faithful*. A godly spouse will never abandon us in adversity no matter what the costs are (Prov 17:17; 18:24; 27:10). In the early twentieth century, Russian Orthodox thinker Pavel Florensky gave us this apt observation about friendship that certainly applies to godly spouses: "friendship . . . is chiefly expressed in the bearing of the *infirmities* of one's friend, without limit, in mutual patience, mutual forgiveness."[31]

Deffinbaugh goes on. A true friend is willing to confront us with hard truths about ourselves, to *rebuke* us when we need it (Prov 27:5–6). Despite this, good friends are *sensitive* and *tactful*, desiring to redirect as necessary and encourage us always, not knock us down or discourage us. Thus, quality friends pay attention to *how they talk to friends*, not just the content (Prov 25:20; 27:14). Next, good friends push us to do better in order to be and achieve all of which we are capable. They often draw us much higher than we think we can go (Prov 20:5; 27:17). Further, assuming they are wise, they are able to provide us with good *counsel*, and thus make us wiser (Prov 13:20; 27:9).[32]

Sixth, we should only consider prospective mates who *treat their parents with respect and love* as much as this is possible. I touched on this earlier in my sweep through the Ten Commandments, but this is important to look at specifically. As Deffinbaugh observes, "we can tell much about the character of a person by observing his relationship to his parents."[33] In most cases, this is directly observable or otherwise discoverable. Few people who treat their parents badly will make good spouses. By definition no one is a godly person who dismisses, neglects, or is rude or cruel to his or her parents (Prov 1:8–9; 20:20; 30:17; 1 Tim 5:8; 1 Pet 5:5). Uncorrected,

---

29. Aristotle, *Nicomachean Ethics*, vols. VIII and IX, 4–5.
30. Deffinbaugh, "The Way of the Wise."
31. Florensky, *The Pillar and Ground of the Truth*, 310.
32. Deffinbaugh, "The Way of the Wise."
33. Ibid.

those attitudes and behaviors will tend to creep into the marital relationship. This does not mean that there can be no stresses and strains in a potential partner's relationship with his or her parents. Obviously, many people have suffered badly at the hand of their parents; they may be alienated from them through no fault of their own and may struggle to honor them. I have known people whose parents disowned them for converting to the evangelical faith, abused them brutally, abandoned them, or were actively evil in their lifestyle and pursuits. One cannot expect a potential spouse with that kind of background to relate to their parents in the same manner as those blessed with a sound and loving Christian upbringing, and sometime they may even need to separate from them completely. However, God's command to honor father and mother does not depend on their worthiness, and godly men or women will do everything in their power to do so, within whatever limits they face, in spite of such hindrances.

Finally, we should marry someone who is *self-controlled* (Prov 25:28; Gal 5:23; 1 Tim 1:7). As I have noted, self-control is certainly associated with wisdom and discretion. However, it also deserves distinct attention here in certain areas that commonly destroy marriages.

Your prospective mate should be able to manage passions such as *anger* (Prov 16:32; 22:24–25; 29:11), *jealousy* (Prov 27:4; Jas 3:14–16), and the *urge to control and manipulate* others (Prov 23:7; Rom 16:17–18), all of which can lead to physical, verbal, and emotional abuse. Your partner should be "peaceable, gentle, open to reason" because "a harvest of righteousness is sown in peace by those who make peace" (Jas 3:17b–18). While married women are far less likely to suffer violence at the hand of their partners than women in other types of relationships,[34] some kind of physical abuse takes place eventually in about one in five marriages, which is concerning.[35] Emotional and verbal abuse are more common, and of course, parents may subject children to mistreatment. It makes no sense to marry someone who has already shown him- or herself to be seriously and consistently prone to such behavior.

---

34. In 2010, according to the US Department of Justice Crime Victimization Survey, the figure was 2 per 1,000 married females, versus 6.5 for divorced and widowed, and about the same for single women, 60 for women who were separated from their husbands (Catalano, *Intimate Partner Violence 1993–2010*, 6). In addition, partner violence is much higher in cohabiting than in marital households (Starbuck and Lundy, *Families in Context*, 394). See also Cherlin, *Public and Private Families*, 308.

35. Stith, "Domestic Violence."

Sexual restraint is also very important (1 Thess 4:3–7). Even beyond obvious issues I have already covered, such as pornography, lust, fornication, adultery, and the like, marriage will contain periods in which sexual intercourse can or should not happen. Childbirth, illness, injury, extended travel, and much more can and will intrude on couples' sex lives. One or both of you will not always be emotionally or physically "up for it." It is important that in these times, the desiring partner can be considerate of the other rather than demanding sexual attention.

Finally, moderation in the use of _alcohol_ and avoiding other forms of _drug abuse_ is vital (Prov 20:1; 23:29–35; 31:4–7; 1 Cor 6:10; Eph 5:18). This is notorious for wrecking marriages and destroying families,[36] and strongly related to domestic violence.[37]

No one should expect that people prone to abuse, sexual misconduct, excessive drinking, or using illicit drugs is going to be "fixed" by marriage, no matter how much or how well they are loved. I have seen numerous instances of folks plunging into marriage with partners who have unresolved issues in one or more of these areas, and it has rarely turned out well. No one with these kinds of problems should get married until they have put them well behind, as attested to by leaders and fellow believers in sound and attentive churches they are members in.

We are never going to find or be the perfect prospect or spouse. We can only ask that these character traits are substantially rooted, valued, and that there is growth in them. Nor can we predict the future accurately. Our partner may improve, or decline, in any of these areas. On the other hand, if we value our future marriage and family, we cannot ignore or minimize the importance of these virtues. "Getting it right" affects not only the couple's life and all those directly impacted by it but, through their children, generations well into the future. As an avid, amateur genealogist, I have learned how many ways my great- or even great-great-grandparents' choices affected my life, for good and ill. Among fellow church members and friends, I have witnessed the impact of poor mate-selection choices down to the third generation. As Douglas Wilson rightly said about choosing a spouse, "We cannot make our decision based on what _we_ predict might

---

36. Kaufman and Yoshioka, _Substance Abuse Treatment and Family Therapy_, 21–23.

37. Starbuck and Lundy, _Families in Context_, 395–96. The nature of the relationship between substance abuse and domestic violence is complex, but the association itself is strong.

happen twenty years from now. Rather, we must proceed on what God has revealed in his Word. God *does* know the future so we must obey him."[38]

DO NOT BE UNEQUALLY YOKED

Much that I have said in the preceding section of this chapter assumes that committed believers should only consider potential mates of sound Christian faith. However, many evangelicals do not know about or honor this principle. Sometimes, conservative Protestants have different faiths from their spouses because one but not the other converts. However— whether through disobedience, ignorance, wishful expectation of their partner's imminent conversion, or wrong interpretation of relevant biblical teaching—evangelicals often *choose* to marry non-Christians, nominal or rebellious professed believers, or Christians with whom they have fundamental differences in doctrine or practice that will likely undermine their marriages.

The problem is not new. In 1869, A. A. Hodge called marriages between the "converted and unconverted . . . common."[39] However, as Naomi Schaefer Riley pointed out in an important 2013 study, in American marriages between people of different religious faiths, the latter are dramatically increasing, while the belief that folks should marry within their religion has diminished.[40] She commissioned a survey of about 2,500 married Americans in 2010. As table 5.1 shows,[41] the vast majority of evangelical parents do not consider marriage within the faith to be "very important" to their children. In addition, only 32 percent of them agreed that their religion teaches this, while another 39 percent said it was only "somewhat important" in their churches' teaching.[42] Thus, about three in ten evangelicals do not believe that the Bible commands marriage within the faith. This should not surprise us. Many evangelical churches neglect the topic, and pastors are often afraid to bring it up for fear of offending people.[43]

---

38. Wilson, *Her Hand in Marriage*, 65–66.

39. Hodge, *The Westminster Confession*, 305.

40. Riley, *'Til Faith Do Us Part*, xiii, 6, 35. This is consistent with the findings of a very thorough, recent Pew Research Center report, "America's Changing Religious Landscape," 5.

41. Riley, *'Til Faith Do Us Part*, 35–36.

42. Ibid., 37

43. Ibid., 37–38.

Table 5.1: 2010 Interfaith Survey of 2,500 Married Americans commissioned by Naomi Schaefer Riley. Percentages for Evangelical Protestants Only

Question	Very Important	Somewhat Important	Not Very Important	Not At All Important
"How important is it to *you* that your children marry someone of the same faith?"	32%	29%	23%	15%
"How important is it to *your parents* that you marry someone of your own faith?"	28%	27%	25%	20%

The behavior of evangelicals reflects their attitudes. Riley's survey revealed that "about 30 percent of evangelical Christians are married to someone of another faith."[44] The Pew Research Center's 2015 estimate was 25 percent.[45] The General Social Survey for 2010 through 2016 combined was a bit more positive, with 77 percent of married conservative Protestants indicating that their partner shared their faith. However, those under the age of thirty were closer to Riley's estimate—28 percent were married to someone of a different faith.[46]

The issue is not just poor or sparse teaching on the issue. Mark Regnerus noted, "Quality survey data reveal only two serious, churchgoing evangelical men for every three comparable women. Thus, one out of every three evangelical women is not in a position to marry a man who's her 'spiritual equal,' let alone 'head.'"[47] Riley observes also that, with folks typically waiting into their late twenties to marry, singles usually spend years in a "religious netherworld"

44. Regnerus et al., "Is Interfaith Marriage Always Wrong?"

45. Pew Research Center, "America's Changing Religious Landscape," 47.

46. Variations between this and Pew Research Center's (above) from Riley's results appear to stem from differences in how one's faith is measured, the General Social Survey using an established way to classify certain Protestant denominations as "fundamentalist." For 2010–2016 there were 993 married respondents classified as "fundamentalists"; however, only 81 of these were under thirty, so the latter figure should be interpreted with caution.

47. Regnerus et al., "Is Interfaith Marriage Always Wrong?"

apart from their families and home churches, meeting eligible mates during periods when they are "most secular."[48] The fact that people in other religious traditions are increasingly comfortable with marriage between people of different religions may also mean that, at least for those with "softer" views on less popular evangelical beliefs, there are fewer barriers for conservative Protestants considering marrying outside the faith.

The issue raises important marital, familial, and pastoral questions. Therefore, it makes sense to explore it in depth.

BIBLICAL TEACHING AND CHRISTIAN DOCTRINE
ON MARRYING "ONLY IN THE LORD"

The *Westminster Confession of Faith* states, "It is lawful for all sorts of people to marry, who are able with judgment to give their consent. Yet it is the duty of Christians to marry only in the Lord."[49] This means not only marrying professed believers, but also rejecting those whose life and doctrine are seriously flawed: "neither should such as are godly be unequally yoked, by marrying with such as are notoriously wicked in their life, or maintain damnable heresies."[50] Given what we have already seen about the beliefs and lifestyles of many professed conservative Protestants, especially among younger cohorts, this last warning is certainly appropriate for evangelicals seeking to be married today, even when the person they are considering claims to be a fellow believer.[51]

Conservative Protestantism is not alone in calling on their members to avoid marrying outside their faith community. Roman Catholic teaching, which carefully distinguishes marriages between Catholics and "baptized non-Catholics," from those where there is "disparity of cult" (marriage between a Catholic and a non-Christian), is quite similar in this respect.[52] The Orthodox Church holds comparable views.[53]

---

48. Ibid.

49. 80–81.

50. Ibid., 81.

51. If what we have already covered on evangelical views is not enough, consider the very sobering findings of a February–March 2017 survey of "born again Christians" done by the American Culture & Faith Institute, documenting disturbing levels of disagreement with 17 Christian teachings, many of them historically at the very center of basic Christian orthodoxy. "Where Born-Agains Are Missing the Mark."

52. *Catechism of the Catholic Church*, 407–8.

53. See, for example, Orthodox Church in America, "Marriage," and "Marriage to a Non-Christian."

Westminster's doctrinal stance is clearly justified in Scripture. In the New Testament, the apostle Paul allows that a widow is "free to be married to whom she wishes, *only in the Lord*" (1 Cor 7:39b, emphasis added). Later, in a general discussion of what it means to be holy and set apart to God, he makes this powerful statement: "Be ye not unequally yoked together with unbelievers: for what fellowship hath righteousness with unrighteousness? And what communion hath light with darkness?" (2 Cor 6:14 KJV). The principle, as the *Reformation Study Bible* notes, is not avoiding all friendship and cooperation with unbelievers, but "situations where significant control over one's actions would be willingly yielded to an unbeliever through a voluntary partnership or association" in which "they significantly influence the direction and outcome of our moral decisions and spiritual activities."[54] Obviously, this includes marriage. He is making spiritual application of the Old Testament injunction against yoking an ox and donkey together to plow (Deut 22:10), where they would not pull together in a unified way and clean and unclean animals would be mixed.[55] God similarly forbade his people from marrying non-Jews in the Old Testament (Exod 34:16; Deut 7:3; Mal 2:11–12; Ezra 9–10).

It is not difficult to see why "equal yoking" would be important in Christian marriage. We have already seen that God's purposes for it include not only having children but the "increase of . . . the Church with an holy seed."[56] Remember that God also designed marriage to provide believers with a helpmate who will encourage and assist them in their Christian calling and faith, which they are to express in all areas of their lives.

Regarding rearing faithful children, in unequally yoked marriages, both partners cannot participate together in the instruction of children in the faith, baptism, family prayer, and the like. In a marriage between a believer and an unbeliever, even if the latter is wonderfully supportive and accommodating of his or her partner raising their children in the faith, much is missing and difficulties arise. The situation is even more complex if each partner has strong, but different and even directly contrary, religious beliefs. Says Riley, "Deciding how to raise children is probably the highest hurdle interfaith parents face. . . . There are choices that parents have to make every year—if not every day—about how religion will be

54. 1836.

55. Ibid., 270.

56. *Westminster Confession of Faith*, 80.

practiced in the household, what kinds of ceremonies to adopt, how strict observance should be, how to answer children's questions about important issues like death or sex."[57]

I experienced growing up in a home in which my six siblings and I were raised Roman Catholic, including weekly mass, Catholic schools, and catechism classes. My mother was Catholic and my father a lapsed Protestant. At best an agnostic, he never darkened the parish door except for funerals and baptisms, but rarely directly spoke against what the church taught us. He honored the vow he made that enabled him to marry my mother—that he would support our mother raising us as Catholics—but never joined us in our faith. I appreciate much that this meant, but ultimately it was not the same for me as it was for my peers whose fathers were sitting with them every Sunday, modeling and instructing them in the faith.

As to the second point about husband and wife as mutual helpmates, I cannot imagine walking as a Christian and as a husband and father without the daily encouragement, admonition, and partnership of my wife in matters of faith. There is also the danger that believing spouses will be drawn away from the faith by their mate (Exod 34:16; Deut 7:4), rather than vice versa. Though many religiously-mixed marriages are stable and happy, Riley documents that on average they have higher divorce rates, and much lower levels of marital satisfaction, than "same-faith" ones.[58] Generally, in her study, evangelicals married to non-evangelicals had percentages of divorce that were one-third higher than those married within their faith (48 percent versus 32 percent). Evangelicals married to those of no religion were about twice as likely to be divorced (61 percent).[59] Twenty-nine percent of Catholics who had married within their faith got divorced, compared to over one quarter more (40 percent) who had married evangelicals.

The more Christians believe that Jesus is the only way to salvation rather than holding that there are many paths to God—that is to say, the more orthodox they are—the less happy they are married outside their

---

57. Riley, *'Til Faith Do Us Part*, 80. An excellent article anyone should read who is contemplating marrying outside the faith is Kathy Keller's "Don't Take It From Me: Reasons You Should Not Marry An Unbeliever."

58. Ibid., 119–43.

59. Ibid., 121.

faith.[60] Interestingly, the higher divorce rate and lower satisfaction of marriages between people of different faiths appear to be partly due to conflicts over "raising children [which] seem to provide some of the greatest sources of tension in these marriages."[61]

Moreover, it is difficult for believing partners to participate fully in the life of their church—worship, Bible studies, evangelism, and the rest—without leaving their spouses out of many of their most important activities and socializing while diverting time away from things their partner wants to do. Riley succinctly summarizes this dilemma: "Having to either leave a spouse at home or drag a reluctant spouse along."[62] Unequal yoking or not, honoring the marital relationship and the needs of one's spouse is a sacred calling before God. The commitment is profound and lifelong (1 Cor 7:39). Thus, in even the best situations—understanding spouses who do not share, but do value and abundantly accommodate the spiritual life of their evangelical partners—it is inevitable that the latter will have to curtail their spiritual pursuits.[63] As A. A. Hodge observed, in joining themselves in marriage to unbelievers there is great danger that the believer will be "greatly depressed in his inward spiritual life, and greatly hindered in his attempts to serve his Master in the world."[64]

WHAT THE BIBLICAL PROHIBITION MEANS AND DOES NOT MEAN

The prohibition has nothing to do with non-Christians being generally or necessarily "inferior" to believers beyond the matter of redemption, as important as salvation is. We all know those outside our faith who are admirable and wonderful in many respects, including in many of the basic qualities I have covered here, such as integrity, love, practical wisdom and discretion, work ethic, and the like. It has to do with saving faith and doctrinal compatibility, and all that this means in wedded life, and is not in itself an insult against the sincerity of character of the unbelieving spouse in any other respect.

This principle does not mean that a marriage between people of different faiths is any less of a marriage in the eyes of God, whether one

---

60. Ibid., 126.
61. Ibid., 127.
62. Ibid.
63. "Don't Take It From Me."
64. Hodge, *The Westminster Confession of Faith*, 305.

partner is an evangelical or not. Even though believers should not choose to marry outside their faith, once they have made their vows and consummated their union, their marriage is lawful and valid in every way. This is true for them and, as the *Westminster Confession of Faith* notes, millions of marriages that do not involve believers at all.[65] Even regarding marriage with non-Christians, says A. A. Hodge, "The principle that . . . true believers should not intermarry with the ungodly, touches not that which is essential to the validity of marriage, but that which belongs to its perfection, and brings in question not the reality of the marriage when formed, but the propriety of forming it."[66] Southern Baptist leader Russell Moore advises married Christian converts whose spouses did not embrace the faith: "this is a real marriage and you owe your spouse everything you owed him before—love, fidelity, and understanding. Your marriage is a sanctified union before God."[67]

The New Testament clearly affirms this, and it does not command that church or spouse seek to have such marriages dissolved, as Ezra insisted that (often polygamous) Jewish men do with their "foreign wives" (10:3–5, 11–14). Jesus' teaching on marriage as a one-flesh bond, indissoluble except for the most grievous violations of the marriage vow (Matt 19:3–9; Mark 10:2–12) holds for all true marriages, not just those between two faithful, committed Christians of sound faith. The apostle Paul addressed this clearly:

> To the rest I say (I, not the Lord) that if any brother has a wife who is an unbeliever, and she consents to live with him, he should not divorce her. If any woman has a husband who is an unbeliever, and he consents to live with her, she should not divorce him. For the unbelieving husband is made holy because of his wife, and the unbelieving wife is made holy because of her husband. Otherwise your children would be unclean, but as it is, they are holy. But if the unbelieving partner separates, let it be so. In such cases the brother or sister is not enslaved. God has called you to peace. For how do you know, wife, whether you will save your husband?

---

65. 80.

66. Ibid.

67. Riley, *'Til Faith Do Us Part*, 141.

Or how do you know, husband, whether you will save your wife? (1 Cor 7:12–16)

There are some remarkable things here, which should be a hope and encouragement to believers married to unconverted spouses to press on in the faith, regardless of how their marital situation came about. God is gracious and never abandons his people. Because of the believing spouse, he regards the whole household as being within his covenant. Through him or her the children and parents are exposed to godly influences, including being witnesses to the goodness of God in the life of the believer. Paul even refers to the children as "holy," set apart to God.

The principle of "equal yoking" does not extend to every form of potential incompatibility. Puritans often used the prohibition on unequal yoking to condemn marriages between people who were not equals in areas like the prestige of their families, education, wealth, and social status.[68] Though there may be practical wisdom in considering how differences like this might affect marital suitability or challenges a married couple might face, Scripture does not justify this use of Paul's teaching on the matter.[69] There are many areas in which couples will on average do better if they are roughly similar, but exceptions abound; the correct answer is often "it depends," and these types of things have to do with judgment, not scriptural commands.

So, how far does the principle of "equal yoking" extend, beyond believers not marrying those who are non-Christian or only nominally so, or who, despite claims to faith, are reprobate in life or reject central tenets of the Christian faith? Here, we need to employ a great deal of charity and practical wisdom, and competent biblical counsel. There are no easy rules.

Marriages between evangelicals and Roman Catholics pose serious difficulties, as leaders in both communions admit. Catholics who are *laissez-faire* about the numerous areas of important doctrinal difference that will exist are not of sound or serious faith according to their *own* religion, whether or not their church admits them to the sacraments. If they are serious Christians who now agree with evangelicals in the key areas of disagreement, then they should do as I did, and convert. However, if serious,

---

68. Morgan, *The Puritan Family*, 55.
69. Douglas Wilson agrees; see *Her Hand In Marriage*, 74.

committed Roman Catholics and evangelicals get married, and neither fundamentally alters their religious convictions, partners will pull in opposite directions in numerous critical areas of marriage and family, or one or both will dilute their faith over time. Moreover, the Roman Catholic Church will only bless the union if the evangelical accepts the expectation that the Catholic partner will keep his or her own faith, and will do all in their power to have their children baptized and raised as Catholics.[70] Since 1983, the expectation is less binding and absolute than it was when my parents were married.[71] Still, to an evangelical, agreeing to this is not defensible.

Among conservative Protestants, doctrinal differences between potential partners are common. Douglas Wilson's point that couples should be "doctrinally *like-minded*" regarding "fundamental and deep doctrinal differences"[72] makes sense. These will radically affect the marriage and family. However, he agrees that they need not "agree on everything in the Bible before they marry."[73] After all, "Some things are revealed in Scripture to be less important than others," and sometimes the couple is "clearly on their way to further likemindedness."[74] People also differ on the importance they place on secondary beliefs. Couples who are aware of doctrinal differences and talk about them often settle on reasonable accommodations that do not presume either person has to change his or her convictions. For example, Reformed men and women who differ on infant baptism often marry successfully when the woman agrees to support the man's convictions for them and their future family. If her conscience will not allow that, and he is not going to change his views, then they should not marry.

The requirement that Christians marry "in the Lord" is a solemn one that singles, parents, and churches have too often neglected. No revitalization of Christian marriage practice can ignore it. However, distorting the commandment, and abandoning and condemning those who have violated it, are uncalled for as well.

I will be coming back to the issue of mixed marriage again. In chapter 9, as part of discussing premarital preparation, we will consider what

---

70. *Catechism of the Catholic Church*, 408.

71. Lemmons, "Ecumenical and Interfaith Marriages."

72. Wilson, *Her Hand In Marriage*, 68.

73. Ibid., 69.

74. Ibid.

Christian churches, parents, families, and friends can do when an evangelical young person insists on going forward in marrying outside the faith. In chapter 14, which deals with practical issues in marriage, we will consider how evangelicals in mixed marriages can be constructive and redemptive while living out their faith. In the next chapter, we continue looking at mate selection, focusing on practical matters in which there are not clear biblical requirements.

CHAPTER 6

PRACTICAL WISDOM IN CHOOSING A MARRIAGE PARTNER

*Take special care, that fancy and passion overrule not reason, and
friends' advice, in the choice of your condition, or of the person. I know
you must have love to those that you match with; but that love must
be rational, and such as you can justify in the severest trial, by the
evidences of worth and fitness in the person you love.*

Richard Baxter[1]

A bird may love a fish, but where would they build a home together?

Tevye the Dairyman[2]

I n choosing a mate, we must not turn up our noses at practical wisdom.
Remembering Saint Augustine's famous principle that "all truth is God's
truth," we will find good insights among those outside the evangelical fold,
including unbelievers. However, it is especially important that we pay
attention to the insight of godly men and women.

Wise counsel is critical to any important endeavor. This is particularly
important in decisions like this, where emotional attachments and powerful social-psychological dynamics can cloud human judgment. Honest
advice should be sought not only (where possible) from parents, but also,
for younger people, from faithful older saints, not just age peers. This
should include advisers getting to know potential partners, including

---

1. *A Christian Directory*, 401.
2. From the musical "Fiddler on the Roof," 492.

observing the couple together, and, if possible, in situations in which they are apart from one another.

The book of Proverbs is full of admonitions to be open to teaching and advice, and these include situations, such as forming battle plans, in which the Bible does *not* provide explicit, detailed instructions or rules (cf. 20:18; 24:6). Proverbs often pleads with readers to seek counsel when making important decisions. "Hear, my son, your father's instruction, and forsake not your mother's teaching, for they are a graceful garland for your head and pendants for your neck" (1:8–9). "Where there is no guidance, a people falls, but in an abundance of counselors there is safety" (Prov 11:14). "Without counsel plans fail, but with many advisers they succeed" (15:22). "Listen to advice and accept instruction, that you may gain wisdom in the future" (19:20). The biggest obstacle to accepting wise counsel is pride, which leads to excessive confidence in one's own judgments. "When pride comes, then comes disgrace, but with the humble is wisdom" (11:2). "The way of a fool is right in his own eyes, but a wise man listens to advice" (12:15). People rushing headlong into unwise relationships are often a bit like the enraged mob who stoned Stephen—going to extraordinary effort to block out opinions they do not wish to hear (Acts 7:57) so their plans will not be hindered by uncomfortable truths.

Seeking God directly and earnestly for wisdom is also necessary. He will not disappoint those who do so with sincerity and the determination to submit to him in all things (Jas 1:5–8). This includes resolving to reject advice and teaching that contradicts Scripture (Acts 17:11).

Applying practical wisdom to mate selection also means reading what others have written on the subject, including but not limited to this book in your hand. Anything worth doing well is worth studying, not only through direct observation but also by attentive and critical reading. In doing this, do not be limited by what C. S. Lewis called "chronological snobbery,"[3] which J. I. Packer humorously referred to as the "what is recent is decent" error.[4] After all, modern folks have not been more successful in establishing lifelong marriages than their forebears. While it is true that every culture and time period has its own challenges and

---

3. Lewis, *Surprised By Joy*, 201.
4. Packer, "Is Systematic Theology a Mirage?," 21.

opportunities, the basic elements of making sound marital choices are not new.

The Puritans, who focused on this topic a great deal, are especially helpful, despite their inevitable blind spots. Though they required parental consent in first marriages,[5] they were committed to the principles of free choice and consent in mate selection,[6] guided by biblical boundaries, sober practicality, wise counsel, and experience. While enjoying and appreciating that sometimes people do find their match by "falling in love," perhaps even suddenly and without obvious cause, they also recognized that this was far from universal, nor was this reliable, on its own, in choosing a life partner.[7] As Packer noted, Puritans looked "not necessarily for one whom one *does* love, here and now . . . (such a person . . . might still not be a suitable candidate for a life partnership), but for one whom one *can* love with steady affection on a permanent basis."[8] Moreover, this love was not to be part of some idealized relationship defined by two people seeking personal fulfillment, but rather love lived out in the earthly, day-to-day rigors of marriage as God defines it, for his purposes, as struggling sinners in a fallen world.[9] The great Puritan minister Richard Baxter put it like this:

> Understand well all the duties of your relation before you enter into it; and run not upon it as boys to a play, but with the sense of your duty as those that engage themselves to a great deal of work of great importance towards God and towards each other. Address yourselves therefore beforehand to God for counsel, and earnestly beg his guidance and his blessing, and run not without him, or before him. Reckon upon the worst, and foresee all temptations which could diminish your affections, or make you unfaithful to each other; and see that you be fortified against them all.[10]

In this spirit, I will show, first, what the Puritans commonly said about practical considerations in mate selection. Where possible, I will reflect further

---

5. Morgan, *The Puritan Family*, 57.

6. Fischer, *Albion's Seed*, 78.

7. Packer, *A Quest for Godliness*, 264.

8. Ibid., emphasis in the original.

9. Cf. Ryken, *Worldly Saints*, 51.

10. Baxter, *A Christian Directory*, 404.

on these using Scripture and insights from the social sciences. From there, I will look at factors that are commonly relevant in potential partners, and may affect marital quality and stability, especially if people moving toward marriage ignore them rather than face them knowledgably and realistically. Most of them have to do with ways that two romantic partners may *not* be *similar*.

For every aspect of potential partners we will look at here, it is not a "sin" to marry differently from conventional wisdom or practice, nor is it necessarily unwise to do so. However, these factors do matter and, for anyone eager to find the right partner with whom to build a good marriage, it *is* unwise to ignore them. It is a lot like how we should approach grammar rules. Deviating from them may at times be justified, but one should know when and why one is doing so, and then do so only after realistic consideration of the pros, cons, and possible outcomes.

PRACTICAL WISDOM FROM THE PURITANS

CHARACTER ESTIMATES

Puritans recommended a "character estimate" of potential mates.[11] To do so, they advised those considering the latter to spend a lot of time with them in varying situations, "to find out their reputation, watch how they act in company, how they dress and talk, and note whom they select as friends."[12] Preaching in the late 1500s, Henry Smith recommended that a man considering a wife for marriage should "see her eating, and walking, and working, and playing, and talking, and laughing and chiding."[13]

Certainly, this included looking for character traits that the Bible clearly requires, and so, for example, men could use such Scriptures as Proverbs 31 and 1 Peter 3:1–7 to guide them as they considered possible wives.[14] However, as Henry Smith observed, "It is not enough to be virtuous but to be suitable, for divers women have many virtues, and yet do not fit to some men; and divers men have many virtues yet do not fit to some women; and therefore we see many times even the godly couples to jar when they are married, because there is some unfitness between them, which makes odds."[15] Even

---

11. Packer, *A Quest for Godliness*, 268.
12. Ibid. For example, see Henry Smith's "A Preparative to Marriage," 19.
13. Ibid.
14. Packer, *A Quest for Godliness*, 268.
15. "A Preparative to Marriage," 15–16.

if we all accept that certain qualities are important, not everyone will rate or desire them similarly in possible mates. Smith warned young men that if they did not thoroughly acquaint themselves with a woman before asking for her hand in marriage, they might "have less with her than he looked for, or more than he wished for."[16] Puritans valued "beauty of mind" in a spouse,[17] but this is something that people judge subjectively according to taste and inclination. Puritan ministers identified various ways to check for personal suitability; for example, John Dod and Robert Cleaver suggested that a man look for a wife who typically chooses companions like himself.[18]

Puritan couples also used the time they spent with potential partners to assess the degree to which their mutual bonds of affection were growing.[19] With this, they could also look for evidence that God had called them together and that their mutual love and service would glorify him.[20] Couples discern such things based on insight and reasoning specific to them, such as what kind of signs of affection they are looking for, or what their particular callings before God are. However, it is hard to argue with the value of growing affection or evidence that God is calling them together for couples deciding whether to marry, and it is obvious that a great deal of time and varieties of observations will usually be needed to make such judgments wisely.

EQUALITY OF LIFE CIRCUMSTANCES

Packer notes that, to Puritans, "other things being equal, partners should be of similar *age*, *social position*, *wealth*, and *intellectual ability*."[21] In emphasizing these equalities, they closely echoed John Calvin's earlier advice.[22] William Gouge succinctly advised, "That matrimonial society may prove comfortable, it is requisite that there should be some equality betwixt the parties that are married in *Age, Estate, Condition, Piety*."[23] As Edmund

---

16. Ibid., 19–20.

17. Packer, *A Quest for Godliness*, 268.

18. In their *A Godly Forme of Householde Government*, cited in ibid., 268.

19. Packer, *A Quest for Godliness*, 268.

20. Ibid.

21. Ibid. Although Packer handles these as part of their "character estimates," I do not, as these have to do with aspects of potential mates other than character or personality traits.

22. Witte, "Marriage and Family," 461–62.

23. Gouge, *Of Domesticall Duties*, 188.

Morgan discussed and I touched on in the last chapter, this meant they often used the metaphor of "unequal yoking" for more than matters of incompatibility of religious faith.[24] As one Boston minister advised, "the happiness of marige life consists much in that Persons being equally yoaked draw together in a holy yoak . . . there must be sutable fitness for this Condition equality in birth, education, and religion."[25] Puritan records and letters are filled with concerns about equality of birth, occupation, wealth (including financial negotiations and considerations that preceded marriage), and the like.[26] Perusing these documents reminds one of the constant concern with rank and inheritance one finds in Jane Austen's famous novels.

The emphasis that Puritans placed on some of these things, and sometimes the motives they had for doing so, could be unseemly. Morgan honestly observed that surviving documents show that it was common for Puritan parents to engage in "sordid" haggling over the money and property each family agreed to give the couple and that young people often weighed wealth and social status heavily in assessing potential partners.[27] Widows who inherited tidy sums were highly sought by suitors, and were usually quite direct in establishing prenuptial arrangements to protect their control of these inheritances.[28] To be fair, inherited wealth played a bigger role in peoples' livelihood than it does in today's post-industrial economy. In addition, Puritan ministers did not encourage people's using marriage to advance wealth, and often spoke of its dangers.[29] Moreover, excessive pecuniary and social calculation in choosing mates is common today as well, even among professed believers. The potential for gainful employment and the ability to earn enough income to care for a family are factors that those seeking to get married should realistically consider, but we should not pay excessive attention to status and wealth.

On the other hand, the tendency for people to marry others who are similar to themselves, not only the matters of personality characteristics

---

24. Morgan, *The Puritan Family*, 55.
25. Ibid., archaic spellings in the original.
26. Ibid., 55–59.
27. Ibid., 57.
28. Ibid., 58.
29. Ibid., 80. See, for example, Gouge, *Of Domesticall Duties*, 190.

and preferences we mentioned earlier, but also in terms of these larger social distinctions, makes a lot of sense for many reasons. The Puritans were not the first to discover that, as Henry Smith said, "birds of a feather will fly together,"[30] observing that "like will to like. . . . If they be not like, they will not like."[31]

Social psychologists have abundantly documented the power of perceived similarities for interpersonal attraction.[32] Sociologists refer to this as marital *homogamy*—a type of *assortative mating*—and it is the norm for people everywhere. As Starbuck and Lundy point out, across a broad range of social and personal characteristics including race, class, religion, and education, "The marriage system is largely homogamous, both in the United States and around the world."[33]

To be sure, some aspects of this tendency reflect our fallen natures, including such things as pride, vanity, prejudice and discrimination, inappropriate desire for social approval, status, power, and wealth. However, much assortative mating is due to reasonable causes such as choosing mates from among those with whom we live, worship, go to school and work; relevant compatibilities of lifestyle, taste, and opinion; common interests; the degree to which people interact more comfortably with others of similar intellect and education; and so on. There is a lot of evidence that on average, most of these similarities make a positive difference in marital compatibility, stability, and satisfaction, just as the Puritans asserted. As Andrew Cherlin states, "People who marry others similar to them are less likely to divorce."[34]

AGE DIFFERENCES

With this background and context in mind, let's consider those four ways Packer identified that Puritans wanted brides and grooms to be similar. I will start with one that is a bit more complicated: *age similarity*.

From early settlement and for at least a century after, American Puritans' average age at marriage was roughly twenty-six for men and

---

30. "A Preparative to Marriage," 19.

31. Ibid., 17, 19.

32. Montoya et al., "Is Actual Similarity Necessary For Attraction? A Meta-analysis of Actual and Perceived Similarity."

33. Starbuck and Lundy, *Families in Context*, 234.

34. Cherlin, *Public and Private Families*, 337.

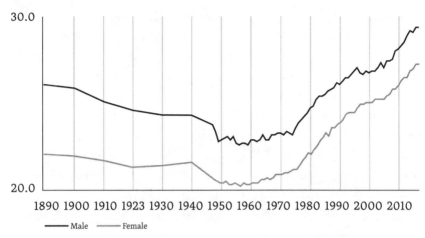

Figure 6.1: Age at First Marriage, Male versus Female, 1890–2016 (US Census)

Figure 6.2: Age Gap at First Marriage, 1890–2016 (Calculated from US Census Data)

twenty-three for women.[35] It is still the norm for husbands and wives to be similar in age, with the male a bit older. Worldwide, the groom is typically about three years older.[36] About 125 years ago there was a median difference of four years but, as figures 6.1 and 6.2 show, it has decreased to about half of that since then. As of 2016, the median age at marriage was 29.5 for men and 27.4 for women, an age difference of 2.1 years.[37] As table 6.1 shows, big

---

35. Fischer, *Albion's Seed*, 76.

36. Starbuck and Lundy, *Families in Context*, 241–42.

37. US Census Bureau, "Table MS-2. Estimated Median Age at First Marriage: 1890 to Present."

differences in age between spouses are not common, especially where the wife is the older partner. In the United States, as of 2017, only 19 percent of wives and 5 percent of husbands were married to someone more than five years older.[38] For Americans, the age gap between males and their partners gets wider each time they get married.[39] One study found that 20 percent of remarried men have wives ten or more years younger, which is about four times higher than in first marriages, and 18 percent have wives who are six to nine years younger, almost twice as many as in first marriages.[40] Among those who remarried, 47 percent of men, and 38 percent of women, had spouses with ages that were more than five years different.[41]

Since men tend to mature more slowly than women,[42] it probably makes sense that women tend to marry somewhat older men. As one gets into large gap in age, on average there will be relevant differences in lifestyle, taste, maturity, friendships, sexual needs, and biographical experience that can impact marital relations. Data from a 2014 study of over 3,000 Americans who were either married or recently divorced[43] shows that the larger the gap in age between husband and wife, the more likely they are to get divorced.[44] Graphs from that research show that, compared to marriages between people of identical age, those ten years apart were 39 percent more likely to be divorced—about twice as likely at twenty years and approaching three times more likely if they were thirty years apart.[45] Other research has yielded similar results.[46]

---

38. US Census Bureau, "Table FG3. Married Couple Family Groups, by Presence of Own Children Under 18, and Age, Earnings, Education, and Race and Hispanic Origin of Both Spouses: 2017."

39. Starbuck and Lundy, *Families in Context*, 242.

40. Livingston, "Tying the Knot Again? Chances Are, There's a Bigger Age Gap Than the First Time Around."

41. Ibid.

42. This is a complex topic, but the observation is sound and hard science suggests there are bases for this in more than just cultural expectation. See, for example, the much-covered 2013 neurological study, authored by Lim et al., with the heavy title "Preferential Detachment During Human Brain Development: Age- and Sex-Specific Structural Connectivity in Diffusion Tensor Imaging (DTI) Data," which documents slower neurological development in males.

43. Francis-Tan and Mialon, "'A Diamond is Forever' and Other Fairy Tales: The Relationship between Wedding Expenses and Marriage Duration."

44. Ibid; see further analysis of Francis-Tan and Mialon's data by Olson, "What Makes for a Stable Marriage? Part 2."

45. Garber, "For a Lasting Marriage, Try Marrying Someone Your Own Age."

46. Cherlin, *Public and Private Families*, 337.

Table 6.1: Percentages of Marriages with Large Age Differences (US Census, 2016)

Which Spouse Is Older?	20 or More Years	15 to 19 Years	10 to 14 Years	6 to 9 Years
Husband:	1%	1.6%	4.8%	11.3%
Wife:	0.4%	0.3%	1%	2.8%

We cannot say for sure that large age gaps *cause* higher divorce, but we should take differences this huge into account, especially knowing spouses often find them challenging to deal with. Some might argue that men marrying much younger women was common in the Bible. Outside of noting that Abraham was ten years older than Sarah (Gen 17:17), the Scriptures do not record the age of both spouses. However, it was common for men to marry much younger women in ancient cultures and in many places with polygamy and arranged marriages, so it was almost certainly so during biblical times. However, these marital situations and cultures are not comparable with those of modern, monogamous cultures. Since this is a matter of practical wisdom and not biblical prescription, it is best to evaluate it relative to our own cultural reality.

INTELLECTUAL ABILITY

The kinds of similarities of *intellectual ability* Puritans recommended are harder to evaluate, since what they meant by this is somewhat different from the various "intelligence quotient" (IQ) scores that we have been enamored with since the twentieth century. However, most studies have found that the IQs of married partners tend to be similar, and not because of changes that happen after they are married.[47] Part of this is due to another factor we will discuss, namely those with similar IQs tend to have comparable levels of education.[48] Although most research suggests those with higher levels of intelligence are less likely to get divorced, that relationship does not seem to be strong or direct, nor is that the same thing as IQ *similarity*. Researchers have not studied the effects of couples'

---

47. See, for example, Mascie-Taylor, "Spouse Similarity for IQ and Personality and Convergence"; Pan and Wang, "Spousal concordance in academic achievements and IQ."
48. Pappas, "Genetic Match? People Marry Those With Similar DNA."

equality of intelligence on marriage quality much, and the little they have done suggests that, in itself, it is not that important compared to other factors.[49] It is safe to say that it makes sense to consider whether two potential partners can converse in an understanding way, being interested in and able to "follow" what each other cares about, and would be able to agree on the type of intellectual climate they desire in their home.

SOCIOECONOMIC STATUS: EDUCATION, CLASS, AND WEALTH

Let's turn now to the issues of education, social class, and wealth, which are strongly and mutually associated with each other, and are often combined under the term "socioeconomic status," or SES. Typically, people's occupations reflect all three. For example, knowing that a person is an auto mechanic, or a federal judge, gives one a good idea of their level of education, social rank, and affluence. Higher levels of socioeconomic status, overall and for each of these three elements of it, are associated with lower divorce rates.[50] This fact is increasing rather than decreasing, as the class differences in marriage and divorce become greater over time.[51] Those who are poorer and less educated face great and growing challenges getting and staying married, a fact that the church serving poor and working-class communities needs to address. This will also affect marriages between people from different socioeconomic levels because all things being equal, the partner of lower SES is more likely to bring background marital disadvantages into the union, while the reverse will be true for those of higher SES.

However, the Puritan concerns focused most directly on inequality between marriage partners on these three dimensions of socioeconomic status, so let's turn to those specifically. Let's start with equality of education, which the Puritans placed great emphasis on, valuing learning highly as a quality in potential spouses.[52] This makes sense, emphasizing as they

---

49. This sparse research was covered pretty well in Holley et al.'s "Outwitting Divorce: How Intelligence Can Keep Couples Together."

50. Starbuck and Lundy, *Families in Context*, 415–16; see also "'A Diamond is Forever'" on the effects of wealth; "Marriage and Divorce: Patterns by Gender, Race and Education," 8–9 on education; and Murray, *Coming Apart*, 156, 167, on social class. See also table 6.3, below, which clearly shows the combined impact of both age at marriage and educational level on divorce rates.

51. Murray, *Coming Apart*, 156.

52. Morgan, *The Puritan Family*, 55.

did the need for spouses to be true friends, companions for life,[53] working as a team educating their children, governing their families, and managing their businesses.[54] Being roughly similar in knowledge and scholarly training enhanced these joint endeavors enormously. Is similarity of education still important to married couples?

Francis-Tan and Mialon found that married couples tended to be alike in their level of education as measured by their highest degree obtained.[55] The General Social Survey years 2000 through 2016 combined shows that 67 percent of currently married partners have about the same degree status,[56] while in another 21 percent one partner had a high school diploma and the other a bachelor's degree. This makes sense, since people interact more often and directly with others with similar educational degrees, including in schools and workplaces. In fact, educational similarity in newly married couples appears to be increasing in the United States.[57] This is partly because, as figure 6.1 showed, people are marrying later, which means they are more likely to pair up with those they work with, who in turn tend to have similar education.[58] Another factor driving this trend is the increasing cultural and residential segregation of Americans along class lines, which includes interacting with and living around those with similar education.[59]

Even controlling for other factors, couples who were similar in education were less likely to split up.[60] Francis-Tan and Mialon's data shows that the percentage divorced was 43 percent higher for marriages where spouses were *not* educationally similar.[61] Just as with big age gaps, different educational levels may be associated with important disparities of life experience, knowledge, tastes, and interests that create difficulties

---

53. Ryken, *Worldly Saints*, 43, 50.

54. Packer, *A Quest for Godliness*, 263.

55. Francis-Tan and Mialon, "A Diamond Is Forever," 1927.

56. Neither finished high school, both finished high school and maybe some college, both had obtained at least a bachelor's degree.

57. Miller and Bui, "Equality in Marriage Grows, and So Does Class Divide."

58. Ibid.

59. See ibid. for how increased residential segregation by class has encouraged educationally similar people to intermarry. On the overall, increasing cultural and geographical division of Americans by social class, at least among whites, see the important recent book by Charles Murray, *Coming Apart*.

60. Francis-Tan and Mialon, "A Diamond Is Forever," 1927.

61. Olson, "What Makes for a Stable Marriage? Part 2."

in some marital relationships. However, educational differences are not as big a factor in marital stability and quality as large age gaps. That may be partly because holding particular diplomas, and being "educated," are not identical. I have known many people without college degrees who—by virtue of reading, experience, and training—are far more "educated" than many holding bachelor's degrees or higher.

We come now to the Puritan preference for equality of *social class* and *wealth* in potential marriage partners. Puritans in America mostly came from the "broad middle class" of England, and while they "preserved its middling distinctions," including in their marriage practices, they did not encourage having extremes of upper and lower class in their settlements.[62] Their preference to marry within social class was not unique; in fact it is nearly universal across cultures.[63] Despite the fact that Americans consciously focus on this less than almost any other society, marriage partners in the United States tend to be from the same socioeconomic background,[64] much as they prefer those who are educationally equal, and for the same reasons. Likewise, as with education, equality of social class and wealth between marital partners has been increasing, and again, because of the same social forces.[65]

Research on how differences in partners' class and wealth affects marital stability and quality, especially *if* their educations are similar, is for the most part inconclusive.[66] However, Starbuck and Lundy note that partners who come from very different social-class backgrounds often face "difficulties with in-laws, friends, and leisure interests."[67] In a study of thirty-six white "mixed class" couples, mostly of working versus middle-class backgrounds, Jessi Streib found that spouses' individual socioeconomic backgrounds strongly influenced them even after years of marriage, leading to many differences of preference, style, and outlook between partners in mixed-class marriages.[68] In an interview, she remarked, "Systematically, strangers who have never met yet who share a class background often have more in

---

62. Fischer, *Albion's Seed*, 177.

63. Starbuck and Lundy, *Families in Context*, 238.

64. Ibid.

65. See, for example, the citations and text connected to endnote 43.

66. Starbuck and Lundy, *Families in Context*, 327; see also Strong et al., *The Marriage and Family Experience*, 290.

67. Starbuck and Lundy, *Families in Context*, 327.

68. *The Power of the Past*.

common with each other than spouses with whom they share their life if they came from different classes."[69]

Puritan beliefs that equality of age, education, class, and wealth matter in potential marital partners continue to make practical sense. It is not morally wrong to marry someone who is much lower or higher on any or all of these four traits, but in making that decision, it makes sense to consider the possible effects of those disparities. This seems especially true where possible mates differ in a number of these areas or in combination with other factors where, as we shall see, differences potentially matter. At the very least, doing so will enable couples to make the right kind of adjustments in thinking, practice, the kind of counsel they seek, and so on, as they move forward together to build a godly marriage.

OTHER PRACTICAL MATTERS TO CONSIDER IN CHOOSING A SPOUSE

RACIAL AND ETHNIC DIFFERENCES

Similar to these other differences we have been considering is the sensitive issue of interracial marriage as well as those between some ethnic groups, particularly Hispanics with non-Hispanics. My guess is that the Puritans' mate selection advice would have addressed that too if they had lived in a time and place when such marriages were likely. This kind of marriage is on the rise and is now widely accepted.[70]

It is important to say that marrying across race or ethnic groups is not in any way morally wrong. I have served as best man in two interracial weddings and have many friends in such unions. Moses was married to a Cushite—a black African—and God affirmed this union directly (Num 12:1–15).[71] Both Ruth and Rahab, having become believers, were foreigners who married Jews and became part of the lineage of Christ (Matt 1:5). The body of Christ is one, and includes every race and ethnicity (Gal 3:28; Col 3:11; Rev 7:9), so marrying in the Lord does not preclude the union of two races as one flesh.[72] If anything, it is a beautiful, living picture of our oneness in Christ.

---

69. Kurtzleben, "If You Grew Up Far Richer Than Your Spouse, It Will Likely Change Your Marriage."

70. Starbuck and Lundy, *Families in Context*, 235–36.

71. Piper, "Racial Harmony and Interracial Marriage."

72. Ibid. See also the nice summary from BibleInfo, "What Does the Bible Say About Interracial Marriage?"

In 1960, less than 1 percent of all American marriages were interracial.[73] As of 1970, about the time when the US Census Bureau began independently tracking Hispanic marriages, less than 2 percent of married couples were Hispanics married to non-Hispanics.[74] Over the next decades, these percentages exploded. By 2010, almost 7 percent of marriages in the United States were interracial, and a little over 4 percent involved Hispanics married to non-Hispanics.[75] By 2010, about 27 percent of married Hispanics had a non-Hispanic partner.[76] Among newlyweds in 2010, 9 percent of whites, 17 percent of blacks, 26 percent of Hispanics, and 28 percent of Asian Americans got married to someone of another race or ethnicity.[77]

In such marriages, some combinations of race and ethnicity are more common. Table 6.2 shows what percentages of husbands and wives within each major racial or ethnic group, in 2017, were married to spouses in each of the other categories, showing quite a range.[78] For example, while over 15 percent of Asian wives had white husbands, and about 16 percent of Hispanic wives were married to non-Hispanic whites, only four-tenths of a percent of Asian husbands had black spouses. While almost 13 percent of Hispanic and almost 9 percent of black husbands had non-Hispanic white wives, only four-tenths of one percent of white husbands had black wives, and only about 3 percent were married to Hispanics. Overall, among whites and Hispanics, there are not significant gender differences in intermarriage. However, among African-Americans males are more likely to do so, while among Asians females are. In fact, Asian females were about three times more likely than Asian men to be in intermarriages.[79]

---

73. Starbuck and Lundy, *Families in Context*, 235.

74. United States Census Bureau, *Statistical Abstract of the United States: 2012*, 55. Percentage calculated by author from raw numbers.

75. Ibid., and Lofquist et al., "Households and Families: 2010," 17–18.

76. United States Census Bureau, *Statistical Abstract of the United States: 2012*, 55. Percentage calculated by author from raw numbers. That percentage was actually slightly higher, at 30 percent in 1970. The percentage of marriages involving a non-Hispanic and Hispanic went up not because more Hispanics were entering such mixed marriages, but because of the huge increase in the proportion of Hispanics in the United States. On the latter, see Pew Research Center, "The U.S. Hispanic Population Has Increased Sixfold Since 1970." On the increase in racial and ethnic intermarriage generally, see also Wang, *The Rise of Intermarriage*, 5.

77. Ibid., 10.

78. Calculated by the author from data in "Table FG3. Married Couple Family Groups, by Presence of Own Children Under 18, and Age, Earnings, Education, and Race and Hispanic Origin of Both Spouses: 2017." Read table left to right, by row.

79. See also *The Rise of Intermarriage*, 9.

Table 6.2: Percentages: Husbands and Wives by Race and Ethnicity of Spouse (US Census, 2017)

	White Spouse	*Black Spouse*	*Hispanic Spouse*	*Asian* Spouse*
WHITE				
Husband:	93.5%	0.4%	3.3%	1.4%
Wife:	94.9%	0.9%	2.6%	0.4%
BLACK				
Husband:	8.5%	85.4%	3.4%	1.1%
Wife:	3.9%	93%	1.9%	0.4%
HISPANIC				
Husband:	12.7%	0.9%	84.7%	N/A**
Wife:	15.7%	1.7%	81.1%	N/A
ASIAN*				
Husband:	5.3%	0.4%	N/A	94%
Wife:	15.5%	1.2%	N/A	82.3%

Italics are used where both spouses are members of same racial or ethnic category.

*   Because of the way the Census data was presented, Asian marriages to whites or blacks here includes a small percentage of marriages to white or black spouses who also identify as Hispanic. However, in all other percentages in this table, whites and blacks are non-Hispanic.

** In the Census data used here, where Asians are broken out separately, Hispanics are not, and so information specifically on Hispanic-Asian marriages was not available.

Due to rounding, the exclusion of an "Other" category, and inclusion of white and black spouses who also identified as Hispanic in the Asian percentages here, totals left-to-right will not add up to 100.

Very few Americans now believe that racial and ethnic intermarriage is a bad thing. For example, in one 2011 survey the highest percentage for any subgroup believing that more racial intermarriage was "a change for the worse" was 19 percent of those sixty-five and older.[80] In 2009, 83 percent thought it was fine for blacks and whites to date each other.[81] Most indicated

---

80. Ibid., 33.
81. Ibid., 35.

they would have no problem with a family member marrying outside his or her race or ethnicity, and those who remained indicated it would bother them at first but they would get over it. Only 6 percent of whites and 3 percent of blacks said they would refuse to accept it.[82] As we would expect, younger people were more accepting.[83] Much depended on the race or ethnicity of the person being married. Respondents were less likely to say they would be "fine" with a family member intermarrying with a black (66 percent), than with a Hispanic (73 percent), Asian American (75 percent), or white (81 percent).[84]

Acceptance of racial and ethnic intermarriage has improved a great deal, and all trends point toward even greater progress. However, people involved in such unions still face prejudice and resistance in their families and personal networks, and it would be foolish to ignore and fail to prepare for the potential social and interpersonal challenges involved in some interracial or interethnic marriages. These situations involve careful consideration of cultural context, family and friends, and children, especially in societies that are less accepting of such unions or even some families that are more hostile.

Significant percentages of people—especially those who are older—admit they would have a difficult time adjusting to such a marriage in their family, and it is likely that people present a more optimistic picture on surveys than might be true in real life. For example, in the above survey, 59 percent of whites sixty-five and older, and 45 percent ages fifty to fifty-four, admitted they would have a tough time with a family member marrying an African-American. Among Hispanics ages thirty to forty-nine, 38 percent felt the same way. For elderly blacks, 39 percent would struggle with a family member marrying an Asian American.

In some situations, people face a higher divorce risk marrying outside their race or ethnicity, especially if they are marrying someone from a group that has higher divorce rates than their own.[85] For example, Asian Americans have lower rates of marital dissolution, while African-American

---

82. Ibid., 36.

83. Ibid., 38.

84. Ibid., 36. Obviously, respondents were not asked about marriage to someone in their own racial or ethnic group.

85. Zhang and Hook, "Marital Dissolution Among Interracial Couples," 105.

marriages are more likely to break up,[86] so whites marrying Asian Americans should face lower risk of divorce, while those marrying blacks should face higher. Reality roughly corresponds with this. As Wang notes, results vary quite a bit depending on the specific combination of gender and race or ethnicity.[87] The most recent, and strongest, study that she cited found that—with other relevant factors such as age, education, number of children, and so forth taken into account—the most elevated divorce levels among mixed marriages were between blacks and whites, followed by white-Hispanic, while Asian-white couples were less likely to divorce than if both were white.[88] The most likely to break up were marriages between black husbands and white wives, though this was no different from those where both partners were black.[89]

What about when one spouse is foreign-born, which is true for over one-third of racially or ethnically mixed couples?[90] Overall, despite the large cultural differences between spouses in these marriages, it does *not* appear they are more likely to get divorced.[91]

How can we turn these complex divorce findings into practical advice for those considering a partner of another race or ethnicity? People marrying into a high-divorce group, particularly black-white couples especially where the wife is white, should especially do realistic assessment and prepare for any heightened risk of divorce. There is good anecdotal evidence regarding higher levels of racial hostility and social isolation faced by this last type of couple.[92] Even in the relatively tolerant United States, people who are considering marrying someone of another race or ethnicity should look at their own interpersonal situation honestly, be prepared to make some adjustments, have some difficult conversations, and weather the occasional difficulty. I mentioned earlier being the best man at two interracial marriages. In one of them, the groom was white and the bride African-American. I was one of only three other white people there—most of his family, including his parents, refused to attend. That

---

86. Starbuck and Lundy, *Families in Context*, 415.

87. *The Rise of Intermarriage*, 12.

88. Ibid., "Marital Dissolution Among Interracial Couples," 101.

89. Ibid., 104.

90. Ibid., 99.

91. Ibid., 102–3.

92. Ibid., 95, 104–5.

was decades ago and things have changed, but these kinds of mixed marriages still face hurdles.

Solid premarital counseling from someone tuned in to the special issues involved here is very important.[93] It would also be wise to spend time with other racially or ethnically mixed couples and share experiences and support. Being that much more committed to uniting together with Christ and supported by his people is essential too, though that is critical for all Christian married couples no matter what they face.

AGE AT MARRIAGE

It is clear that marrying too young significantly increases the risk of being divorced. One major study based on data from 7,357 people born between 1957 and 1964 and tracked since 1979 found that the younger people were when they first got married, the more likely they were to get divorced.[94] This was not only because people who married later had more education, as table 6.3 makes clear.[95] For example, even among those with college degrees, those who married earlier were much more likely to get divorced than those who married later. Obviously, education matters, but age at marriage does as well.

However, in looking at these kinds of statistics, we must consider some important qualifications. First, the fact that people are waiting longer than ever to marry—as we have seen, a median age of first marriage of almost thirty for men and over twenty-seven for women—has been associated with a lot of premarital sex, multiple partners, and cohabitation, as Mark Regnerus and Jeremy Uecker have documented abundantly.[96] This means a lot of relational instability, out-of-wedlock pregnancies, failed cohabitations, sexually transmitted diseases, and other negative consequences occur outside of marriage and divorce for late-marrying adults. Given human frailties, in or out of the professing church, we will not be successful

---

93. I will deal with this specifically in chapter 9.

94. "Marriage and Divorce," 12–13.

95. Ibid. Calculated by author from percentages in the original that were expressed as percent of marriages still in effect. The category of respondents who got married between ages thirty-five and forty, and the other category of those who married between forty-one and forty-six, were not included here. In the latter none had completed ten years since their first marriage, and for those thirty-five to forty at marriage, many of them had not.

96. Regnerus and Uecker, *Premarital Sex in America*, 2, 111, 169, 200, 232.

Table 6.3: Percentage of First Marriages Ending in Divorce Within Ten Years for Those Born Between 1957–1964 (NLSY, US Bureau of Labor Statistics)

Age at Marriage	Less Than High School Diploma	High School Diploma	Some or 2-Year College	4-Year College Degree
15–22:	44.4%	39.5%	41.5%	30%
23–28:	37.6%	35.5%	33.3%	20.8%
29–34:	38.8%	34.6%	33.9%	19.1%

getting most young people to "wait until marriage" if that means delaying until they are nearly thirty. As we have seen, the apostle Paul admonished people to choose marriage over fornication if they cannot exercise sexual self-control (1 Cor 7:9), which appears to apply especially to those in relationships in which such temptation will be great. Yet, as Russell Moore pointed out in his book *Onward*, many Christian young people and their parents quietly accept ongoing premarital sex in non-marital relationships that they prolong, often for many years, postponing marriage until after they meet numerous other personal and financial goals.[97]

Second, and given all of this, is it true that the 31 percent of young women, and 23 percent of young men, who married before age twenty-four[98] were ill-advised, bearing unacceptable risks, and so on? What about the 49 percent of women, and 36 percent of men, among self-identified conservative Protestants who were married by the time they were twenty-four, many of them attempting to obey the biblical admonition about how to maintain sexual purity that was just discussed? Today, many young people, and even their parents and other elders, treat getting married before their late twenties as not only dumb but as Regnerus and Uecker point out, "a *moral mistake* in which the odds of failure are perceived as too high to

---

97. 174–75.

98. Regnerus and Uecker, *Premarital Sex in America*, 176–77. This was as of 2011, for those twenty-four to twenty-eight years old. For blacks, the percentages marrying before age twenty-four were 15 percent for both males and females, and for Hispanics, there were 30 percent for both. For Asians, 29 percent of women and 22 percent of men married by age twenty-four, and for whites these percentages were the highest, at 36 percent for females and 24 percent for males.

justify a risk."[99] For many evangelicals, this even includes justifying fornication and cohabitation, if that is what it takes to marry later.

The problem is that this is an exaggeration and even distortion of the kind of statistics we looked at in table 6.3. These and similar analyses tend to lump together larger age groups. For example, the percentages in this table put those who married at twenty-two in the same category as those who married as teenagers, along with those who waited until after graduating college with those who married before even starting it and then tried to handle marriage and college at the same time.

Regnerus and Uecker point out that when looked at more closely, the huge divorce dangers are for those who marry prior to age twenty.[100] A standard way to approach this is to look at what percentage had divorced within ten years of their first marriage. Using this measure, for those who marry at age twenty-one, the risk of divorce is about average. From ages twenty-three through twenty-nine, there is only a tiny decrease in divorce risk for each additional year they wait until marrying, and this only applies to women. Men gain little or nothing by waiting beyond age twenty-three.[101] Regnerus and Uecker summarize things like this, "The most *significant leap* in avoiding divorce occurs by simply waiting to marry until you're twenty-one. The difference in success between, say, marrying at twenty-three and marrying at twenty-eight are just not as substantial as many emerging adults believe them to be. And among men, there are really no notable differences to speak of."[102]

Although this is not true in every individual case, at the social level late marriage is associated with seeing matrimony as mostly about self-fulfillment than about legitimizing sex or parenting or building the foundations of a life together. Andrew Cherlin notes that young people today view marriage as a "capstone experience," something one builds toward after not only completing education and establishing a career and financial security, but after becoming sexually active, living together, and even beginning parenting.[103] This is very different from the traditional way of

---

99. Ibid., 179, emphasis in original.

100. Ibid., 180.

101. Ibid.

102. Ibid.

103. Cherlin, *Public and Private Families*, 201.

seeing marriage as the foundation for adult life for most people, not an optional add-on. The latter view is much more consistent with accepting and wanting to live by the Christian sexual ethic and understanding marriage's definition and purposes. Christians should not marry when they lack the requisite maturity and preparation, but neither should they prolong marriage unnecessarily when they have found the right person, particularly just to climb one or two more rungs of a career ladder, or as I see so often, to save up for an expensive wedding. This is especially true if they are in love and facing strong sexual temptation in their relationship. Like Regnerus and Uecker, I "have no interest in dragging immature men and women into marriages for which they are unprepared" but do think they should "think twice" before deciding, after meeting the right person, that "they're just not ready" for marriage.[104]

ISSUES OF FAMILY STRUCTURE

Many of the impacts of divorce and out-of-wedlock parenting upon children last well into adulthood. Unfair as it seems, escalating the risk that, should they marry, they will have serious marital difficulty and divorce themselves is one of them. Starbuck and Lundy state flatly, "Adults whose parents divorced, or who grew up with a never-married parent, are more likely to end their own marriage by divorce."[105] Respected family scholar Paul Amato likewise points out that both divorce and being born out of wedlock are consistently associated with higher divorce rates in the children when they reach adulthood.[106] There is a lot of research to support these claims, which few if any family scholars dispute. For example, Kelly and Emery state the obvious regarding divorce, "Higher divorce rates for children of divorced families compared with those in still-married families are substantiated in a number of studies."[107] Cherlin notes that the death of a parent does not have this effect.[108] It is not wise to ignore these realities in moving forward with a potential marriage partner.

---

104. Regnerus and Uecker, *Premarital Sex in America*, 249.

105. Starbuck and Lundy, *Families in Context*, 417.

106. Amato, "Research on Divorce," 653. See also Amato and Cheadle, "The Long Reach of Divorce," which show negative marital impacts extending all the way to adult *grandchildren* of divorced couples.

107. Kelly and Emery, "Children's Adjustment Following Divorce," 356.

108. Cherlin, *Public and Private Families*, 334, 337.

Still, I have seen many successful marriages among those who come from broken family situations. God is gracious and he is fully able and willing to bestow his blessings on the marriages of all his children, including those who come from less than ideal home environments. I have known many people from disrupted home situations who have formed wonderful marriages. Most children from such family situations do as well as others. The point is that they are at *greater risk* of marital discord and divorce. The key is acknowledging the challenges and handling them in wise and godly ways.

Scholarly literature on the greater marital problems of those who were from divorced homes or born out of wedlock suggests that they are more likely to have attitudes, practices, or experiences that directly undermine their chances of a successful marriage. Children from divorced homes are more likely to cohabit, get married too early, or have children out of wedlock.[109] On average, they have weaker interpersonal communication skills, are more prone to conflict, perform less well educationally and financially, and tend to have a weaker commitment to the ideal of lifelong marriage and weaker ties with their parents.[110] In addition to this, we know that often, training and role models for having a successful marriage are lacking, while they have grown up with examples for things like getting divorced or having children out of wedlock.[111]

People considering marriages with folks who have divorced or unmarried parents should honestly look at these things. How many of the outcomes in the last paragraph are serious problems in a potential mate, and how resistant to change are they? If people cannot answer these questions in a positive way about a potential spouse, it is generally best not to move further toward marriage unless or until these issues are significantly addressed and improved.

Of course, *all* couples should avoid things like marrying too early or cohabiting, as we have already indicated. If the biblical qualities that we discussed in chapter 5 are present, including a strong and active Christian

---

109. Kelly and Emery, "Children's Adjustment Following Divorce," 356.

110. Amato, "The Effects of Divorce and Marital Discord on Adult Children's Psychological Well-Being," 902–904; see also Whitton et al., "Effects of Parental Divorce on Marital Commitment and Confidence."

111. Starbuck and Lundy, *Families in Context*, 417.

commitment and involvement in a solid local church, the framework for handling the challenges of partners coming from a damaged home environment will be there. Beyond that, skilled premarital counseling, which is always a good idea, thoroughly delves into the family background of both partners, dealing with known problem points that are associated with them, including those tied to having divorced or unmarried parents.[112] Spending time with older, sound, established Christian married couples also often helps people from broken home situations who are progressing toward marriage.

PROSPECTIVE SPOUSES WITH PREVIOUS MARRIAGES AND CHILDREN

A major issue in considering potential marital partners is previous divorce. Assuming that, upon due consideration of the biblical teachings on the matter, along with pastoral counsel, the potential partners' divorce is valid and they are able to remarry in the Lord,[113] there are still important practical wisdom issues to be faced.

Such marriage decisions become especially complicated when prospective mates (usually women) will bring children from previous relationships into the new household. As anyone who has gone through this could attest, these situations are often complex and prone to numerous conflicts and practical problems, not all of which are easy to anticipate. It is incredibly important to go forward in such relationships only after carefully considering the costs and risks, with a clear understanding of what kinds of challenges one will face.

Summarizing the relevant research on these issues is hard, but we can accurately sketch out the main lines here. First, the easy part is describing the current reality. Remarriages make up a growing proportion of all marriages, the percentage having almost doubled since 1960.[114] Currently, about 40 percent of new marriages involve remarriage, and in half of these, namely 20 percent, *both* spouses were previously married.[115] Divorce is a

---

112. Again, I will be discussing premarital counseling specifically in chapter 9.

113. I will tackle the vital issue of what Christianity teaches about divorce and remarriage in chapter 10.

114. Pew Research Center, *Four-in-Ten Couples Are Saying "I Do," Again*, 4.

115. Ibid.

big reason for remarriage, as is the increasing proportion of older people, many of whom are widowed and wish to remarry.[116] Meanwhile, the proportion of those getting married for the third time or more is also higher than most people realize. Among newlyweds, 8 percent have been married at least twice before.[117] According to the General Social Survey for the years 2006 through 2016, 30 percent of all married conservative Protestants were previously divorced, and another 3 percent widowed. That GSS data also shows that among evangelicals between the ages of thirty and forty-five, 25 percent of those married are previously divorced, 22 percent are currently divorced or legally separated, and almost 90 percent of the latter have children. Remarriage is a big and growing issue in our congregations, and many church leaders are not adequately helping members who are considering such marriage think through and prepare properly for it.

Paul Amato succinctly points out the well-established risks associated with remarriage and bringing children into new marriages: "the major risk factors for divorce . . . include . . . having a premarital birth, bringing children from a previous union into a new marriage (especially among mothers) . . . being in a second- or higher order marriage."[118] Remarriages are more likely to end in divorce despite having the advantage of the partners being older, on average, than in first marriages.[119] However, not all remarriages are equally prone to divorce. One major study found that women remarrying before age twenty-five were at much higher risk than those who were older than that.[120] The probability of divorce is higher in remarriages than in first marriages when the woman (but not the man) brings a child from a previous union into the household.[121] There is also some evidence that remarriages where only one partner was previously married are as successful as first marriages, while there is *much* greater risk of divorce if both partners were previously married.[122]

---

116. Ibid.

117. Ibid., 7.

118. Amato, "Research on Divorce," 651.

119. Kreider and Ellis, "Number, Timing, and Duration of Marriages and Divorces: 2009," 17.

120. Bramlett and Mosher, "First Marriage Dissolution, Divorce, and Remarriage: United States," 11–12.

121. Teachman, "Complex Life Course Patterns and the Risk of Divorce in Second Marriages," 302–303.

122. Starbuck and Lundy, *Families in Context*, 428.

Addressing many of the problems associated with remarriage and bringing children into a new marriage involves tackling the other risk factors we have already discussed. For example, as we touched on earlier, remarriages are also much more likely to involve large gaps in age,[123] and are more likely to have significant differences in religious beliefs and education.[124] There is some evidence that people being remarried are more likely to "rush into it" than in first marriages. If they have premarital sex they do so more quickly, and their engagements tend to be shorter.[125] Divorced people are more likely to cohabit prior to marriage and to have histories of multiple cohabitations.[126] Paying attention to all of the other things we have said in this chapter, therefore, may practically help when remarrying.

It is also important to anticipate the greater number of problems one is likely to encounter in remarriage situations, especially when children are involved. Conflict over the latter is much greater in stepfamilies than in first marriages, and the legal and other rights, obligations, and expectations for stepparents are often ambiguous.[127] Fighting between children and their stepparents is common, and there is a strong tendency for the biological parent to side with their child against their spouse.[128] There are also issues with the prior spouse or other biological parent that frequently undermine peace and stability in the newly formed home[129] and, even if things are ideal with him or her, require a lot of planning and delicate communication. Evelyn Husband Thompson, who remarried after being widowed, provides this wisdom: "Remarriages are more complicated than first marriages. Children are already in the picture. Patterns for communication, attitudes towards work vs. leisure time, financial goals (including spending and saving), and spiritual beliefs are much more deep-seated."[130]

---

123. Pew Research Center, *Four-in-Ten Couples Are Saying "I Do," Again*, 7.

124. Starbuck and Lundy, *Families in Context*, 427.

125. Ibid.

126. "Complex Life Course Patterns and the Risk of Divorce in Second Marriages," 294–295.

127. Sweeney, "Remarriage and Stepfamilies: Strategic Sites for Family Scholarship in the 21st Century," 667, 669; see also Saint-Jacques, "The Processes Distinguishing Stable From Unstable Stepfamily Couples: A Qualitative Analysis," 546–47.

128. Ibid., 546.

129. Ibid., 547.

130. From her "Foreword," in Deal and Olson's *The Remarriage Checkup*, 12.

It is not wise to rush into a relationship with these kinds of potential challenges and statistical realities without due consideration and preparation, solid pastoral support, a lot of honest conversations with one's potential spouse, and excellent premarital counseling and other resources especially tuned to issues facing remarriage[131] and, if appropriate, stepfamily life. There is no reason marriage following a previous divorce or involving children from prior relationships cannot be a great one for everyone, and a real blessing to the kingdom, provided everyone handles things wisely and prayerfully.

PHYSICAL ATTRACTION

The Bible is full of warnings urging believers to be careful of allowing physical attractiveness to divert their attention from things that are more important and permanent. The apostle Peter admonished women to focus not on outer adornment but rather on "the imperishable beauty of a gentle and quiet spirit" (1 Pet 3:3–4). Paul directed Timothy to advise women similarly, suggesting they beautify themselves with "good works" rather than with "braided hair and gold or pearls or costly attire" (1 Tim 2:9–10). God reminded Samuel, "man looks on the outward appearance, but the LORD looks on the heart" (1 Sam 16:7). King Lemuel's mother advised her son, "Charm is deceitful, and beauty is vain, but a woman who fears the LORD is to be praised" (Prov 31:30). "Vain" here means fleeting, like the wind, and vapor. Good looks cannot be trusted, this last verse tells us—they can deceive us, and then they will fade. For godly marriages, we need partners with more essential virtues.

One of the reasons the Scriptures warn us about the dangers of focusing too much on physical appearance is because we are so prone to do just that across a wide spectrum of judgments and decisions we make about other people, including a potential mate. As Hunt et al. point out, "physical attractiveness . . . is for both men and women one of the most highly desirable characteristics in a romantic partner."[132] The evidence is strong and consistent for this claim.[133] To be sure, people do not consider physical

---

131. For example, ibid.

132. "Leveling the Playing Field," 1046–47.

133. Eastwick et al., "The Predictive Validity of Ideal Partner Preferences," which reviewed and analyzed a huge number of studies spanning decades.

attractiveness as heavily when they have known someone for a good while before becoming romantically involved.[134] Moreover, consistent with our emphasis here on the power of similarity, whatever they seek initially, ultimately people tend to settle on partners who are roughly similar in levels of physical attractiveness.[135]

Recall that the Scriptures we looked at warned of beauty as being somewhat deceptive. One aspect of this is that when people focus too much on appearance, they often do not pay enough attention to other important aspects of someone. In the passage from Samuel above, the danger was that the prophet would focus on size and strength so much that he would ignore heart qualities that matter more in the king of a nation that ought to fear God. Another deceptive tendency with physical attractiveness is that it has been consistently associated with something social psychologists call the "halo effect." The halo effect is the human tendency to *assume* things about a person that are actually unknown based upon and consistent with known characteristics. Interpersonally, it leads to "more positive impressions of more attractive people" than may be warranted by the facts.[136] Starbuck and Lundy point out that in considering possible romantic partners, "A person's attractiveness can affect the way others evaluate aspects of their personality. Both men and women perceive attractive persons to have more socially desirable personality traits than less attractive ones are supposed to have."[137]

The answer to overemphasizing, being deceived, or being blinded by good looks is *not* treating physical attraction as if it is not important. The lovers in the Song of Songs certainly find each other to be comely and bodily appealing, and the book unfolds amidst detailed praise of each other's beauty (cf. 4:1–7) but without losing sight of other virtues. Genesis informs us without negative comment about the beauty of Abraham's, Isaac's, and Jacob's wives (12:11–15; 24:16; 29:17). Douglas Wilson is correct

---

134. "Leveling the Playing Field," 1051.

135. In ibid., the researchers still found the tendency toward similarity in levels of physical attractiveness. See also the helpful discussion by Swanson, "The real reason some people end up with partners who are way more attractive." See also Starbuck and Lundy, *Families in Context*, 211.

136. Zebrowitz and Franklin, "The Attractiveness Halo Effect and the Babyface Stereotype in Older and Younger Adults," 375.

137. Starbuck and Lundy, *Families in Context*, 211.

when he points out that sexual desire is an integral and good part of marriage, so "the beauty of the bride" should be "alluring to the bridegroom," and "they should both be pleased at the prospect of sleeping together."[138] Therefore, "Christian young people should court someone, or be courted by someone, whom they find to be sexually attractive, in a broad sense."[139]

The key is for those seeking a spouse to consider all the other important aspects of a potential mate, particularly those things associated with godliness, and not allow physical desire to overcome their judgment. Being physically attracted to someone, and looking for someone compatible and of good character, are "both-and," not "either-or." Nor are they remotely equal in value. Being physically attractive is a "lesser good," a fleeting, temporal quality compared to the greater good associated with godly character. In this, it is important for those getting married to remember the absolute nature of the covenant they will be entering. God calls them to love and be faithful to this person for the rest of their lives. Beauty, handsomeness, health, and mortal life itself are fleeting, while true moral goodness will sweeten, mature, and grow over time.

Each of the points of practical wisdom I have addressed in this chapter is not a matter of right or wrong, sinfulness or purity, but rather of intelligent judgment; suitability; weighing pluses and minuses; being realistic and informed; and preparing for a strong, godly, productive, joyful marriage based on knowledge. That is what being mature means, at least partially—being willing to make important decisions prudently without a clear rulebook directing every particular and relieving one of the need for careful deliberation, wise counsel, earnestly praying for wisdom, and (ultimately) accepting a certain degree of uncertainty. Deciding whom to marry this way won't work out perfectly—nothing does—but it will certainly work out better than deciding foolishly.

138. Wilson, *Her Hand In Marriage*, 73.
139. Ibid.

CHAPTER 7

A CALL TO PREMARITAL
SEXUAL INTEGRITY

*God's choice must needs be far better for us, than our own. . . . Lawful
and ordinate enjoyments, are as honey without the sting. Forbidden
pleasures, are embittered and extinguished by these regrets and
reflections of the conscience. They are like those pleasant fruits, which
the Spaniards found in the Indies, which are sweet to the taste, but so
environed, and armed on every side with dangerous briars and thorns,
that they tore not only their clothes off their backs, but the skin off
their flesh, to come to them. And therefore they called them "comfits in
hell." And such are all forbidden, and unlawful pleasures.*

John Flavel[1]

*All created things cease to fulfill their potential if they are removed
from the place God assigned to them.*

Douglas Wilson[2]

C onsider Leonardo Da Vinci's famous painting, the *Mona Lisa*. A cura-
tor who hangs this portrait in a context suited to it wonderfully
enhances its stunning beauty and richness, enabling people to appreciate it accurately and fully, unleashing its positive potential. On the other
hand, someone who slapped that painting onto the wall in a filthy public
restroom, like a cheap poster, would turn this exquisite work of art into

---

1. *The Whole Works of the Reverend Mr. John Flavel*, 386–87. I modernized some spelling.
2. Wilson, *Reforming Marriage*, 101.

something ludicrous, even obscene. People who had only seen the *Mona Lisa* in this grotesque setting might even find it difficult to appreciate it appropriately in a fine art gallery, that negative association now burned into their consciousness.

Sex is a lot like that. As we saw in chapter 3, God designed sex for marriage and only in that context—and even then, only if they approach it properly—can humans experience all its marvelous possibilities. Outside of that, sex is a particularly powerful form of sin that harms us individually and collectively, and ultimately, if not repented of, leads to spiritual death.

In helping professing believers prepare for godly marriage, it is essential that we address the issue of premarital sex. This is especially true given the disturbing statistics on premarital behavior and beliefs among evangelicals discussed in chapter 3 and the fallout in our churches in the form of abortion, rise in out-of-wedlock births, and single mothers documented in chapter 4. In England of the late 1600s, John Flavel mourned "how the sin of uncleanness should grow so epidemical and common as it does," claiming that "never was any age more infamous for this sin."[3] One can only imagine what he would say today where, as Mark Dever has observed, "The shame, shock, disgrace, and danger once associated with fornication . . . have declined. . . . In fact, if we are honest, marriage these days is not viewed as the permanent *introduction to* sex, but as the temporary *limitation* of it!"[4] When one-fourth of weekly church attenders between the ages of twenty-four and thirty-five will not reject the statement that "consensual polyamory is OK," and about three in ten feel the same way about sex with absolutely "no strings attached,"[5] the church faces serious challenges in helping young people embrace the most basic tenets of biblical teaching on sex.

In this chapter, we will first cover some areas of sexual activity outside of wedlock that we have not considered yet, particularly various practices and beliefs among teenagers and single young adults, and the scandal of pornography, which undermine future marriages and are big problems among professing evangelicals today. Next, we will look at the degree to which sexually transmitted diseases (STDs) are issues and why, in the process

---

3. *The Whole Works of the Reverend Mr. John Flavel*, 388.
4. "Christian Hedonists or Religious Prudes? The Puritans on Sex," 247. Emphasis in original.
5. Regnerus, *Cheap Sex*, 186. See chapter 1, footnote 5 for a definition of polyamory.

challenging ludicrous "safe sex" myths. Finally, I will lay out some positive things that singles, and their parents, can do to maintain or recapture premarital sexual integrity, and so build a stronger foundation for future marriages. To be sure, there is much the church can do as well; however, these will be addressed in my overall recommendations to churches in chapter 15.

PREMARITAL SEX AMONG TEENS AND YOUNG ADULTS

PREMARITAL SEXUAL INTERCOURSE

Since 1991, the Centers for Disease Control and Prevention (CDC) has conducted a biannual Youth Risk Behavior Surveillance (YRBS) study on a random sample of high school students nationally. The 2017 version included over 14,956 teens.[6] In that year, 57 percent indicated they had engaged in sexual intercourse prior to graduation, about the same for males and females.[7] Just under half (47 percent) had done so before completing the eleventh grade.[8] About one of five (17 percent female and 23 percent male) were already having intercourse before entering the tenth grade.[9] Almost 45 percent of both sexes said they were "currently sexually active" as of their senior year.[10] Moreover, 16.5 percent of females, and 19.5 percent of males, had sexual intercourse with four or more partners by the time they graduated high school.[11] Across the board, percentages were highest for African-American males.[12]

The YRBS does not capture information about religious beliefs, but the National Survey of Family Growth (NSFG) does.[13] I combined the last two

---

6. Kann et al., "Youth Risk Behavior Surveillance: United States, 2017," 5.

7. Ibid, 321.

8. Ibid.

9. Ibid.

10. Ibid., 330.

11. Ibid, 327.

12. Ibid., 321, 327, 330.

13. This survey, conducted in various forms since 1974, captures information about marriage, family life, sex, and so on. It is conducted by the Centers for Disease Control and Prevention's (CDC) National Center for Health Statistics (NCHS). Sampling males and females separately, the 2014 version, conducted from September 2011 to September 2013, involved 10,416 respondents between the ages of fifteen and forty-four; and the 2016 release, conducted from September 2013 to September 2015, involved 10,205 respondents between the ages of fifteen and forty-nine. See National Center for Health Statistics, "About the *National Survey for Family Growth*."

survey cycles (2011–13 and 2013–15) to assemble a random national sample of 1,271 males and 1,190 females who were singles between the ages of fifteen and seventeen, and of 1,492 females and 1,586 males who were singles between eighteen and twenty-two. Table 7.1 shows the percentages who have had sexual intercourse overall, for those who identified as evangelical Protestants, then by church attendance and how important they felt religion was in their daily lives.[14]

With the exception of females ages fifteen to seventeen, overall evangelical singles had engaged in sexual intercourse somewhat less than average. Across the board, weekly church attenders did much better than average, especially compared to those who went to church less often or never. Rating religion "very important" in their daily lives mattered too. Especially among those eighteen to twenty-two, youth who did so were much more likely to be virgins than those who considered religion to be

Table 7.1: Percent of Never-Married, Ages 15–17 and 18–22, Who Have Had Sexual Intercourse. Overall and Along Various Religious Dimensions (NSFG 2014 and 2016)

	Males 15–17	Females 15–17	Males 18–22	Females 18–22
OVERALL:	34%	29%	75%	75%
Evangelical Protestant:	29%	27%	64%	64%
CHURCH ATTENDANCE				
Weekly:	23%	22%	56%	61%
Monthly:	34%	31%	80%	75%
Less Than Monthly:	40%	26%	83%	81%
Never:	41%	39%	80%	83%
IMPORTANCE OF RELIGION				
Very:	28.5%	23%	67%	66%
Somewhat:	37%	28%	79%	79%
Not:	34%	33%	81%	83%

14. In doing these analyses summarized in tables 7.1, 7.2, and 7.3, I am following a fine rubric used earlier by Mark Regnerus, but with later data, *Forbidden Fruit*, throughout.

only "somewhat," or "not," important. Still, overall, the percentages are disappointing. This should not be surprising. Only 26 percent of eighteen-to twenty-two-year old evangelicals in the 2006 through 2016 General Social Survey said that premarital sex was "always wrong," just 22 percent of those who said they were raised in evangelical homes. Our youth look more like the current cultural norm than they do believers striving for holiness (Heb 12:14), and our churches and parents need to take responsibility for their part in that.

Mark Regnerus recounts a teenage girl whom his research team interviewed in 2002 or 2003. She was actively involved in Young Life, described her relationship with her two married parents as good, attended a Baptist church (though she and her family often skipped), considered herself religious, claimed to "respect" the Bible, prayed regularly . . . and was sexually active.[15] When she described why her sexual activity was not wrong, it is hard to see a moral anchor or reference point beyond comparing herself with peers and not being like the "really bad" ones.

> Well, just, like, what the Bible says, you know, not having sex 'til you're married. But at the same time, like, so many kids have had sex. . . . Kids make up their own morals, too, and of, like, what is right and wrong, so it's not necessarily like, you know, you're always gonna go by what the Bible says or what your parents say or stuff like that. It's sort of, like, a half-and-half thing, like, you know, you make up your own rules and combine them with what your parents say and mix and match. . . . I've only had sex with, like, one person. And like, we were, like, together in a relationship for like three months. So it's not as if like I'm, like, a slut or anything. Like with other girls and stuff like that, they go out and like screw many guys 'cause I have friends that are that way.[16]

Happily, there are many Christian young people out there with solid beliefs about premarital sex who, if they fail in this area, repent and strive to submit to biblical teaching with the help of their churches, parents, and youth groups. Regnerus relays the story of just such an evangelical teenage

---

15. Ibid., 32.
16. Ibid.

girl he described as trying to "'reclaim' her virginity in some sense"[17] who gave him this accurate statement about Christian teaching on sex: "You're not to have sex before you marry. Like it's a gift from God to have when you're married and, you know, to enjoy between a wife and a husband."[18] Unfortunately, as the polls and statistics show, youth like that in their late teens have been swimming against the current for many years now, not only in the larger culture, but within too much of our evangelical subculture as well.

OTHER FORMS OF SEXUAL ACTIVITY

Here I want to look briefly at two other forms of sexual activity that are more common among our youth than we wish or typically want to think about—oral and anal sex. This is not an easy subject to broach, but one that we need to tackle, not only in this chapter, but also as parents and in the church to speak intelligently to and minister to our young people. I am not alone here. In his extensive study of "sex and religion in the lives of American teenagers," Mark Regnerus also found these to be important topics.[19] These activities are more common among our *heterosexual* single teens and young adults, and far riskier, than most seem to understand. In fact, as I wrote this the *Journal of Adolescent Health* had just released an explosive new study based on over 45,000 interviews of British young people ages sixteen to twenty-four. It showed that, among those who are sexually active, the number who say they have engaged in anal and/or oral sex increased from one in ten in 1990 and 1991, to one in four males and one in five females in 2010 through 2012. Since 2000, the largest increase in this activity was among those sixteen to nineteen years of age.[20] As we shall see, these activities are an increasing issue in the United States as well.

Religious youth may try to justify these activities by claiming they are "not really" sex.[21] For example, in one study, 71 percent of youth ages thirteen to nineteen said that someone who has had oral sex but not intercourse is still a

---

17. Ibid., 41.

18. Ibid., 28.

19. Ibid. (throughout); see also Regnerus and Uecker, *Premarital Sex in America*, 32–39.

20. Summarized by MacMillan, "Teenagers Today Are Having More of This Type of Sex." Full research article is Lewis et al., "Heterosexual Practices Among Young People in Britain: Evidence From Three National Surveys of Sexual Attitudes and Lifestyles."

21. Ibid., 33; Regnerus, *Forbidden Fruit*, 30.

"virgin."[22] Scholars refer to this as "'technical' virginity,"[23] a kind of everything-but-intercourse-is-OK approach. However, Regnerus relied on the 2002 NSFG to assert that the best evidence is that—regardless of what they believe constitutes "real sex"—most evangelical young people do *not* engage in oral or anal sex because they are consciously trying to have sex without "losing their virginity."[24] Looking at single evangelicals between fifteen and twenty-two in the most recent cycles of the *NSFG*,[25] I also found little evidence for it: only 11 percent of the males, and 13 percent of the females, had never engaged in vaginal intercourse but had been involved in heterosexual oral or anal sex.

Oral Sex

As Mark Regnerus points out, oral sex is "not addressed in the Bible at all" whether in or out of marriage.[26] However—given scriptural teaching on lust, purity, and every other form of sexual activity outside of marriage—it would be a stretch to claim that married people engaging in oral sex with someone other than their spouse is *not* adultery, or that between unmarried persons it does *not* constitute fornication.[27] Regardless, many young people view it as a substitute for intercourse, and it is the most common first sexual experience for those who begin sex by age sixteen.[28] Youth commonly justify it as a way to avoid pregnancy and by asserting a mistaken idea that oral sex carries minimal risk of sexually transmitted diseases.[29] Moreover, as Regnerus and Uecker point out, when it comes to oral sex, many religious youths are *"selectively permissive."*[30] That is, "the moral rule remains right and good and in effect, yet it does not apply to them at present, for reasons too difficult and nuanced for them to adequately describe."[31]

22. Bersamin et al., "Defining Virginity and Abstinence," 184.

23. Regnerus, *Forbidden Fruit*, 167; Regnerus and Uecker, *Premarital Sex in America*, 21–22. "Technical virginity" patterns are "everything but" approaches to sex—engaging in petting, oral, and anal sex while avoiding intercourse.

24. Regnerus, *Forbidden Fruit*, 167–68.

25. The same groups I combined in tables 7.1 through 7.4, here.

26. Ibid., 20.

27. Ibid.

28. Ibid.

29. Ibid., 30, 180. As we shall see later, the risk of sexually transmitted diseases with oral sex is significant.

30. Regnerus and Uecker, *Premarital Sex in America*, 35.

31. Ibid.

Table 7.2: Percent of Never-Married, Ages 15–17 and 18–22, Who Have Engaged in Heterosexual Oral Sex. Overall and Along Various Religious Dimensions (NSFG 2014 and 2016)

	Males 15–17	Females 15–17	Males 18–22	Females 18–22
OVERALL:	43%	34%	76%	72%
Evangelical Protestant:	39%	34%	66%	65%
CHURCH ATTENDANCE				
Weekly:	33%	28%	58%	58%
Monthly:	46%	37%	78%	67%
Less Than Monthly:	48%	32%	80%	80%
Never:	46%	42%	79%	78%
IMPORTANCE OF RELIGION				
Very:	36%	28%	66%	63%
Somewhat:	45%	35%	77%	74%
Not:	42%	31%	83%	84%

The truth about what is happening with young singles in this area may not be as bad as many seem to think, but there are reasons for concern.[32] Table 7.2 shows that, once again, there are more differences between evangelicals and the overall average among the older, eighteen- to twenty-two-year-old group. Still, over a third of evangelicals fifteen to seventeen, and roughly two-thirds of those eighteen to twenty-two, have engaged in some form of oral sex with a member of the opposite gender. Those who attend church weekly do better, as do those who regard religion as very important in their daily lives. Still, the picture is dismal, even among weekly attenders. Oral sex is clearly not an issue we should set aside out of embarrassment, and it is certainly not a secret to our youth.

---

32. Regnerus, Forbidden Fruit, 41.

Anal Sex

As I write this chapter, the internet is ablaze with emotional discussion of *Teen Vogue's* disturbing "Guide to Anal Sex" for teenagers.[33] The decision to sell this to teenagers was repulsive and irresponsible in the extreme, and the article's text clearly indicates that the author means to not only instruct but also to normalize it, and not just for gay males. However, we should not be surprised given not only the overall decline in our culture, but also the fact that for at least a couple of decades, internet pornography has become the new sex education for teens,[34] and anal sex is hardly rare in the world of virtual smut. As Regnerus observes, "Sexual practices like anal sex no doubt receive a boost from their online visibility."[35] How bad is it? Isn't this really something only gay males do? Let's look at table 7.3 and see.

Table 7.3: Percent of Never-Married, Ages 15–17 and 18–22, Who Have Engaged in <u>Heterosexual</u> Anal Sex. Overall and Along Various Religious Dimensions (NSFG 2014 and 2016)

	Males 15–17	Females 15–17	Males 18–22	Females 18–22
OVERALL:	8.5%	6%	24%	24%
Evangelical Protestant:	8%	8%	21%	20%
CHURCH ATTENDANCE				
Weekly:	7%	6%	15%	17%
Monthly:	8%	6%	22%	19%
Less Than Monthly:	8%	9%	25%	26.5%
Never:	11.5%	7%	29%	31%
IMPORTANCE OF RELIGION				
Very:	7%	4%	16%	18%
Somewhat:	8%	8%	27%	24%
Not:	10%	9%*	23%	31%

* Only 2 respondents, interpret cautiously.

---

33. Engle, "Anal Sex: What You Need to Know, How to Do It the RIGHT Way."
34. Regnerus, *Forbidden Fruit*, 180.
35. Ibid.

The patterns are almost the same as for intercourse and oral sex—evangelicals slightly better (except for females fifteen to seventeen), weekly church attendance and placing high importance on religion in daily life both associated with lower percentages of having engaged in anal sex. However, especially given the high risks associated with this activity,[36] knowing that "only" one-fifth of evangelical singles ages eighteen to twenty-two have at least tried anal sex, compared to one-quarter overall, is not comforting. Can we really use the term "only" to describe the 15 percent to 18 percent of young adults who attend church weekly or consider religion important engaging in, of all things, anal sex? There is also solid evidence that this practice is on the rise among young people.[37] Again, we should not ignore something this potentially destructive, sinful, and common among our young people. We must find ways to address this.

Pulling This Together

Table 7.4, similar to the last three tables, shows percentages who have engaged in one or more of the sexual activities we have discussed here. Remember that this does *not* include what used to be called "petting" and is now more known as "mutual masturbation." We see that except evangelical single *males only* have done somewhat better than the overall averages, but very clearly weekly church attendance is associated with the lowest percentages, followed by those who say religion is very important to them.

Note here how clearly something stands out that we have seen in the previous three tables as well—the advantage for those who attend church *weekly*. Sporadic church attendance is not good enough. Scholars can legitimately argue that perhaps the relationship between spending time in public worship week after week, and having less non-marital sex, is accidental—that people who go to church regularly tend to have other qualities that lead to abstinence. This is the "chicken-egg" issue, and yes, correlation is not the same thing as cause. Moreover, some churches are biblically faithful while others are not. However, it is not hard to see that

36. More on this later in this chapter.

37. Regnerus and Uecker, *Premarital Sex in America*, 36.

Table 7.4: Percent of Never-Married, Ages 15–17 and 18–22, Who Have Engaged Heterosexually in Any of the Following: Sexual Intercourse, Oral or Anal Sex. Overall and Along Various Religious Dimensions (NSFG 2014 and 2016)

	Males 15–17	Females 15–17	Males 18–22	Females 18–22
OVERALL:	51%	42%	82%	82%
Evangelical Protestant:	46%	41%	72%	81%
CHURCH ATTENDANCE				
Weekly:	40%	36%	65%	70%
Monthly:	52%	45%	86%	82%
Less Than Monthly:	58%	37%	85%	87%
Never:	56%	52.5%	84%	86%
IMPORTANCE OF RELIGION				
Very:	42%	38%	73%	74%
Somewhat:	53%	43%	83.5%	85%
Not:	52%	44%	86%	87%

in ways that matter both in and out of the formal services, being with the people of God weekly at least encourages us, sustains us, and makes it easier for others to minister to us. It helps us to stay or get back on track. It is no accident that the famous admonishment in the book of Hebrews about "not neglecting to meet together" (Heb 10:25) is sandwiched between pointing out how Christians are to "stir up one another to . . . good works" (v. 24) and not to "go on sinning deliberately after receiving the knowledge of the truth" (v. 26). These are connected. The apostle Peter warned believers, "Your adversary the devil prowls around like a roaring lion, seeking someone to devour" (1 Pet 5:8b). Predators pick off strays. Packs of wolves often separate the young from adults who are defending them. If it really is true that those who attend church regularly just have more of the qualities that keep them from engaging in premarital sex, then by God's grace we should cultivate those qualities, and attend church.

Pornography

There is no doubt pornography use generally, and among younger adults in particular, has reached epidemic proportions with the rise of free 24/7 access to virtually any forms of it, with at least the perception of anonymity, on the internet. This has hit both genders, but males particularly are susceptible to its dubious temptations. The evidence for this is everywhere, and I cannot do better than to quote a 2011 statement by Regnerus and Uecker[38]:

> So is porn an issue among emerging adults? Absolutely. Pornography use is highest among this demographic. In one of the most rigorous and reliable studies of online porn use and norms, researchers interviewed 813 emerging adults—undergraduate and graduate students from six colleges and universities ranging in age from 18 to 26. Two out of three men agreed that porn use was generally acceptable, while the same was true of half the women. On usage, however, the genders differ significantly. The survey revealed that 86 percent of men 'interact' with porn at least once a month, while 69 percent of women reported no porn use at all. Just under half of men watch porn weekly, while only 3 percent of women say the same.

With regard to porn, statistically there is some good news for evangelicals, though there is still cause for alarm. The General Social Survey regularly asks about watching an entire pornographic movie within the past year. This is a much higher threshold than a lot of internet porn viewing. Among those ages eighteen to twenty-three, 54 percent of males admitted doing so, as did 32 percent of females. Among conservative Protestants in the same age group, the percentages were 47 and 30, which is better but not by much. However, a large 2002 through 2003 survey showed that 7.5 percent of evangelical adolescent boys viewed internet porn at least monthly. This was much lower than almost every other religious group; for example, those with no religion hit 22 percent.[39] Church attendance and the importance of religiosity were generally more powerfully associated with reduced porn viewing—8 percent for those attending church weekly versus 22 percent for those who rarely did, and 5 percent for those

---

38. Ibid., 95.
39. Regnerus, *Forbidden Fruit*, 176.

who regarded religion as very important versus 26 percent who said it was "not important at all."[40] This was roughly fifteen years ago, and internet porn viewing has gone up dramatically since then.

Today, while the percentages are much higher across the board, it does appear that patterns for religious commitment remain similar. For example, a 2015 Barna Group survey found that among those thirteen to twenty-four years old, 41 percent of actively Christian males had sought out pornography on the internet in the past month, compared to 72 percent of males who were not practicing Christians.[41] For females the differences were much smaller—17 percent versus 14 percent. One concerning finding in this survey was that, for all age groups combined, only 29 percent of practicing Christians who used porn said that they felt guilty about it.[42] This was higher than for others, to be sure, but *all* Christians should experience guilt when they sin. In fact, one of the overwhelming facts that emerged in this survey was the "cavalier" attitude toward porn among teens and young adults.[43] Many more of them found "not recycling" to be immoral (56 percent) than they did "viewing pornographic images" (32 percent).[44]

Mark Regnerus looked at a large national survey conducted in 2014 that asked, among many other topics, whether respondents believed that "viewing porn is OK." Only a little over 60 percent of twenty-four- to thirty-five-year-olds disagreed with this statement.[45]

There are many effects of widespread exposure to pornography among singles bound for marriage that should concern us. We cannot list them all here. Viewing pornography is a potentially addictive sin that, if not dealt with, can alienate Christians from God and sap their spiritual vitality, encourage them toward moral compromise and drift, and desensitize them to increasingly more extreme forms of sexual depravity. One of the biggest problems is that many males believe that porn is real sex education.[46]

---

40. Ibid.

41. "Porn in the Digital Age: New Research Reveals 10 Trends."

42. Ibid.

43. Ibid.

44. Ibid.

45. Regnerus, *Cheap Sex*, 186.

46. Regnerus, *Forbidden Fruit*, 179.

Regnerus points out "that it provides a false picture of what sexually intimate relationships are like" including males viewing themselves as naturally aggressors relative to submissive women, and that they can and
ought to demand often degrading sexual activities with women, who (they
believe) will typically end up enjoying them.[47] If porn use continues into
marriage, it will of course undermine marital intimacy.[48]

As a long-term evangelical college professor who teaches courses on
marriage and family, I have observed internet porn move from technically non-existent to a major issue of profound importance among my
male students. Viewing porn seems to be the most common struggle they
deal with in their accountability groups. I am heartened to see young men
intelligently battling these temptations. This is certainly a reason why we
are doing better than those who are not practicing Christians. However,
porn has ensnared too many believers. We cannot afford to evade this topic
or stop trying to apply more effort, skill, teaching, and prayer to fighting
the encroachment of this awful, degraded industry into the lives of God's
people.

DESTRUCTIVE MYTHS ABOUT PREMARITAL
SEX COMMON AMONG SINGLES TODAY

Regnerus and Uecker note that their research uncovered ten destructive
lies believed by many singles today, fostered by these kinds of questionable
influences.[49] I would like to briefly overview seven of them here, those that
appear most pertinent to evangelicals who *do* hope to build strong marriages someday that we do not tackle elsewhere.

First, we will consider four lies that easily become what sociologists call "self-fulfilling prophecies," namely they *become* true at least
partly *because* we believe them. We start with the notion that long-
term, faithful, and exclusive sexual relationships are a "fiction," despite
data such as those we have seen that show that most married people
do *not* commit adultery.[50] Moreover, people have a difficult time trusting a potential partner who has had numerous sexual partners in the

---

47. Ibid.
48. Ibid., 174.
49. Regnerus and Uecker, *Premarital Sex in America*, 242–50.
50. Ibid., 242–43.

past,[51] so acting on this belief undermines marriage. It is not fair, but "women especially are sanctioned for their sexual past."[52]

Closely associated with this last myth is another, namely that women cannot expect men to be as committed and self-controlled sexually as they would wish, that it is somehow natural for males to expect sex "with no strings attached."[53] However, as Regnerus and Uecker observe, "this scenario is *not* fixed . . . boys will be boys *if nothing different is expected of them.*"[54] What seems normal in our current environment, where sex outside marriage and porn are readily available, is not acceptable when the rules change.[55] As I have witnessed repeatedly, if a man sincerely wants a godly Christian wife, he will hold off sexually if she, and God, expects him to.

Third is the idea that gender equality means women thinking and acting in the same way as men do about sex. This does not work, because males and females are sexually different.[56] When women try to act like men sexually, they typically cannot maintain it for long and be happy or true to themselves.[57] Regnerus and Uecker respond this way to the common complaint that "women should be held to a higher standard": "On the contrary, perhaps it ought to be lauded that women generally *do* set higher standards for their relationships."[58]

Fourth is the stubborn belief that introducing sex will strengthen a new or troubled relationship.[59] Research overwhelmingly shows the opposite is true, that sex actually makes breakdown more likely.[60] Here is another example of self-fulfilling prophecy. Because people act as if this lie is true, they initiate sex, thus bringing on the very breakdown they fear.[61] Besides, if sex outside marriage is the price of keeping someone, he or she is not a

51. Ibid., 243.
52. Ibid.
53. Ibid., 244–45.
54. Ibid., 244 (emphasis added).
55. Ibid., 245.
56. Ibid., 243–44.
57. Ibid., 244.
58. Ibid.
59. Ibid., 243.
60. Ibid.
61. Ibid.

person whom a Christian should want to marry. Relationships with people like that tend to fail anyway.[62]

The last three myths I will address here are tied less to the self-fulfilling prophecy problem, but they are dangerous. The first is the belief that other singles are having lots of sex, and that those who are chaste feel left out, or odd.[63] Singles who think this are often highly overestimating,[64] but the key thing for believers is that they are better off not involved in fornication no matter how popular it is. The Lord and solid believers struggling alongside us will be joining us. Besides, while believers should reach out to all kinds of people in love, if they are part of a close friendship network in which they feel odd maintaining biblical standards of sexuality, they need to rethink being that close to these peers and seek out more friendships with people who are serious about following the Lord.

The sixth myth is the assertion that pornography will not "affect your relationships."[65] Yes it does, including, as we discussed, fostering demands men make upon women sexually that the latter often find unappealing or even degrading.[66] Under the influence of porn, what men want from women sexually seems to keep expanding while what they are willing to give emotionally to their partners "seems to be diminishing."[67] Marriage and marital sex requires at times, real effort, but porn teaches people to expect effortless thrill.[68] Beyond this, for increasing numbers of males today, porn literally competes with, and thus devalues, real sex.[69]

Finally, there is the belief that casual sex without emotional commitment need not be harmful.[70] The fact is that for women especially who hope to build a solid marriage and family today, it hurts a lot. Sex as "just fun" degrades both males and females. God did not design sex to be a form of recreation between two non-committed people.

---

62. Ibid.
63. Ibid., 247.
64. Ibid.
65. Ibid., 246.
66. Ibid.
67. Ibid.
68. Ibid.
69. Ibid
70. Ibid.

THE ONLY SAFE SEX IS MARRIED SEX

Loving sex between a faithful husband and wife is not only beautiful and godly; it is also about as "safe" as sex is ever going to be. Outside of marriage—despite all the education, technology, and medical advancement we have thrown at it—sex is not "safe." We see this in the extraordinarily high levels of out-of-wedlock pregnancy we discussed in chapter 4. Consider the amount of non-marital sexual activity, in terms of frequency and the number of sex partners that we have documented in chapter 2 and in this chapter. Under that onslaught, no amount of low-cost, highly available modern contraception is going to prevent singles experiencing a high number of pregnancies despite all the assurances we have heard for years from progressives. That is why the latter remain so adamant to keep abortion on demand legal and far from rare.

The same thing is true about STDs. Only condoms or similar "barriers"[71] can prevent STDs. They make sex "safer" but just as with other forms of contraception and pregnancy, condoms do have a failure rate. The more sex people have—even if they use them perfectly and consistently—the more likely they will experience condom failure. That is simple mathematics. Only abstinence is one hundred percent effective against pregnancy. With the exception of a monogamous relationship with an uninfected partner, it is also the only sure-fire protection against sexually transmitted disease.

CONDOMS

There are many misconceptions about the effectiveness of condoms.[72] One is that they work on all forms of STDs. The fact is, they protect better against some diseases than others because some STDs—such as syphilis, genital herpes, and human papillomavirus (HPV)—can be transmitted in skin-to-skin contact that is not always covered by condoms even if they are used properly. Condoms work best for preventing diseases spread by genital secretions, such as HIV (which causes AIDS), gonorrhea, chlamydia, and trichomoniasis.[73] So even if they worked perfectly, they do not protect against STDs completely.

---

71. For example, special latex devices, like condoms, called "dental dams" for preventing STD transmission during oral sex.

72. For simplicity, unless stated otherwise, I will be referring to condoms worn by men, not "female condoms" or other such devices.

73. Centers for Disease Control and Prevention, "Condoms and STDs: Fact Sheet for Public Health Personnel."

However, according to the Association of Reproductive Health Professionals, in terms of pregnancy prevention, male condoms have a 2 percent failure rate with *perfect* use, and about an 18 percent failure rate with *typical* use.[74] What this means is that on average, 18 of every 100 women using condoms in the typical manner experience an unintended pregnancy within a year,[75] down to a low of 2 percent for those whose partners always use them and do so perfectly. Looking up rules for "perfect use" helps one understand why it is not typical—they are hard to follow. Expecting that kind of consistency and attention to detail in using condoms while having sex, from teens and young adults, is unrealistic. Moreover, notice that the risk of eventual pregnancy rises the longer women are sexually active,[76] and will be higher for those with more sexual activity than average. Someone starting as a teen and continuing a typical pattern of non-marital sex until marriage in the middle or late 20s will most likely experience condom failure.

This bears on STDs because for these hypothetical eighteen women of every one hundred to get pregnant in a year, sperm had to have passed the latex barrier, usually more than once. This also means, logically, that this happened to some unknown number of women who did *not* get pregnant as well; they were just "lucky." Each time sperm passes through due to condom failure, whether or not pregnancy results, vaginal mucous membranes contact "male secretions" and perhaps female secretions do the same with the penis. Either means a risk of STD transmission. Anal sex raises the danger astronomically, as both the risk of infection due to the tearing of blood vessels and tissue, and the chance of the condom breaking, are much higher, even with lubrication.[77] We do not have firm percentages of STD transmission across all types of sex and condoms, and situations. There are simply too many variables. What we do know is that wearing condoms, especially regularly and

---

74. "Choosing a Birth Control Method: Male Condom." This is consistent with CDC estimates, see next note.

75. Centers for Disease Control and Prevention, "How Effective Are Birth Control Methods?"

76. If 18 percent of one hundred women get pregnant within a year, then of the remaining eighty-two, should they continue having sex, another fifteen will get pregnant, making the risk 33 percent at two years, and so on.

77. New York State Department of Health, "Frequently Asked Questions (FAQs) About Condoms."

properly, *will* make sex outside committed marriage physically *safer*, but it is still far from "safe."

With this in mind, consider the facts in table 7.5 regarding the number of sexual partners in the past five years, and frequency of sex over the past year, for single *GSS* respondents, aged eighteen to twenty-nine, in the years 2006 through 2016. Few had less than two sex partners, and almost 70 percent of males and 55 percent of females had three or more. Meanwhile, 56 percent of males and 59 percent of females were having sex weekly or more often. In that environment, even if everyone used condoms, pregnancy and STDs are going to flourish. Considering that only 63 percent of sexually active unmarried males (61.5 percent for evangelicals) between the ages of fifteen and twenty-seven in the last two cycles of the *NSFG* indicated they used a condom the last time they had intercourse (much less used them *every* time), the outcome is predictable. Skyrocketing out-of-wedlock pregnancies, as we have seen, and loads of STDs.

Neither condoms, nor humans, are perfect. The world of sexually active singles is not a safe place. God's best and safest venue for sex is as it always has been—monogamous marriage.

Table 7.5: Percent of Non-Virgin Singles Ages 18–29 Who Have Engaged in Sex. By Number of Partners in Past Five Years and Frequency Over Past Year (GSS 2000–2016)

	Males	*Females*
# PARTNERS PAST 5 YEARS		
One:	19%	27%
Two:	12%	18%
Three or More:	69%	55%
FREQUENCY IN PAST YEAR		
None:	6%	4%
Once or Twice:	13%	10%
1 to 3 per Month:	24%	28%
Once a Week:	15%	17%
2 to 3 per Week:	25%	29%
4 or More per Week:	16%	13%

ORAL SEX IS NOT SAFE

While few people seem to think that anal sex is safe compared to vaginal intercourse, the idea that oral sex is low risk appears to be widely held, as we have seen. According to the Centers for Disease Control, people can and do get STDs this way, and both males and females can do so either by performing or receiving oral stimulation.[78] Oral sex can transmit HIV, syphilis, herpes, gonorrhea, chlamydia, trichomoniasis,[79] and HPV. In fact, as one Harvard Medical School headline warned, "HPV transmission during oral sex" is now a "growing cause of mouth and throat cancer."[80] The only protection—and again, it is not perfect—is condoms and, for women receiving oral sex, dental dams. Among singles between fifteen and twenty-seven in the last two *NSFG*, only 10 percent of males and 9 percent of females indicated they had used condoms the last time they had oral sex, and all of *these* certainly did not do so every time.[81]

THE STD EPIDEMIC

This brings us to the sad, predictable result. In March of 2008, the CDC released shocking news that 38 percent of sexually active teenage girls between the ages of fourteen and nineteen had at least one of five sexually transmitted diseases (gonorrhea, chlamydia, herpes simplex, HPV, and trichomoniasis).[82] Amazingly, 20 percent of those who claimed they had only ever had one sex partner were infected.[83] Fully 24 percent of teenage girls overall were infected.[84] Considering that results would have been at least slightly worse if more sexually transmitted afflictions had been considered, and occurred after decades of sex education and pushing condoms to teenagers, these percentages are awful.

The news has not been getting better. In a disturbing 2015 release, the CDC noted that as of 2014, cases of chlamydia, gonorrhea, and syphilis had

---

78. Centers for Disease Control and Prevention, "STD Risk and Oral Sex."

79. Ibid.

80. Lewine, "HPV Transmission during Oral Sex a Growing Cause of Mouth and Throat Cancer."

81. For males this was receiving oral sex from females; the female question pertained to the male wearing a condom while she performed it on him.

82. Forhan et al., "Prevalence of Sexually Transmitted Infections among Female Adolescents Aged 14 to 19 in the United States," 1505.

83. Ibid.

84. Ibid.

all risen, some dramatically.[85] HPV vaccinations have brought down HPV rates, the most common form of genital herpes had declined,[86] but trichomoniasis and other vaginal infections appeared to be rising slightly after several years of decline,[87] and a less common type of genital herpes was increasing among the college-aged population.[88] Overall STDs and the rise in them disproportionately affect younger populations. Those ages fifteen to twenty-four "acquire half of all new STDs" and "are at a higher risk of acquiring STDs for a combination of behavioral, biological, and cultural reasons."[89] That means that those who will get married and maybe are in the process of planning for it are hit the hardest.

All three of the STDs that were the focus of this CDC report can have adverse impacts upon pregnancy and fetuses, as can genital herpes.[90] Chlamydia and gonorrhea often do not produce symptoms in women, who must have screening to detect it.[91] Symptoms of syphilis infections typically appear in ten to ninety days.[92] This means that those infected with these and other STDs can spread them for some time before they even know that they are carrying them.

Even if the rates of these STDs decline, the sheer risk and incidence of these are too great to ignore. For example, in 2014 for every 100,000 women ages fifteen to twenty-four, there were 3,309 reported cases of chlamydia (that is 3.3 percent).[93] In many states, the rate was much higher.[94] Consider that: this is just one of many STDs, health professionals had not detected all chlamydia cases, many uninfected women would become so in subsequent years, and this is hitting females as they are just getting into marriage and having children.

---

85. CDC, *Sexually Transmitted Disease Surveillance 2014*, 1–2. The report points out that gay males have driven a lot of the increase, but by no means all of it, especially the more recent spikes.

86. Ibid., 41–42.

87. Ibid., 49.

88. Ibid., 42.

89. Ibid., 60.

90. Ibid., 52.

91. Ibid., 52–53.

92. CDC, "Syphilis."

93. CDC, *Sexually Transmitted Disease Surveillance 2014*, 60.

94. Ibid., 62.

The responses of modern, secular professionals to the STD problem, like those of CDC physician Jonathan Mermin, are predictable and understandable: "America's worsening STD epidemic is a clear call for better diagnosis, treatment, and prevention."[95] Of course, prevention mostly means "using condoms consistently and correctly" and "limiting the number of sex partners."[96] This is a bit like encouraging smokers to cut back and use weaker cigarettes, rather than to quit. However, calls for abstinence until marriage and faithfulness afterward are rare and mostly limited to the religious community, and as we have seen, many of *them* have abandoned those convictions as well.

Evangelicals must keep in mind that their sexually active young adults are as susceptible to STDs and their consequences as everyone else is. If we love them, we cannot ignore this.

REASONS VIRGINS HAVE NOT HAD SEX

So how important are some of the risks we have raised, versus moral convictions or other consideration, in explaining why young singles have *not* become sexually active? The *NSFG* asks respondents who have not had sex to give their reasons for abstaining. I have provided them below for singles fifteen to twenty-two years old who have never engaged in vaginal, oral, or anal sexual relationships, comparing evangelicals to the overall percentages. It is encouraging that evangelicals, particularly females, were more likely to cite their religious and moral beliefs as reasons for remaining abstinent; but the percentages, especially for males, were disappointing. Males were actually more concerned than females about pregnancy, a fact that is difficult to explain. Surprisingly, fear of STDs was a minor factor across the board. Meanwhile, many evangelical virgins indicated they would have premarital sex under the right circumstances.

These percentages help us to see the challenges ahead for those of us who want to help turn things around among evangelicals. Among our young singles who are not sexually active, substantial percentages are just waiting for the right opportunity and many of them care more about physical consequences than upholding God's moral law.

---

95. CDC, "Reported Cases of STDs on the Rise in the U.S."
96. Ibid.

Table 7.6: Singles, Ages 15–22, Who Have Not Engaged in Vaginal, Oral, or Anal Sex. Percent Providing Different Reasons for Not Having Sex (NSFG 2014 and 2016)

	Evangelical Males	Evangelical Females	Overall Males	Overall Females
REASONS GIVEN FOR NOT HAVING SEX				
Against Religion or Morals:	47%	63%	23%	29%
Don't Want to Get/ Make Girl Pregnant:	11%	8%	17.5%	20%
Don't Want to Get an STD:	7%	2%	6%	8%
Haven't Found Right Person:	20%	12.5%	33%	24%
Have Right Person but Not Right Time:	4%	7%	7%	6%
Other:	10%	7%	14%	12%

POSITIVE STRATEGIES FOR SINGLES AND PARENTS

Having biblically grounded beliefs and practices about premarital sex is vitally important, central to important aspects of the Christian life, and yet we continue to lose ground in this area. What can we do? Here, I would like to lay out some common-sense, realistic things that singles and their parents can do to retain or recapture sexual integrity. As I indicated earlier, there are many positive roles for the church too, and much I have to say here clearly assumes that, but I will address these in my overall recommendations for churches in the final chapter of this book. First, however, we must get our priorities in order.

Helping singles avoid STDs, out-of-wedlock pregnancies, and other fallout of sexual promiscuity that will harm them but also undermine their future marriages, is a vitally important, loving motivation for helping them do much better with sexual purity, whether or not they appreciate the dangers. There is a lot of other human damage caused by the modern breakdown of moral restraint, such as how pornography wrecks the viewers and those they view. We should mourn over this harm to so many people, including ourselves, and desire something better for ourselves, our children, our fellow Christians, and the unbelievers too.

However, as the Larger Catechism points out, "the chief and highest end of man" is to "glorify God, and fully to enjoy him forever."[97] The human costs of sexual indulgence are terrible, but the spiritual consequences are far more important. Widespread sexual promiscuity and its acceptance, among professing believers, dishonor God because his people are openly treating his righteous demands as trivialities or encumbrances rather than the righteous order given to them by a loving parent. Sexual immorality, said the apostle Paul, is a "leaven" that "leavens the whole lump" (1 Cor 5:6), corrupting our families and churches as it spreads and we become comfortable with it. As we saw in chapter 3, the beliefs of most professing evangelicals today about premarital sex suggest a people who believe they are wiser than God is. Godliness is a necessary foundation for Christian life, including marriage, and sexual chastity is indispensable to that. A people who wink at sexual sin are not a godly people. Moreover, at least two of God's purposes for marriage—that he desires that we have our children and our sexual fulfillment under its covenantal protections—relate directly to reserving sex for marriage.

None of this means we have to be harsh or judgmental with others, our children, their peers, or ourselves. Most of us have failed in precisely these areas, in one way or another. The pull of sexual temptation is a powerful force to most of us, particularly in a sex-saturated culture that takes premarital sex for granted and provides numerous opportunities and inducements. In helping others, including our children, conform their beliefs and practices on premarital sex to biblical teaching, we must embrace the fact that we are sinners helping sinners. We should be direct and honest, but with humility, patience, mercy, grace, and prayer. We have or can fall too, and so we must preach to ourselves as well. We must keep the apostle Paul's admonition in mind: "Brothers, if anyone is caught in any transgression, you who are spiritual should restore him in a spirit of gentleness. Keep watch on yourself, lest you too be tempted" (Gal 6:1).

We must also address our failings with sexual beliefs and practice with reasonable expectations, knowing we must start where we are at,

---

97. *Westminster Confession*, "The Larger Catechism," 3.

not where we wish we were. Moreover, nothing we do will guarantee that our loved ones will not fail sexually. Human freedom does not work like that. However, many of us can do more, and do better.

With this framework, let us consider some practical strategies. You will notice that many encourage holiness across the Christian life, not just the sexual arena. That makes sense. After all, the best defenses against all sin and error are the consistent application of the common means of grace empowered by the Holy Spirit and done in Christian joy. This is not an exhaustive list, and I cannot give much detail about anything on it in this brief space. I will, however, cover things that are essential, and that seem most connected to helping us to see sex as God does—a beautiful part of godly marriage infused with powerful spiritual significance, meaning, and imagery, but outside of matrimony, a physically and spiritually destructive snare.

A GIFT FROM GOD

CHURCH ATTENDANCE

In this chapter and elsewhere, we have repeatedly seen powerful statistics attesting to the association of weekly church attendance with less sex outside marriage and its consequences. No singles intent on holiness or parents desirous of helping them can responsibly ignore this duty. It makes sense. The best church teachings do Christians no good if they are not there to hear them. Parents need to ask what they are modeling when they regularly skip church. It is inconsistent and even hypocritical for them to ask their children to sacrifice their personal desires in order to submit to biblical teaching about sex if they are not willing to do the same with regard to regular participation in public worship (Heb 10:25). In *The Benedict Option*, Rod Dreher observes, "Every Christian family likes to think they put God first, but this is not always how we live."[98] He gives the example of putting sports and recreation ahead of Sunday worship, noting that living out faithful Christianity "means putting the life of the church first, even if you have to keep your kid out of a sports program that schedules games during your church's worship services. Even more importantly, your kids need to see you and your spouse sacrifice attendance at events if they conflict with church. And they need to see that you are serious about the

---

98. 124.

spiritual life."[99] Parents and singles, examine yourself in this vital area. What comes first?

Assuming churches are biblically sound and believers are not merely spectators or there to be entertained but instead are active participants, every element of the experience builds us up. Teaching and preaching, singing, prayer, the sacraments—all encourage and instruct. There is the fellowship and example of fellow believers, including other singles struggling to be chaste and older saints who can be sources of modeling and instruction for singles and parents. Ministers and others can see brethren being tempted and falling, and address sin issues before they become monstrously difficult. Taking advantage of opportunities to serve means having hands that are busy doing good works, which is a basic curative to temptation, and necessary for all saints, single or otherwise, to live out their callings and be spiritually healthy. As the apostle Paul noted, "For we are his workmanship, created in Christ Jesus for good works, which God prepared beforehand, that we should walk in them" (Eph 2:10). Most importantly, God himself ministers to us directly in the prayers and worship of his people.

FOSTERING STRONG MARRIAGES

In chapter 4, I discussed the overwhelming social-science research on the effects of separating children from homes headed by married biological or adoptive parents. This included higher incidence of marital disruption, conduct disorders, and sexual promiscuity. One group of researchers flatly asserted, "Children raised without a biological father in the household have earlier average ages of first sexual intercourse than children raised in father-present households."[100] James Q. Wilson points out that "Children in one-parent families are twice as likely as those in two-parent ones to have an out-of-wedlock birth."[101] This relationship holds in all income groups.[102] Waite and Gallagher connect the last two points when they point out that, "One reason children in single-parent families are at

---

99. 125.

100. Mendle et al., "Associations Between Father Absence and Age of First Sexual Intercourse," 1463.

101. Wilson, *The Marriage Problem*, 7.

102. Ibid.

great risk for out-of-wedlock births is that they start having sex at much earlier ages."[103] For example, one study found that girls who were not living with both married biological parents were between about 2 to 2.6 times more likely to start having sex between the ages of twelve and fourteen.[104]

Using the last two cycles of the NSFG analysis, I looked again at the percentage of fifteen- to seventeen-year-olds who had been involved in heterosexual vaginal, oral, or anal sex. Among males who had always lived with both of their biological or adoptive parents, the percentage was 40 percent, versus 76 percent for those who had not. For females, the percentages were 30 percent versus 59 percent. For both genders, not living with their parents almost *doubled* the incidence. In the GSS for 2000 to 2016, single male eighteen- to twenty-two-year-olds who were living with both parents at age sixteen were almost two times more likely to be sexually abstinent in the past five years and 36 percent *less* likely to have had three or more sex partners. Females who lived with both parents at age sixteen were 2.2 times more likely to abstain in the past five years, and 37 percent less likely to have had three or more sex partners.

The fact is, in family life, what happens upstream shapes what happens downstream. We can add to the benefits of encouraging people to delay childbearing until marriage—and to build strong, permanent marriages—that this will radically lessen the risk of sexual promiscuity and its consequences in the youths raised in those milieus. I am old enough to see these consequences work out across generations many times.

Parents, your children need you to demonstrate to them what it means to be faithful and sacrificial spouses committed in adversity. Singles, you need to see how sinful choices you make now can have ramifications for your children and even their children down the line. The solution to the fallout of illicit sex is not condoms or abortion but reserving sex until you are in a strong marriage and your children can be born under its protection.

What about those single-parent or blended families created by divorce and out-of-wedlock births we have now and that we will continue to have? Although many wonderful exceptions occur, the task of premarital sexual purity is often going to be harder, as the statistics show. However, God is

---

103. Waite and Gallagher, *The Case for Marriage*, 137.
104. Ibid.

a gracious God, and where the parents and singles are willing to humbly commit themselves to biblical order, where there has been sin openly repent, and draw on willing and qualified fellow believers to help them, a great deal of good can happen. The parents must work together to emphasize and model faithful marriage and chastity to the children, as the apostle Paul said, "forgetting what lies behind and straining forward to what lies ahead" (Phil 3:13b). We must start, wherever we are, with teaching and modeling a radical commitment to God's design for sex and marriage, and parents and singles in these situations must be doubly conscientious in applying means for avoiding sexual sins such as we are looking at here.

HEALTHY AND HONEST "SEX EDUCATION"

We have already seen that most "sex education" that young people get today comes from peers, porn, media of all forms that reflect a damaged and wayward culture, and morally questionable formal instruction. Dangerous myths abound, such as those we have confronted here about condoms, oral sex, STDs, and the seven sexual misperceptions that Regnerus and Uecker have identified. It is important to learn what is honest and godly while confronting and minimizing the influence of what is false and destructive. We also must draw out others and honestly reflect ourselves to discover and confront lies we have embraced.

Parents and singles need to short-circuit all of these deceptive influences and beliefs in several ways. First is to talk about sex at relatively young ages, using solid and God-honoring materials, and being unafraid to talk frankly and openly about the kinds of facts and myths we have covered here. It is worth doing some research to find useful, age-appropriate resources as well. Eventually, young singles need to learn the facts about condoms, pregnancy, and STDs. These subjects lend themselves to honest reflection about God's world and the folly of attempting to use technology to defy his loving limitations. Singles need to clearly see sex as good, but only in marriage, and why and how this is so. My wife and I found *Passport to Purity* materials by Dennis and Barbara Rainey to be very helpful, but there are others.

Where sex education is a subject at school, especially in the public system, parents need to find out what educators are teaching or doing there, and both youth and their parents need to talk about it together honestly. Sometimes, this may result in removing a student from the class or a school. There are sex education materials and teachers out there that no Christian young person should be required to "follow," much like the instructions in *Teen Vogue* about how to have pleasurable anal sex discussed earlier. Often, however, the best way to deal with it is for parents and their children to go over lessons together in light of the facts and God's word. Nothing taught in schools should be off-limits to parents and a private matter between teachers and students, and this is especially true of sexual education.

Next is to seize control of negative cultural influences in film, music, the internet, and more while encouraging engagement with more positive media. This means filtering, monitoring, and limiting exposure to the internet and other media, while asking and being willing to answer tough, penetrating questions, and communicating honestly. To work, without minimizing standards, honesty must be safe for both parties, and everyone must be humble enough to accept the need for accountability and oversight in navigating a world of seductive temptation and lies. Again, there are many good resources, including filtering and monitoring software and devices that can be useful, though none is a panacea, and nothing can replace face-to-face involvement.

Finally, parents need to be willing to discover things about their children that they do not want to know but must if they are going to help them. It means asking tough questions, checking computer histories, knowing what is in the drawers and closets. Within reason, unless they are adults now on their own, this is part of parenting. There are often signs when children are hiding things, normally involving sudden changes in behavior including becoming guarded or hostile overall or in certain types of situations. It may be nothing, but it is important to find out. What you do not know *can* hurt you and, most importantly, keep you from helping *them*.

EARLY DATING

The overwhelming majority of adolescents who become sexually active have sex for the first time with someone they are dating. This is especially true for females, and the most concerning is having a steady, not occasional, dating partner. In the *NSFG* among sexually active fifteen- to nineteen-year-olds in the last two cycles, 50 percent of males and 72 percent of females had their first sex in a steady dating relationship; 14 percent of males and 8 percent of females did so with someone they had dated once in a while. Meanwhile, almost half of eighth-graders have already begun dating.[105] Immaturity coupled with heightened opportunity and temptation to have sex is a bad combination.

Thus, it is not surprising that earlier dating is associated with early sex. The National Survey of Children (NSC) followed almost 1,250 children from 1976 into 1987. Analyzing this data, I found that among those who started dating by age fourteen, 56 percent of males and 36 percent of females had sex before or by age fifteen, and only 15 percent of males and 32 percent of females waited until they were eighteen or older. Meanwhile, among those who did not start dating until age seventeen, only 7 percent of males and 6 percent of females had sex by age fifteen, while 63 percent of males and 60 percent of females did not have sex until age eighteen or later. More disturbingly, 18 percent of females who started dating by age fourteen were forcibly raped. This was more than double the rest of the girls combined. More recently, another study analyzed surveys of over 2,500 students, from 1997 through 2000, who had been virgins in the seventh grade and found that steady dating in the seventh grade, especially with someone older, significantly increased the likelihood of having sex by the ninth grade.[106]

In the next chapter, we will look at modern dating in more detail. Here, however, it is enough to make the common-sense observation that encouraging or tolerating romantic involvement between younger youths especially invites disaster.

UNNECESSARILY DELAYING MARRIAGE

Finally, as I covered in detail in the last chapter, couples who are ready for marriage and have found the right partner should not then delay, often for years, while they assemble the perfect educational, career, and financial situation. Good marriages, and sexual faithfulness, are vastly more important than lavish weddings or ranch homes in desirable suburbs. This is not a call for those who are immature to rush into ill-advised unions, but rather for those who are mature enough not to presumptuously extend romance

---

105. Wildsmith et al., "Dating and Sexual Relationships," 1–2.
106. Marin et al., "Boyfriends, Girlfriends and Teenagers' Risk of Sexual Involvement."

outside marriage for years, either expecting to remain chaste despite that or not caring if they do. Godly marriage is an excellent platform upon which to build a life of productive and successful service to God. It does not need a platform of material success, beyond the basic ability to earn a living, to rest upon itself.

The perils of sex outside marriage are many and the technical solutions of the modern world cannot and have not eliminated them, nor will they change the righteous demands of a loving God. Why would we, as professed believers, want to begin marriage with disobedience rather than faithfulness to his sexual design? Where we have succeeded, let us "take heed lest [we] fall" (1 Cor 10:12); where we have stumbled let us forsake our own ways and turn to God, who "will abundantly pardon" (Isa 55:7). God wants to forgive and strengthen us. He blesses the marriage bed of his saints in ways that those having sex outside of this covenant can never know. Those who wait actually have nothing to lose, and everything to gain.

CHAPTER 8

CONFRONTING THE DATING CULTURE

And now, my sweet Love, let me a while solace myself in the remembrance of our love, of which this spring time of our acquaintance can put forth as yet no more but the leaves and blossoms, while the fruit lies wrapped up in the tender bud of hope; a little more patience will disclose this good fruit, and bring it to some maturity. Let it be our care and labor to preserve these hopeful buds from the beasts of the field, and from frosts and other injuries of the air, lest our fruit fall off ere it be ripe, or lose ought in the beauty and pleasantness of it. Let us pluck up such nettles and thorns as would defraud our plants of their due nourishment, let us prune off superfluous branches; let us not stick at some labor in watering and manuring them— the plenty and goodness of our fruit shall recompense us abundantly. Our trees are planted in a fruitful soil; the ground and pattern of our love is no other but that between Christ and his dear spouse, of whom she speaks as she finds him, "My well-beloved is mine and I am his."

John Winthrop, letter to Margaret Tyndal[1]

The starting point for most of our marriage relationships, the modern recreational dating system, can be safely considered as bankrupt.

Douglas Wilson[2]

A bout thirty years ago—when I was a young, brand-new Christian college instructor—I was asked a serious, honest question by a male student whom I knew well. He had a steady girlfriend with whom he was

---

1. *Some Old Puritan Love-letters: John and Margaret Winthrop, 1618–1638*, 32–33. I modernized some spelling and sentence structure.
2. Wilson, *Her Hand in Marriage*, 7.

trying to maintain a "godly" dating relationship. This meant exclusivity, holding hands, kissing, other physical contact and romance, but hopefully nothing more sexual than that. He had repeatedly expressed his amorous (not just platonic) love for her as she did for him and was enjoying the relationship as long as it lasted. However, he was certain that she was not the woman he was going to marry. Whether she thought *he* was "the one" was unclear. This was only *recreational* romantic intimacy, without lasting commitment, which he knew would break up like his previous steady dating relationships. In his world, even among evangelicals, Christian singles routinely had boyfriends and girlfriends like this, often from their early teens, without any long-term intentions or plans. In my Marriage and Family class I had questioned the wisdom or morality of this type of "recreational dating," and he wanted to talk to me about it further, troubled a bit by the suspicion that what he was doing was wrong for him, unfair to her, a bit dishonest, and otherwise out of harmony with biblical teaching.

For at least a couple of decades now, serious Christians have been questioning modern dating practices and, as we shall see, for good reasons. They are not the only ones who are discontent with the increasingly sterile palette of choices available to single men and women seeking to form romantic attachments. Many young people more interested in marriage than in endless series of "relationships" are thinking that perhaps, as Amy and Leon Kass asserted, "Anyone interested in improving relations between men and women today and tomorrow must proceed by taking a page from yesterday."[3] Often, this means rejecting "dating" in favor of "courtship."[4] This latter term calls to mind the classic idea of a man "courting" the woman he hopes to marry, emphasizing traditional sex roles, purity, parental oversight, and the like. To the extent that people are considering traditional courtship practices because they find it tiresome and destructive to form amorous bonds with a series of people they are not likely to marry, that is wonderful. We ought to reject romance disconnected from the pursuit of marriage. Seeking suitable spouses as men like Fitzwilliam Darcy, Colonel Brandon, and John Knightley did in Jane Austen's novels, or as Gilbert Blythe wooed Anne Shirley in Lucy Maud Montgomery's *Anne*

---

3. "Proposing Courtship," 32.
4. Ibid.

of Green Gables, is infinitely preferable to chasing after significant others by mimicking singles from television sitcoms like *Friends*, *The Big Bang Theory*, or *New Girl*.

On the other hand, it is too easy to be concerned more with labels than substance. The origins of the term "courtship" were in medieval "courtly" romance that was typically adulterous.[5] Meanwhile, a great deal of what people have called "dating" since the term first emerged among the working class in the 1890s has been perfectly fine, despite anxieties many people had about the practice in the early years.[6] It mainly meant a male and female going out together in public, at the invitation of the boy, with him paying for whatever it was they were going to do together.[7] People acted morally or badly, wisely or foolishly, on "dates." As Douglas Wilson observes, with a little humor, "Some couples who 'date' are in closer conformity with biblical principles than other couples who embrace the 'courtship' model. . . . If a courting couple goes on a *date*, we should not all panic and relegate this horror to the same category as nation rising up against nation."[8]

In this chapter, we will look, first, at the emergence and development of modern recreational dating. Next, we will consider problems associated with modern recreational dating practices, in light of biblical morals and teachings on marriage. Finally, we will consider some better practices rooted in sound biblical principles and common sense, guided by an understanding that the end goal is forming godly marriages.

THE EMERGENCE OF RECREATIONAL DATING

Among the Puritans, as we have seen, there was no "dating" as we know it. Unmarried men sought out wives, considering such things as godliness and good reputation, practical considerations including someone well suited, equal in essentials, with whom they could share life happily as lovers, partners, and friends. The ideal was developing affection guided and controlled by reason. With some exceptions such as widows, women went from the care of their fathers to that of their husbands. Said Edmund Morgan, "Marriage . . . resulted not from falling in love, but from a decision to enter

---

5. Wilson, *Her Hand in Marriage*, 15–16.

6. Coontz, *Marriage, a History*, 199–200.

7. Ibid., 200.

8. Wilson, *Her Hand in Marriage*, 16.

a married state, followed by the choice of a suitable person."[9] Except for older people, parents were typically involved, and parental consent was normally required for first marriages.[10] However, Puritans also strongly objected to parents forcing their children to marry someone they did not want.[11] Theirs were *not* "arranged" marriages.

Following this and prior to the actual wedding, the couple typically developed their emotional attachment for one another. This did not lead to a "dry form of love," Morgan pointed out, but, "The love which proceeded from Christian charity, conceived in reason and conscious of God's sacred order, was warm and tender and gracious."[12] The letter from John Winthrop to his betrothed, with which we opened this chapter, is a vibrant example of the kind of love that Morgan described.[13] The Puritans were not alone in wanting to see emotional attachment develop in couples headed toward matrimony; for example, Quakers also sought this.[14] People developed courtship practices designed to nurture these intimate bonds between the future husband and wife. The desire to give couples time alone together despite limited indoor space and cold weather sometimes went as far as "bundling," where couples would spend the night in bed together, typically fully clothed and often with a board or other material separating them.[15]

Patterns of courtship and mate selection such as this, scripted by society and closely supervised by parents and other elders, were dominant through the nineteenth century.[16] Most people lived in small farming communities. Older people created numerous opportunities for young unmarried people to get to know each other, in dances, church picnics, work parties, and the like.[17] As society became more industrialized, more people lived in cities and worked away from the home. Here, at least among the middle or upper class, interaction between single men and women became

9. Morgan, *The Puritan Family*, 59.

10. Ibid., 57.

11. Ibid., 83–84.

12. Ibid., 60.

13. Morgan also cited Winthrop as an example. See ibid. See also Ryken, *Worldly Saints*, 50–51.

14. Starbuck and Lundy, *Families in Context*, 226.

15. Ibid., 68, 72, 226.

16. Ibid., 226; see also Cherlin, *Public and Private Families*, 184.

17. See Shorter, *The Making of the Modern Family*, 120–48 on European practices; in America there were many similar practices and parallels.

more formalized, and was still heavily regulated by parents and elders.[18] For the most part, young men visited women they were interested in, in their homes, sometimes at the invitation of girls' mothers. Single men and women only "went out" together in groups.[19]

When modern dating first emerged among the urban working class at the end of the nineteenth century,[20] it made sense in light of certain facts about their lives in the new industrial America, as compared to small-town and farm life. Homes were often crowded and lacked private places for young people to meet, and it was harder for parents and elders to supervise their children.[21] Interestingly, for all the appearance of "liberation" in this, women and their parents actually had less control and now the male suitors played a much bigger leadership role.[22]

By the 1920s the broader middle classes had embraced dating as well.[23] With young people in schools longer, the rise of the teenage years as a distinct stage of life receiving a lot of attention,[24] and more mingling of the sexes in workplaces away from home, the mold was set.[25] The "peer group" was now in charge of dating, and set the rules, with parents and other older people playing diminishing roles.[26] By the mid-twentieth century, most dating had little to do with finding and securing a marriage partner.[27] It was now a youthful recreational activity, and even a vehicle for interpersonal competition and increasing one's status.[28] Falling in love, going steady, breaking up, and then starting the cycle with a new partner became a new "normal" for youth. Most individuals now went through this several times before engagement.[29] By 1960, the vast majority of school kids had started dating by the ninth grade.[30] It is interesting that we now completely take

---

18. Starbuck and Lundy, *Families in Context*, 226.
19. Ibid.; Cherlin, *Public and Private Families*, 184.
20. Coontz, *Marriage, a History*, 199.
21. Starbuck and Lundy, *Families in Context*, 226; Cherlin, *Public and Private Families*, 184.
22. Cherlin, *Public and Private Families*, 185; Coontz, *Marriage, a History*, 199–200.
23. Starbuck and Lundy, *Families in Context*, 227; Coontz, *Marriage, a History*, 199.
24. Cherlin, *Public and Private Families*, 185.
25. Starbuck and Lundy, *Families in Context*, 227.
26. Cherlin, *Public and Private Families*, 185.
27. Ibid.
28. Starbuck and Lundy, *Families in Context*, 227.
29. Ibid.
30. Cherlin, *Public and Private Families*, 185.

dating for granted, despite the fact that it was almost unknown before the early twentieth century. Most people view abstainers from this dating scene who still hold to the older ideals and goals as abnormal, even strange.

Dating as I have described it here continues to be popular. However, in the prolonged adolescence of college and even a bit beyond, it appears that many singles are turning toward practices often called "getting together" and "hooking up."[31] As two researchers noted, hooking up does not mean young singles are having sex more, just that they are increasingly doing so with casual dates, folks they just met, or just friends—that is, with no romantic intentions at all.[32] The new patterns, resting alongside the old dating model, are more spontaneous, less committed or romantic, with reduced emphasis on clear gender roles.[33] Meanwhile, given the late and rising marriage ages discussed in chapter 6, even steady high school dating is increasingly detached from marital aspirations.[34] The fact that cohabitation is now the preferred next step beyond dating further pushes marriage back in time.[35] Moreover, close to a quarter of heterosexual men and women now use the internet to meet partners,[36] and this is likely to grow.

CONCERNS ABOUT DATING
AND ITS OFFSPRING

BIBLICAL QUESTIONS AND ISSUES

The Bible does not prescribe processes for dating, courtship, or whatever we wish to call it. As with so many other areas of life, God's word provides room for many approaches, across cultures and historical periods. We have numerous examples of people connecting and getting married in the Bible, and these shed some light. However, when the Scriptures relay what happened in the past, they do not necessarily direct us to do things exactly the same way in the present, even if the outcome was a good one. The story of how Abraham and his steward brought Isaac and Rebekah together (Gen 24) is lovely, for example, and there are lessons

---

31. Starbuck and Lundy, *Families in Context*, 228.

32. Monto and Carey, "A New Standard of Sexual Behavior? Are Claims Associated With the 'Hookup Culture' Supported by General Social Survey Data?," 605.

33. Starbuck and Lundy, *Families in Context*, 228.

34. Cherlin, *Public and Private Families*, 185.

35. Ibid.

36. Ibid.

we can glean from it. However, it would usually be difficult and probably unwise for twenty-first-century American fathers to find wives for their sons exactly the same way.

However, as we have seen, there are applicable biblical precepts. Older systems of courtship mostly upheld these principles, while many aspects of modern recreational dating systematically and increasingly violate them. I am not speaking of every date and person, of course, but of the larger framework of contemporary dating, and now for some hooking up, characterized by a series of partners, many of them steady, extending from early teens well into adulthood, most of which is disconnected from marriage.

Wise Counsel and Supervision from Parents and Elders

I opened chapter 6 by focusing clearly on what the Scriptures teach about counsel, the value of experience, parental guidance and authority, and more. Biblically, those who operate outside this protection are foolish and suffer for it. We do not need to repeat these Scriptures and arguments here. The point is that anyone involved in the godly pursuit of a spouse, as with any critically important decision, should seek guidance from the wise. For younger people especially, this normally means parents (Prov 1:8–9; 23:22, 25). The normal biblical pattern is for parents or guardians to have a strong and direct role in the marriage decisions of their children (cf. Gen 24:2–4; 28:1–2; Deut 7:3; Jer 29:6), guided by godly wisdom and love. Requiring the willing consent of both the bride and groom is critical and is an important part of the Christian understanding of valid marriage, as I touched on in chapter 1.[37] We see a beautiful example of this balance—loving parental guidance and the consent of the partners to be married—in the record of the marriage of Rebekah and Isaac that we just mentioned.

Meanwhile, as we touched on earlier, one of the most fundamental features of modern dating as a whole is the replacement of oversight and boundary setting by parents and elders, with ever-changing informal rules set by peers and reduced parental monitoring. Andrew Cherlin summarizes this well: "Dating . . . shifted power from parents to teenagers and

---

37. Stipulated in both the Anglican and Presbyterian traditions. See *Westminster Confession*, 80, chapter 24:3 and the public profession of consent for both bride and groom in the Book of Common Prayer, 313.

young adults. The movement of activity away from public gatherings and the home made it much harder for parents to influence the process. Rather, adolescents became oriented toward the dating system of their peer group—the other adolescents in the local school or neighborhood. With the triumph of dating, courtship moved from a parent- and other-adult-run system to a peer-run system where the participants made the rules and punished the offenders."[38]

When King Rehoboam rejected the good counsel of his father's elderly advisers in favor of the rash and uninformed opinions of his age peers in 1 Kings 12:6–14, the result was not good. Similarly, in the modern dating world, we find sixteen-year-olds listening to the collective wisdom of peers in making critical emotional and sexual decisions, apart from and even hidden from their parents. They will also often experience the consequences of this folly. The point is *not* that peers do not ever give good advice or even accountability—if a young person has godly friends, their counsel can be quite helpful and they will also be willing to give timely admonitions and rebukes if need be. It is that peers should not *replace* parents and other elders.

Finally, the Scriptures do not simply teach children to submit to the authority and wisdom of their parents but require parents to *take* this kind of responsibility for their offspring. Indeed, God has made this one of the gravest, most important responsibilities adults with children have (Deut 4:9; 11:19; Ps 78:5–6; Prov 1:8–9; 13:24; 19:18; 1 Tim 3:4; 5:8; Heb 12:7). The Lord requires fathers to bring their children "up in the discipline and instruction of the Lord" (Eph 6:4b), to manage their households well while keeping their children submissive (1 Tim 3:4). Women are to love their children well (Titus 2:4), which includes imparting to them godly teaching (Prov 1:8). Again, many parents who allow their children to "date" do so while admirably fulfilling their high callings as mothers and fathers. However, much if not most of what modern recreational dating involves cannot be reconciled with wise parenting. For example, it is hard for me to see how parents concerned with the purity and Christian maturation of their children in godliness can embrace their ninth-grade children entering into exclusive, amorous, private, intimate dating relationships. Yet I see it

---

38. Cherlin, *Public and Private Families*, 185.

all the time, and in families in which the parents have the best intentions and seem to want to steward their children for God.

There are exceptions to parents having a significant role in guiding and monitoring young singles' relationships. The parents may be deceased or otherwise separated from the person, or the parents themselves may be unwise, ungodly, or unloving. They may not wish to be involved. In sad situations such as these, a committed Christian single ought to seek out the advice and accountability of loving and wise older saints, and still not depend solely on peers. The overarching lesson here is that those who want to make important decisions wisely must place their actions and plans before the wise.

Meaningless and Even Dishonest Vows

The Bible is full of strong warnings about making false or rash vows and promises (Num 30:2; Prov 19:5; 25:14; Matt 5:37; Jas 5:12). Yet while casual dating is perhaps not so prone to this, most *steady* romantic relationships involve confessions and even exchanging physical symbols of committed love, which one or both parties violate when the relationship breaks up. Too often, singles make vows—sometimes seriously, but often casually, rashly, even falsely and manipulatively—and then abandon them. A lot of what goes on in the dating world is false and insincere, and yet in Romans 12:9 the apostle Paul states simply that, "Love must be genuine" (or, "sincere"). When Christians engage in this kind of behavior, what are they saying to the world about the nature of God's honest and committed love? Moreover, having developed the habit of treating vows this casually, how easy will it be, later, for the same people to give appropriate weight to those they make at their weddings?

Romance as Recreation or Worse?

The only biblical examples that show anything remotely similar to recreational romance involve illicit relationships and even prostitution. For the Christian romantic love, often identified as "eros" or "erotic" love, finds its legitimate expression in marriage only. As we have seen repeatedly, God calls the human race to nurture and protect this kind of love within a framework of unreserved covenantal commitment. We are not to be lovers based upon empty promises with no direction to our relationships other than mutual enjoyment or emotion. We are not to embrace emotional intimacy disconnected from covenantal obligations.

Moreover, those we embrace as our lovers are not to be means to any ends but God's ends, including their best and holiest welfare. How can the self-sacrificing love he calls us to be reconciled with developing a romantic relationship for fun or pleasure, then abandoning the person when the good times are no longer there? Even worse is dating someone to enhance one's status and popularity. I want my sons and daughters to know joy, gratification, and pleasure with the one they marry. However, these great feelings and experiences ought to be the products, not foundations, of their marriage. In most marriages dark times will come and feelings will dry up in some seasons. The relationship at points will be more work than fun. How will the modern dating ethos prepare them to weather those inevitable hardships and disappointments, and come out with their marriages intact or even stronger?

Feelings Overrule Practical Considerations

Starbuck and Lundy underscore the degree to which an unrealistic understanding of, and dependence upon, romantic love has replaced "more practical reasons" in the modern practice of going steady as a basis for eventual marriage.[39] The way that Edward Shorter put it is that "a rush of sentiment swept over mating and dating, replacing familiar and prudential considerations with 'inclination,' 'affection,' and finally 'romance'."[40]

Affections are of course a good thing, when they are more than just powerful feelings, and when they are subject to reason and Christian precept. However, biblical love expresses itself primarily not in emotion, but in action. The apostle Paul makes this abundantly clear in 1 Corinthians 13. Love of any sort is mainly about what we choose to do for, or choose not to do to, the ones we love. It sacrifices self, including, when necessary, good feelings. When we reduce affection to romantic feelings, we tend to lose sight of that. Self-centeredness creeps in, we find it hard to be loving and committed in the absence of this emotional stimulation, and we do not have a secure or scriptural foundation for lasting love. Robert Bellah

---

39. Starbuck and Lundy, *Families in Context*, 227.
40. Shorter, *The Making of the Modern Family*, 120.

and his colleagues discuss the challenge this focus on individual gratification and feelings poses to the stability of modern romantic relationships in detail, contrasting it with the ways that evangelicals and other seriously religious people have tended to understand love.[41] The classic Gordon Lightfoot song *If You Could Read My Mind* captures well the feeling-centered nature of modern romantic attachment. Explaining how he knows that the marriage with his first wife is over, he sings, "I don't know where we went wrong, but the feeling's gone, and I just can't get it back."

Moreover, any Christian grounded in biblical teaching about human nature needs to approach feelings, emotions, and advice to simply "follow our hearts," with a great deal of suspicion. After all, as Jeremiah pointedly informs us, "The heart is deceitful above all things, and desperately sick; who can understand it?" (17:9). Jesus, reflecting a claim made in the book of Genesis (6:5), said this, "For from within, out of the heart of man, come evil thoughts, sexual immorality, theft, murder, adultery, coveting, wickedness, deceit, sensuality, envy, slander, pride, foolishness" (Mark 7:21–22). A redeemed heart, dedicated toward God, repentant, and guarded, is a marvelous thing, and the affectionate thoughts and feelings generated within it can be a wonderful part of the love between a man and a woman. However, in themselves (separated from biblical principles, reason, wise counsel, and caution), heart feelings are not a reliable guide or foundation for a godly, lasting marriage, nor are they trustworthy in informing us of how to act with and toward the object of our affections.

Flirting with Sexual Temptation

The apostle Paul told both the Corinthian church and his co-laborer Timothy what to do with "sexual immorality" and "youthful passions" (or, "lusts"). They were to *flee* from them (1 Cor 6:18; 2 Tim 2:22). The Christian, deeply appreciative of both the seriousness of this sin and his or her susceptibility to fall sexually, is to literally bolt away from sexual temptation.

However, most of what now occurs within the modern dating system goes completely contrary to Paul's loving command here. Willfully and repeatedly placing oneself in intimate, private affectionate contact with someone whom one is deeply attracted to is not a wise pathway to holiness.

---

41. Bellah et al., *Habits of the Heart*, 108–10.

This is especially the case when one is immature, inexperienced, perhaps years away from marriage in a relationship that is completely disconnected from it. To believe otherwise is to be hopelessly naive or blindly arrogant. Yet many Christian parents and elders who really do care about young singles allow and even encourage privacy and intimacy while simultaneously asking young singles to "just say no." This is unrealistic and the results should not surprise us. Group dating, chaperoned events, and the like do not create these kinds of sexual pressures and temptations. Private, often steady, recreational dating does.

CONCRETE OUTCOMES

The modern system of private, recreational, serial, and steady dating is associated with negative outcomes that match the biblical concerns raised above. That should not surprise us, since God's framework for mate selection, handling temptation, making critical life decisions, and the ultimate nature and purposes of marriage, fits the way he designed humans to function individually and corporately. It is interesting that secular and even progressive social scientists continue to demonstrate these connections. The difference between the latter and thoughtful conservative evangelical observers is not so much in noting what these practical consequences are, as in judging whether the latter are actually harmful or not.

The onset and spread of modern recreational dating practices have accompanied skyrocketing divorce rates. Given what we know, some of this association is almost certainly more than accidental. There is much about common dating practices that appears to, directly or indirectly, undermine marital quality and permanence.[42]

Premarital Sexual Promiscuity

In chapter 7 we looked in detail at the relationship between early recreational, private dating—particularly steady relationships—and early onset of premarital sex. There is no need to reexamine that here, except to also remind the reader that girls who begin dating too young are also at dramatically higher risk of being victims of forcible rape. For example, the NSC survey discussed in chapter 7 shows that almost one in five girls who

---

42. Cf. Stanley and Rhoades's popularly written overview of some relevant research literature, "The Perils of Sowing Wild Oats."

started dating by or before age fourteen reported a male forcibly raped them. This was double or higher than any group of females who started dating when older, and true among both whites and African-Americans.

Social historians have directly tied the rise in modern recreational dating to dramatic and almost immediate increases in premarital sexual activity. As Starbuck and Lundy dryly observed regarding changes in the first few decades of the twentieth century, "The dating process allowed more opportunity for sexual experimentation."[43] Research in the late 1930s showed that the percentage of women who had sexual intercourse prior to marriage literally *tripled* from women born before 1890 to women born after 1910.[44] Among the latter group, by about 1940, about 70 percent had sex before marriage.[45] Things have advanced, and as we have seen, premarital sex is now almost universal. Parents and elders used to expect that most young people with steady dating partners would not go beyond "petting," but most quietly abandoned even that modest goal decades ago.[46]

The modern dating system has not only brought us more singles having sex, but with more partners. As we pointed out in chapter 2, well into the 1950s people who had sex before marriage did so with the person they ended up married to. That is no longer remotely true. For example, in the last two cycles of the NSFG, among those twenty-three to thirty-two years old in their first marriages, almost two-thirds of women, and almost three-quarters of men, had more sex partners than just their spouse. In fact, 41 percent of females and 53 percent of males had three or more sex partners *other than* their spouse.

That is a lot of sexual baggage. As Regenerus and Uecker have pointed out, there are a range of emotional difficulties tied to sexual activity for women and most of all for those cycling through numerous relationships.[47] This is true even if premarital sex does not bring on the obvious, terrible effects of STDs, unplanned pregnancy, or abortion.

All of this sex outside wedlock is also associated with much higher risk of divorce when people do get married. There is a long line of research

---

43. Starbuck and Lundy, *Families in Context*, 227.
44. Ibid.
45. Ibid.
46. Cherlin, *Public and Private Families*, 185.
47. Regnerus and Uecker, *Premarital Sex in America*, 135–68.

that supports the idea that premarital sex generally, and especially having multiple sex partners prior to marriage, is associated with higher risk of marital dissolution and even greater likelihood of committing adultery.[48] In research on the most recent NSFG, Nicholas Wolfinger found that those who have sex before marriage, and especially those who have had multiple sex partners, are more likely to get divorced.[49] He notes that as of the year 2000 and later, compared to women who married as virgins, the chance of divorce after five years of marriage increased about *fourfold* even for women who only had sex with their spouse before marriage.[50] Those who had one *other* partner in addition to their husband were almost *six times* more likely than those who abstained from sex before marriage to get divorced in that time frame.[51] The highest divorce rates were for those who had ten or more sex partners before marriage.[52] Typical modern dating practices, by encouraging premarital sex and having multiple partners, undermine marriage.

Choosing Spouses as If They Were Recreational Dating Partners

With typically a decade or more of recreational dating prior to marriage, it should come as no surprise that people increasingly pick spouses based on dating aspirations and values rather than looking for the kinds of qualities we discussed in chapters 5 and 6. Given the relative absence of parents and elders as counselors and guides, the strong reliance on peers, and the focus on romantic feelings, this should not surprise us. For example, drawing on an interesting study comparing preferences for romantic partners among adolescents in four countries including the United States,[53] Starbuck and

---

48. Stanton, "Premarital Sex and Greater Divorce Risk." See, for example, Teachman, "Premarital Sex, Premarital Cohabitation, and the Risk of Subsequent Marital Dissolution Among Women." Teachman found that multiple partners are the main problem. He did not find that women who had only had sex with their husbands before marriage had heightened risk of divorce. See also Rhoades and Stanley, *Before "I Do": What Do Premarital Experiences Have To Do With Marital Quality Among Today's Young Adults?*, 6, 8–9.

49. Wolfinger, "Counterintuitive Trends in the Link Between Premarital Sex and Marital Stability."

50. Ibid.

51. Ibid.

52. Ibid. Interestingly, those who had three to nine sex partners were less likely to get divorced than those who had two before marriage, though again virgins were *much* more likely to stay married. Explanations for this are tentative and go beyond what we need to deal with here.

53. Gibbons et al., "Adolescent's Opposite-Sex Ideal in Four Countries."

Lundy pointed out that American teens looked for "being fun, being sexy, and having money" rather than qualities those from more traditional societies favored, such as "liking children and being a good parent."[54] They go on to warn, "Americans . . . are likely to carry their adolescent perceptions of the ideal opposite-sex person well into adulthood. These ideals might not be the best criteria for selecting a lifelong partner."[55] Not only are obvious practical considerations being downplayed, but qualities specifically tied to the time-honored goals of marriage—practical support, sexual honor, the desire and ability to have children and raise them well—have little to do with modern dating.

Mastering the Art of Breaking Up

When I typed the phrase "how to break up" into the Google search engine a moment ago, I got 313,000,000 hits in less than one second. From the first several pages of links that I was offered, the intent of my query, namely "How do you end a romantic relationship?" was clearly "understood" by Google. I got it all—how to break up with nice people or jerks, how to "dump someone," how to do it kindly, and so on. One professional counseling site even offered an easy, sure-fire three-step method. Another focused on helping teenagers break up. Of course, if having a series of steady romantic partners for a decade or more is now the norm, becoming skilled at handling relationship breakdown, and even getting used to it, is a necessary survival adaptation. As I write, there are probably millions of Americans using the internet to think through how to drop some lover from their lives. On the other hand, there will be many whose lives are about to be turned upside down and do not know it yet.

This prompts the question—could all this learning, practice, and acceptance of breaking up make it easier to contemplate the same kind of ending for our marriages as well? Has having numerous steady lovers before marriage gotten people used to walking away from their romantic relationships, often for trivial reasons, making it easier to take this "get out when things are not great anymore" mentality into wedlock? As Rhoades and Stanley point out, "A history of multiple breakups may make people take a more jaundiced view of love and relationships."[56]

---

54. Starbuck and Lundy, *Families in Context*, 230.

55. Ibid.

56. Rhoades and Stanley, *Before "I Do,"* 8.

We do know that there is an emotional and psychological cost to all this. It complicates life for young people when they need to be focusing on gaining education and skills or simply enjoying youth, and may lead to even worse. In adolescents, romantic involvement and especially breaking up has been linked to depression,[57] separation from old friends, loss of social standing, jealousy, and interpersonal conflicts.[58] Young males often react to "being dumped" with retaliation, up to at times committing acts of violence.[59] No one reading this who has ever had someone they love end a powerful romantic relationship can deny the level of hurt and disruption this can bring. Should sixteen- or seventeen-year-olds facing finals and trying to improve their grades to get into good colleges really be dealing with that, often with little input and support from parents?

POSITIVE SOLUTIONS FOR DATING MADNESS

Unshackled from pressure to thoughtlessly accept or reject any practices associated with either modern dating or older-style courtship, let us consider some "dos and don'ts." These will make use of common sense and factual evidence within a biblical framework.

WHAT WE SHOULD NOT DO

First, allowing young people to engage in private, intimate dating at an early age is almost criminally irresponsible. This is especially true of allowing young girls to go out with older boys. A young man and woman going together to a chaperoned and supervised event such as a dance or church picnic can be fine. However, children and parents should avoid even these if the end is likely to be the formation of a romantic attachment between two people so young as to be many years from marriage, particularly if either would not be suitable as a spouse for reasons beyond current age and maturity level.

Second, relaxing our guard because an event is "Christian" or church-related is unwise. Without the proper safeguards in place—particularly wise rules applied by trustworthy adults who are playing a direct, hands-on

---

57. Szwedo et al., "Adolescent Romance and Depressive Symptoms: The Moderating Effects of Positive Coping and Perceived Friendship Competence."

58. Pickhardt, "Adolescent Breakups."

59. Ibid.

role—a lot of mischief can happen in such settings. In fact, it is often precisely because we tend to assume they are safe that teens often use these to mask other, less benign, purposes. What I, and others, have heard in bathrooms and locker rooms from professed Christian singles who were unaware of our presence about what they are doing or hope to do with their dating partners, and how they view them, has at times been deeply disappointing.

The same rules apply to blindly trusting that because parents will be in charge of some gathering, for example in a home, others letting their children go do not need to be cautious. Nothing is further from the truth. Whether because of negligence, naivety, or even parents who allow their children to engage in things like substance abuse and casual sex, many mothers and fathers have found out the hard way that other parents— even professed believers—cannot necessarily be trusted. In her undercover foray into the lives of middle and high school students from 1992 to 1995, journalist Patricia Hersch witnessed this repeatedly.[60] As a high school student over forty-five years ago, I was aware of "cool parents" who accepted or remained negligently unaware of teens doing things in their homes that would have horrified most adults. Whether or not parents are "in charge," the Russian proverb "Trust, but verify" applies.

Third, young people should be discouraged from exclusive, steady dating relationships with anyone they are not actively considering becoming engaged to. To do otherwise is to invite strings of sexual relationships and broken hearts. This means helping them understand that romantic feelings are not the ultimate basis for lasting unions. Those emotions can and ought to be subject to reason and wisdom, nor are they a sufficient guide to choosing a lover. It is important that young people learn that it is possible for a romantically interested male and female to develop a relationship beyond simple friendship without becoming completely committed romantically. In this context, if the relationship does not work out, there is no need to feel as if they failed, or to have to go through an emotional breakup. Rather, the two people have found out that they were not the right choice for each other without being devastated. They can now try again, with someone else, without all the unhealthy sexual and emotional baggage from past relationships, as we see too often.

---

60. *A Tribe Apart*, 147–48, 173.

Fourth, "missionary dating" ought to be completely off limits. This is dating an unbeliever in hopes of drawing him or her toward the faith. Given strong scriptural grounds to marry "only in the Lord" (1 Cor 7:39b) that I discussed at length in chapter 5, there is no warrant for this. We ought to reach out to the unbelieving world as Christians and as friends, but not as regular dating partners. If romance becomes almost unavoidable in relationships between believer and unbeliever, the Christian ought to pull back, focus more on getting the other person to church, into relationships with other saints, and so on.

Next, couples ought to avoid any situation that heightens sexual temptation or allows a couple to hide inappropriate sexual intimacy. A dance or public theater followed by coffee and conversation might be a lot less problematic, for example, than going swimming together at night in a private lake. Most of this is a matter of sober self-reflection and common sense.

WHAT WE SHOULD DO

First, it is critical that pastors, elders, and parents encourage couples who are romantically interested in one another to become or remain fully integrated into the life of the church. They ought to be attending church together as regularly as possible, be involved in healthy activities with Christian peers, and study the Scriptures together as a couple or in larger groups. This does not preclude lots of "normal" recreational activities or opportunities for intimate, private communication upon which to build their relationships. However, if God is going to be the center of their lives when and if they marry, his people ought to be important to them even in their period of dating or courtship.

These are great opportunities not only to judge, but also to build, Christian character. Sociologists often talk about religion having its greatest impact when lived out within "moral communities" in which group practice and religion help to shape action and belief more profoundly. This seems particularly true in an area like dating and dealing with sexual temptation,[61] in which Christian teaching and aspirations are so countercultural in the modern world. It also means that more peers influencing the couple will be religiously committed as well. Then, not only will parents, pastors,

---

61. Cf. Regnerus, *Forbidden Fruit*, 196–98.

and elders shape them, but friendship networks in their church or other Christian ministries and activities will do so as well.[62] Many of those peer relationships will bless them well into their adult life as spouses and parents, as I have had the joy of seeing come true for my married children.

Similarly, couples seeing each other romantically should not be shy about praying together. If Christ is going to be the third party holding their marriage together, should God direct them to wed, prayer is going to be an essential part of that. Now is the best time to develop that habit and to unleash the power that a godly couple has to realize Jesus' teaching that, "where two or three are gathered in my name, there am I among them" (Matt 18:20). Again, this gives both partners a chance to witness the other's character and grow together in the faith.

Next, singles exploring one another as potential mates, or getting more serious than that, should spend time with each other's families. To most of us, this seems natural, but couples often neglect it and parents sometimes fail to encourage it. Potential marriage partners need to get to know those who may become their in-laws. They also need to know how their possible future spouse interacts with his or her parents, siblings, and others in his or her home.

Fourth, parents and elders need to provide a lot of opportunity for singles to get to know one another and identify potential marriage partners in enjoyable group settings. We mentioned earlier that one of the factors driving many Christian women to marry unbelievers is a shortage of mature, single men of faith. Ensuring that young people have opportunity to meet one another is vital. In some situations, this requires creative thinking, for example, in small churches where no available and acceptable marriage opportunities exist for the singles who are there. This is an effective use of our homes—hosting opportunities for young people to get together. I have seen many "matches" flowing out of things as simple as the weekly Sunday night Bible study and fellowship time a former pastor of ours hosted in his home, or an elder and his wife who made their house a popular gathering place for Christian college students.

Fifth, teens and young adults need to be challenged to reject the idea that romantic intimacy and exclusivity can ever be justified as a recreational

---

62. Ibid., 197.

activity separated from marriage, especially as one used for any instrumental, purely personal ends such as status striving or sex. They need to be encouraged to develop or maintain a positive desire for holiness and appreciation of their vulnerability to sexual temptation. With this, we need to teach them the beauty of marriage in God's natural order, and desire to know it, *with* the right person, *as* the right person, *at* the right time. Someone we are courting does not "belong to us" outside of the covenant of marriage. For two people to make demands and depend upon each other almost as if they are a married couple, while they are still youths and not ready for the full demands of marriage, is not liberating, but stifling.

Sixth, as I touched on in the last chapter, we must have the courage to learn about what our young people are really thinking and doing in their relationships with the opposite sex. Most of them have learned the right "Sunday school" answers. We have to dig deeper than that. In her time posing as a modern adolescent among middle and high school kids, Patricia Hersch learned that many lived, as the title of her book stated, as *A Tribe Apart* from the adult world. The degree to which parents and others were ignorant, often willfully, of what was going on in the world of the adolescents she interacted with over several years was often terrible and sad.

Finally, parents and singles alike need to trust their wise and loving God to provide a suitable marriage partner in due time. So often, I see young men and women leaving our Christian college despondent because they have not yet become engaged or married, and they believe their quest for a godly spouse is now about to become even harder. This is especially so for those who saw a relationship they hoped would end in engagement not lead to that result. Yet I and so many others I know found wonderful, believing partners in the midst of secular environments and pursuits, especially in as much as we remained committed members of biblical churches. God is faithful, if marriage is in his plan he will bring it to pass, and it is enough to rest in that.

FINISHING THAT STORY

At the beginning of this chapter, I recounted the story of the student I had as a young professor. Popular Christian books questioning dating were still years in the future, but he was beginning to awaken to some of the same concerns and conflicts between accepted dating practices and the whole biblical picture of marital love and preparation. I am not sure he ever adopted the language of "courtship" to describe the changes he made, and I doubt they were instantaneous or perfect. However, so far as I could see, he did begin the process of being even more jealous of his purity and that of the women in his life, and became more intentional about discovering his calling and finding a partner in life who could be his helpmate, sexual partner, and mother for his children. Many years later, I had the delight of sharing lunch with him, hearing about his excellent and dynamic church and pastoral ministry, and seeing pictures of his wife and children. I doubt he would say he missed much by making the choices he did, and after about a quarter-century of marriage, it seems to have turned out well. God honored his decision to pursue a godly wife, not fun dating partners, and blessed others through that as well.

CHAPTER 9

DOING PREMARITAL
PREPARATION THE RIGHT WAY

If God call you to a married life, expect all these troubles, or most of them; and make particular preparation for each temptation, cross, and duty which you must expect. Think not that you are entering into a state of mere delight, lest it prove but a fool's paradise for you. See that you be furnished with marriage strength and patience, for the duties and sufferings of a married state, before you venture into it. . . . To marry without all this preparation, is as foolish as to go to sea without the necessary preparations for your voyage, or to go to war without armour or ammunition, or to go to work without the tools or strength, or to go to buy meat in the market when you have no money.

Richard Baxter[1]

Preparing well for marriage means asking each other all the hard questions.

David Mathis[2]

Even after a man and woman have decided that they ought to marry one another, and even if they have chosen their intended mate with godly wisdom, they need to prepare carefully for their upcoming marriage. God wants his people to live joyfully with their spouses, their marriages a fount of reliable help and comfort through the challenges of life, not a

---

1. Baxter, *A Christian Directory*, 401.
2. "Editor's Preface," in John Piper, *Preparing for Marriage*, 1.

source of uncertainty, anguish, or pain (Prov 5:18; Eccl 9:9). Choosing one's partner wisely *and* intelligently preparing for marriage to him or her is the most likely path to such a happy outcome. Yes, even if we wisely choose, plan, and prepare, our marriage may still go awry. We live in a fallen world. However, we ought to make every effort to set up our future marriages for success, as doing so will usually lead to better results than proceeding in foolishness or haste.

A godly marital covenant is a deep, solemn, lifelong, demanding commitment to another flawed, sinful human being. This is not easy to get ready for and may even scare us. The Gospel of Matthew informs us that the level of commitment Jesus demanded in marriage even unnerved his earthly disciples (19:10). Yet it is also true that God has designed most human beings to desire and need to be bound to a spouse in this way. We cannot realize the rich rewards most of us hope to gain from matrimony without accepting its obligations. Therefore, our appreciation of what marriage will require from us should not lead us to avoid it, or to try to replace it with some less demanding arrangement. That would be self-defeating. Instead, as the old Anglican matrimonial service admonishes, understanding the nature of this covenant should motivate us to approach marriage "reverently" and "deliberately" rather than "unadvisedly or lightly."[3]

We have already examined many factors and practices that people should consider if they wish to choose marriage partners wisely and be prepared for marriage. We also looked at what they ought to avoid. In this final chapter in our section on mate selection and preparation for marriage, we will look at processes and practices that can be of great value in helping couples who are seriously considering engagement, or who are perhaps already betrothed, make final, practical preparations to embark on their marital journey. If done properly, these can also give them a final opportunity to identify and turn aside from ill-advised marital decisions.

However, before we cover that we must consider a couple of modern problem areas that keep most modern unmarried Americans from preparing for marriage well. The first are the difficulties many singles today have committing to marriage in the first place. This leads them to delay

---

3. Book of Common Prayer, 311.

and avoid it, and to do so in ways that make marital success less attainable. The second is *premarital* cohabitation. When couples connect living together to marriage at all, they often use it as a form of marital preparation or at least think it is a lifestyle choice that might help, and certainly will not hurt them since they are planning to get married anyway. We will confront such popular but erroneous perceptions with the facts.

MODERN OBSTACLES TO WISE MARITAL PREPARATION

FEAR OF COMMITMENT

Some pundits have claimed that, when it comes to marriage, a lot more of today's young singles are "commitment-phobes" than in earlier generations.[4] Many indicators support this claim. In the last chapter, we looked at how often singles today disconnect sexual activity from marriage or any romantic attachment at all. And as we saw in chapter 6, people are also waiting much longer to get married today than has been true in recent decades. Marriage rates have fallen dramatically, even among those twenty-five and older.[5] Only 53 percent of all never-married adults in 2014 say they are sure they want to marry someday; this number had dropped 8 percent from only four years earlier.[6] Another 2014 survey suggested that about 69 percent of unmarried millennials say they want to marry someday.[7] This is better, but hardly a resounding affirmation of matrimony. Projections suggest that by the time today's young adults are in their mid-forties to mid-fifties, 25 percent of them will have never married.[8] In the General Social Survey (GSS), 84 percent of those twenty-five to thirty-four from the years 1972 through 1980 had been married; that figure for 2008 through 2016 was just 50 percent.

Cohabitation is an attempt to get many of the benefits of marriage without making the same level of commitment. As discussed briefly in chapter

---

4. Landau, "Commitment for Millennials: Is It OK, Cupid?"

5. Wang and Parker, "Record Share of Americans Have Never Married."

6. Ibid.

7. Pew Research Center, "Millennials in Adulthood." Roughly, "millennials" became adults in the early twenty-first century, being born from about the early 1980s through the early 2000s.

8. Wang and Parker, "Record Share of Americans Have Never Married."

2, most research suggests that on average, it fails to do so, mainly due to lack of stability, commitment, and definition.[9] Still, it has skyrocketed in the past several decades. The number of such couples between the ages of eighteen and thirty-four rose 24 percent between 2007 and 2016 alone.[10] As of 2017, there were about 7,752,000 opposite-sex cohabiting couples in the United States.[11]

Moreover, referring to cohabitation as "premarital" is often inaccurate. Most people who move in with their lover are not planning to marry each other at all. Looking at the last two cycles of the National Survey of Family Growth (NSFG), of current cohabiters who had never been married, 61 percent of males and 68 percent of females admitted that they had moved in together with no plans to marry. Engaged couples made up 10 percent of those who moved in together, while the rest claimed to have "definite plans" to marry when they commenced cohabiting. Even worse, by the time of the survey 26 percent of males and 15 percent of females who had been engaged to their partner when they moved in together, and 28 percent of males and 24 percent of females who had definite plans to marry at that time, were no longer certain they would marry their partner. Typically, these wafflers now said marriage would "probably" happen. I wonder if their partners knew how they felt.

One group of researchers found that 72 percent of married people who had lived together prior to getting married were not engaged when they began cohabiting.[12] A smaller study asked cohabiting partners to name their most important reason for living together. Over 60 percent said, "I wanted to spend more time with my partner," and 18.5 percent said, "It made the most sense financially."[13] Only 14 percent said it was to test their

---

9. As was mentioned in a note in that discussion, some research claims that an *engaged* couple who cohabit do match the benefits of married couples. As we shall see here, this does not describe most cohabitation, certainly not those we are discussing here as marriage avoidant. We will also see that engaged couples are still better off waiting to live together until after marriage.

10. Stepler, "Number of U.S. Adults Cohabiting With a Partner Continues to Rise, Especially Among Those 50 and Older."

11. US Census Bureau, Table UC3, "Opposite Sex Unmarried Couples By Presence Of Biological Children Under 18, And Age, Earnings, Education, And Race And Hispanic Origin Of Both Partners: 2017," *America's Families and Living Arrangements: 2017.*

12. Rhoades et al., "The Pre-Engagement Cohabitation Effect," 107. Showed 59.5 percent had lived together prior to marriage, 43.1 percent of whom had done so prior to becoming formally engaged.

relationship to determine if they should get married.[14] A 2014 poll by a legal firm found similar trends in the United Kingdom; only one in four couples who moved in together said it was a step toward marriage.[15] Most cohabitation is not *preparation* for marriage. It is substituting for or avoiding it, while enjoying the benefits of a shared domicile and ready sexual access.

The reasons for marital-commitment phobia among many unmarried people today are complex. They include such factors as financial expectations; growing gaps between more highly educated women and less educated men among singles; increasing numbers of young adults who don't see marriage as positive or necessary; and little social pressure for those who want to have sex, children, or live together to marry.[16] Almost 60 percent of millennials describe themselves as "self-absorbed,"[17] something that makes marriage difficult.[18] They also tend to see themselves as having many possible mate choices, which makes it harder to commit to one person.[19]

A huge factor is fear of having a bad marriage or getting divorced. Liz Higgins, a professional premarital counselor writing for the Gottman Institute, made this observation: "Millennials . . . are turned off by the idea of divorce. Some . . . grew up in single-parent homes or juggled the balance of living between divorced parents. The economic, emotional, and relational implications of divorce are enough to make millennials want to find that sense of certainty before walking down the aisle. If that means taking 10 more years to find it, then so be it. . . . I hear from many millennial couples that they want to . . . make sure they 'don't end up like their parents' or 'to make sure we are doing everything we can to avoid divorce later on'."[20] This should not surprise us given the increasing numbers who have seen their parents get divorced. In the *GSS*, among those eighteen to twenty-nine in the years 1972 through 1980, 12 percent had experienced the divorce or separation of their parents by age sixteen. That figure was 2.5 times higher—30 percent—by the years 2008 through 2016. Even those

---

13. Rhoades et al., "Couples' Reasons for Cohabitation," 246.
14. Ibid., 247.
15. Bingham, "Only One in Four Couples Living Together Plan to Marry."
16. Wang and Parker, "Record Share of Americans Have Never Married."
17. Pew Research Center, "Most Millennials Resist the 'Millennial' Label."
18. Higgins, "3 Reasons Millennials Are Waiting to Get Married."
19. Ibid.; Landau, "Commitment for Millennials: Is It OK, Cupid?"
20. Higgins, "3 Reasons Millennials Are Waiting to Get Married."

today whose parents have good and stable marriages have witnessed what happened to peers whose parents did not. Moreover, with divorce rising among those over the age of fifty, many singles in their 20s and 30s are just now witnessing the collapse of their parents' marriages.[21] I recently knew a young man quite well whose parents decided to divorce during his engagement. That kind of thing is becoming more common.

The experience of parental divorce directly undermines the ability of young adults to form lasting romantic attachments,[22] as we shall see in chapter 12. Meanwhile, people who are already divorced are often reluctant to remarry, not wishing to go through marital collapse again. One study found that of currently divorced adults in 2014, 45 percent said they definitely do *not* wish to be married again, while only 21 percent were sure they did.[23]

Considering all of these factors that discourage marriage among young singles today, there appears to be more *fear* of committing to marriage, than a lack of desire to do so.[24] In fact, I suspect that many who say they do not want marriage feel this way at least partly because they are afraid of it, or are at least concerned they would be less happy than if they stayed single or simply cohabited. The unmarried are often afraid of marrying the wrong person, of having to choose between getting divorced or staying in a bad marriage, of what this will do to their children, and of not being prepared for marriage in many ways—psychologically, financially, and spiritually. Unfortunately, the ways that young people today are preparing for marriage, and trying to protect themselves from its risks, are mostly negative. Too few are taking the route of Higgins' clients and getting good premarital counseling,[25] while too many are engaging in counterproductive, intimacy-without-commitment practices that make the outcomes they fear *more* likely. Once again, living together prior to marriage is among the worst.

---

21. Binzer, "Millennial Children of Divorce: Fear, Anxiety and Determination to End the Cycle."

22. Cf. Ming et al., "The Effect of Parental Divorce on Young Adults' Romantic Relationship Dissolution: What Makes a Difference?" and Jacquet and Surra, "Parental Divorce and Premarital Couples: Commitment and Other Relationship Characteristics."

23. Pew Research Center, *Four-in-Ten Couples Are Saying "I Do," Again*, 5.

24. Ibid.

25. Higgins, "3 Reasons Millennials Are Waiting to Get Married." See below on couples not pursuing premarital counseling.

PREMARITAL COHABITATION

In chapter 1, I mentioned briefly that more than 40 percent of self-identifying Christians agree that premarital cohabitation is a "good idea."[26] The last two cycles of the NSFG certainly make the commonness of this view among evangelical singles abundantly clear. Table 9.1 shows the percentages of singles who *disagreed* with this biblical statement: "A young couple should *not* live together unless they are married."[27] Evangelicals, especially those who attend church weekly, are less likely to disagree with the Scriptures on cohabitation. However, the percentages are discouraging to evangelical parents and leaders who expect their single, professing children and church members to agree with this statement overwhelmingly.

Meanwhile, as table 9.2 shows, most evangelical Protestant singles think that cohabitation before marrying can possibly lower their chances of divorce. The picture is not as dismal among those who attend church weekly, but it is still quite bad. The worst thing is that they are not only morally wrong, but they are also seriously factually misguided.

Living together prior to wedlock is certainly *not* associated with better marriage outcomes. No research supports the notion that cohabitation *increases* marital success. To the contrary, under most circumstances premarital cohabitation is associated with higher risk of divorce, less marital satisfaction, less commitment to marriage as an institution, and poorer marital communication and problem solving.[28] I touched on this and looked at a number of other problems in cohabiting relationships in chapter 2.

Defenders of cohabitation often correctly state, "Correlation does not prove cause." That is certainly true, and it is unlikely that anyone will ever "prove" that cohabitation in itself harms marriage. There are numerous ways that cohabiters are different from non-cohabiters that partially explain why the marriages of people who live together prior to marriage, on average, do worse.[29] Social scientists often call this explanation for the negative associations of cohabitation the "selection hypothesis." Since they

---

26. Barna Group, "Majority of Americans Now Believe in Cohabitation." This was based on 1,097 respondents. "Practicing Christians" are those who self-identify as believers and attend religious services at least once per month.

27. Emphasis added.

28. Starbuck and Lundy, *Families in Context*, 246.

29. Ibid., 247.

Table 9.1: Singles, by Age Group, Religious Affiliation, and Church Attendance, Who Disagreed with the Statement, "A Young Couple Should NOT Live Together Unless They Are Married." (NSFG 2014 and 2016)

	15–22	23–32	33–44
MALES:			
Evangelical:	59%	64%	67%
Other:	75%	79%	75%
Evangelical Weekly Church Attenders:	47%	41%	57%*
Other Weekly Church Attenders:	57%	60%	53%
FEMALES:			
Evangelical:	60%	71%	45%
Other:	78%	83%	80%
Evangelical Weekly Church Attenders:	51%	53%	37%**
Other Weekly Church Attenders:	59%	57%	66%

*   This percentage is based on only 37 of 65 respondents who fit all the criteria and must be interpreted with caution.

**   This percentage is based on only 16 of 43 respondents who fit all the criteria and must be interpreted with caution.

Table 9.2: Singles, by Age Group, Religious Affiliation, and Church Attendance, Who Agreed with the Statement, "Living Together Before Marriage May Prevent Divorce." (NSFG 2014 and 2016)

	15–22	23–32	33–44
MALES:			
Evangelical:	55%	65%	63%
Other:	71%	76%	76%
Evangelical Weekly Church Attenders:	45.5%	39%	53%
Other Weekly Church Attenders:	56%	60%	61%
FEMALES:			
Evangelical:	49%	56%	57%
Other:	64%	72%	69%
Evangelical Weekly Church Attenders:	38%	36%	46%
Other Weekly Church Attenders:	47.5%	58%	58%

move in together before marriage, some researchers have also claimed that, if they do get married, they go into a post-marriage "slump" earlier than those who do not start living together until after their wedding.[30] However, so far, researchers who have compared "apples to apples" have still usually found that marriages preceded by cohabitation have lower levels of quality and stability.[31] Even in countries like Sweden where cohabitation is widely accepted, marriages preceded by it are much more likely to end in divorce.[32] One Australian study of over 5,600 married couples controlled for both when couples moved in together, and background differences between individuals who cohabited and those who did not. Their findings are typical: "The increased risk of separation [for cohabiters] remained significant after the control variables were introduced, regardless of whether marriage duration or union duration was examined."[33] A study by the CDC points out that the tie between cohabitation and higher divorce rates has lessened as cohabitation has become more common, but it has not gone away.[34] Claims such as Andrew Cherlin's that "premarital cohabitation no longer increases the risk of divorce"[35] are premature and far too broadly stated.

One difficulty about cohabitation that many singles fail to consider is the well-established observation that once a couple moves in together, they often "slide" into marriage, as they typically slid into living together, without the kind of wise deliberation such a decision ought to entail.[36] Cohabiters who "slide" into marriage like this have especially elevated risk of marital problems and divorce.[37] Once a couple starts living together, it is harder for them to break up, even when perhaps they should.[38] Rhoades and Stanley summarize this: "In short, living together creates a kind of inertia that makes it difficult to change course."[39] These facts about the

30. Weston et al., "Premarital Cohabitation and Marital Stability," 4.

31. Starbuck and Lundy, Families in Context, 247.

32. Ibid.

33. Weston et al., "Premarital Cohabitation and Marital Stability," 10.

34. Copen et al., "First Marriages in the United States," 2, 8.

35. Cherlin, Public and Private Families, 337.

36. Rhoades and Stanley, Before "I Do," 10.

37. Ibid.

38. Ibid.

39. Ibid.

dynamics of cohabitation directly contradict the notion that cohabiting usually leads to *better* preparation and choice, despite what so many people today seem to believe.

Exceptions to cohabitation being associated, on average, with higher divorce rates and poorer marital quality may exist. Some studies have found that if a couple gets engaged before they move in together,[40] or a woman's cohabiting male partner is the first man she has ever had sex with,[41] their marriages are no more likely than average to end in divorce.[42] Couples who are intentional and deliberative about their plans to live together, who then marry, also do as well as others on average.[43] In looking at women who had first married approximately ten to twenty years prior to being surveyed in the last two cycles of the NSFG, I found that the percentage divorced or legally separated was about the same for non-cohabiters and those who did so after becoming engaged or having definite plans to marry. However, the marriages of those who had cohabited with no marital plans were almost 25 percent more likely to fail.[44] The danger of cohabitation appears to be "front-loaded" as well.[45] Once a couple has been married many years, whether they cohabited first makes little difference.[46] Being honest with the research means pointing out these possible caveats, even though I believe, and the Bible teaches, that sex before marriage, which cohabitation obviously involves, is morally wrong. So how to respond to this research?

First, not all the research supports the notion that engaged cohabiters are just as well off as those who refrain from living together until marriage. A major study by the CDC using 2006–2010 NSFG data found that for women, the risk of divorce within twenty years of a first marriage was much higher for those who lived with their spouse first, *whether or not they were engaged or had definite plans to marry* when they moved in together.[47] Another study examined the total scores of 14,000 engaged cohabiting

---

40. Cf. Kline et al., "Timing Is Everything," 311, 315–16; Rhoades et al., "The Pre-Engagement Cohabitation Effect," 107, 109–110.

41. Teachman, "Premarital Sex, Premarital Cohabitation, and the Risk of Subsequent Marital Dissolution Among Women," 444, 453.

42. Starbuck and Lundy, *Families in Context*, 246.

43. Rhoades and Stanley, *Before "I Do,"* 10.

44. This is with no additional controls, just "straight" frequencies and percentages.

45. As we shall see in chapter 11, that is true about the danger of getting divorced overall.

46. Starbuck and Lundy, *Families in Context*, 247. They cite one study that says about eight years or more. That is a bit dated, but no doubt the main thing is that the threat is in the earlier years of marriage.

couples versus over 18,000 engaged couples living apart who completed a widely used and well-validated premarital inventory in 2010.[48] Of the four categories of couples this instrument defines, compared to those who were cohabiting while engaged, those who were engaged but not cohabiting were 15 percent more likely to fall into the most positive group, and about 2.6 times less likely to be in the group that had the highest risk of divorce.[49]

Second, if our goal is to have a *godly* and *Christ-centered* marriage, starting it out in flagrant disobedience to God's word makes no sense. I recall a student telling me years ago that his brother wanted to have a Catholic wedding and marriage without giving up sex or cohabitation prior to marriage. He and his fiancée simply lied to their priest, even using caller identification to screen their calls to keep their priest from discovering their deception. Lying to one's priest to secure a Catholic wedding without having to follow church teaching seems a bit self-defeating. I have seen evangelicals proceed in the same manner, often with parental support.

Third, most cohabitation does not fit the ideal circumstances laid out above. As we have seen, few cohabiters moved in together already engaged to one another, and most did not even have definite marriage plans. Many who did still were not sure they would go through with the wedding, though their partner may not have known that. This last fact suggests that many people begin cohabitation believing that their marital futures are more certain than they really are.

Fourth, at best some research indicates that premarital cohabiters who move in together engaged or with definite plans to marry will have marital outcomes and divorce that are *no worse* than average. How does this meet the lofty goals of preparing, screening, testing the relationship, and so forth to *reduce* the risk of divorce and *improve* marital outcomes? The average marriage today carries an unacceptably high risk of divorce.[50] Would it not be better to engage practices that produce better than ordinary results, rather than one that just *might* not be worse?

Meanwhile, moving in together means risking having this relationship fail after carrying on a deep, sexual, co-residential partnership. After all, if

---

47. "First Marriages in the United States," 8.

48. PREPARE, which I will get into more below.

49. Larson and Olson, *Cohabitation Reduces Relationship Quality for Dating and Engaged Couples.* For comparisons of these two categories, see Olson et al., *The Couple Checkup*, 24, 27.

50. More on that in chapter 11.

one is "test-driving" a relationship, the assumption is not sticking with it if it falls short of expectations, regardless of what intentions were in place at the start. Meanwhile, there is a strong chance that pregnancy will occur during this "trial process." One CDC study found that, as of about the mid-2000s, about one in five women gets pregnant during her first cohabitation.[51]

There are much better ways to determine if someone is the "right fit" that carry less risk and produce better results than cohabitation. Galena Rhoades and Scott Stanley crystallized why living together may not be the best path, even for engaged couples with no religious scruples who have good reason to believe it will not harm their eventual marriage. There is solid wisdom here that matches much that I have pointed out up to this point, and this serves as an excellent introduction to our discussion of *wise* premarital preparation:

> If it is risky to live with someone you don't wind up marrying, but you want to test the relationship or get to know each other's habits before deciding whether to get married, what can you do? As we have noted . . . cohabiting may not be a good test of a relationship because constraints (e.g., merging finances, sharing friends, adopting a pet) may make it more difficult to end the relationship when you realize a partner has failed the test. Other ways to test a relationship, without increasing constraints, may be more beneficial: plan a trip together, meet each other's parents, observe your boyfriend/girlfriend in many different settings, or seek other people's opinions.[52]

QUALITY APPROACHES TO
MARITAL PREPARATION

Proverbs teaches us that "the horse is made ready for the day of battle, but the victory belongs to the LORD" (21:31). I love the balance this verse represents. It takes an enormous investment of time and skill to prepare a true warhorse, but one would be foolish to ride anything less into battle. We cannot expect God to bless that kind of reckless presumption. At the same time, if the Lord is not in our venture, and if we do not rely on him,

---

51. "First Premarital Cohabitation in the United States," 5–6. The risk was greatest for younger women, lowest for older ones.

52. Rhoades and Stanley, *Before "I Do,"* 11.

we will fail despite our skill and preparation. Both things are true in every aspect of life, including marriage.

Good premarital preparation must meet some general criteria. First, it must follow sound mate-selection and courtship practices, and indeed, complete them. Second, it must include solid teaching of and reflection upon biblical teachings about marriage, such as those we addressed in the first four chapters of this book. Third, as the wedding approaches couples need education or counseling with a clear practical focus on habits, practices, expectations, and so on that are most likely to build up or tear down the marriage, particularly in its early years. This will typically provide a final opportunity for couples to determine if they should marry this person at this time.

One counselor does not need to provide all of this practical preparation. In fact, it is best that the couple benefits from a "multitude" of counselors (Prov 11:14; 15:22; 24:6). It will take *time*. Married couples need a lot more than the perfunctory two or three one-hour meetings with a pastor that many churches require.[53] Finally, it ought to use methods based upon empirical evidence as to what hurts and helps marriage, using content, delivery, and a kind of "curriculum" that has actually been shown to identify problems and strengths, while improving marital outcomes. We will focus on this kind of practical, fact-based premarital preparation here.

TIMING FORMAL PREMARITAL PREPARATION

Must Couples Do This before Their Engagement?

Some Christians assert that premarital preparation ought to occur *before* the couple becomes engaged to be married. One reason for that is that the best premarital preparation will lead many couples to decide that they should *not* get married.[54] However, if one views engagement as a solemn vow to marry, then breaking it is tantamount to divorce, much as the gospel of Matthew describes Joseph deciding to "divorce" his "betrothed," Mary, when he found out she was pregnant (1:18–19). *If* we start from that premise, engaging in any process that could lead a couple to forsake their engagement "vows" is immoral.

---

53. McManus, *Marriage Savers*, 138–39.

54. Ibid., 138; Scott et al., "Reasons for Divorce and Recollections of Premarital Intervention," 142.

I agree that if a couple decides they should not marry, it is better for them to make that decision earlier than later. It is certainly not wrong for couples to complete a rigorous premarital preparation process before engagement, and it is probably a good idea. It is also clear that couples should not delay formal premarital education or counseling until close to their weddings, when it becomes very difficult for them to back out of an ill-conceived union.[55]

However, our culture does not assign the same meaning to engagement as Jews of Jesus' time gave to betrothal, which, as John Ortberg pointed out, "was a legal act . . . so to end it required an act of divorce."[56] For us, formal engagement is a *contingent* arrangement in which either partner can end the relationship without formally finding serious fault in the other. As one pastor friend of mine likes to say—for us, "Engagement is the already and not-yet of marriage."[57] Discouraging engaged couples from undertaking premarital preparation or from breaking up if it is clear they should not marry, due to such technicalities, is incredibly shortsighted.

The Solution for the "Front-loaded" Danger of Divorce

Divorce is heavily "front-loaded" in the life of a marriage. One classic study that followed a large group of married women over about ten years found that, for those who got divorced, over half did so within five years of getting married, and over 80 percent did so by the end of their tenth year of marriage.[58] A recent US Census study found that the median duration of marriages that end in divorce is eight years, and the median time to legal separation is only seven years.[59] Meanwhile, as we shall see, the major factors that contribute to divorce are well known,[60] and quality premarital preparation tackles these issues directly with the couple before they are married.

---

55. Ibid.

56. Ortberg, "Leader's Insight: There's Something about Joseph."

57. Nathaniel Devlin, associate pastor of Beverly Heights Presbyterian Church in Pittsburgh, PA.

58. South and Spitze, "Determinants of Divorce over the Marital Life Course," 587–88. The methods allowed them to look at young and mature women, combining thirty years of marriage. Of the 21.3 percent total who got divorced, 12.2 percent (57 percent of the total) did so in the first five years of marriage, and 17.7 percent (83 percent of the total) did so in the first ten years.

59. Krieder and Ellis, "Number, Timing, and Duration of Marriages and Divorces: 2009," 15, 18.

60. Cf. Barna, *The Future of the American Family*, 73.

That means that, done well, couples can get the specific marriage preparation they need, when they need it the most.[61] Unfortunately, it appears that most engaged couples do not receive any type of premarital education.[62] Of those who do, many may not be getting high-quality counseling, nor investing a sufficient amount of time.

WHAT THE BEST PRACTICAL AND APPLIED
PREMARITAL COUNSELING INCLUDES

Premarital counselors or educators should directly target the most important building blocks of hindrances to a successful marriage. Ideally, they should work within established, evidence-based systems that ensure they tackle each thoroughly, in ways tailored to the individuals and couples they are serving. Future spouses need to reveal their beliefs, attitudes, and experiences in a range of important areas to the person who is counseling them, and to each other. Trained counselors or educators must provide sound instruction, training, and practice to teach necessary skills and guide discussions that will need to take place then and in the future. If the process is not demanding, at times exhausting or even a bit scary, it is probably not sufficient. However, there is also a lot of delight in a good premarital counseling process.

So what content areas should the couple and their counselors or teachers address? To identify those that are necessary, I draw upon the premarital counseling system I trained in and use called PREPARE, produced by Life Innovations. David Olson, a former president of the National Council on Family Relations, created this approach.[63] It employs an inventory that functions almost like an "X-ray" of two partners and their relationship.[64] PREPARE has been in use for over thirty-five years; is available in twelve languages; and has been used by over 100,000 counselors or pastors, and over four million couples, many of them providing feedback and results.[65] I also rely heavily upon the Prevention and Relationship Enhancement

---

61. McManus, *Marriage Savers*, 105–6.

62. Stanley et al., "Premarital Education, Marital Quality, and Marital Stability," 119; Williamson et al., "Does Premarital Education Decrease or Increase Couples' Later Help-Seeking?," 113.

63. McManus, *Marriage Savers*, 106.

64. Ibid., 26. See David Olson et al.'s *The Couple Checkup*.

65. See www.prepare-enrich.com.

Program (PREP), which is an educational approach[66] that can also be used in counseling.[67] As of 2010, about 500,000 couples had participated in PREP education, and about 14,500 professionals had trained in it.[68] Both of these approaches have materials specifically for Christians. PREPARE even has tailored materials for Protestants and for Catholics.[69] There are many fine approaches out there, but between the two of these, both of which rely heavily upon many years of empirical research and have systematic training for counselors or educators, we can get a solid idea of the areas that premarital preparation needs to address. I will supplement these with additional insights.

Note that it is critical to focus not only on problems or challenges a couple faces, but also to help them identify, appreciate, and build upon their strengths.[70] No premarital preparation should focus exclusively on the negative. Where possible, a positive emphasis is best.

Family of Origin

The experiences people had growing up shape them and their approach to marriage in numerous ways.[71] These include marital expectations. In fact, it is hard to discuss what they hope marriage will bring without getting into family-of-origin issues.[72] As we have seen, other aspects of partners' family backgrounds can affect their marriage, including significantly increasing their risk of divorce. Important things to learn about and address are obvious ones, such as whether the person grew up with two biological married parents or some other arrangement, family size, and religious belief. Also significant are matters that most of us are less prone to think about, such as how parents related to each other and their children, whether the families were close-knit, how flexible versus rule-based and organized their households

---

66. Markman et al., *Fighting for Your Marriage*, 2. See also the PREP home page: www.prepinc.com.

67. Ibid.

68. Markman et al., *Fighting for Your Marriage*, 2.

69. Cf. Stanley et al., *A Lasting Promise*, tied to the PREP program; and The Center for Marriage and Family Studies and Life Innovations, *Bible Verses for the PREPARE/ENRICH Program*.

70. McManus, *Marriage Savers*, 109; Olson et al., *The Couple Checkup*, 15–16.

71. McManus, *Marriage Savers*, 112.

72. Markman et al., *Fighting for Your Marriage*, 326–29. We will get into marital expectations below.

were,[73] gender roles, approaches to parenting, and so on. Beyond that, coun-seling may need to get into darker matters: domestic abuse, alcoholism or other misuse of substances in the home, parental conflict, and the like.

Another critical thing here is if the partners' families support their marriage. Opposition by parents, siblings, grandparents, and so on is not a deal breaker, but it cannot be ignored either. Meanwhile, their support can be a source of great strength. A related issue is their view of marriage in general, as well as areas such as sex, divorce, and children. These will often become relevant, for example, as partners strive to maintain their purity, struggle with difficulties in their marriage, have or do not have children, and so on.

Peers

Friends' views on marriage and related issues and values in general are important.[74] Do they believe in and value the institution of marriage and its permanence, or are they cynical and questioning about such matters? What about their views of sex and procreation? As with families, whether or not a couple's friends support their potential marriage also matters, and can be a positive and encouraging influence or a set of difficulties to over-come. When my wife and I were progressing toward marriage, we enjoyed the enthusiastic support of many friends, some of whom are still part of our lives more than thirty-six years later. Had it been otherwise I am sure our relationship would have been a lot harder, our foundation less secure.

Personality Types and Personal Styles

The PREPARE premarital counseling approach gauges the personal styles, habits, and personalities of each partner, and explores ways these create both compatibilities, complementary strengths, but also potential conflict and dissatisfaction.[75] For example, if one partner tends to be moody, nega-tive, withdrawn, unreliable, controlling, or prone to publicly embarrass-ing behaviors, this tends to lead to marital unhappiness and breakdown.[76]

---

73. Olson et al., *The Couple Checkup*, 164; *PREPARE/ENRICH: Workbook for Couples*, 23–24. More on closeness versus flexibility below.

74. Wilcox and Marquardt, *When Baby Makes Three*, 26–30.

75. McManus, *Marriage Savers*, 107; Olson et al., *The Couple Checkup*, 213.

76. Ibid., 218–19.

Other areas that PREPARE researchers have found are important for couples to explore include: introverted versus extroverted, highly organized versus spontaneous and impulsive, open to change versus more conventional and stable, quick to agree and yield versus forceful, calm versus more prone to react.[77] Notice that these are not good or bad, just different. However, they will affect preferences, activities, and decisions in many areas of life, and partners will often need to discuss, negotiate, and compromise how to handle different decisions and situations in light of their natural tendencies.[78] The personality tendencies can create problems if they are not balanced,[79] and even if partners share the same trait. For example, when both partners are introverted and this is imbalanced, the couple can become isolated, while extroverts could compete for attention and popularity if they take things too far. Forcefulness can become bullying, and folks may easily take advantage of those who are too agreeable.

Considering the effect personality traits can have upon how future marriage partners will deal with life is not a new discovery. Consider Mr. Bennet's congratulation of his daughter Jane upon her engagement to Charles Bingley in Jane Austen's *Pride and Prejudice,* "I have not a doubt of your doing very well together. Your tempers are by no means unlike. You are each of you so complying, that nothing will ever be resolved on; so easy, that every servant will cheat you; and so generous, that you will always exceed your income."[80]

Personal History and Self-Disclosure

Getting into personal history and background, and talking about this with or as a couple, can be very simple and pleasant and involve reflecting on some wonderful, positive, formative experiences. However, in some cases these matters can be quite painful and may bring up a host of complex matters the couple must explore and resolve.[81] A classic work by psychologist Sidney Jourard correctly asserted that appropriate, mutual self-disclosure is necessary for a relationship to grow in closeness and trust.[82] It is vital

---

77. Ibid., 220.

78. Ibid., 221.

79. Ibid.

80. Austen, *Pride and Prejudice,* 328.

81. Harris, *Boy Meets Girl,* 169–72.

82. *The Transparent Self,* 65–66.

that neither betrays those confidences.[83] He noted, not surprisingly, that on average males find this harder than do females, and will need more help opening up.[84] The Scriptures clearly say that this kind of disclosure needs to happen among trusted Christians (cf. Jas 5:16). This applies even more to future husbands and wives.[85]

Besides, there are things prospective spouses have the right to know about each other before consenting to marriage. Has either been married before, had live-in relationships, or been engaged to someone else? What about existing children, custody arrangements, or plans for the future stepparent to adopt? Are there any previous romantic relationships that continue to affect one or the other partner, and if so which and how? These need to include previous sexual relations, enough to get the facts into the open but not getting into unnecessary details. What about vices, including gambling or substance abuse? A common issue that comes up these days is pornography, which most males have been exposed to and some a lot more, not to mention women. Has the female partner had an abortion, or given up a child for adoption? What about sexually transmitted diseases, or in fact, any relevant medical conditions? Many of these not only require uncomfortable discussions, but thoughtful decisions. Some couples will have no major issues related to any of these things, but others may be carrying many of them. It is important not only to handle these things honestly but with grace, always in the light of Christ's incredible power and redeeming love. Marriage will involve many confessions, so teaching partners to do so, learning and practicing forgiving and trusting one another, is critical.

Abuse

At the level of the couple, it is critical to find out if there are problems with physical or emotional abuse, misusing substances, pornography or aberrant sexual behaviors, or other serious problems of that sort.[86] If singles have been careful in selecting their mate as we have discussed especially in chapter 5, these types of issues are less likely to be present. However,

---

83. Ibid., 66.
84. Ibid., 35–36, 218.
85. Cf. Olson et al., *The Couple Checkup*, 46.
86. Cf. Scott et al., "Reasons for Divorce and Recollections of Premarital Intervention,"136, 140–41.

couples and counselors should still explore them in formal practical pre-marital preparation. The PREPARE inventory delves into these kinds of issues directly.[87] There is no perfect answer as to how the couple or their counselors should address any problems that may come to light, as the nature of the problems and circumstances can vary so much between cases. However, we must always take them very seriously and expect nothing less of guilty parties than clear repentance and some ongoing accountability if the relationship is going to move forward. Many counselors will need to refer some cases to professionals with more experience and training in areas such as sexual addictions, domestic violence, and so on.[88] In some cases, one or both partners may decide that they should postpone or cancel the marriage. Counselors and couples should pursue matters such as these compassionately but forthrightly.

Balancing Closeness and Flexibility

A large national survey conducted by David Olson and his colleagues revealed that the balance of closeness and flexibility in a couple's rela-tionship was a major predictor of future marital success.[89] As with so many other areas of life, it is easy for couples to fall off one side of the log or the other on either or both of these relational traits. They can smother each other or be too rigid on the one hand,[90] or be too separate or disorga-nized on the other.[91] David Olson humorously notes that two well-known television shows, The Osbornes and Everybody Loves Raymond, depict the opposite extremes.[92]

As touched on earlier, family background influences a person's pref-erences and expectation as to how much togetherness or independence, change and spontaneity or rules, structure, and planning they desire in their marriage and future family. Regardless of where these expectan-cies come from, in premarital counseling it is worthwhile for partners to

---

87. PREPARE/ENRICH: Sample Facilitator Report, 7.
88. Stanley et al., A Lasting Promise, 286.
89. Olson et al., The Couple Checkup, 163.
90. Barna's research revealed that "feeling smothered by the partner" was a common reason respondents gave for why they ended their marriage. See The Future of the American Family, 73.
91. Olson et al., The Couple Checkup, 164–72.
92. Ibid., 175–76.

learn how each other views these, how it will affect their daily lives, and to begin reaching agreement—to begin finding consensus and balance in these areas if it is not there already. PREPARE's "Couple and Family Maps," and the questions they use to place people on these maps, are useful tools for helping them do this.[93] Premarital counseling is also a great time to help couples learn how and why the amount of closeness and flexibility they will want and need will change over the life of their marriage.[94] Sickness, unemployment, job changes, children, and so on will all affect these.

Finances

Financial problems regularly land on lists of top reasons for divorce.[95] These contribute both directly and indirectly to marital breakdown, as they lead to stress, interpersonal conflict, and even health problems, and substance abuse.[96] A systematic and comprehensive review of partners' financial expectations, situation, budget plans, planning, and knowledge is critical. Wise financial instruction is invaluable.[97] The reality for many singles today is that they will have less abundance in their early marriages than they experienced living with their parents. It is easy for them to expect more than they can actually afford, rather than adjust their lifestyle "downward." Easy credit and lack of experience creating and sticking to budgets is a frequent, related issue as well.[98] Many Americans have also succumbed to idolatry of wealth—the subtle belief that happiness requires material abundance and security rests in money.[99] They have forgotten Jesus' warning that "one's life does not consist in the abundance of his possessions" (Luke 12:15b). The money management skills that engaged and newlywed couples will need include: establishing godly priorities, giving to charities and the church, saving, controlling spending and debt, maintaining

---

93. Ibid., 172–73. *PREPARE/ENRICH: Workbook for Couples,* 23–26.

94. Ibid., 177.

95. *The Future of the American Family,* 73; McManus, *Marriage Savers,* 164; Olson et al., *The Couple Checkup,* 80; Markman et al., *Fighting for Your Marriage,* 409–10; Scott et al., "Reasons for Divorce and Recollections of Premarital Intervention," 134, 136, 141.

96. Ibid., 136.

97. Olson et al., *The Couple Checkup,* 79–98.

98. Ibid., 86–89.

99. Ibid., 89–90.

appropriate forms of insurance, and relying on God rather than stressing over money.[100] Recognizing that all wealth belongs to the Lord (Ps 24:1), to be stewarded for his purposes rather than our gratification (Matt 25:14–30), is a good place to start.[101]

Recreation and Leisure

Years ago, my wife and I were touring a house we were considering buying. I noticed an enormous amount of expensive turkey-hunting gear, clothing, and trophies. The husband seemed to be almost fanatically obsessed with the sport, which at this advanced level requires a lot of time and travel. When the realtor informed us that the sellers were divorcing, I was not surprised. This level of dedication to the sport was not compatible with a healthy marriage unless they lived on inherited wealth or both of them were childless and madly in love with hunting turkeys.

It is easy to overlook learning about, and discussing, the leisure interests of future spouses. However, these are important aspects of our lives, and couples need to address this in quality premarital counseling.[102] Though their interests will probably change over their lifetime, it is a good idea to find out what things they like to do together, or on their own, and find healthy balance. I do not expect my wife to enjoy hunting, nor does she harbor the belief that she will ever convince me to take up quilting, but it has been wonderful that we both enjoy doing activities together such as camping, shopping at discount warehouses, travel, spending time with our grandchildren, and dining out. It is important for spouses to go out from time to time, and that means identifying things both partners can enjoy together.[103] Folks should also willingly engage in activities they are not "naturally" interested in when doing them together is important to their partners. They also need to consider how to indulge their recreational interests modestly rather than allowing these to deprive their partner of needed help, support, and companionship.

---

100. McManus, *Marriage Savers*, 162–64.

101. I am grateful to ibid., 163, for these Scripture applications.

102. Cf. McManus, *Marriage Savers*, 107; see also *PREPARE/ENRICH: Sample Facilitator Report*, 13.

103. *PREPARE/ENRICH: Workbook for Couples*, 16.

Marital Expectations

One key area to look at is the expectations prospective spouses have for marriage and each other.[104] Of particular concern are unrealistic expectancies, where folks are going into marriage with proverbial "rose-colored glasses." PREPARE calls this "ideological distortion."[105] This leads to disappointment with outcomes that are actually normal and good, but not expected. Disagreement about expectations is a challenge couples need to explore, as are negative expectations that suggest deeper underlying problems.[106] Regardless, partners must know what each other expects, and be clear with one another about these beliefs. Where it is reasonable, moral, and possible, they should be willing to try to meet their partner's positive expectations. It is also important that they prepare for some aspects of their future life to fall short of their aspirations. Because we are fallen human beings in a broken world, some of these will go unmet. This can be hard. "Hope deferred makes the heart sick, but a desire fulfilled is a tree of life" (Prov 13:12). To be committed to an imperfect being, as Christ is toward each of us, means preparing to handle in circumspect and godly ways those moments in life when reality falls short of our dreams.[107]

Sex and Intimacy

As discussed in chapter 3, a healthy and regular sexual life, rooted in sacrificial love and enjoyable intimacy, is vital to a happy and godly marriage.[108] They foster this by exercising godly decisions and self-control prior to marriage, but also by addressing these issues constructively in premarital education and counseling. This is more about art, attitude, effective communication, and making the other person one's main priority than it is about sterile techniques.[109] Partners typically have a lot to learn about

---

104. Scott et al., "Reasons for Divorce and Recollections of Premarital Intervention,"141.

105. Cf. *PREPARE/ENRICH: Sample Facilitator Report*, 5; and *PREPARE/ENRICH: Workbook for Couples*, 20, for statements and inventory items that show common types of such distortion.

106. Markman et al., *Fighting for Your Marriage*, 321–25; *PREPARE/ENRICH: Workbook for Couples*, 20.

107. Markman et al., *Fighting for Your Marriage*, 337–38.

108. See also Olson et al., *The Couple Checkup*, 105.

109. Cf. Markman et al., *Fighting for Your Marriage*, 275–76.

each other's sexual perceptions, expectations, and aspirations. Couples often do not understand how or how not to communicate affection and approach each other sexually, or how to talk about what each finds desirable or unappealing. Future spouses need to understand basic differences between the way men and women approach sexual relationships. For example, misunderstanding can occur because men expect physical intimacy to come before emotional connection, while women expect the opposite.[110] They may fail to understand how and why unresolved conflict undermines sexual intimacy, how to deal with "performance anxiety," or how to understand and adjust to the different levels of sexual desire and need that they will experience across the life of their marriage.[111] In addition, couples often need to discuss their birth-control beliefs and preferences. It is ironic that in the midst of so much fake "sexual liberation," many believing couples find sex so difficult to discuss. Quality premarital counseling deals with these issues thoroughly and systematically.[112]

One area that is too easy to neglect is marital infidelity,[113] which is of course a major relationship destroyer. One group of researchers found that adultery was often the "final straw" that broke marriages.[114] It is important to explore any ideas, fantasies, or actions that may have already happened in a relationship that could make this a concern.[115] Couples need to learn what seasons and situations make infidelity most likely and how to manage those. These include times of stress and separation, low periods in marital satisfaction or romance, pregnancy, inappropriate relationships with coworkers and friends of the opposite sex, extensive travel, and the like.[116] This subject requires tact and caution, since it may be difficult for couples in their most romantic period, leading up to their wedding, to consider the possibility of adultery and the need to prevent it.[117] That is OK—married couples can also explore this in later education or counseling.

---

110. McManus, *Marriage Savers*, 94.

111. Olson et al., *The Couple Checkup*, 108–18; Markman et al., *Fighting for Your Marriage*, 277–92.

112. Cf. *PREPARE/ENRICH: Workbook for Couples*, 17.

113. Scott et al., "Reasons for Divorce and Recollections of Premarital Intervention,"140.

114. Ibid., 136–37, 140.

115. Olson et al., *The Couple Checkup*, 105.

116. Scott et al., "Reasons for Divorce and Recollections of Premarital Intervention," 140.

117. Ibid.

Children

It stands to reason that if the procreation and nurture of children is central to marriage that, except for couples who cannot have them due to age or infirmity and the like, discussing children ought to be vital in preparing for marriage. The notion of "dealing with that when the time comes" is foolish. PREPARE gets into how many children each partner wants, and when. It also encourages the couple to think about and discuss their ideas, and disagreements, with regard to how the children will be disciplined, educated, spiritually formed, and the respective roles the father and mother will play in all of that. Doubts or concerns, but also confidence and affirmation, each partner has of the other as a future parent are addressed directly.[118] Couples are also encouraged to be realistic about how having children will affect their relationship and home, to maintain their marriage as the first priority, and to support one another as co-parents, through all the challenges and joys of raising children.[119]

Gender Roles and Division of Labor

On average, even in dual-earner households, women tend to pick up a larger, even unfair, share of the housework, and this is a frequent source of conflict.[120] Partners' expectations about who will do what in their future marriage, including the degree to which these fit "traditional" expectations, are influenced by many factors, including religious beliefs, family of origin, peers, and more.[121] People can and will argue back and forth about whether couples ought to adopt roles in their marriages associated with labels such as "traditional," "egalitarian," "complementarian," "patriarchal," and the rest. These issues are important, but here my main concern is to encourage couples to work through each other's expectations and beliefs and find equitable solutions. There ought to be healthy individual variation, depending on preference, gifts, interests, and circumstances. A key thing is that neither partner should abuse, neglect, or cut the other one out of vital decision-making.[122] Rigid, one-size-fits-all

---

118. *PREPARE/ENRICH: Sample Facilitator Report*, 19.

119. Olson et al., *The Couple Checkup*, 191–96, 200–206.

120. Markman et al., *Fighting for Your Marriage*, 69–70.

121. Olson et al., *The Couple Checkup*, 127–29.

122. Ibid., 128–30.

rules, whether of the feminist or patriarchal mold, do not make much sense.

In the PREPARE system, couples are encouraged to consider how their household will be organized, decisions made, if both will be pursuing careers, and so on. PREPARE counselors direct them to explore together where their ideas about sex roles come from, and how much they are using traditional role models or simply want to assign tasks, in their household, based on ability and interest.[123] This curriculum does not impose a particular approach upon them, and couples end up varying quite a bit, knowing too that future exigencies will change things.[124]

Religious Beliefs and Values

If couples have considered the kinds of qualities that I covered in chapter 5, both partners will have already settled issues of spiritual compatibility. However, there can still be important issues of doctrine and practice to discuss, even between committed believers of generally sound faith. For example, I have counseled partners who disagreed on the issue of infant baptism, who comfortably settled that the future husband's convictions would prevail and the future wife would be able to fully honor and support that. Other couples may differ somewhat in their doctrine of salvation. These are important issues, central to any godly marriage. Sometimes partners can readily disagree and respect each other's views on some religious matter, while for some people or topics this may be difficult or impossible.[125]

It is vital to get specifics about doctrinal belief and practice out in the open and for couples to talk them through thoroughly before tying the knot. They should not be lulled into thinking that they can defer such discussions until after marriage. Couples often find a great deal of encouragement in considering their faith commitments and beliefs together, as they typically discover how much they have in common and the degree to which their shared commitment to God, particular callings, and doctrines strengthens

---

123. *PREPARE/ENRICH: Workbook for Couples*, 18.

124. See, for example, the *PREPARE/ENRICH: Sample Facilitator Report*, 16, for an idea of what kinds of issues are addressed: decision making, assigning household tasks, the place of career, if and how power will be shared, and more.

125. Markman et al., *Fighting for Your Marriage*, 307–13.

their relationship.[126] The PREPARE inventory walks couples through a set of items that help them consider such matters as how much they share spiritual beliefs, how satisfied they are with this aspect of their relationship, the degree to which each is committed to public worship, and more.[127]

Marital Commitment

One of the principals behind the PREP premarital education system describes marital commitment this way, "Are you sticking together, or do you just feel stuck?"[128] Commitment has to do with the willingness to work on difficulties, to stick together no matter what. It is necessary to prevent divorce and to generate and sustain true marital happiness.[129] I have placed this topic here, near the end of our list, to underscore its importance. A spouse who is strongly dedicated to his or her marriage will be motivated to deal with any other issue when and if doing so will preserve or improve his or her relationship.[130]

PREP educators talk about two types of commitment, both of which have a place in marriage. The first, *"personal dedication,"* is rooted in the desire and will of each partner to do their best to "maintain or improve the quality of their relationship for the mutual benefit of both partners."[131] The second, *"constraint commitment,"* consists of "either external or internal pressures" that make "ending the relationship more costly—economically, socially, personally, or psychologically."[132] If a couple has personal dedication they will also make decisions that naturally increase internal and external constraints as well, such as having children, maintaining joint finances and home ownership, and the like. They will even welcome them as a source of strength and comfort, as additional "glue" when their wills feel depleted.[133] People who are constrained to remain in their marriage

126. Olson et al., *The Couple Checkup,* 149–51.

127. *PREPARE/ENRICH: Sample Facilitator Report,* 17.

128. Markman et al., *Fighting for Your Marriage,* 372.

129. Ibid., 372. See also Scott et al., "Reasons for Divorce and Recollections of Premarital Intervention,"135.

130. Ibid., 372–73. I touch on this again in chapter 12, in pointing out that this type of commitment is less likely to be strong in those raised in divorced homes, which in turn leads to higher risk of divorce.

131. Ibid., 377.

132. Ibid.

133. Ibid.

with no sense of personal dedication feel "stuck." The key is to have both forms of commitment, flowing out of personal dedication and, beyond that, our larger desire to serve, please, and enjoy God.

I discussed infidelity earlier. Both dedication and constraints help spouses resist these kinds of sexual temptations.[134] Committed couples will seek to "affair proof" their marriages.

Premarital counseling should explore how much commitment is present and growing, while teaching partners ways that they can nurture it. For example, the PREPARE inventory has several items that measure how committed each person is to doing what is needed to keep their marriage happy and sticking with it for a lifetime, as well as how confident they are that their partner is strongly dedicated to the marriage as well.[135]

Communication and Conflict

Like the last topic, I saved communication and conflict for the end not because they are less important but because they are critical and central as foundations for a good marriage. Like marital commitment, they are vital to addressing every other element that involves building a good marriage, and resolving problems, requires. Without adequate skills, practices, and habits in communicating generally and addressing disagreement in particular, spouses will not be equipped to solve or prevent problems in any of the other areas we have discussed here, or even to understand each other well. If a couple did nothing prior to marriage but establish a radical commitment to their relationship, rooted in love under Christ in service to him, and joined this to excellent skills and habits in communicating and dealing with conflict, they would be prepared to have a happy marriage and handle any challenges to it.

I am dealing with conflict and communication skills together rather than separately because they are logically interrelated. The best premarital counseling or education focuses very heavily on diagnostics, teaching, and training on communication and conflict-management skills, which are naturally connected.[136]

---

134. Ibid., 383–84.

135. *PREPARE/ENRICH: Sample Facilitator Report*, 7.

136. McManus, *Marriage Savers*, 107, 110–11, 124–28; Markman et al., *Fighting for Your Marriage*, 87–213; *PREPARE/ENRICH: Workbook for Couples*, 3–5, 9–11; Olson et al., *The Couple Checkup*, 33–78; *PREPARE/ENRICH: Sample Facilitator Report*, 4, 6, 9–10.

Like so much we have dealt with about what couples, educators, and counselors need to address in premarital preparation, it is not possible to cover all of the elements of effective versus poor communication and conflict skills here. However, there are some general areas to be aware of that couples ought to be sure they consider, as they get ready for married life.

First, effective communication means learning to be assertive and clear in stating needs and concerns, giving opinions, and sharing feelings. It also means, on the part of hearers, mastering the skills of actively listening so that a person understands the other and communicates to him or her clearly that he or she has done so.[137] A person who is actively listening is able to paraphrase what their partner said in a manner that he or she agrees is accurate.[138]

Second, the best marriages are not those with less conflict; they are those in which spouses handle conflict promptly, constructively, and honestly. As David Olson points out, "Conflict is a natural and inevitable part of human relationships. . . . In fact, more intimate relationships will often have more conflict. If handled in a healthy way, that conflict will strengthen the relational bond, but if handled wrongly, it can break down the relationship."[139] Two of the worst ways of handling conflict are avoiding it[140] or, as Olson notes, "attacking the person rather than the problem."[141] Beyond this, couples can never spend too much time learning effective ways to handle their disagreements so that they build, rather than break down, their marriage.[142] Couples often point out that chronic, escalating conflict and poor communication wear away their relationship, frustrating them and alienating them from one another.[143]

Next, note how cultivating, by God's grace, basic godly virtues is important. Among the chief of these are kindness, patience, and humility. Given

---

137. Olson et al., *The Couple Checkup*, 39–40, 42; PREPARE/ENRICH: *Workbook for Couples*, 304.

138. Olson et al., *The Couple Checkup*, 47–48.

139. Olson et al., *The Couple Checkup*, 59.

140. Stanley et al., *A Lasting Promise*, 40–42; Olson et al., *The Couple Checkup*, 59–60.

141. Olson et al., *The Couple Checkup*, 60.

142. Cf. Olson et al., *The Couple Checkup*, 63–73 for excellent pointers about what to do and what *not* to do. For a much lengthier and more in-depth practical discussion of effective communication and dealing with conflict constructively, see the five chapters in Markman et al., *Fighting for Your Marriage* from pages 87–214.

143. Scott et al., "Reasons for Divorce and Recollections of Premarital Intervention,"135.

that all of us sin in what we do or fail to do, forgiveness is vital to any marriage. True, godly forgiveness requires the grace of God, and we must rely on his assistance to find healing and restoration. However, couples ought to take the time to get some practical ideas about how to forgive, and what not to do.[144] Regardless, forgiveness is necessary in all human relationships, including marriage, and is not an option for believers. Those entering marriage often need Paul's admonition to, "Put on then, as God's chosen ones, holy and beloved, compassionate hearts, kindness, humility, meekness, and patience, bearing with one another and, if one has a complaint against another, forgiving each other; as the Lord has forgiven you, so you also must forgive" (Col 3:12–13).

Finally, couples need to learn about and appreciate how sex differences affect how men and women approach communication and conflict.[145] The authors of *Fighting for Your Marriage* identify several important ones. Men tend to withdraw more easily, while women are more anxious to open up issues and talk about them.[146] In general, women guard their relationships more, are more sensitive to disruption to or threats in them, and as a result are more anxious to discuss issues.[147] Men are more competitive and more likely to put winning ahead of preserving a relationship, while women are more willing to accept loss in order to preserve a relationship.[148] On average, men do not handle marital conflict as effectively as women do, even as women react more physically to it.[149] While both men and women crave intimacy with their spouse, women tend to focus more on *dialogue*, while men think of closeness as doing things together.[150] Howard Markman makes this accurate generalization: "Men would be wise to focus on their beloved's feelings, needs, and interests . . . Women may need to understand that men want the same things women want: closeness, friendship, and intimacy."[151]

---

144. Stanley et al., *A Lasting Promise*, 264–82 has a chapter that is concrete, provides exercises, and approaches forgiveness within marriage from an explicitly Christian and biblical orientation.

145. McManus, *Marriage Savers*, 126.

146. Markman et al., *Fighting for Your Marriage*, 71–74, 81–82.

147. Ibid., 78.

148. Ibid., 70.

149. Ibid., 76.

150. Ibid., 74.

151. Ibid., 82.

DOES MARITAL PREPARATION WORK?

We have good evidence that good marital preparation can significantly improve marital quality and reduce the risk of divorce. For example, research on PREP and PREPARE and other empirically-rooted approaches to premarital education and counseling has shown high levels of couple satisfaction with them, a solid ability to predict which couples are most likely to get divorced, lasting benefits in terms of knowledge and skills gained, and lower risk of marital breakdown for those who complete these programs.[152] One study reviewed twenty-three others and concluded that, "the average person who participated in a premarital prevention program was significantly better off afterwards than 79 percent of people who did not participate. Stated differently, the average participant in a premarital program tends to experience about a 30 percent increase in measures of outcome success."[153] One of the key problems is that those most in need of such help are least likely to seek it out or receive it.[154]

There are numerous methods for doing this, and couples must consider which one fits them best and is available to them locally, led by folks they trust with compatible Christian beliefs and approaches to marriage. Here are some that are better known. Many Protestant and Roman Catholic churches sponsor Engaged Encounter retreats.[155] A premarital inventory called FOCCUS[156] (Facilitating Open Couple Communication, Understanding, and Study), which is guided by a trained facilitator with follow-up, is another popular approach. Its creators originally designed it for use in Catholic churches and Pre-Cana programs, but there are versions tailored for other Christian or even secular settings.[157] The

---

152. McManus, *Marriage Savers*, 113–18; summary of research in Scott et al., "Reasons for Divorce and Recollections of Premarital Intervention," 131–32; Futris et al., "The Impact of PREPARE on Engaged Couples," 70–71, 81–82; Olson et al., "PREPARE/ENRICH Program"; Markman et al., *Fighting for Your Marriage*, 12–14; FOCCUS USA, "Evidence of Reliability and Validity for FOCCUS Fourth Edition Pre-Marriage Inventory"; Stanley et al., "Premarital Education, Marital Quality, and Marital Stability."

153. Carroll and Doherty, "Evaluating the Effectiveness of Premarital Prevention Programs," 105.

154. Doss et al., "Differential Use of Premarital Education in First and Second Marriages," 268.

155. McManus, *Marriage Savers*, 137–38.

156. Ibid., 133.

157. FOCCUS USA, FOCCUS Pre-Marriage Inventory.

Relationship Evaluation Questionnaire (RELATE) is a popular tool used by couples alone, or preferably as part of more comprehensive premarital counseling.[158]

There are also some excellent Christian books and workbooks that can be used, with counseling or as part of couple's education if desired, to prepare for marriage. Each covers many or most of the major areas that I outlined in the last section of this chapter, including the most critical ones. They include the *Getting Ready for Marriage* book and workbook by Jim Burns and Doug Fields; *Preparing for Marriage* book, leader guide, and devotional materials from Dennis and Barbara Rainey's FamilyLife Ministries; *Before You Say "I Do"* by H. Norman Wright and Wes Roberts; and Wayne Mack's *Preparing for Marriage God's Way*. A short guide by John Piper, *Preparing for Marriage*, is less comprehensive but quite popular and helpful.

Many churches also link up seriously courting or engaged couples with marriage mentors, who are married couples who have volunteered and been trained as guides and models, able to encourage, counsel, identify problem areas, and so forth.[159] I highly recommend premarital couples hook up with a mentor couple even informally, if a formal, church-based program is not available to them. This can be as simple as forming a friendship with an older Christian couple with a great marriage and asking if they would be willing to spend time together, provide counseling, advice, and a sounding board. Even with premarital education and counseling, mentoring couples are an excellent resource. This is a very biblical approach to helping engaged couples. In the book of Titus, Paul indicates, for example, that these kinds of relationships ought to exist between older and younger women in the church (2:3–5).[160]

The key is to get some form of sound premarital preparation that addresses the issues we laid out in the last section of this chapter in a solid, thorough way, led by a wise counselor or educator with sound faith and solid experience. As has often been pointed out, young couples are

---

158. Relate Institute, "The Relate Assessment."
159. McManus, *Marriage Savers*, 319–24.
160. Ibid., 320.

willing to invest huge amounts of time and money in planning a *wedding*, while investing little in formally preparing for *marriage*.[161] A great wedding day is wonderful, but how much more important is it to build a solid foundation for a lifetime together as covenant partners leading a family and serving God together?

---

161. Ibid., 119.

PART 3

DIVORCE AND REMARRIAGE

INTRODUCTION TO PART 3

Except where marriage has little meaning, divorce is always major surgery.

Harold Haas[1]

I f we correctly understand marriage to be a most holy covenant, one that a husband and wife have entered into voluntarily and publicly before God to love, support, and be faithful to each other through every trial, difficulty, and disappointment of life until death separates them, then divorce is a truly horrendous way to conclude the marital bond. A man and a woman, united by God himself as one flesh in a relationship that represents the mystical union between Christ and his church, have dissolved their marriage. In some way or another, one or both of them, not God, chose to separate what he had joined (Matt 19:6; Mark 10:8-9), grievously violating the solemn vows once voiced to their spouse and to their Lord (Mal 2:14-16).

In a fallen world, divorce may be necessary, but it is always a tragedy; something the Lord hates (Mal 2:16a). The One who loves us selflessly and is perfectly wise despises it thoroughly. Therefore, it should not surprise us that divorce is horribly destructive, harming spouses, their children, their other intimates, and society generally. Yet modern people, including many professing believers, seem to have made peace with it. They have come to accept a shockingly high divorce rate and embraced the morality of the action itself on numerous grounds, many trivial, that are found nowhere in Scripture. How else do we find purchasing cakes and holding parties to *celebrate* divorce trending

---

1. Haas, *Marriage*, 33.

today?[2] This relaxed view of divorce emanates from a deficient view of marriage and a shrunken, distorted view of its Author.

In this section of this book, we will plunge into the difficult but necessary topic of divorce and remarriage. In the current chapter, we will look at what the Scriptures teach about this, and various doctrines, opinions, and disagreements about this among conservative Christian thinkers and leaders. This will include a thumbnail introduction of the relationship of Christian belief and then Enlightenment reasoning to divorce law. In chapter 11, we will tackle trends and current realities in divorce rates and risk, as well as reviewing the main causes for divorce, and public opinion about it, comparing evangelicals to others. Finally, in chapter 12, I will detail the terrible consequences of divorce. This will shatter popular misconceptions about the so-called good divorce. Many folks exposed to these facts find renewed motivation to avoid divorce at all costs, finding in them good cause to take those matters discussed in the last section of this book even more to heart. An ounce of prevention is worth a pound of cure.

---

2. In simply searching the term "divorce cake" on Google, I got thousands of hits, along with a list of related search ideas for parties and other confections, all of them finding cause for humor, joking, and fun, plus many articles from modern magazines applauding this sick trend. It struck me as macabre as having "Aren't you glad he's dead?" cakes and parties.

CHAPTER 10

THE BIBLE AND CHRISTIAN DOCTRINE ON DIVORCE AND REMARRIAGE

We have indeed seen that the priests . . . had violated the marriage pledge, which was to wholly destroy the very order of nature; for there can be . . . no chastity in social life except the bond of marriage be preserved, for marriage . . . is the fountain of mankind.

John Calvin[1]

It is a general rule that man must not go about to put asunder what God hath joined together. . . . If the yoke of marriage may not be thrown off at pleasure, it does not follow that therefore we must not come under it; but therefore, when we do come under it, we must resolve to comport with it, by love, and meekness, and patience, which will make divorce the most unnecessary undesirable thing that can be.

Matthew Henry[2]

T he Scriptures formed the basis for divorce laws in the West for many centuries. Under Roman Catholicism, given their interpretation of biblical teaching, in the eyes of the law marriage was indissoluble so long as both spouses lived. Otherwise, those wishing to dissolve their union had to obtain a declaration of annulment from the church, meaning that their marriage had never fulfilled the criteria for being a true, valid marital

---

1. Calvin, "The Commentaries of John Calvin on the Prophet Malachi," 552.
2. Henry, *Commentary on the Whole Bible*, 269, 270.

union.[3] Historians point out that the process by which those wishing to have their marriages dissolved was often corrupt, the rich and powerful using bribes and lobbying to get annulments that, for everyone else, were impossible to obtain.[4] The law increasingly allowed for legal separation, usually based on serious moral breach such as adultery, but this was not a true divorce and neither party was free to remarry.[5] Many predominantly Catholic nations had no legal divorce well into the twentieth century.[6] Chile did not legalize it until 2004[7] and, as of this writing, the Philippines still had not.[8]

With the onset of the Reformation about five hundred years ago, legal divorce began to emerge in Western nations. Along with denying that marriage was a sacrament of the church, most Protestants found limited grounds for divorce in the Scriptures, either directly or through logical inference. Since this was not merely legal separation, this understanding of biblical teaching allowed remarriage after dissolution of the marriage, at least for the innocent party. In Protestant countries, laws allowing divorce for serious breaches of the marital covenant—such as adultery, cruelty, or desertion—followed these doctrinal changes.[9] This happened first in continental Europe, for example in parts of Germany during the time of Martin Luther.[10] England proceeded much more slowly[11] and, except for a handful of private divorces granted by Parliament,[12] did not fully allow legal divorce until 1857.[13] For the most part, before that date English law only provided legal separations with no right to remarriage,[14] as in Catholic countries. However, as far back as the 1600s, in New England the Puritans went in opposite directions. They forbade permanent legal separations but granted divorce that allowed the innocent party to remarry in cases such as adultery,

---

3. Starbuck and Lundy, *Families in Context*, 67–68.

4. Stone, *A History of Divorce*, 1.

5. Rheinstein, "Trends in Marriage and Divorce Laws of Western Countries," 3–4.

6. Ibid., 3.

7. Hundley and Santos, "The Last Country in the World Where Divorce Is Illegal."

8. Tiglao, "Do What All the World Does: Have a Divorce Law."

9. Ibid., 10–11.

10. Witte, "The Reformation of Marriage Law in Martin Luther's Germany: Its Significance Then and Now," 336–46.

11. Ibid.

12. Stone, *A History of Divorce*, 20.

13. Ibid., 2.

14. Morgan, *The Puritan Family*, 34.

desertion, and long absences, and rarely in other situations such as when husbands refused to support their wives.[15] Like the Continental Reformers, the New England Puritans based their reasoning on the Scriptures.

Some Reformers advocated legal divorce for broader reasons than those laid out in the Bible, on utilitarian grounds such as making allowances for people to escape misery caused by stubborn and obstinate spouses. The idea was protecting people and maintaining order, making allowance for sinful people to prevent even greater sin[16] much as the Mosaic law had done (Matt 19:8; Mark 10:5). They asserted that while true Christians should abide by the strict teaching of the Scriptures regarding divorce, societies had to make allowance for unbelievers in unwanted marriages who did not embrace the same beliefs, motivations, and grace.[17]

Given all of this, we cannot deny that Protestantism helped to pave the way for the explosion of divorce, and secularization of divorce law, that we have seen since the early twentieth century. However, the Reformers did not anticipate this, nor would they have supported it. The extensive liberalization of law and public opinion related to divorce in modern countries is really more a direct product of the Enlightenment[18] than of the Reformation. Many Enlightenment philosophers emphasized secular reason over what they regarded as religious superstition. They also advocated removing any encumbrances to individuals' pursuit of happiness so long as they did no harm to anyone else, or to the state. This secular Enlightenment approach to individual rights began influencing divorce legislation as far back as the late 1700s in the French Revolution and Prussia.[19] As Max Rheinstein said, "This right had clearly to include the freedom of the individual to shake off the tie of an unhappy marriage and to pursue marital happiness with a new partner."[20] This quote succinctly summarizes modern thinking about divorce.

In the matter of divorce and remarriage, as in all other aspects of marriage, the committed Christian must submit to God's requirements,

---

15. Ibid., 34–38.
16. "The Reformation of Marriage Law in Martin Luther's Germany," 339–40.
17. Ibid., 339.
18. "Trends in Marriage and Divorce Laws of Western Countries," 11–12.
19. Ibid., 12–13.
20. Ibid., 12.

whatever their nation's law or public opinion may allow. His way is also the best way. So let's turn now to the key scriptural passages on divorce that informed these doctrinal stances and debates in Christian history, weighing competing ideas about what they meant and how they ought to be applied by God's people.

SCRIPTURAL TEACHING ON DIVORCE

OLD TESTAMENT

We must have some familiarity with the Old Testament regulations in order to make sense of New Testament teaching about divorce and remarriage. John Witte asserted that, "The Mosaic law had permitted divorce for indecency and incompatibility of all kinds."[21] This is similar with what some of the Pharisees claimed in Jesus' time (Matt 19:3, 7; Mark 10:4). Is this interpretation of the law accurate? To some extent perhaps, but not completely. The only Old Testament passage that specifically regulates divorce is Deuteronomy 24:1–4a:[22]

> When a man takes a wife and marries her, if then she finds no favor in his eyes because he has found some indecency in her, and he writes her a certificate of divorce and puts it in her hand and sends her out of his house, and she departs out of his house, and if she goes and becomes another man's wife, and the latter man hates her and writes her a certificate of divorce and puts it in her hand and sends her out of his house, or if the latter man dies, who took her to be his wife, then her former husband, who sent her away, may not take her again to be his wife, after she has been defiled, for that is an abomination before the LORD.

First, God is not commanding or even encouraging divorce here. He is only *allowing* it.[23] In fact, at the end of the Old Testament, the prophet Malachi tells Jewish men that much of their divorce, though perhaps technically "legal," was hateful to God and viewed by him as a serious oath violation (2:13–16).[24] Moreover, hearkening back to the creation of

---

21. "The Reformation of Marriage Law in Martin Luther's Germany," 338.

22. Murray, *Divorce*, 3.

23. Ibid., 6–8; Köstenberger and Jones, *God, Marriage, and Family*, 224–25; Instone-Brewer, *Divorce and Remarriage in the Bible*, 143–44.

24. Murray, *Divorce*, 16.

marriage in Genesis 2:24, there is no doubt that God intended wedlock to be permanent.[25] Almost all references to divorce in the Old Testament are negative.[26]

Second, this divorce was supposed to be a decision the *husband* made, not the wife. A woman could ask her spouse for a divorce, but only he could initiate the proceeding.[27] So we see that in cases where divorce was *not* allowed, the command is directed at the husband, as in "he may not divorce her" (cf. Deut 22:19, 29).

Third, the "indecency" mentioned here could not have been adultery, since that was punishable by death (Deut 22:20).[28] John Murray convincingly points out that it could not have referred to any kind of sexual uncleanness.[29] He believes that it probably applied to some kinds of unspecified shameful conduct,[30] certainly not any reason at all.[31] D. A. Carson suggests that it referred to "lewd, immoral behavior" of a serious nature.[32] Despite what some Jewish teachers were claiming during the time of Christ, given how ancient Israelites viewed marriage it is not likely that husbands were free to divorce their wives for trivial reasons.[33]

Fourth, this law protected the wife and restrained the husband. The divorce certificate gave her the right to remarry and protected her in various ways.[34] The fact that he could not take her back if she remarried would discourage him for divorcing her impulsively or hastily.[35] While the divorce was optional, the protection of this bill of divorcement was not.[36]

---

25. Köstenberger and Jones, *God, Marriage, and Family*, 33–34.

26. Ibid., 225; Murray, *Divorce*, 8. There may have been exceptions, such as Abraham's divorce of Hagar (Gen 21:12), though this is an extraordinary case given Sarah's role in demanding it. See Instone-Brewer, *Divorce and Remarriage in the Bible*, 23.

27. Köstenberger and Jones, *God, Marriage, and Family*, 170.

28. Ibid., 224; Instone-Brewer, *Divorce and Remarriage in the Bible*, 10; Murray, *Divorce*, 10.

29. Ibid., 11–12.

30. Ibid., 12; see also Adams, *Marriage, Divorce, and Remarriage in the Bible*, 63–64; and Instone-Brewer, *Divorce and Remarriage in the Bible*, 10.

31. Murray, *Divorce*, 15.

32. Carson, "Matthew," 467.

33. Köstenberger and Jones, *God, Marriage, and Family*, 225; see also Adams, *Marriage, Divorce, and Remarriage in the Bible*, 64.

34. Köstenberger and Jones, *God, Marriage, and Family*, 170; Murray, *Divorce*, 9; Instone-Brewer, *Divorce and Remarriage in the Bible*, 29.

35. Ibid., 32–33; Adams, *Marriage, Divorce, and Remarriage in the Bible*, 62–63; Murray, *Divorce*, 9.

36. Ibid., 9.

THE GOSPELS

John Murray identified seven "cardinal passages of Scripture upon which any treatment of the biblical teaching [on divorce and remarriage] must turn."[37] We have already examined one (Deut 24:1–4). Now we will look at the four found in the Gospels.

Luke 16 and Mark 10. We will start with Luke 16:18, the shortest of these: "Everyone who divorces his wife and marries another commits adultery, and he who marries a woman divorced from her husband commits adultery." Then there is the longer Mark 10:2–12:

> And Pharisees came up and in order to test him asked, "Is it lawful for a man to divorce his wife?" He answered them, "What did Moses command you?" They said, "Moses allowed a man to write a certificate of divorce and to send her away." And Jesus said to them, "Because of your hardness of heart he wrote you this command-ment. But from the beginning of creation, 'God made them male and female.' 'Therefore a man shall leave his father and mother and hold fast to his wife, and the two shall become one flesh.' So they are no longer two but one flesh. What therefore God has joined together, let not man separate." And in the house the disciples asked him again about this matter. And he said to them, "Whoever divorces his wife and marries another commits adultery against her, and if she divorces her husband and marries another, she commits adultery."

Both of these passages deal not just with divorce, but also remarriage. This makes sense, since a true divorce would have to leave at least the inno-cent partner free to marry again, as if their former spouse was dead. In the Mark text, we see that our Lord does not go back to where the Pharisees started, namely Moses. Instead, he builds where God started, namely, in the original marriage bond between Adam and Eve in Genesis (2:24), his true, creational intention for marriage.[38] As Paul did later in Ephesians 5:31, Jesus took them right to the fact that in marriage, God has united the two as one flesh. If God himself has joined a man and a woman together, how

---

37. Ibid., 2.

38. Adams, *Marriage, Divorce, and Remarriage in the Bible*, 68. See also "Matthew," 466–67.

can mere humans have the temerity to separate them? Such an improper divorce would not be valid, the original marriage would still be binding, and thus remarriage would be adultery. Why then did Mosaic law permit divorce for at least some number of reasons? As a concession to their sinfulness, and as we have seen, to restrain the effects of sin, including upon the vulnerable woman.

As Jay Adams has noted, the Pharisees are clearly trying to stretch the law of God, to give themselves wiggle room by narrowly focusing on what is legally acceptable.[39] This is far from attempting to discover God's perfect will, to find out what he delights in and how to find grace to fulfill it. Yet we see that approach to divorce and remarriage among many professing Christians today. We often, like the Pharisees, want a formal list of escape clauses, of technicalities to get out of an unwanted marriage.

Some might note, in response to Luke 16:18 and Mark 10:11, that in Hebrew society a man who married another woman could *not* be committing adultery, even if he had improperly divorced his first wife. Since the law allowed polygamy, he could have more than one wife. The best answer to that is that Jesus clearly rejected polygamy here as well: "the *two* shall become one flesh."[40] Another possible objection to these verses is that under Mosaic law, adultery was always a crime against the husband; technically the latter could have sex with others under various conditions without it being legal adultery. The answer to that is that Jesus was ending that loophole forever, again, by returning to the creational intent set forth in Genesis 2:24. David Instone-Brewer points out that in these passages Jesus makes clear that, "Marriage was meant to be monogamous, which meant that both husband and wife owed exclusive faithfulness to each other, and either could be the victim of adultery."[41]

One more possible objection is that women could not divorce their husbands, meaning that Mark 10:12 is either nonsense or refers to non-Jews. However, historical evidence shows that Jewish wives could sue for divorce during the time of Christ. If they prevailed, their husbands were required to divorce them by writing them the necessary certificate.[42] Regardless,

---

39. Adams, *Marriage, Divorce, and Remarriage in the Bible*, 68.
40. Instone-Brewer, *Divorce and Remarriage in the Bible*, 151.
41. Ibid., 151.
42. Ibid., 151–52.

again, here Jesus is equalizing the two sexes in matters of marital faithfulness and divorce.

The solutions to these objections show that in this teaching Jesus was affirming the sacredness of the marriage bond beyond just the question of divorce and remarriage. By focusing attention away from Old Testament regulations and toward God's original design for marriage, Jesus fit his teaching on divorce into the rich covenantal, spiritual realities of holy wedlock that reached back to the beginnings of the human race. In doing this, the logic of Christian marriage, and regulations on divorce and remarriage, become more applicable and comprehensible to gentiles living outside the Mosaic order, many of whom would soon join his church.

Matthew. Matthew 5:31-32 and 19:3-9 are well known for providing what is regarded by most Protestants as an "exception clause" to what appears, in Luke 16:18 and Mark 10:2-12, to be an absolute prohibition of divorce and remarriage.[43] The English Standard Version translates this apparent exception as "sexual immorality" in both of these Matthew passages.

Here is what Jesus said as recorded in Matthew 5:31-32: "It was also said, 'Whoever divorces his wife, let him give her a certificate of divorce.' But I say to you that everyone who divorces his wife, *except on the ground of sexual immorality*, makes her commit adultery, and whoever marries a divorced woman commits adultery" (emphasis added). Matthew 19:3-9 embeds this teaching in the larger context of the Pharisees grilling Jesus, trying to force him to take a position that would get him into trouble with at least some important group, and force him to take sides between two influential rabbinical schools:[44]

> And Pharisees came up to him and tested him by asking, "Is it lawful to divorce one's wife for any cause?" He answered, "Have you not read that he who created them from the beginning made them male and female, and said, 'Therefore a man shall leave his father and his mother and hold fast to his wife, and the two shall become one flesh'? So they are no longer two but one flesh. What therefore God

---

43. Such a qualification of general principles in some special cases would not have surprised ancient audiences, for whom this was common practice. See Keener, . . . *And Marries Another*, 31–32.

44. Carson, "Matthew," 465–66.

has joined together, let not man separate." They said to him, "Why then did Moses command one to give a certificate of divorce and to send her away?" He said to them, "Because of your hardness of heart Moses allowed you to divorce your wives, but from the beginning it was not so. And I say to you: whoever divorces his wife, *except for sexual immorality*, and marries another, commits adultery." (emphasis added)

Mark 10:2–12 and Matthew 19:3–9 are very similar, though we find a few differences such as the Pharisees asking about divorce "for any cause" or saying that Moses "commanded" men to give their wives certificates of divorce in some cases.[45] However, in terms of Jesus' teaching here, the most important thing introduced in these two passages in Matthew that we do not find in the Luke and Mark passages above is that critical insertion, "except for sexual immorality." What does this mean? The answer is not simple.

"Sexual immorality" here certainly *includes* "adultery." Many scholars assert that first-century Jews would have *assumed* that Jesus would have allowed divorce in cases of adultery unless he said otherwise.[46] Some offer this as an explanation for why Luke and Mark do not mention this exception; namely, there was no need to. The Mosaic punishment for adultery was death, ending the marriage.[47] First-century Jewish law also *required* men to divorce adulterous wives.[48] Both the practice and God's approval of divorce in such instances is seen in the Prophets (cf. Jer 3:8), and in Joseph's plan to divorce Mary when he assumed she was pregnant due to being unfaithful to him (Matt 1:19).[49] Rather than charging the wife with a capital offense, her husband could divorce her. Going further, other scholars have even reasonably stated that in Matthew, Jesus was replacing the death penalty for adultery with divorce.[50]

---

45. Murray, *Divorce*, 29–30.

46. Ibid., 33; Carson, "Matthew," 473.

47. Cf. Richards, "Divorce and Remarriage under a Variety of Circumstances," 229; Murray, *Divorce*, 27; Newheiser, *Marriage, Divorce, and Remarriage*, 212–13.

48. Köstenberger and Jones, *God, Marriage, and Family*, 228; "Matthew," 470.

49. Adams, *Marriage, Divorce, and Remarriage in the Bible*, 70–73; Newheiser, *Marriage, Divorce, and Remarriage*, 213.

50. "Matthew," 472; Murray, *Divorce*, 27. See also Newheiser, *Marriage, Divorce, and Remarriage*, 212.

However, it appears that Jesus had more in view here than adultery.[51] The phrase rendered "sexual immorality" in both Matthew passages comes from the Greek *porneia*, which covers a range of sexual sins, not just adultery.[52] Scholars often translate it as "fornication," as we discussed briefly in chapter 3. If that were not the case, Jesus could have used the more specific term for adultery, *moicheia*.[53] Remember that a married person must have sexual intercourse with someone other than his or her spouse to commit adultery.[54] This would leave out potentially serious sexual sins like bestiality, homosexuality, non-intercourse incestuous acts, child molestation, and the like. As Jay Adams noted, Jesus would have certainly included such sins, and not just technical adultery, as an exception here, given the gravity of those sexual acts.[55]

Thomas Edgar argues, to the contrary, that *only* adultery and not these other sexual sins would be included under "sexual immorality" since Jesus' context is married couples.[56] Sadly, as we see all around us, married people do commit such sins. It seems ludicrous to claim that a married man having intercourse with a woman other than his wife would fall under Jesus' use of *porneia* here, but not one who committed sodomy or engaged in bestiality. We could also point out that folks today would consider such acts committed by married people to be variant forms of adultery anyway, and among the Jews they would have been capital offenses. Sadly, there are other sexual acts that people can and do engage in outside of marriage such as oral sex, petting, various forms of perversion, extreme levels or forms of use of pornography, and more.[57] If we accept the exception clause in the Matthew passages as including a wider form of sexual offenses than technical adultery, they could also constitute grounds for divorce.[58]

---

51. Keener, . . . *And Marries Another*, 22–25.

52. Murray, *Divorce*, 20–21; Carson, "Matthew," 468; Köstenberger and Jones, *God, Marriage, and Family*, 231; Adams, *Marriage, Divorce, and Remarriage in the Bible*, 53; Wilson, *Reforming Marriage*, 133.

53. Adams, *Marriage, Divorce, and Remarriage in the Bible*, 53; Carson, "Matthew," 468.

54. I touched on this briefly in footnote 66 in chapter 1, pointing out why in England and Wales same-sex couples cannot legally commit adultery, as they would not be having sexual intercourse with the non-marital partner, at least not homosexually.

55. Adams, *Marriage, Divorce, and Remarriage in the Bible*, 54–55. See also Richards, "Divorce and Remarriage under a Variety of Circumstances," 230; and Instone-Brewer, *Divorce and Remarriage in the Bible*, 158–59.

56. "Divorce & Remarriage for Adultery or Desertion," 162.

57. Newheiser, *Marriage, Divorce, and Remarriage*, 239–41.

58. Noting, as we already have, that pastorally these not be handled as "escape clauses," and that in many if not most cases the best solution is still going to be repentance and reconciliation.

In the first-century Jewish context, and certainly all we understand about marriage rooted in reasonably informed consent, fornication committed before marriage and hidden from the spouse could be included in Jesus' use of *porneia*.[59] In the Old Testament, a woman claiming to be a virgin at marriage who was not could be put to death (Deut 22:20–21).[60] This is not the sole meaning of *porneia* here, as some claim,[61] but it almost certainly is included.

However, there are dangers in broadening the meaning of *porneia*.[62] In all such cases, given the complexity of sin and of the human heart, and the power of emotions, people should seek wise pastoral counsel when they are confronting any sexual sin in their spouse.

D. A. Carson notes that allowing divorce only for *porneia* is more limited than what could have been accepted under the Mosaic law.[63] It also fits Jesus' focus on marriage as "one flesh," something that as we have seen is expressed in the sexual union. A violation of this is most serious, and while not requiring divorce, it certainly is consistent with biblical marriage that it gravely strikes at the heart of a marriage such that Jesus would at least allow divorce where a spouse has been sexually promiscuous outside the bonds of marriage.[64]

Some argue that Matthew added in the exception clauses later, that Jesus never actually verbalized this exception.[65] Thus, they say, we should ignore "except for sexual immorality" and adopt an absolute "no divorce, no remarriage" position. There are numerous problems with this stance, including what I said above about why first-century Jews would have assumed Jesus was allowing for an adultery exception unless he specifically rejected it. These are part of inerrant Scripture regardless; there is no

---

59. Wilson, *Reforming Marriage*, 133. D. A. Carson points out that some think that is *all* Jesus was talking about here, a position he rejects, "Matthew," 468.

60. Newheiser, *Marriage, Divorce, and Remarriage*, 242.

61. Carson, "Matthew," 468.

62. Newheiser, *Marriage, Divorce, and Remarriage*, 240–41.

63. Carson, "Matthew," 472.

64. Carson, "Matthew," 472; Wilson, *Reforming Marriage*, 133.

65. For example, Johnson and Buttrick, "The Gospel According to St. Matthew," 480–81 make this argument forcefully, asserting that Jesus never actually said this (see Murray, *Divorce*, 46; "Matthew," 469). A variant on this, discussed in the latter source, is to say that the text really means that Jesus is specifically *excluding* adultery as a cause for divorce, based on tortured linguistic analysis. Not many have adopted this view.

doubt that the "except clauses" are part of the original Matthew text.[66] This position, though "conservative" in impact, actually involves a subtle rejection of the doctrine of biblical inerrancy.[67] There is no concrete evidence that Matthew made this up and did not accurately capture what Jesus said.

Others argue that all Jesus is referring to are incestuous marriages.[68] Nothing in the text suggests that.[69] Besides, in this culture, such a "marriage" would not have ever been valid.[70]

Others argue that the sexual immorality exception applies to divorce but does not allow the innocent party to remarry.[71] To summarize a highly technical scholarly debate involving logic, translation, and Greek grammar, there is no way to render the text this way that makes good sense.[72] This also would require we abandon the normal meaning of divorce, substituting for it a permanent separation.[73] The "except for sexual immorality" applies to both divorce and remarriage.[74] This also fits the normal sense of "divorce" at that time.[75] Remarriage is not adultery if it follows a divorce enacted for permissible reasons.

Douglas Wilson suggests that any offense that would have carried the death penalty under biblical law is grounds for divorce, since if the state was fulfilling its proper functions the offender would be executed and the marriage ended. He uses murder as an example.[76] Although he does not specifically tie this to the Matthew passages or *porneia*, it flows from some of the logic for including sexual sins other than adultery that would have carried the death penalty, and so is worth mentioning here. It is not hard to see why innocent parties could possibly divorce spouses guilty of such crimes as murder, witchcraft, kidnapping, and so on. However, given the long list of capital offenses in the Old Testament, I would want to

---

66. "Matthew," 467, 473; Köstenberger and Jones, *God, Marriage, and Family*, 227; Murray, *Divorce*, 46–47.

67. "Divorce & Remarriage for Adultery or Desertion," 166.

68. Carson, "Matthew," 468.

69. Newheiser, *Marriage, Divorce, and Remarriage*, 213.

70. Carson, "Matthew," 469.

71. Ibid., 470.

72. Murray, *Divorce*, 36–43, 48–50; Carson, "Matthew," 470.

73. Newheiser, *Marriage, Divorce, and Remarriage*, 215.

74. Carson, "Matthew," 470–71; Adams, *Marriage, Divorce, and Remarriage in the Bible*, 52–53.

75. Newheiser, *Marriage, Divorce, and Remarriage*, 179–80, 222–23.

76. Wilson, *Reforming Marriage*, 134–36.

see this more qualified and biblically defended than is evident in Wilson's brief discourse. Still, his general point appears to fit the overall teaching of Scripture, and biblically informed common sense.

What we do know is that if we embrace the exception clause, God does not command or even prefer divorce. He *permits* it.[77] In the larger context of Christian revelation, there is no doubt that where possible, the best outcome is one in which the guilty party fully repents and the innocent spouse forgives, and both work to restore the marriage.[78] However, it is not always possible, and even if the wronged spouse truly forgives his or her partner, it may not be advisable or otherwise desirable for the innocent party to remain in the marriage. If that happens, there is no basis for accusing the divorcing spouse of being unforgiving, rigid, ungodly, and so forth.

PAUL'S LETTERS

The last two of the passages that John Murray called "cardinal" for understanding what the Bible teaches about divorce and remarriage come from Paul's epistles: Romans 7:1-3 and the most well-known and pivotal of the two, 1 Corinthians 7:10-16.[79] Neither one mentions the exception clause from Matthew. We will begin with Romans.

Romans 7. James Montgomery Boice pointed out that in Romans 7:1-3, the apostle Paul uses "the illustration of marriage law to show how Christians have been freed from the law in order to be married to Jesus Christ."[80] We will not focus on this central point, but at what Paul seems to be assuming about divorce and remarriage[81] in this text: "Or do you not know, brothers— for I am speaking to those who know the law—that the law is binding on a person only as long as he lives? For a married woman is bound by law to her husband while he lives, but if her husband dies she is released from the law of marriage. Accordingly, she will be called an adulteress if she lives with another man while her husband is alive. But if her husband dies, she is free from that law, and if she marries another man she is not an adulteress."

---

77. Murray, *Divorce*, 21; Adams, *Marriage, Divorce, and Remarriage in the Bible*, 56.

78. Adams, *Marriage, Divorce, and Remarriage in the Bible*, 56–59; Wilson, *Reforming Marriage*, 133.

79. *Romans*, 716. See also Murray, *Divorce*, 2, 55.

80. Ibid., 78.

81. Ibid., 78.

The marital situation that Paul refers to here was true under the Mosaic law.[82] However, the obligations of a wife to her husband presented here are universal and not just applicable to Jews.[83] Paul appeals to gentiles here to consider the same thing that Jesus based his teachings about marriage and divorce on (Luke 16:18; Mark 10:11–12; Matt 5:32; 19:9), pointing back to God uniting the first man and woman as recorded in Genesis 2:23–24.[84] In any valid marriage, God has joined the two as one flesh. If a widow remarries, there is no sin, but if a woman leaves her husband to live with another man, she violates that covenant and commits adultery.

Taken out of context, Romans 7:2–3 seems to imply that Paul assumed that only death ends marriage and frees someone up to remarry, that he is saying that remarriage following divorce is always adultery. This would make this incompatible with the Matthew passages we discussed earlier, unless we were to interpret the exception clause as meaning something other than allowing divorce and remarriage for sexual immorality.[85]

However, as we shall soon see, Paul does seem to provide an exception to the general prohibition against divorce and remarriage in 1 Corinthians 7:15.[86] If this is the case, then in Paul's teaching he did not intend for the principle set forth in Romans 7:2–3 to be absolute. He was merely stating a general reality, not applying this to every possible exception.

The key thing to remember is that, as Köstenberger and Jones note, Paul's aim here was "not to give an exhaustive discourse on the morality of divorce and remarriage but rather to illustrate a deeper truth regarding . . . the atonement."[87] To sidetrack the discussion into the intricacies of rules regarding divorce and remarriage would have meant pursuing a tangent at the expense of his main point.[88] It is for the same reason that he focuses on the obligations of the woman here and not her husband. Only she can represent the believer in this metaphor.[89]

---

82. Harrison and Hagner, "Romans," 114–15.

83. Murray, *Divorce*, 81; *Romans, Volume 2*, 717.

84. Murray, *Divorce*, 81.

85. Ibid., 82.

86. Ibid., 86, 88–89.

87. Köstenberger and Jones, *God, Marriage, and Family*, 233. See also Murray, *Divorce*, 91.

88. Ibid., 93–94; Instone-Brewer, *Divorce and Remarriage in the Bible*, 210–11, 283.

89. Murray, *Divorce*, 94–95. Because Christ's death frees the woman from the law, she is free to "marry" another, namely, Jesus Christ.

Given this, there is no reason to believe that the sexual immorality exception given by Christ in Matthew, or the situation addressed in 1 Corinthians 7:15, cannot be an exception to the general rule described in Romans 7:2–3.[90] We cannot expect Paul to detail exceptions to the prohibition on divorce while using the general rules about remarriage to illustrate a totally different doctrine, even those exceptions he is aware of and accepts.

1 *Corinthians 7*. The last of what John Murray referred to as the "cardinal passages of Scripture" dealing with divorce is in 1 Corinthians 7:10–16. Here is what Paul said here:

> To the married I give this charge (not I, but the Lord): the wife should not separate from her husband (but if she does, she should remain unmarried or else be reconciled to her husband), and the husband should not divorce his wife. To the rest I say (I, not the Lord) that if any brother has a wife who is an unbeliever, and she consents to live with him, he should not divorce her. If any woman has a husband who is an unbeliever, and he consents to live with her, she should not divorce him. For the unbelieving husband is made holy because of his wife, and the unbelieving wife is made holy because of her husband. Otherwise your children would be unclean, but as it is, they are holy. *But if the unbelieving partner separates, let it be so. In such cases the brother or sister is not enslaved. God has called you to peace.* For how do you know, wife, whether you will save your husband? Or how do you know, husband, whether you will save your wife? (emphasis added)

The first point that Paul makes here (vv. 10–11), concerning marriages in which both partners are believers,[91] is that husbands and wives must not divorce. By specifying that this command is from the Lord, he hearkens back directly to Matthew 5:32 and 19:9, Mark 10:11–12, and Luke 16:18.[92] What if they sin and separate contrary to this command?[93] Then, he says,

---

90. Ibid., 90.

91. Verbrugge, "1 Corinthians," 317; Fee, *The First Epistle to the Corinthians*, 323.

92. Verbrugge, "1 Corinthians," 317; Fee, *The First Epistle to the Corinthians*, 323–24; Instone-Brewer, *Divorce and Remarriage in the Bible*, 199.

93. Murray, *Divorce*, 61–62; Fee, *The First Epistle to the Corinthians*, 326.

they should seek to be reconciled and not go on to remarry, as this would be adulterous.[94] As Charles Hodge notes, this suggests that there will be occasions in which a Christian will be justified in separating from his or her spouse over reasons that "do not justify divorce."[95] Pastors see this all too commonly.

Paul's expression of the Lord's command here without mentioning the exception for sexual immorality that Jesus mentions in Matthew 5:32 and 19:9, does not mean that he was unaware of it.[96] As John Murray notes, Paul is clearly referring here to a situation in which the couple should not permanently separate,[97] which does not mean that he includes all possible divorce. This would not include a situation where an innocent party left a philandering spouse, for example, where the above teachings in Matthew would teach us that the aggrieved party is *not* required to seek reconciliation.[98] Murray reasonably argues that having just talked about the need to avoid fornication and marriage as a remedy for that, it would be "incongruous" for Paul to have brought up two Christians divorcing because of serious sexual sin in that context.[99]

In a short bridge statement following verse 11, Paul says, "To the rest I say (I, not the Lord)." The "rest" he is talking about are those in mixed marriages, most created when one partner has converted but the other has not.[100] The "I, not the Lord" does not mean that this is merely human opinion, as some mistakenly think. It means, as Jay Adams points out, that he is "taking up an issue that Jesus did not discuss."[101] That is not surprising, since it was not Christ's purpose to deal with every possible divorce situation from every angle,[102] and the audience and issues facing it were so different.[103]

94. Newheiser, *Marriage, Divorce, and Remarriage*, 219.

95. Hodge, *1 & 2 Corinthians*, 113–14.

96. Murray, *Divorce*, 57–58; Hodge, *1 & 2 Corinthians*, 113.

97. Murray, *Divorce*, 56.

98. Ibid., 56.

99. Ibid., 57; "Divorce & Remarriage for Adultery or Desertion," 188–89.

100. Adams, *Marriage, Divorce, and Remarriage in the Bible*, 45; Keener, . . . *And Marries Another*, 55, 57.

101. Adams, *Marriage, Divorce, and Remarriage in the Bible*, 45.

102. Ibid.

103. Keener, . . . *And Marries Another*, 54.

Now we have a frame of reference for Paul's second point (vv. 12-14), which is that no Christian should divorce his or her spouse merely because he or she is an unbeliever.[104] In fact, though the salvation of the latter is not a certainty (1 Cor 7:16), God might use the conduct of the believer to win over the unregenerate partner (v. 16).[105] Regardless, God's grace will extend to the family of the believer (v. 14),[106] and it is certainly not improper to remain in this relationship.[107] Mixed marriage or not, God has made them "one flesh," and the children are those of a believer.[108] Given the clarity of this teaching, it is amazing that Tim Challies lists "My spouse isn't a Christian" as a common reason evangelicals give for seeking a divorce.[109]

The third point, in verse 15, is the one that is most central to the question of whether or not Paul is allowing another reason for a Christian to divorce his or her spouse and remarry.[110] There is little argument about the fact that Paul says here that, if the unbelieving spouse chooses to leave, the believer should not stop them and is no longer bound to them. The believer has not driven out his or her spouse, which Paul forbade in verses 12-13. He or she has left willfully.[111] The language here suggests Paul is rendering a decisive judgement upon the one leaving and erasing the marital obligations of the believing husband or wife.[112]

What scholars mainly dispute is what Paul means by, "In such cases the brother or sister is not enslaved" (often translated, "not under bondage"), and that in such situations Christians are "called to peace." I believe the best answer is that he means the innocent spouse should allow the marriage to be dissolved, and is then free to remarry.

Certainly, the language here is ambiguous enough for sincere, faithful biblical scholars to disagree.[113] We cannot absolutely disprove the argument

---

104. Murray, *Divorce*, 65; Hodge, *1 & 2 Corinthians*, 114; Verbrugge, "1 Corinthians," 318-19; Fee, *The First Epistle to the Corinthians*, 329.

105. Ibid.

106. Murray, *Divorce*, 65.

107. Verbrugge, "1 Corinthians," 319; Fee, *The First Epistle to the Corinthians*, 329.

108. Hodge, *1 & 2 Corinthians*, 116-17.

109. "10 Common but Illegitimate Reasons to Divorce."

110. Murray, *Divorce*, 2.

111. Ibid., 68, 77.

112. Ibid., 69.

113. Verbrugge, "1 Corinthians," 319; Köstenberger and Jones, *God, Marriage, and Family*, 235. See, for example, the next footnote.

that Paul is allowing separation only, without remarriage, in the cases he is addressing here.[114] Even though I disagree with this view, I also agree that we must not lose sight of the overall weight of Paul's argument, namely that mixed marriage or not, believers should strive mightily to maintain their marriages, even at great personal cost if need be.[115] The innocent spouse and the church should always make sincere, prolonged attempts at reconciliation before giving up.[116]

However, the position that in such desertion the abandoned partner is free to divorce and remarry is the stronger one. Most evangelical scholars agree with that view.[117] The exact term that Paul uses to say "not *bound*" is stronger than what he uses in verse 39 to describe a wife bound to her husband until he dies.[118] This implies that the deserting spouse is now, as the husband in verse 39, "dead" to his or her partner.[119] Paul uses the same word for "separates" here that Jesus uses in Matthew 19:6 to refer to divorce, meaning that Paul is talking about the unbeliever divorcing the believer.[120] Jim Newheiser notes that "both Jewish and Greco-Roman bills of divorce explicitly stated the divorcée's freedom to remarry."[121] Thus, this would have been the natural assumption of Paul's audience regarding "not bound" unless he specified otherwise. There is also the pictured futility of bringing any Christian argument or church discipline to bear upon the deserter to bring about reconciliation—the situation is essentially hopeless.[122] Indeed, no interpreter denies that a divorce has essentially happened, initiated by the deserting spouse, not the innocent one.[123] Not allowing divorce and

---

114. Verbrugge, "1 Corinthians," 319–20. Gordon Fee makes that argument in his highly regarded *First Epistle to the Corinthians* (329), stating that the call to "peace" in this passage means to "maintain the marriage in the hope of the unbelieving spouse's conversion." However, he does not dig into and exegetically defend that statement. He later (334–39) sets forth a longer and more detailed defense of the proposition that Paul is not dealing at all with remarriage here, that the weight is to the maintenance of the marriage at all costs even in the face of desertion. See the charitable summary of this competing view in Köstenberger and Jones, *God, Marriage, and Family*, 234–35.

115. Fee, *The First Epistle to the Corinthians*, 338–39.

116. Köstenberger and Jones, *God, Marriage, and Family*, 236.

117. Ibid., 234.

118. Murray, *Divorce*, 74–75; "Divorce and Remarriage for Adultery or Desertion," 189–90.

119. *God, Family, and Marriage*, 234.

120. Newheiser, *Marriage, Divorce, and Remarriage*, 221.

121. Ibid., 223. See also Heth, "Remarriage for Adultery or Desertion," 67.

122. Murray, *Divorce*, 75; Adams, *Marriage, Divorce, and Remarriage in the Bible*, 45–46.

123. Köstenberger and Jones, *God, Marriage, and Family*, 235.

remarriage in the case of desertion can harm the innocent spouse and any children they had together. Both Jay Adams[124] and Jim Newheiser[125] make this point compellingly using concrete cases. Yet biblical standards about divorce are supposed to protect the innocent,[126] and otherwise restrain the effects of sin. Moreover, why would Paul *only* tell the abandoned spouse that he or she is free to separate? If this has already occurred due to their partner's action, that seems unnecessary.[127] Are they to implore their former partner to return indefinitely, even if he or she remarries?[128] The freedom, and the peace, Paul has in view seems to be complete, meaning the innocent spouse can remarry.[129] As Douglas Wilson says, "Not bound means *not bound.*"[130]

If true then desertion would have the same effect as the sexual immorality mentioned in Matthew 5:32 and 19:9. Would this, in turn, bring Paul into conflict with the teachings of Christ on divorce in the Gospels?[131] Not at all. In the case Paul is dealing with, it is not the believer "putting away" his or her spouse as it is in the Matthew passages, but the latter willfully "going away" and the believer accepting it.[132] Second, the situation Jesus deals with in the divorce passages in Luke, Mark, and Matthew is of two people who are both part of the covenant faith where, as Paul said in verses 10 and 11, they should resolve separation and other difficulties by reconciliation, not divorce and remarriage.[133] Most of us have seen believing spouses separate over some ongoing disagreement or incompatibility, and understand how that is different from one willfully deserting the other and rejecting the faith. To expect the teaching of Christ in Matthew to cover the particular situation Paul is addressing is

---

124. Adams, *Marriage, Divorce, and Remarriage in the Bible*, 49.

125. Newheiser, *Marriage, Divorce, and Remarriage*, 190–91.

126. Ibid., 191.

127. Instone-Brewer, *Divorce and Remarriage in the Bible*, 201.

128. Ibid.

129. Ibid., 202; Adams, *Marriage, Divorce, and Remarriage in the Bible*, 48–50. As Craig Keener notes, if Paul meant divorce but not remarriage, the way he put it would have suggested to his audience the opposite of what he meant. . . . *And Marries Another*, 61.

130. Wilson, *Reforming Marriage*, 134, emphasis in the original. Charles Hodge certainly agrees; see *1 & 2 Corinthians*, 118.

131. Murray, *Divorce*, 69–70.

132. Ibid., 70; "Divorce & Remarriage for Adultery or Desertion," 190.

133. Murray, *Divorce*, 70–71.

unreasonable.[134] Finally, as with our discussion of Romans 7:1–3 above, there is no reason for Paul to bring in the adultery exception here, though he was doubtless aware of it, because it was a given.[135]

If there is a freedom to divorce and remarry in response to one spouse willfully and obstinately deserting the other, does it apply to two believers, or only in the religiously mixed marriages addressed here? After all, we must not carelessly extend this teaching to other types of cases.[136] However, if a professed believer has deserted a spouse who has not forced him or her out, and absolutely refuses to repent or reconcile, the church should treat him or her as an unbeliever. This person has abandoned not only their spouse, but also the Christian faith.[137]

THE WESTMINSTER CONFESSION OF FAITH VERSUS CATHOLIC AND PROTESTANT "PERMANENCE" POSITIONS

The *Westminster Confession of Faith* states the following:[138]

5. Adultery or fornication committed after a contract, being detected before marriage, giveth just occasion to the innocent party to dissolve that contract. In the case of adultery after marriage, it is lawful for the innocent party to sue out for a divorce, and, after the divorce, to marry another, as if the offending party were dead.

6. Although the corruption of man be such as is apt to study arguments unduly to put asunder those whom God hath joined together in marriage: yet nothing but adultery, or such willfull desertion as can no way be remedied by the Church, or civil magistrate, is cause sufficient of dissolving the bond of marriage: wherein, a public and orderly course of proceeding is to be observed; and the persons concerned in it not left to their own wills and discretion in their own case.

---

134. Ibid., 71; Wilson, *Reforming Marriage*, 136.

135. "Divorce & Remarriage for Adultery or Desertion," 188–89.

136. Murray, *Divorce*, 75.

137. Ibid., 76; Newheiser, *Marriage, Divorce, and Remarriage*, 223–24. I find this more convincing in dealing with the case of a professed believer who deserts his or her spouse than the tentative argument made by Thomas Edgar that mixed marriages are as valid as non-mixed marriages and so desertion would be the same in both. That lets the church "off the hook" for dealing with the professed believer who abandons his or her spouse to implore them to repent and then excommunicate them should this fail.

The *Westminster Confession of Faith* allows divorce and, for the innocent party, remarriage on limited grounds through an orderly process. In the main I believe that this statement, while not perfect, generally captures the teaching of the Scriptures, as I have set it out in this section. It would be better if those who drafted it had used a more general term than "adultery," though there is little doubt they would have included in this such sexual offenses as bestiality and homosexuality. Douglas Wilson's points about divorcing spouses guilty of heinous non-sexual offenses such as homicide, kidnapping, and the like are reasonable, as I pointed out, but not addressed here. It does not tackle such hard subjects as what to do about serious abuse, or believers who have sinfully divorced and remarried, including those who were guilty parties in the initial divorce, as we will discuss below. However, Scripture does not *specifically* address those topics either.

The Roman Catholic position is that absolutely no divorce or remarriage is permissible, and that all remarriage following divorce is adultery. The Church does not cut off divorced and remarried Catholics and their families from mass or from the care and fellowship of the Church, but it does bar them from receiving the sacrament of communion.[139] The latter is currently a subject of intense debate among Catholic leaders.[140] The Church agrees that physical separation may at times be necessary, as well as *legal* divorce to provide for "certain legal rights, the care of the children, or the protection of inheritance."[141] Freedom to marry following divorce only exists for those who have successfully petitioned the Church to *annul* their first marriage, that is, declared that it was never fully valid under Church law. This has led to the multiplication of grounds for annulment,[142] determined through an often complicated and time-consuming process.[143]

---

138. 81–82.

139. To review the Roman Catholic position on the indissolubility of marriage, forbidding divorce and remarriage, see the *Catholic Catechism*, sections 1614 (p. 403), 1640 (p. 409), 1646–51 (pp. 411–12), 1664–65 (pp. 414–15), 2382–86 (pp. 573–74), 2400 (p. 576).

140. Cf. Rocca, "Pope Francis Opens New Phase in Church's Debate on Divorce."

141. *Catholic Catechism*, section 2383 (p. 573).

142. That issue is a long-standing concern. See, for example, "Trends in Marriage and Divorce Law of Western Countries," 10.

143. United States Conference of Catholic Bishops, "Annulment," gives a brief overview.

Pastors and scholars often refer to Protestant positions that forbid all divorce with right to remarry as "permanence" views. These hold that even spouses who have been faithful to their marital vows who have suffered adultery or desertion are bound for life, without the support of a spouse, to their spouses even if reconciliation is no longer viably possible. Well-known exponents of this view are John Piper,[144] Gordon Wenham,[145] J. Carl Laney,[146] and Daryl Wingerd and the other authors of *Divorce and Remarriage: A Permanence View.*

The *Westminster Confession of Faith* rejects the Catholic and Protestant permanence approaches that, while sincere and often carried out with real compassion, burden innocent parties to uphold an absolute restriction that our Lord does not require. Consider the case of former US Congressman Robert Bauman, a Roman Catholic, closeted actively gay man who had a wife and four children. Upon discovery of his private activities, and given that he did not intend to, or believe he could, change his orientation or action, his wife sought to end the marriage. Under the *Westminster Confession of Faith*, her church would have recognized her right to divorce and remarry based on her spouse's unrepentant and serious sexual immorality, which appears to be a clear application of Matthew 5:32 and 19:9. In a "permanence" Protestant church, she would have been required to remain bound to him for life, probably separated, even as he continued his active gay lifestyle. As a Catholic, his wife had the original marriage declared to be less than totally valid, following a lengthy nullification process, based on the fact that he had a "defect of character," including that he was homosexually inclined, at the time they were married.[147] The Catholic approach struck me as a distortion of the concept of marital validity and annulment, while the Protestant permanence position would have burdened this innocent woman for life because of her husband's flagrant violation of his marital vows. The application of the exception clause given by Jesus would have been more straightforward, merciful, and honest.

---

144. "Divorce & Remarriage." Note that Piper does not impose this view on his church; the elders govern more by the standards on divorce and remarriage laid out in the *Westminster Confession of Faith.*

145. "No Remarriage after Divorce."

146. *The Divorce Myth*; also "No Divorce and No Remarriage."

147. Romano, "Bob Bauman, After the Fall."

At the same time, the *Westminster Confession of Faith* also rejects the trend in modern times to multiply grounds for divorce recklessly and without regard to Scripture according to the private whims and desires of married persons seeking to leave their spouses.[148] For desertion, it makes very clear that people should exhaust all reasonable efforts at reconciliation before a divorce is accepted. It assumes that not everything that makes a marriage hard is a sound reason to dissolve it. It masterfully captures a lot of biblical information in a very brief, balanced way.

CONCLUDING THOUGHTS ON DEBATES OVER SCRIPTURAL TEACHINGS ON DIVORCE AND REMARRIAGE

I would like to make a final point here that applies to debates over the "exceptions" that have led to these competing stances. These are difficult, complex passages and issues. Serious, orthodox believers who hold that there are *some* legitimate grounds for Christians to get divorced and remarry do not necessarily have a lower view of marriage than those who hold to an absolute "permanence" position.[149] The latter should not marginalize or heap guilt on Christians who have suffered desertion or adultery and eventually divorced and remarried because they accepted and acted upon the majority evangelical position.[150] Conversely, those who believe in these limited grounds for divorce should not accuse their brethren who do not of being hard-hearted, legalistic, and the like. Most that I have encountered are trying to be faithful to a reasonable reading of the Scriptures that has formed their convictions. That is something we all must do. We can add that while "permanence" advocates are asking fellow believers to endure some hard things for the sake of obedience to Christ, all faithful Christians understand that living in his kingdom may cost us dearly.[151] This can include remaining in difficult marital situations where there are no valid grounds for divorce and remarriage, which is what vowing "for better, for worse" means.

---

148. Hodge, *The Westminster Confession*, 302.
149. That is, no divorce and no remarriage, or divorce but no remarriage.
150. Köstenberger and Jones, *God, Marriage, and Family*, 236.
151. Newheiser, *Marriage, Divorce, and Remarriage*, 206.
152. Much more commonly the husband, by the way.

DIFFICULT CASES

Numerous cases do not fit neatly into the Scriptures we have looked at, nor into the *Westminster Confession of Faith* clauses that summarize them. Believers, their families, and churches wrestle with these matters, even when they take biblical teaching seriously and sincerely want to honor God in their marital decisions. How they handle these choices affects the lives of many Christian adults and children for good or ill. These types of puzzling, complex situations will become more numerous in the coming years, given rapid liberalization of marriage law.

It is impossible to deal with every perplexing circumstance here. No one should attempt to address difficult questions and decisions about divorce and remarriage without benefit of the oversight and counsel of wise Christian counselors and pastors who have experience with such matters and a robust, orthodox doctrinal foundation. For those in search of good resources to sort through thorny problems, I heartily recommend two books that take a pastoral approach, are sound, and are readable. The first is the Jay Adams classic *Marriage, Divorce, and Remarriage in the Bible: A Fresh Look at What Scripture Teaches*. The second, which is more detailed, accessible, and up-to-date, is Jim Newheiser's excellent *Marriage, Divorce, and Remarriage: Critical Questions and Answers*.

When it comes to cases that the *Westminster Confession of Faith* does not clearly address, I read about and personally encounter these two the most. The first is serious *abuse*, including spouses recklessly and needlessly putting their partners and children in situations that put them in danger or that subject them to constant, severe personal or moral degradation. The second is *divorces and remarriages that are not easy to justify biblically*. How to handle remarriage in these cases has been a major issue among believers and churches for many years.

ABUSE AND CLOSELY RELATED MATTERS

Marriages in which one spouse is guilty of a pattern of seriously abusing the other, or the children, are far too common. Similar situations, often accompanying directly abusing spouse and children, can arise due to a husband or wife's[152] criminality or substance abuse that undermines or

---

153. Ibid., 261, 264; Keener, "Remarriage for Circumstances Beyond Adultery and Desertion," 112; Heth, "Remarriage for Adultery or Desertion," 77.

endangers the innocent partner and perhaps children living in the household. These latter actions are also a form of abuse. There is no doubt that in many of these cases, *the only responsible course of action will involve physical, residential separation from the offending spouse* at least for some period of time, in addition to the many interventions that will be needed, including not only counselors and pastors but often police and the courts.[153] However, does the innocent spouse have biblical grounds to divorce his or her spouse, with freedom to remarry?

At least in terms of abuse, many evangelicals today say they do.[154] David Instone-Brewer defends divorce with the right to remarry in the case of abuse in a convoluted manner that makes logical leaps outside of Scripture at least twice.[155] First, in Exodus 21:10, if a man takes another wife and diminishes his provision of food, or clothing or conjugal love to his first wife, she can leave him.[156] Second, Paul pointed out that supplying these things was a marital duty, in 1 Corinthians 7:3–5 and 32–34.[157] Not only Jews but also the Greco-Roman world accepted these as grounds of divorce.[158] Thus, even though he never affirms or even mentions divorcing for these reasons, Paul's audience would have known he was thereby confirming that failure to provide these things is grounds for divorce.[159] This is "neglect." He then goes on to use these as basis for expansive grounds for divorce— lack of enough physical affection, sufficient material support beyond basic needs, and so on.[160] "Neglect" becomes abuse at a certain point and, because neglect is grounds for divorce, then so is abuse.[161] Others simply argue that serious abuse is a grave violation of the marital covenant, like adultery, and so is grounds for divorce with freedom to remarry,[162] a view that is compatible with the Instone-Brewer analysis.

This argument neglects to establish a single direct statement from Paul or Jesus, and assumes that they were accepting many of the basic

---

154. Newheiser, *Marriage, Divorce, and Remarriage*, 259.

155. Instone-Brewer, *Divorce and Remarriage in the Church*, 103–6.

156. Ibid., 98–99.

157. Ibid., 99.

158. Ibid.

159. Ibid.

160. Ibid., 101.

161. Ibid., 102–5.

162. Keener, "Remarriage for Circumstances Other Than Adultery and Desertion," 112–13.

assumptions about divorce held by not only the Jews, but also the pagan world. It is not a convincing or credible argument.

Other evangelicals try to argue that abuse, and thus some of the related situations that I have mentioned, is a form of *porneia*. As such, it falls under the exception clause Jesus gives us in Matthew 5:32 and 19:9. These arguments appear to stretch the meaning of *porneia* to the breaking point and rely on flawed logic. A widely cited example among evangelicals today is Beth Felker Jones' argument.[163] She says, essentially, that since *porneia* is to break faith with one's spouse, and abuse does that too, then abuse is *porneia* and the exception for sexual immorality applies to abuse. Here is a key quote: "Like the one who commits adultery, anyone who would batter and bruise a husband or a wife sins against his or her body. The batterer, like the adulterer, denies the reality that the spouse is truly, faithfully, united to him or to her, and the batterer, like the adulterer, embodies a false image of what God intends faithfulness to look like in this world. Porneia is sin against fidelity."[164] This is flawed logic and exegesis. It would not take much imagination to use this to justify divorce over a host of nonsexual violations.

Aimee K. Cassiday-Shaw, from a more evangelical feminist perspective, makes an even worse argument for treating abuse as *porneia* in making it a ground for divorce. She states that in the Bible, sexual unfaithfulness is often used as a metaphor for idolatry, and therefore all idolatry is sexual unfaithfulness.[165] Since domestic violence is idolatry, then all abuse is *porneia*.[166] Given how many things can be idols or motivated by idolatry (greed, even excessive love of country or family, etc.) that would mean that just about everything can be *porneia*.

If *porneia* can mean anything then it means nothing. It is just not possible to stretch the definition of this word to include domestic abuse.

To try to solve the issue of abuse is hard. There are many different types of abuse—physical, sexual, emotional, verbal, and so on—and many

---

163. *Faithful.*

164. Ibid., 44.

165. *Family Abuse and the Bible: The Scriptural Perspective*, 120.

166. Ibid.

167. Cf. "Remarriage for Circumstances Other Than Adultery and Desertion," 112–13.

degrees of severity.[167] Establishing facts or blame is often difficult, as pastors or counselors who have dealt with such cases can attest.[168] This is *not* to say that both parties are always to blame in whole or part, just that abuse cases tend to be complicated.[169] The fact that churches often badly mishandle them, or fail to involve civil authorities when they should, compounds the difficulty. There is no way to minimize how awful patterns of abuse in marriage and family can be or the private anguish and pain that too many endure. We need to treat these seriously and protect the innocent.

The best way to defend divorce with right to remarry in response to abuse is through application of Paul's teaching about desertion in 1 Corinthians 7:15, as we have laid it out above and as it is summarized in the *Westminster Confession of Faith*. This means, following the latter, that all reasonable attempts have been made, by the church and if necessary the civil magistrate, to fix the situation, to no avail. If the abusive spouse is unrepentant, eventually the church must treat him or her as an unbeliever. Meanwhile, regardless of who remains in the joint residence, if an abusive spouse has driven out his or her partner, the responsibility for this rests with the abuser, not with the innocent party.[170] For example, a wife who flees a violent husband who continues his depredations despite the intervention of church and perhaps the civil authorities, exhausting all attempts at achieving repentance and restoration, is not deserting him. He has deserted her.

This reasoning does not mean that any spouse who feels abused, or who believes that their partner's behavior has created unacceptable discomfort or risk for the family, has a blanket "right" to divorce and remarriage. That would open the door to numerous illegitimate claims for divorce.[171] However, if a spouse ends his or her marriage due to serious abuse that no one has been able to remedy, in which separation has become necessary, and where church leaders have been appropriately involved, the church should accept this.

---

168. Newheiser, *Marriage, Divorce, and Remarriage*, 259–60.
169. Ibid., 260.
170. Ibid., 262–63.
171. Ibid., 263.
172. Ibid., 287–88.

"GUILTY PARTIES" IN REMARRIAGES

Here are some realistic situations, each of them versions of cases I imagine many of us have encountered. First, a woman leaves her husband because she feels he is not ambitious enough, then later marries someone else. The second is a married man and woman who have an affair, leave their respective spouses, and marry each other. In the third, a man's wife divorces him because he committed adultery repeatedly, and he eventually remarries. All of these people are now in marriages they were not biblically free to enter. They may have committed their wrongful actions before they were believers, or sinned grievously after professing faith in Christ.[172] These situations are complex, often mixing their sin and the church's failure to intervene and counsel appropriately;[173] but then, as Jay Adams has observed, "sin complicates life."[174] Regardless, they now appear to be seriously repentant, and wish to serve the Lord and be in fellowship with his people. Most churches face situations like this.

Some Christians would argue that in such cases, the current marriage is not valid, and the remarried persons should dissolve it and seek to restore their broken marriage.[175] I have met some who claim that this is true even if the remarried persons have had children together.[176] However, most evangelical leaders and scholars, even those who believe in the permanence view and believe *all* remarriage is sinful, say that dissolving remarriages increases rather than reduces the damage caused by sin.[177] I believe that this is the view with the best scriptural support.

Wrongful divorce and remarriage, like every other sin, is forgivable.[178] David and Bathsheba married on the heels of their adultery and David's act of murder to hide it (2 Sam 11:27). Neither God nor the Scriptures passed lightly over the awful sins involved in this union. There were terrible consequences and God demanded profound, serious, heartfelt repentance

---

173. Adams, *Marriage, Divorce, and Remarriage in the Bible*, 87–89.

174. Ibid., 87.

175. Newheiser, *Marriage, Divorce, and Remarriage*, 285.

176. One example of this view, written in an inflammatory style, is Jesus Is Lord, "Divorce and Remarriage: Profaning the Covenant of Marriage."

177. Cf. John Piper's "Divorce & Remarriage," and *Divorce and Remarriage: A Permanence View*, 114.

178. Newheiser, *Marriage, Divorce, and Remarriage*, 289–90; Strauss, "Conclusion: Three Questions for You to Answer," 141; Adams, *Marriage, Divorce, and Remarriage in the Bible*, 93–94.

(2 Sam 12:1–23; Ps 51). In spite of these awful beginnings, the marriage of David and Bathsheba was blessed by God, producing the next king of Israel, and ultimately continued the lineage of Christ himself (2 Sam 12:24; Matt 1:6).[179]

This helps us to think about how Christians should handle unbiblical divorce and remarriage. Leaving a spouse for unbiblical reasons or causing a divorce by sinful violation of the marriage covenant is a grievous sin, with serious earthly consequence that God does not completely erase even if one truly repents.[180] The church should accept the remarried persons provided they have truly repented and done all in their power to seek forgiveness from, and make amends to, those they have wronged, with the full involvement of the church.[181] Consistent with Paul's general principle that believers should remain in the condition in which God called them (1 Cor 7:20),[182] such couples need to be as fully committed to their present marriage as they should have been to the one that they sinfully destroyed.[183]

What about those who have sinfully caused or gotten a divorce and are now single, who have repented honestly and wish to be remarried with the blessing of the church? This is tougher.

Most evangelicals would agree that if reconciliation is possible and their former spouse is still single, the believers in this situation should seek it by God's mercy and grace (1 Cor 7:11).[184] So long as their former spouse is also single, and there is any chance of reconciliation, no matter how distant, they must not remarry another person but seek to be reunited.[185] This is difficult, but no more so than a married person caring for a seriously physically or mentally disabled spouse. Like the latter, God will give them grace to bear up in their loneliness and need.[186]

Jay Adams argues from the fact of their repentance and forgiveness that, like the innocent parties in divorces, the church should accept and

---

179. Adams, *Marriage, Divorce, and Remarriage in the Bible*, 95.

180. Newheiser, *Marriage, Divorce, and Remarriage*, 285–86.

181. Ibid., 287–88; Adams, *Marriage, Divorce, and Remarriage in the Bible*, 95–96; Wilson, *Reforming Marriage*, 137–38.

182. Adams, *Marriage, Divorce, and Remarriage in the Bible*, 92.

183. Newheiser, *Marriage, Divorce, and Remarriage*, 288.

184. Ibid., 284.

185. Ibid., 284–85.

186. Ibid., 279.

bless them remarrying.[187] In fact, since God has forgiven them, they are no longer a "guilty party."[188] Driving this point home, he points out that if one can marry someone who used to be a liar or murderer or slanderer, than one can marry someone who was divorced for adultery.[189] Adams makes it clear that the church must treat the prior sin seriously, and be sure that true repentance has taken place.[190]

However, the call to seek reconciliation, and the teaching that those who have wrongfully divorced must not remarry, is strong (Luke 16:18; Mark 10:11–12; Matt 5:32; 19:9; 1 Cor 7:10–11). If the former spouse is still single, the latter should give him or her every opportunity to reunite. However, if the former spouse remarries or enters into some kind of sexually immoral relationship, he or she has irrevocably ended the original covenant of marriage as much as death would, and reconciliation is not possible. Then, as Jim Newheiser argues, the divorced brother or sister in question may remarry.[191]

Some have suggested that if the former spouse is an unbeliever, the call to seek reconciliation does not hold until and unless he or she comes to Christ. They base this on the idea that the call to marry "only in the Lord" discussed at length in chapter 5 would overrule the call to reconciliation. Jay Adams makes this case,[192] as do others. Others argue that God had united them by covenant as one flesh, and this is a solemn calling irrespective of their former spouse's faith.[193] I personally believe the divorced believer in question should reconcile or remain unmarried unless their former spouse dies or is remarried, just as would be the case if both of them were believers. After all, in the case we are considering their unbelieving former spouse did not violate the marital covenant; they did. However, this is something believers and churches will need to sort out.[194]

What about a believer returning to their former spouse after one or the other has remarried and then this latter marriage ended in divorce

---

187. Adams, *Marriage, Divorce, and Remarriage in the Bible*, 93–94.
188. Ibid., 94.
189. Ibid.
190. Ibid., 95.
191. Newheiser, *Marriage, Divorce, and Remarriage*, 279.
192. Adams, *Marriage, Divorce, and Remarriage in the Bible*, 87.
193. *Divorce and Remarriage*, 114.
194. Newheiser, *Marriage, Divorce, and Remarriage*, 281.

or death? Assuming that both parties are biblically free to remarry, there are different answers. Some argue that one should not return to a former marriage after remarrying, deriving this from the moral principle underlying Deuteronomy 24:4. However, others, including John Murray, point out that applying this to the New Testament situations is problematic.[195] King David was also free to remarry Michal after her father, Saul, had given her in marriage to someone else (2 Sam 3:13-16). This is not an easy situation to sort out. Jim Newheiser's perspective seems sound, "While I am uneasy with encouraging a remarriage in such circumstances, I would regard it as a matter for the couple to work out in their own consciences with the guidance of their church leaders."[196]

The last remarriage case is also too common—both parties to the original divorce contributed to it through adultery or some other gross sexual immorality. In this case, both should try to reconcile, and go through serious repentance and counsel. However, if that fails, each has essentially released the other through *porneia*. Upon evidence of saving faith and with great care that they have dealt with the earlier sin at the root, they should be free to remarry.[197]

Too many churches simply accept divorced and remarried believers into their midst, or accept members remarrying following divorce, with no inquiry, passing over things that God takes very seriously. Others refuse to accept such persons or insist on treating them as second-class citizens in the kingdom of God. Certainly, sin has consequences.[198] For example, ordained ministry may not be open to those who have sinfully divorced and remarried, or who have been the guilty party in a valid divorce. This is outside our purview here, though we will consider this topic in chapter 15. At the same time, those of us who have repented and turned to Christ have been set free (Gal 5:1), and we have become new creations for whom the old things have passed away (2 Cor 5:17). A balanced approach that takes both sin and forgiveness following true repentance seriously, rooted in a careful understanding of Scripture and a sincere desire to live by its precepts, gives us the foundation to deal with the complexities of divorce and remarriage.

---

195. Murray, *Divorce*, 113–14.

196. Newheiser, *Marriage, Divorce, and Remarriage*, 196.

197. Ibid., 280.

198. Ibid., 290–91.

Thoughtful, committed believers with a high view of Scripture will often disagree about divorce and remarriage. What we can agree on is that divorce is always a tragedy and the result of sin. The state may believe in "no fault" divorce, but children of the kingdom of God know there is no such thing.[199]

However, we are not going to achieve strong marriages and foster a pro-marriage culture mainly by knowing, accepting, and applying what the Bible teaches about divorce and remarriage, as important as that is. We are going to get there by marrying wisely, then doing all we can to strengthen, enrich, and where necessary, heal our marriages. The point is not *only* to stay married. The point is to have marriages that are delightful, fruitful blessings that truly if imperfectly symbolize to the world the beauty of the love of Christ for his people, a love that he also offers to them freely. That is what gospel marriage, kingdom matrimony, is.

---

199. I touch on this in chapter 12.

CHAPTER 11

THE MODERN DIVORCE PLAGUE

For trouble here is owing solely to the fact that men do not regard marriage according to God's word as his work and ordinance, do not pay regard to his will, that he has given to every one his spouse, to keep her, and to endure for his sake the discomforts that married life brings with it; they regard it as nothing else than a mere human, secular affair, with which God has nothing to do. Therefore one soon becomes tired of it, and if it does not go as we wish, we soon begin to separate and change. Then God nevertheless so orders it, that we thereby make it no better; as it then generally happens, if one wants to change and improve matters, and no one wants to carry his cross, but have everything perfectly convenient and without discomfort, that he gets an exchange in which he finds twice or ten times more discomfort, not alone in this matter but in all matters.

Martin Luther[1]

I do my thing and you do your thing.
I am not in this world to live up to your expectations,
And you are not in this world to live up to mine.
You are you, and I am I,
and if by chance we find each other, it's beautiful.
If not, it can't be helped.

Frederick S. Perls, "The Gestalt Prayer"[2]

---

1. Luther, *A Compend of Luther's Theology*, 195–96. This quote excerpted from Luther's *Commentary on the Sermon on the Mount*, originally published in 1532.

2. Perls, *The Gestalt Therapy Verbatim*, 4.

THE RISE OF THE DIVORCE CULTURE

T he majority of modern people would find the previous, extensive discussion of what the Bible teaches on divorce and remarriage to be at best quaint and irrelevant, or at worst a mean-spirited and offensive entrapment in archaic regulations and religious superstitions that undermine human freedom and happiness. Recall the powerful insight of Robert Bellah and his colleagues in *Habits of the Heart* that I have touched on elsewhere in this book. The modern "therapeutic" orientation to marriage emphasizes self-realization, personal fulfillment, psychological gratification, and autonomy, making it difficult to articulate commitments beyond that which might involve significant sacrifice.[3] In this orientation, it is difficult for people to submit to the dictates of a social institution with established roles and obligations that emanate from something other than a contingent interpersonal contract. Without a well-grounded, biblical understanding of matrimony, it is even harder for modern people to comprehend and embrace the fact that in their marriages they publically and voluntarily entered into a covenant whose terms were established from the beginning by God, united by him and not their own wills as one flesh, until death separates them. Social approval for divorce for just about any reason that makes sense to one or both spouses, and high rates of it, are the corollaries we would expect to the therapeutic view of marriage. That is just what we see.

TWO MAJOR SHIFTS IN THE TWENTIETH CENTURY

In *The Divorce Culture*, Barbara Dafoe Whitehead traced two major shifts in views about divorce in American life during the twentieth century. Each new shift in opinion was associated with lower barriers to, and higher levels of, divorce.

First, she says, in the opening few decades of the last century we had the *democratization of divorce*, in which it moved from a practice of the wealthy to something affordable and acceptable to those in the middle and lower classes, while people turned more to secular experts than to religion for guidance about it.[4] Figure 11.1 shows what happened with

---

3. Bellah et al., *Habits of the Heart*, 85–112.
4. 18.

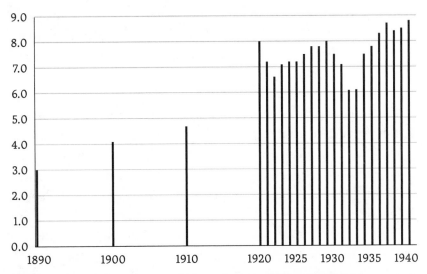

Figure 11.1: Divorces per 1,000 Married Women Ages 15 and Older, 1890 to 1940[5]

divorce rates from the late 1800s into this period, which was roughly from 1900 to 1940.

Materialism and inflated expectations became rampant as prosperity increased. People now saw many goods and experiences as needs rather than luxuries. Dissatisfaction and disputes about money became more of a problem for married couples, divorce became less shameful, and growing female employment made it economically plausible for dissatisfied wives to leave their husbands.[6] Robert and Helen Lynd clearly laid out each of these realities about divorce in Middle America during that era in *Middletown*, their 1929 classic sociological study of everyday life in Muncie, Indiana.[7] At the same time, the public still viewed divorce negatively, and saw it as destructive to children except in instances where it protected them from parental cruelty or moral corruption.[8] As divorce became more common, however, people looked for ways to accommodate and destigmatize it without fully accepting it, keeping it private and controlled.[9]

---

5. Data is from the Department of Health, Education and Welfare in *100 Years of Marriage and Divorce Statistics, United States, 1867–1967*, 24.

6. Ibid., 20–23.

7. *Middletown*, 120–23; 126–30.

8. Whitehead, *The Divorce Culture*, 23–30, 35, 38.

9. Ibid., 30–31, 36–37.

After the prosperity of the Roaring Twenties, the severe financial restraints of the Great Depression artificially held marriages together, temporarily reducing divorce rates, but then they began rising again. This is clearly visible in figure 11.1. From the peak of 1929, divorce rates begin to decline starting in 1930, before beginning a new ascent in 1934.

Then, following a sharp spike amidst the massive marital disruptions of World War II, marital stability improved for a while, accompanied by a huge swell in births now known as the Baby Boom.[10] However, the advance of divorce, in practice and in public approval, was only in remission. Soon, the social upheavals of the 1960s would change the landscape profoundly.

Figure 11.2 shows divorce rates from 1940 to 2016. As it makes clear, a virtual divorce tsunami began during the 1960s, something very different from the previous boom-and-bust war spike in the mid-1940s. This marked Whitehead's second major shift in American perspectives on marital break-ups, what she called the rise of *expressive divorce*.[11]

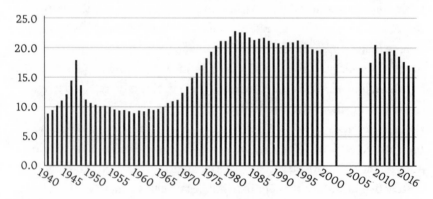

Figure 11.2: Divorces per 1,000 Married Women Ages 15 and Older, 1940 to 2016[12]

---

10. Ibid., 42–44.

11. Whitehead, *The Divorce Culture*, 53.

12. All data through 1997 are National Vital Statistics. Data from 1940 to 1967 are National Vital Statistics (NVS) reported in *100 Years of Marriage and Divorce Statistics, United States, 1867–1967*, 24. Data for 1968 to 1990 are from Clarke, "Advance Report of Final Divorce Statistics, 1988 and 1990," 9. Data for 1991 and 1992 come from "Annual Summary of Births, Marriages, Divorces, and Death: United States, 1992," 4. Data for 1993 and 1994 come from Singh et al., "Annual Summary of Births, Marriages, Divorces, and Death: United States, 1994," 4. Data for 1995 and 1996 come from National Center for Health Statistics, "Births, Marriages, Divorces,

Whitehead pointed out that during this period "an inner revolution . . . created a new way of thinking and talking about divorce."[13] This change was part of the shift to the therapeutic orientation toward marriage discussed by Robert Bellah,[14] what Andrew Cherlin calls "individualized marriage."[15] As Philip Rieff observed in 1966, this era witnessed "the triumph of the therapeutic," one in which new "needs" could be endlessly generated, then satisfied outside the demands of strict moral codes,[16] guided only by the dictates of relativism and the self.

People were increasingly embarking on personal journeys in pursuit of elusive and subjective goods, such as personal fulfillment and life satisfaction, focusing on nourishing their psychological interiors rather than meeting basic material needs or obligations.[17] As we have already seen, people came to view marriage as a vehicle for this quest and, when it failed to deliver, divorce and whatever lay beyond, usually remarriage, also became part of their search for self-realization. Psychological experts became guides for both the marriage and divorce journey.[18] Even pastoral counseling became more like mental health therapy than spiritual instruction and support.[19] People came to view moral teachings and restrictions pertaining to marriage and divorce more as limiting than furthering happiness, a trend that even affected evangelicals.[20] In fact, much of popular American evangelicalism evolved into actually encouraging views that

---

and Deaths for 1996," 3. Data for 1997 come from National Center for Health Statistics, "Births, Marriages, Divorces, and Deaths for 1997," 3. Vital Statistics stopped calculating and distributing this particular rate in 1997, and after that researchers calculated it from raw marriage and divorce Census data, with serious attempts to make them compatible. Thus, while close, post-1997 numbers are not perfectly comparable to the older Vital Statistics numbers. Then for 2000 and 2005 they were calculated by The National Marriage Project, *State of Our Unions 2011*, 68. 2008 through 2016 numbers are from US Census, American Community Survey data using the standard formula employed by Anderson, "Divorce Rate in the United States: Geographic Variation, 2015." That is: number of married women divorced / (currently married including separated + number of married women divorced).

13. Whitehead, *The Divorce Culture*, 45–46.
14. Bellah et al., *Habits of the Heart*, 85–112.
15. Cherlin, *The Marriage-Go-Round*, 88.
16. Rieff, *The Triumph of the Therapeutic*, 239–40.
17. Ibid; Whitehead, *The Divorce Culture*, 46–48.
18. Ibid., 48.
19. Ibid.
20. Ibid., 48–50.

made divorce in pursuit of personal fulfillment more likely.[21] Divorce was now "an individual experience," focused on the inner self.[22] Experts and laypeople increasingly saw it, says Whitehead, as "a psychologically healthy response to marital dissatisfaction," an opportunity "to build a stronger identity and to achieve a more coherent and fully realized sense of self."[23] Like marriage, divorce was now all about "expressive individualism."[24] This message was evident in 1970s and 1980s television comedies such as *One Day at a Time* and *Kate and Allie*.

The close of the 1960s also brought us a new legal reality that represented a final departure from any major hold of Christian doctrine on divorce and remarriage—the no-fault divorce revolution. This began in California in 1969 with a bill signed, ironically, by then-Governor Ronald Reagan.[25] Since then, no-fault divorce laws have swept across the United States, with New York State, the last holdout, adopting this in 2010. Although particulars vary, under these statutes either partner can initiate divorce by claiming that the marriage has broken down irremediably.[26] That is, the divorce may be unilateral, accomplished without mutual consent.

Scholars have not settled whether these laws *caused* increases in divorce, or if they were merely associated with the latter.[27] However, no-fault divorce laws certainly have not *decreased* divorce, as some early proponents claimed they would.[28] They have eliminated the idea of blame for causing marital failure so that it no longer exists much in either law or in public opinion.[29] For example, there is no penalty imposed for adultery. Even where only one partner is unfaithful, either can seek the divorce, and

21. Regnerus, *Cheap Sex*, 188; Cherlin, *The Marriage-Go-Round*, 34, 105–7, 109.

22. Whitehead, *The Divorce Culture*, 53–54.

23. Ibid., 54.

24. Ibid., 66.

25. Cherlin, *The Marriage-Go-Round*, 95.

26. Ibid.; Starbuck and Lundy, *Families in Context*, 409.

27. Cherlin, *The Marriage-Go-Round*, 97. Cf. the assertion that it does in James Q. Wilson's *The Marriage Problem*, 162–63, 175–76 versus Stephanie Coontz's contrary assertions in "Divorce, No-Fault Style." These are brief examples of a fierce and complex debate about empirical studies. I lean toward the argument that these laws, while bad in different ways, did not actually directly cause divorce to increase.

28. Wilson, *The Marriage Problem*, 165–66.

29. Ibid., 162.

in most states, both have at least equal entitlement to a share of the joint property, child custody, and even spousal support payments.[30] One twist that even supporters admit is a problem is that ironically, no-fault divorce disadvantages the spouse who is most committed to the marriage.[31] They can lose everything they have invested, even if their spouse did little to improve or preserve the marriage and then actively destroyed it. Judges can consider this when they settle things like custody and property, but they are not required to. Thus, under no-fault there is a perverse incentive for spouses to reduce their investment in their marriages since they could lose it all even if they are innocent of any wrongdoing. Thus, no-fault divorce has helped encourage and solidify a culture that cheapens marriage and yawns at divorce. It helps to blur the differences between marriage and cohabitation, between divorce and "breaking up" any serious relationship. It has promoted and reflected the tendency to see divorce and marriage in self-centered ways, and it has helped to undermine the obligations and structures of traditional marriage. No-fault is the legal capstone of the modern, expressive, divorce culture.

DECLINES IN DIVORCE—GOOD NEWS AND BAD NEWS

Though there is a lot of fluctuation, divorce rates have been declining since the early 1980s, as figure 11.2 makes clear. This is good news. There are caveats and context to this slide in divorce rates that darken the rosy outlook, however.

First, due to various flaws in data collection and measurement, the true number of divorces is always higher than what the government reports. For various reasons, this error has been greater since about 1990 than during the peak years from 1969 through the late 1980s.[32] Some data sources show much smaller declines in the divorce rates than others, and some top scholars argue that the better information shows less reduction.[33]

To complicate matters, analysts usually record currently separated persons as still married, not divorced, even though most are in the process of divorcing. The fact that roughly 6 percent of permanent separations are

---

30. Ibid.
31. "Divorce, No-Fault Style."
32. Kennedy and Ruggles, "Breaking Up Is Hard to Count," 589.
33. Ibid., 592.

never resolved through a formal divorce,[34] though the couples have dissolved their unions, complicates matters even more. The way divorce tabulators handle separations inadvertently underreports marital dissolution.

Next, divorce rates are not declining or are even increasing in many age groups. Divorce has been increasing among the middle-aged.[35] Researchers have also shown clearly rising divorce among those over fifty.[36] A lot of this is because many in this age group were divorced and remarried during their younger adult years and remarriages are more likely to end in divorce than first marriages.[37] Pastors with older congregations, take note.

Perhaps the most important fact is that much of the general decline in divorce is because fewer people are getting married.[38] One has to get married to get divorced. This means that those who get married are a more select group, less likely to get divorced.[39] Meanwhile, people are increasingly living together and having children outside of wedlock, and much of this involves a lot of relational instability.[40] As Kennedy and Ruggles wryly point out, "Because cohabiting unions are more unstable than marriages, we expect that the rapid rise of cohabitation among the young will neutralize any decline of divorce."[41] With high levels of cohabitation, we underestimate things like how many children are watching their parents break up, how many households are dissolving, and so on, by just looking at formal divorce.[42]

We could argue that the decline of marriage and the rise in cohabitation and out-of-wedlock birth represents the next logical stage in therapeutic, individualized marriages and expressive divorce—skipping marriage entirely. Unfortunately, this is frequently the choice of the poorer and less educated, who are a lot less likely to get married, more likely to have

---

34. Schoen and Canudas-Romo, "Timing Effects on Divorce," 756.

35. Kennedy and Ruggles, "Breaking Up Is Hard to Count," 593–96.

36. Stepler, "Led by Baby Boomers, Divorce Rates Climb for America's 50+ Population"; Brown and Lin, "The Gray Divorce Revolution."

37. Ibid., 731.

38. NMP, *State of Our Unions 2012*, 63

39. Kennedy and Ruggles, "Breaking Up Is Hard to Count," 596; NMP, *State of Our Unions 2012*, 69; Hymowitz, "Divorce Rates Are Falling—But Marriage Is Still on the Rocks."

40. Ibid.

41. Kennedy and Ruggles, "Breaking Up Is Hard to Count," 596.

42. Cherlin, *Public and Private Families*, 330.

children, to cohabit, and to get divorced if they do marry. Those with better incomes and college degrees continue to choose marriage and to stay that way, especially if they have children.[43]

POPULAR PERSPECTIVES ON DIVORCE

Following the General Social Survey (GSS) since the 1970s suggests that, following a period of less acceptance of divorce, opposition to divorce has been softening in recent years. This may be because many people no longer see divorce rates as a national crisis, as was true a couple of decades ago. Figure 11.3 shows changes in the percentage agreeing that it should be "more difficult" to obtain a divorce. After twenty-two years where the percentage only dipped below 50 percent once, in 2006 support for this proposition began sliding dramatically, and was at 39 percent in 2016.

Both the National Survey of Family Growth (NSFG) and the *GSS* have asked respondents to indicate whether they agreed or disagreed with this statement: "Divorce is usually the best solution when a couple can't seem to work out their marriage problems." Table 11.1 shows the results for the

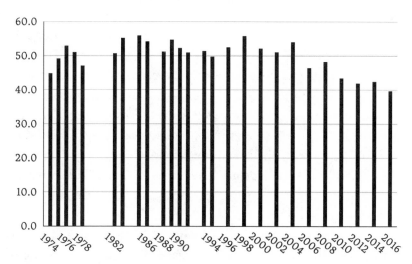

Figure 11.3: Percentage Agreeing It Should Be "More Difficult" to Obtain a Divorce (GSS 1974–2016)

---

43. Wilcox and Wang, *The Marriage Divide*, especially pages 3–8; Hymowitz, "Divorce Rates Are Falling—But Marriage Is Still on the Rocks." This is one of the central arguments in Charles Murray's book *Coming Apart*.

Table 11.1: Percentage Agreeing: "Divorce is usually the best solution when a couple can't seem to work out their marriage problems." (GSS 1994, 2002, and 2012)

	1994	2002	2012
Overall:	**48%**	**43%**	**51.5%**
Has Been Divorced or Legally Separated:	57%	52%	62%
Evangelical:	**44%**	**39%**	**48%**
Evangelical Weekly Church Attenders:	34.5%	29%	43%
Other Weekly Church Attenders:	**43.5%**	**35%**	**40%**

three years that GSS used this item, 1992, 2002, and 2012. As with the percentages in figure 11.3, GSS results suggest that support for divorce may be growing again after dropping for a while. The percentages follow the same pattern over time, and are surprisingly high, for professed evangelicals and regular churchgoers. Those who have been divorced or legally separated were most likely to agree with this statement; for example, 62 percent did in 2012.

Interestingly, responses in the NSFG, which extend from 2002 into 2015, show an opposite trend. In the NSFG support for divorce *dropped* from 47 to 40 percent among women, and 46 to 42 percent among men, between the 2002 and 2013–15 cycles. NSFG respondents are younger, from fifteen to forty-four years of age as compared to the GSS extending from eighteen through old age. However, that does not explain the differences in results. When I compare males and females eighteen to forty-four in the two surveys, support for divorce still increased in the GSS but decreased in the NSFG, though both locate support around 40 percent for the period around 2011 to 2013.

However, age variation in support for divorce is interesting and important. In the GSS, in each of the three years that agreement with this divorce statement was tested, support for it increased steadily with age. The same is true among adults in the NSFG. Part of this is because older people are more likely to have been divorced, but there is more to the age difference than that. Table 11.2, which focuses on differences in support for divorce between those who have been divorced and have not, by age, in

Table 11.2: Percentage Agreeing: "Divorce is usually the best solution when a couple can't seem to work out their marriage problems." (GSS 2012, by Age and Ever-Divorced)

	18–39	40–59	60–79
Been Divorced:	**49%**	**61%**	**69%**
Never Divorced:	41%	45%	56.5%

the GSS makes this clear. Whether people have been divorced or not, the older they are, the more likely they are to support divorce.

The degree to which, among ever-married people, support for divorce is much higher among those who have ever been divorced, is worth focusing on. Combining 2002 and 2012 in the GSS, we find that 43 percent of those who married and have never divorced or legally separated agreed with this statement, compared to 57 percent who had split up at least once. It would be hard for analysts to prove that liberal attitudes on divorce "cause" marital dissolution, but there is no doubt that they strongly go together. It seems obvious that strengthening people's resolve to not divorce at all costs, while helping them find other ways to resolve marital problems, is vital.

Americans as a whole seem to feel that divorce is not a moral problem. A 2012 Pew Research Center poll found that 48 percent believed it was "not a moral issue," and another 23 percent said it was "morally acceptable," while only 21 percent saw divorce as "morally wrong."[44]

In 2004, the Barna Group conducted a survey that asked respondents to indicate whether they agreed that, "when a couple gets divorced without one of them having committed adultery, they are committing a sin."[45] Among "born-again Christians" 52 percent disagreed with this, as did 74 percent of others.[46] There were no significant differences by age.[47] While this is helpful, it is not clear that believers who disagreed with this item did not still have restrictive views of divorce—for example, as we have laid out here, allowing it in cases of desertion and serious abuse but still rejecting most grounds that people use for divorce.

---

44. "Values."
45. "Born Again Christians Just as Likely to Divorce as Are Non-Christians."
46. Ibid.
47. Ibid.

The fact that pollsters survey attitudes about divorce as little as they do, in and out of the professing church, is in itself telling. The public has come to accept high divorce rates, and is morally comfortable with divorce, despite the widespread negative effects of it that we will discuss in chapter 12. Partly they are ignorant of the damage it causes. Few want to strongly condemn, or point out the serious pitfalls, of actions that they or so many around them, including many people's parents, have taken. For these and other reasons, politicians of both parties avoid the topic.[48] In general and in the professing church, our high divorce rate is a major, but largely silent, problem.

DIVORCE RISK

OVERALL

The main divorce fact that most people, and the media, focus on and wonder about is, "What is the probability that marriages will end in divorce?" Scholars refer to this as the *average marital risk*.[49] What it means, literally, is what percentage of marriages that began during a particular time-period— for example, a year or set of years—will eventually end in divorce.[50] That group of marriages is a marital *cohort*, which researchers then track over time.

The only way to get a fully accurate divorce percentage this way is to wait until everyone in a particular marital cohort is dead. So for example, we know what the average marital risk was for everyone married between 1905 and 1910, because their entire life experience, including their divorces, has now been lived. While this is of value to historians, the rest of us are generally looking for something a lot more current. The way that research- ers get more up-to-date estimates is to look at the experience of a cohort up to a certain point, for example the ten- or fifteen-year mark. They then use sound demographic projections to estimate how many who are not cur- rently divorced, will be at some point in the future. For example, we pointed out in chapter 9 that most divorce is "front-loaded," with marriages that end in divorce having a median length of eight years, and only a median of seven years to separation preceding the divorce.[51] One classic study we

---

48. Whitehead, *The Divorce Culture*, 6–7.

49. Starbuck and Lundy, *Families in Context*, 411.

50. Ibid.

51. Krieder and Ellis, "Number, Timing, and Duration of Marriages and Divorces: 2009," 15, 18.

discussed there found that, in surveys of groups of women over nine-year periods in the late 1960s and 1970s, a little over 80 percent of marriages that ended in divorce did so by the tenth year.[52] *If* that were to hold generally and today, that would mean that if 39 percent of all marriages begun in a given year had ended in divorce by the tenth year, then the percentage divorced for that cohort would eventually reach about fifty percent.

Using those *kinds* of estimates, calculated in various ways, researchers typically estimate average marital risks from over 40 percent, to 50 percent or higher, for those married in recent decades.[53] Especially given that most legal separations are permanent, but government officials or researchers do not normally include them in official divorce rates, a marital dissolution rate of at least close to 50 percent is a sound estimate.[54] This is contrary to claims of 20-percent to 25-percent divorce percentages by some Christian authors.[55] Yes, percentages in the 43-percent to 46-percent range, not including separations, are "projections" and the outcome will almost certainly be a little different, better or worse, but these are as accurate as projections can be.

A 2009 US Census Bureau study found that 40 percent of *all* married women had seen their first marriage end in divorce by their fiftieth anniversary.[56] This included many women who had been married during low divorce cohorts, and did not include subsequent divorces following the remarriages of many of those who divorced. Thus, that 40 percent is not a projection, and it is an optimistic percentage. As of 2010, over 45 percent of ever-married Americans ages fifty-five to fifty-nine had already divorced or separated.[57] Many who had not seen their marriage break up by 2010, have seen it do so by now, or may experience that in the future.

In the last two cycles of the *NSFG*, 39 percent of ever-married females ages thirty-three through thirty-four had experienced a divorce or annulment,[58] not counting separations. Notice that this would include many who

52. South and Spitze, "Determinants of Divorce over the Marital Life Course," 587–88.

53. Cherlin, *Public and Private Families*, 331; Cherlin, "Demographic Trends," 405; Amato, "Research on Divorce," 651; "Breaking Up Is Hard to Count," 588; NMP, *State of Our Unions 2012*, 72.

54. Amato, "Research on Divorce," 651.

55. Cf. Feldhahn, *The Good News about Marriage*, 20–28, 37–38; Barna, *The Future of the American Family*, 68.

56. "Number, Timing, and Duration of Marriages and Divorces: 2009," 15.

57. "Breaking Up Is Hard to Count," 595.

had only recently married, and that some sizable, though not perfectly known, percentage of those who had not been divorced or widowed would get divorced in the future. Among ever-married *GSS* respondents from 2006 through 2016, ages thirty to sixty-nine, 49 percent have been divorced or legally separated at some point. Again, this lumps together many different categories of people, from those who have not been married long to others who married in the highest divorce periods. There are no perfect percentages in this paragraph, but they do suggest, along with all the other research that is out there, that America has a huge divorce problem.

NOT EVERYONE HAS A HIGH RISK OF DIVORCE

In the face of these dismal statistics, it is important to point out that whatever the "real" overall average marital risk is for people getting married in a given time period, many people face *much* better odds, and even minimal risk of divorce.[59] Conversely, others face elevated likelihood of marital dissolution. It is vital that we consider these factors when assessing our own situation or those of others to whom we are ministering.

Here are some factors that affect a couple's real statistical risk of divorce. You may notice that I addressed many of these in previous chapters. In chapter 5, I noted that interfaith marriages are more likely to break up than those in which both partners share the same religious beliefs and commitments.[60] In chapter 6, I covered many factors that elevate the chances of divorce. I discussed issues of *age*, marrying too young,[61] and large age gaps between husband and wife.[62] In addition, I covered *socioeconomic* factors—the more income and education, the lower the risk of divorce.[63] It also helps

---

58. Annulment being quite rare.

59. Feldhahn, *The Good News about Marriage*, 20, 28–31; NMP, *State of Our Unions 2012*, 72, 74–75.

60. Riley, *'Til Faith Do Us Part*, 119–43.

61. Aughinbaugh et al., "Marriage and Divorce," 12–13; NMP, *State of Our Unions 2012*, 74; and Feldhahn, *The Good News about Marriage*, 28.

62. Francis-Tan and Mialon, "'A Diamond is Forever' and Other Fairy Tales," 1927 and see further analysis of Francis-Tan and Mialon's data by Olson, "What Makes for a Stable Marriage? Part 2"; also, Garber, "For a Lasting Marriage, Try Marrying Someone Your Own Age"; and Cherlin, *Public and Private Families*, 337.

63. Feldhahn, *The Good News about Marriage*, 28; NMP, *State of Our Unions 2012*, 74; Starbuck and Lundy, *Families in Context*, 415–16; see also Francis-Tan and Mialon, "A Diamond is Forever" on the effects of wealth; "Marriage and Divorce," 8–9 on education; and Murray, *Coming Apart*, 156, 167 on social class.

if partners have similar levels of education.[64] I considered important *family history* influences. People whose parents were divorced or who were born out of wedlock are more likely to get divorced.[65] So are those who have been divorced and remarried themselves.[66] This is especially true if both partners were previously divorced,[67] and if one is bringing children into the marriage.[68]

I looked at *sexual and non-marital relational history*. This included the ways that having children out of wedlock,[69] cohabitation[70] and, as touched on in chapter 8, having numerous sexual partners prior to marriage,[71] all increase the possibility of marital dissolution. In chapter 6, I also touched on *racial* issues. For example, African-Americans have higher rates of divorce and separation, while Asians have among the lowest. *Some* inter-racial marriages, such as those between blacks and whites, are more likely to dissolve.[72]

There are other important factors. In chapter 9 and above, I noted that the longer a couple is married, the lower their risk of marital breakdown. Americans in the South and West are more likely to divorce than in other regions.[73] While the divorce rate is the same or higher among professing

64. Olson, "What Makes for a Stable Marriage? Part 2."

65. Starbuck and Lundy, *Families in Context*, 417; Amato, "Research on Divorce," 653; Amato and Cheadle, "The Long Reach of Divorce"; Kelly and Emery, "Children's Adjustment Following Divorce," 356; Cherlin, *Public and Private Families*, 334, 337; NMP, *State of Our Unions 2011*, 74.

66. Amato, "Research on Divorce," 651; "Number, Timing, and Duration of Marriages and Divorces: 2009," 17; Feldhahn, *The Good News about Marriage*, 28.

67. Starbuck and Lundy, *Families in Context*, 428.

68. Teachman, "Complex Life Course Patterns and the Risk of Divorce in Second Marriages," 302–303.

69. NMP, *State of Our Unions 2011*, 74.

70. Starbuck and Lundy, *Families in Context*, 246–47; Weston et al., "Premarital Cohabitation and Marital Stability," 10; NMP, *State of Our Unions 2012*, 78; Copen et al., "First Marriages in the United States," 2, 8; Rhoades and Stanley, *Before "I Do,"* 10; Feldhahn, *The Good News about Marriage*, 30. Note that, as we discussed in chapter 9, recent data seems to suggest that couples who move in together after becoming engaged or otherwise establishing firm plans to marry may not be more likely to divorce, though they are not better off, either.

71. Stanton, "Premarital Sex and Greater Divorce Risk"; "Premarital Sex, Premarital Cohabitation, and the Risk of Subsequent Marital Dissolution Among Women"; Rhoades and Stanley, *Before "I Do,"* 6, 8–9; Wolfinger, "Counterintuitive Trends in the Link Between Premarital Sex and Marital Stability."

72. Wang, *The Rise of Intermarriage*, 12; Zhang and Hook, "Marital Dissolution Among Interracial Couples," 101.

73. NMP, *State of Our Unions 2011*, 72.

evangelicals as for the population as a whole,[74] regular church attenders have much lower percentages of broken marriages.[75] Supportive family and friends make a positive difference as well,[76] though personal networks that have a negative influence can do great harm.[77] Sexual satisfaction, and high levels of commitment to the marriage, also improve marriages and help divorce-proof them.[78] Substance abuse increases the risk of divorce,[79] as does spousal abuse.[80] Finally, as I emphasized strongly in chapter 9, good premarital counseling can reduce divorce,[81] particularly in helping couples through those high-risk, early years of marriage.

I took the GSS from 2006 and 2016, looking at the total percentage of ever-married respondents between the ages of thirty and sixty-nine who had *ever* been divorced or legally separated. My intention is *not* to arrive at the perfect percentage for any marriage cohort, but just to help you see how much the relative risk of divorce and separation changes for different groups of people based on their background and actions.

As shown in figure 11.4, note that the overall percentage ever-divorced or legally separated for this large age group during these years is 49 percent. Holding evangelical affiliations and beliefs is *not* associated with lower risk of marital dissolution, but attending church weekly most definitely is. Those who rarely or never attend church have a 12 percent higher percentage than those who do so at least weekly. Self-identified *evangelicals*

---

74. Barna Group, "Born Again Christians Just as Likely to Divorce as Are Non-Christians."

75. Feldhahn, *The Good News about Marriage*, 30; NMP, *State of Our Unions 2012*, 74; NMP, *State of Our Unions 2011*, 41.

76. Ibid., 26–30, 40; Feldhahn, *The Good News about Marriage*, 31–32.

77. NMP, *State of Our Unions 2011*, 28.

78. Ibid., 40–41.

79. Cf. Cranford, "DSM-IV Alcohol Dependence and Marital Dissolution," 520–21, 524, 526; Amato and Previti, "People's Reasons for Divorcing," 602, 604–605, 615–16.

80. Cf. Bowlus and Seitz, "Domestic Violence, Employment, and Divorce," 1113–14, 1119–20, 1133–34, 1141–42.

81. McManus, *Marriage Savers*, 113–18; Scott et al., "Reasons for Divorce and Recollections of Premarital Intervention," 131–32; Futris et al., "The Impact of PREPARE on Engaged Couples," 70–71, 81–82; Olson et al., "PREPARE/ENRICH Program"; Markman et al., *Fighting for Your Marriage*, 12–14; FOCCUS USA, "Evidence of Reliability and Validity for FOCCUS Fourth Edition Pre-Marriage Inventory"; Stanley et al., "Premarital Education, Marital Quality, and Marital Stability"; Carroll and Doherty, "Evaluating the Effectiveness of Premarital Prevention Programs," 105.

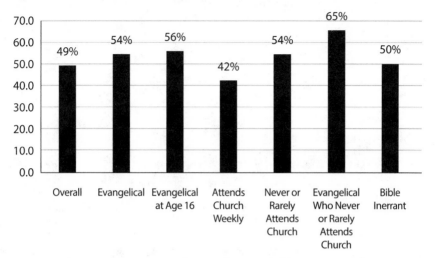

Figure 11.4: Percentage Ever-Divorced or Legally Separated (GSS 2006–2016), Ages 30–69, Ever-Married Respondents Only. *Religious Beliefs and Actions.*

who do not attend church had a whopping percentage of 65 percent, the worst on that graph. Also, sometimes I am asked if evangelicals overall would have had lower divorce rates if researchers accounted for the fact that many people have a conversion experience after divorce. However, we see here that respondents affiliated with evangelical Protestant churches at age sixteen had a percentage that was just as high. The key thing is *action* versus mere belief, as James said (Jas 2:14–24). The data in figure 11.6 match those of numerous studies that have shown that *nominal* evangelicals have *higher*-than-average rates of divorce and separation. Said sociologist W. Bradford Wilcox, who has studied this extensively, *"Lukewarm Christianity is a disaster* for family life. . . . Nominal conservative Protestants and evangelicals do worse in their marriages than other Americans."[82]

In figure 11.5, we can see how big a difference having a married mother and father makes. The differences based on educational attainment, and subjective class identification, are also obvious and powerful. The percentage divorced or separated for middle-class respondents was less than two-thirds of what it was for the lower class, and the number for those

---

82. Zylstra, "Are Evangelicals Bad for Marriage?" (emphasis added).

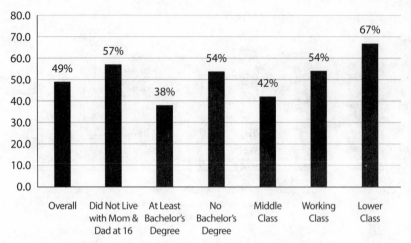

Figure 11.5: Percentage Ever-Divorced or Legally Separated (GSS 2006–2016), Ages 30–69, Ever-Married Respondents Only. *Social Status & Family Background.*

with college degrees was only 70 percent of what the percentage was for those without them.

A couple of other figures are worth mentioning that are simpler to present outside a graph. First, among females, for those who had a child between the ages of thirteen and nineteen, the percentage divorced or legally separated was 67 percent. Second, among all respondents who admitted to having sex with someone other than their spouse while they were married, 74 percent had experienced marital dissolution.

Age at marriage is important, as many researchers have pointed out. The *GSS* asked about age at first marriage from 1972 through 1994, and then in 2006. So switching to earlier years, 1984 through 1994, we get the break-down of those who have ever been divorced or legally separated according to how old they were when they first wed, in figure 11.6. Notice that the overall percentage for those years, for ages forty-five to sixty-nine, is 38 percent.[83] Those who married younger were at a distinct disadvantage. I should note that these age categories do hide some realities worth point-ing out. For those married at age twenty-two, the percentage divorced or

---

83. I chose forty-five as the youngest age of respondent here, so that even those married at ages thirty to thirty-five would have had a significant amount of time pass. Including younger respondents would mean that many who married older would be virtual newlyweds when they were surveyed.

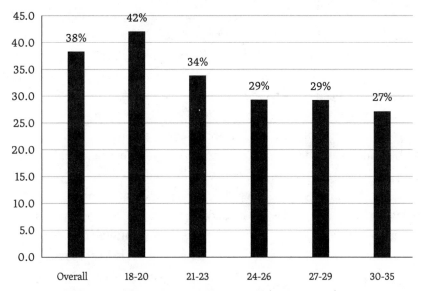

Figure 11.6: Percentage Ever-Divorced or Legally Separated (GSS 1984–1994), Ages 45–69, Ever-Married Respondents Only. *Age at Marriage.*

separated by ages forty-five to sixty-nine was 32 percent, compared to 29 percent for ages twenty-three through twenty-nine combined. The key cutoff, as we pointed out in chapter 6, is about age twenty, with little difference from age twenty-two on up.[84]

Obviously, all of these factors are intertwined, so reality is not as simple as I have presented it here. For example, people who marry older are more likely to have college degrees, be middle class, and so on. Women who had children as teens are less likely to get college degrees or be members of the middle class. Still, as I have discussed earlier, much research has shown these factors to have an impact upon divorce, even when it has considered the other variables. What I am doing here is illustrating how important these things are. The average risk someone looking at marriage has of getting divorced in the future is not that of some overall ever-married population, but of those who are most similar on the constellation of factors such as those we have considered in this chapter.

---

84. Regnerus and Uecker, *Premarital Sex in America*, 179.

Let's consider how these factors add up among typical people, for good or ill. As we saw, the percentage ever divorced or separated for thirty- to sixty-nine-year-olds in the GSS in 2006 through 2016 is 49 percent. However, for the middle and upper class combined, it is 42 percent. Add to that attaining at least a bachelor's degree and we are now down to 34 percent. Now, we take respondents who are middle to upper class *and* have a college degree, *and* in addition attend church weekly, and now we are down to 28 percent. Take *those* and assume they lived with their biological mother and father at age sixteen, and now we have reduced that percentage to 26 percent. Taking one more step, let's also assume that we are dealing with people who will not be committing adultery. That takes us to 21 percent. A sexually faithful, college-educated, regular church attender who is doing well financially and grew up in a two-parent home is in a select group that has less than half the average marital risk. That is without taking into account further reductions for those who also avoid promiscuous sex and cohabitation, marry later, are thoughtful and wise in mate selection, are not involved in substance or spousal abuse, and participate in high-quality premarital counseling.

Taking it in the other direction, and again starting with that 49 percent overall, if the group is lower to working class, their divorce and separation percentage jumps to 56 percent. Further assuming they did not get at least a bachelor's degree, we go up slightly to 57 percent. Take those folks who, in addition, never or rarely step foot in a religious service, and now we are at 62 percent. If our lower- to working-class respondents without a college degree who do not attend church also were not living with two biological parents at age sixteen, we move to 65 percent. We hope that sexual infidelity will not come into play, since if this group commits adultery they will hit 78 percent. We can safely assume that adding in domestic violence or substance abuse would push this even higher.

PULLING IT ALL TOGETHER

Our immediate world—the people around us, our communities, what sociologists would call our "reference groups"—strongly shapes our perception of marriage and divorce. People involved in a fundamentalist church in a defunct coal town in West Virginia are going to see, expect, and accept very different realities than those in a socially elite Presbyterian church near Princeton, New Jersey. For churchgoers, the fact that they mingle most with others of similar commitment often makes it hard for them to understand how much divorce there is in the broader evangelical world. This can even hold true for the members of their churches they do not see much, those who only sporadically attend but are on the rolls. Divorce may not be high among those evangelicals they *see regularly*, so they make wrong assumptions about evangelicals generally. Ministry to engaged or married couples is going to look very different in Neon, Kentucky, than in a suburb of Hartford, Connecticut. It is important we grasp the larger picture, what is going on with our brothers and sisters outside of our familiar worlds.

How do we apply these pictures of average marital risk at the personal level? We see that some people are at a very high risk of getting divorced, and others are not. Just as we do in life insurance and other areas of life, it is worthwhile to see which "risk group" we are in, as well as those we care for, so we can respond appropriately. However, even in the best situations, the real statistical probabilities are great enough that any courting or engaged couple should do everything in their power to build a solid foundation for their life together. Moreover, the point is not to just stay married, but to have a wonderful, God-honoring marriage.

Some people start out with all the right advantages, and yet fall short. Others begin their adult life with serious challenges such as poverty, childhood in a single-parent home, a prior divorce, past drug problems, or even coming to Christ after having messed up sexually and experiencing consequences such as having a child or an STD. Yet I have seen folks with all these "strikes against them" go on to establish and enjoy fantastic marriages and families. The grace of God, humility and repentance for past sins, and walking in intelligent obedience to Christ within the embrace of his people in a solid, ministry-oriented, Bible-believing church are always going to be key to godly marriages, no matter the starting point.

Looking at the risks can be sobering, but it should motivate, not discourage, us. Those who have solid advantages should build on them, and then use those gifts as a platform to help others as well. Those who face serious challenges should face those soberly and wisely, relying on the guidelines such as we discussed in our section on mate selection and marital preparation, as well as principles and approaches that will be touched on in the fourteenth chapter.

Few of us who come to a good understanding of how to do anything enjoy the luxury of beginning at the place we wish we could start from, at least not in every aspect. We must begin where we are. God meets us *there*, not in some hypothetical ideal reality, just as he met the cohabiting, repeatedly divorced Samaritan woman where she was (John 4:6–29). Then he leads us from there to another, better, reality. He can do that for our marriages *if* we are willing, by his grace, to follow him.

CHAPTER 12

RUIN AND WRECKAGE: THE EFFECTS OF DIVORCE

Divorce . . . introduces disorder into the family and into society. This
disorder brings grave harm to the deserted spouse, to children traumatized
by the separation of their parents and often torn between them, and
because of its contagious effect which makes it truly a plague on society.
                                    Catechism of the Catholic Church[1]

The divorced family is a new kind of family. . . . Relationships with
stepparents, visiting parents, stepsiblings, and lifestyles that include
joint custody have no counterpart in the intact family. Moreover . . .
when the marital bond is severed, parent–child relationships are likely
to change radically. . . . Both childhood and parenthood are challenged
and often heavily burdened within the divorced family, at the same
time that many adults are set free from unhappy and sometimes tragic
situations. . . . The impact of these far-reaching changes on the society
as a whole, as well as on the many individuals whose lives have been
profoundly affected, has been hardly addressed or even appreciated.
                                    Judith S. Wallerstein and Julia M. Lewis[2]

I f the Scriptures teach us anything, it is that our God's wisdom and lov-
ingkindness are limitless (Job 12:13; Ps 147:5; 1 John 4:8). Thus, what he
proclaims to be right and good is far superior to any alternative that we

---

1. *Catechism of the Catholic Church*, 573.
2. "The Unexpected Legacy of Divorce," 353.

might construct for ourselves (Isa 55:8-9). Indeed, it is pure folly to substitute our judgment for his. No matter how good some choice might seem to us at the time, to refuse what he calls good or embrace what he identifies as evil brings destruction and death (Prov 14:12). God clearly declares that he despises divorce (Mal 2:16),[3] that it tears apart two who have become one flesh by solemn covenant (Gen 2:24; Matt 19:5-6; Mark 10:7-9; 1 Cor 6:16; Eph 5:28-31). Thus, we would anticipate the effects of our culture of rampant, easy divorce to be negative and enslaving rather than wholesome and liberating. We would expect that divorce, and those things that lead to it, would harm the adult actors and their dependents. It would not shock us if the effects upon society were similar to those of many forms of epidemic violence, as this latter verse from Malachi suggests. That is precisely what the research shows.

Being honest about the damage divorce causes is important because it encourages us to do everything in our power to avoid it, through sound practices and counseling before and after marriage, and discouraging divorce for unbiblical reasons. It also equips us with the knowledge we need to love, support, and assist those who are divorced, especially those innocent parties and their families. If we continue to pretend that divorce usually harms no one, or that its damage is temporary or trivial, we will fail not only in diagnosis, but also in treatment.

The legal term "no-fault divorce" implies that divorce just happens, as if it is just "one of those things." If we take the covenant of marriage, and God's teachings on divorce, seriously, that is simply not true. As Stanley Grenz has pointed out, the term "no-fault divorce" is a legal fiction because there is always fault and failure, at some point and level, in every divorce.[4]

As we saw in chapter 10, however, this does not mean that the fault or failure always lies with the spouse who files for divorce. It is true that most divorce does not involve clearly biblical rationale, or even compelling circumstances in which there really are no better solutions to whatever

---

3. The immediate context in Malachi appears to be condemning men for causelessly putting away faithful wives, which shapes how the English Standard and International Standard versions render this passage. However, compare the same passage in the New King James, American Standard, or Revised Standard versions. Also Luke 16:18, Mark 10:2-12, Matthew 5:31-32 and 19:3-9, all discussed extensively in chapter 10.

4. Grenz, *Sexual Ethics*, 127.

problems led to it. However, in many divorces there really is an innocent party making the best choice in awful circumstances. To fling phrases like "God hates divorce" accusingly at a spouse whose partner has committed adultery, abandoned, or viciously abused them, is unfair. On the other hand, it is just as wrong to pretend that in such circumstances the marital split, along with the gross covenantal violations that preceded it, will not have negative consequences.

In this chapter, I will catalogue the major consequences of divorce. In doing so, I will examine those consequences upon adults who divorce, and then their children. This is a bit artificial, of course, because most of what negatively affects parents will also harm their children. However, it does help to organize and think through the effects of divorce. Before launching into this, however, I want to address some important, broad matters and questions that will help frame this discussion about the negative results of divorce properly.

GENERAL CONSIDERATIONS

The first thing to remember is that both direct and indirect effects are important. For example, perhaps following her divorce, a woman with several children must work outside the home full-time, paying for day care for the toddlers and after-school sitters for the older ones, while carrying the family alone in the evening. These demands follow directly from losing a partner and full-time provider whose own income leaves little money for child support after meeting his own needs and those of his new wife and family. This diminishes the quantity and quality of the time she can give the children and so, with her former husband now mostly absent, they receive less supervision, rotating caretakers not all of whom share her values, more exposure to peer influence, and so on. If circumstances force her to move hundreds of miles to be close to relatives to get the help she needs, this may separate the children from their father even more, perhaps breeding resentment. Most negative impacts lead to other challenges downstream.

The next thing to consider is that, as I will also show in more detail below, single-parent and stepparent homes arising out of different causes are not the same and do not lead to identical results. Divorce, out-of-wedlock birth, and widowhood do not have the same impacts practically, experientially, or morally. Losing your father because he died suddenly of a heart attack is not the same as having him live somewhere else because your parents got divorced after he, your mother, or both had an affair. Having one's mother remarry when both she and her new husband are sharing custody of their biological children with former spouses is not the same as the marriage of a widow to a single, childless man. In the latter, there are no potential conflicts with "exes," disputes over whether the former husband or lover should relinquish parental rights so the man his children now live with can adopt them, custody-based living restrictions, and so on. We can easily multiply scenarios that illustrate the often-profound differences between single-parent and stepparent families arising from these different causes. For example, as David Blankenhorn observed, "Though paternal death and paternal abandonment are frequently treated as sociological equivalents, these two phenomena could hardly be more different in their impact upon children and upon the larger society. To put it simply, death puts an end to fathers. Abandonment puts an end to fatherhood."[5]

Next, consider statistical probabilities, averages, tendencies, not certainties. Many adults and children from divorced situations do just fine. Meanwhile, having two biological, married parents is certainly no guarantee of moral goodness or success in life. Sometimes a custodial parent and his or her children are better off following divorce. Growing up in a household led by two married parents, one of whom is abusive or otherwise morally degenerate, is not a positive good just because it is statistically an "intact home." We should understand the negative effects of divorce in balanced ways that provide warnings and strategies for action without sucking out hope or, conversely, leading anyone to a false sense of security. However, these insights—that no one is doomed by divorce or protected by marriage alone—do not nullify the powerful and real challenges, and higher risk of a number of negative outcomes, faced by those in divorced homes. Just as we do not say that cigarette smoking is "safe" because not everyone who does so gets cancer or heart disease, so we cannot say that divorce is harmless just because many who experience it wind up all right in the end.

---

5. Blankenhorn, *Fatherless America*, 23. See pages 22–24 in this book for a wider discussion of this.

It is certainly possible for a divorced mother to raise her children just as well as two parents in a healthy marriage, but it is a lot harder for her to do so, and she is less likely to succeed. We have to be honest about that. Applying this to research about the welfare of children, psychologist Wade Horn framed it this way: "That does not mean that some marriages aren't awful for both children and adults. Domestic violence and child abuse, unfortunately, are not strangers to married households. In such cases, children and adults are better off if the marriage dissolves than if it stays together. Still, domestic violence and child abuse are less likely in married than non-married households. Marriage may not confer absolute protection against these social ills, but it offers better protection than any other family arrangement."[6]

Fourth, it is simply not true that all of the ill effects associated with divorce are actually simply a result of the negative realities that existed prior to the marital split. Repeatedly, research that considers the impact of both pre- and post-divorce factors shows that divorce itself is associated with numerous negative outcomes. While it is certainly true that problems in the lives of divorced people and their children were often there prior to their marriages dissolving, divorce typically adds new difficulties of its own. Moreover, many of the problems present before a divorce may continue, and even worsen, after it.[7]

A deeper problem with this last argument is that it treats divorce as a distinct event that occurs at one specific place in time, with a clear "before" and "after." That is not how it works. Divorce is a process that begins unfolding long before the legal paperwork is final. This includes a separation process that is often both lengthy and contentious. As Paul Amato wisely observes, "If one views divorce as a process that unfolds gradually rather than as a discrete event that happens on a specific day, then the troubled family relationships that often precede marital dissolution can be conceptualized as part of the dissolution process."[8]

Fifth, commonsense observation and social-science research strongly support the fact that divorce is, in a sense, contagious, just as the *Catholic*

---

6. Horn, "Wedding Bell Blues."

7. Cf. the excellent review of research in Waite and Gallagher, *The Case for Marriage*, 143–48. See also Starbuck and Lundy, *Families in Context*, 421; Cherlin, *Public and Private Families*, 340–47; Anderson, "The Impact of Family Structure on the Health of Children."

8. Amato, "Research on Divorce," 655–56.

Catechism quote at the opening of this chapter claimed. It is not true that only the divorcing couple and their children are affected. One study looked at data collected on two samples of over 5,000 people each followed over decades.[9] People directly connected as family or friends to one divorced person were 75 percent more likely to get divorced themselves.[10] They were 33 percent more likely to do so if they connected secondarily to a divorced person, for example a friend of a friend.[11] This was true even if the divorced persons lived hundreds of miles apart.[12] This "contagion" effect is especially strong for childless couples.[13] Results like this fit with previous research on the spread of divorce within social networks.[14] It is consistent with many findings that people's personal associations have a strong impact upon their behavior and mores, which some scholars call "social contagion."[15]

A common error is to separate the effects of divorce from problems that commonly attach to it, then claim it is those difficulties, not divorce, that are "really" to blame. Scholars refer to this as "disaggregating" the data. For example, some claim that divorce does not hurt children, but loss of income,[16] or lack of supervision, or stressed moms, or father absence, and so on do. If we could actually separate those kinds of effects from divorce, they might be right. However, we cannot. Barbara Dafoe Whitehead used a brilliant analogy to dismiss this deception: "As one scholar has noted, it is possible, by disaggregating the data . . . to make family structure 'go away' as an independent variable. . . . It is true . . . just as disaggregating Hurricane Andrew into wind, rain, and tides can make it disappear as a meteorological phenomenon."[17]

Normally, scholars who push this look to government to fill the gaps and correct the problems caused by divorce with programs such as free

---

9. McDermott et al., "Breaking Up Is Hard to Do, Unless Everyone Else Is Doing It Too," 497.

10. Ibid., 504.

11. Ibid.

12. Ibid., 504–5.

13. Ibid., 513.

14. Booth et al., "Social Integration and Divorce," 221.

15. Morin, "Is Divorce Contagious?"

16. Cf. Waite and Gallagher's observation that "controlling for income may underestimate the true impact of divorce, since in the real world, lower income is one of the most predictable consequences of the breakup of a marriage." *The Case for Marriage*, 147.

17. Whitehead, "Dan Quayle Was Right," 80.

universal day care, draconian child-support enforcement, more financial support and benefits for single mothers, and so on. Poor government policy, not divorce, is "really" the villain, they say. As one letter to the *New York Times* quoted by Barbara Dafoe Whitehead said, "Let's stop moralizing or blaming single parents . . . and give them the respect they have earned and the support they deserve."[18] In an article with the revealing title "Good Riddance to 'The Family'," sociologist Judith Stacey used that argument to rebut those who want to reduce divorce and out-of-wedlock births. She said, "The nostalgia for the family that they peddle is singularly unhelpful to children or to a social policy arena that has been criminally slow to respond to profound family transformation. . . . Family sociologists should be directing public attention to legal, economic, and social policy reforms that could mitigate the unnecessarily injurious effects of divorce."[19] However, no amount of social programs and wealth redistribution can replace a married mother and father in a healthy marriage.

Finally, scholars and the lay public commonly make the claim that divorce is better than continual conflict, with the loaded assumption that this is normally the choice faced by those considering divorce. There are obvious, serious problems with this argument.

The first is that this is a classic example of a false-dilemma fallacy, where the person is essentially claiming there are only two options when there are actually others. As we saw in chapter 9, conflict is normal in marriage, and couples struggling with it can learn good strategies before and after marriage. There are many fine resources and counseling approaches, including those specifically for Christian couples, to help them with marital conflict and communication.

Next, most divorces are not preceded by high levels of marital conflict. In 1997, family scholars Paul Amato and Alan Booth estimated that less than one-third of marriages that ended in divorce were characterized by high conflict—violence, frequent serious quarrels, or disagreements.[20] Another research study found that only 20 percent of children

---

18. Ibid., 47–48.

19. 546–47.

20. Amato and Booth, *A Generation at Risk*, 220.

whose parents divorced saw a high frequency of arguments between them prior to the split.[21] A team of researchers analyzing the National Survey of Family Growth found that among folks who claimed their marriages were "unhappy," 86 percent reported no violence in their relationship.[22] This was true of 77 percent of those who went on to get divorced.[23] For those who remained married, 93 percent reported no violence in their marriages five years later.[24] Interestingly, three of four who said their marriage was "unhappy" had a spouse who was happy with the marriage.[25] The notion that divorce is normally the only option to a marriage characterized by unbearable and unredeemable conflict is false. Moreover, the idea that children in divorced homes are usually rescued from such nightmare worlds is also not true. Normally, they see a marriage end that had been working, at least for them.

Meanwhile, divorce does not necessarily end conflict, and at times worsens it.[26] After all, if couples cannot work out issues when they are married, they may be equally or more conflictual when dealing with disagreements over custody, support, and the like, not to mention trying to settle disagreements over matters such as child discipline while living in separate households. In a large study of divorced adults and their children that was sponsored by a prominent law firm in Britain, 42 percent of children saw bad quarrels, and 17 percent violence, between their divorced or divorcing parents. About one of four children was asked by one parent to lie to the other, while about half of the parents used the courts to mediate disputes over access and living issues related to their children. Half of the parents admitted to drawing out the legal battle to secure a more favorable outcome, and 68 percent confessed to using their children as "bargaining tools" to do so. One of five said they strove to make their ex-spouse's experience as unpleasant as possible, even when and if they knew it hurt

---

21. Morrison and Coiro, "Parental Conflict and Marital Disruption," 631. See also Kelly and Emery, "Children's Adjustment Following Divorce," 353, who estimate 20 to 25 percent of children experience high-conflict marriage prior to their parents' divorce.

22. Waite et al., *Does Divorce Make People Happy?*, 4, 9.

23. Ibid., 4, 10.

24. Ibid.

25. Ibid., 4, 12.

26. Cherlin, *Public and Private Families*, 340; Amato, "The Consequences of Divorce for Adults and Children," 1271–72, 1276, 1280.

their children.[27] This is hardly a picture of "good divorces" resolving years of conflict to pass on to newer, calmer worlds.

Moreover, research strongly refutes the idea that divorce is usually the best solution to marital unhappiness. Waite and her fellow researchers found that, "Even unhappy spouses who had divorced and remarried were no happier, on average, than unhappy spouses who stayed married."[28] Meanwhile, they pointed out, "Two out of three unhappily married adults who avoided divorce or separation ended up happily married five years later. Just one out of five of unhappy spouses who divorced or separated had happily remarried in the same time period."[29]

How did the unhappily married people in their study who stuck it out turn things around? The researchers explored this in focus-group interviews. Many stressors just improved over time. Problems that seemed unbearable disappeared or shrank as the couple endured. Many indicated that they simply worked harder at making changes to improve their marriages. Others made alterations in their lives that made them happier, which brought benefits into their marriages. Many used help from counselors, clergy, or family members, some of the most useful being those who pressured spouses to change problematic behavior.[30] The fact is, as these authors note, "Many happily married spouses have experienced extended periods (typically two years or more) of marital unhappiness, often for quite serious reasons."[31]

The issue is not so much whether or not trouble will come, but how the couple will choose to view and deal with it. Perhaps the key thing is their commitment to their marriages, and deep reluctance to consider divorce.[32] As Amato and Rodgers concluded, based on a study of over 2,000 married people surveyed several times over an eight-year span, "Adopting more favorable attitudes toward divorce appears to undermine marital quality in the long run."[33]

---

27. Study results summarized by Eason, "Bitter Divorcees 'Using Children.'"
28. Waite et al., *Does Divorce Make People Happy?*, 4.
29. Ibid., 5.
30. Summarized in ibid., 24–29.
31. Ibid., 29.
32. Ibid., 30.
33. "Do Attitudes Toward Divorce Affect Marital Quality?," 69.

EFFECTS ON ADULTS

FINANCIAL COSTS OF DIVORCE

The most obvious and immediate negative impact of divorce upon adults is financial. Unlike the wealthy who can absorb the monetary losses associated with splitting up, for most Americans, especially mothers left with custody of children, the results are serious and long lasting. This is often unanticipated by those getting divorced.

For example, in a well-known mid-1980s study, Terry Arendell interviewed sixty divorced women with custody of children, who had enjoyed middle-class status when married. They ranged in age from twenty-eight to fifty-eight, had been divorced at least two years, and were now functioning as single mothers.[34] Most had to spend thousands of dollars, in 1980s value, in legal fees.[35] Despite this, they often got meager child support and most were forced by their ex-husbands' refusal to pay to go to court to collect, which then cost them more money.[36] Only five had automatic cost-of-living increases built into court-ordered support; the rest saw this reduced by inflation over time.[37] Many did not realize until later that normally, when children reach the age of majority at eighteen, no support is required from the non-custodial parent.[38] Despite most of them believing, before the divorce, that their middle-class life could continue, the reality was sadly different. Of the sixty women, fifty-eight experienced substantial loss of income, and fifty-six went down to or below the poverty limit.[39] Even though the median number of years they had been divorced was four, some more and some less, only four were able to go back to a standard of living close to what they had enjoyed before their divorce.[40]

Has reality improved since Arendell's research was completed? Not at all. As a general rule-of-thumb, experts estimate that the household of a divorced woman with custody of two children needs about 80 percent of pre-divorce income to maintain its former standard of living.[41] This is rarely the case.

---

34. Arendell, *Mothers and Divorce*, 8.

35. Ibid., 12.

36. Ibid., 20.

37. Ibid., 22.

38. Ibid., 24–25. This of course remains true today. Cf. William N. Blasser, "How Long Does Child Support Last?"

39. Arendell, *Mothers and Divorce*, 36–37.

40. Ibid., 37.

41. Ibid., 38; Braver, "The Gender Gap in Standard of Living After Divorce," 119–20

Patrick Fagan and Robert Rector reasonably estimated that even among parents who were not poor prior to a divorce, income losses of 50 percent are common, and about half of parents with children go into poverty following divorce.[42] Andrew Cherlin reported a typical drop in standard of living of about 30 percent for divorced, custodial mothers and their households.[43] In one study, over 30 percent of families with above-average incomes saw their standard of living reduced by half. In 2000, 40 percent of households receiving Aid to Families with Dependent Children (AFDC) were divorced or separated.[44]

One US Census report showed that, as of 2013, among those for whom the courts had ordered child support, only 80 percent of divorced, 70 percent of separated, and 75 percent of married custodial parents received *any* of the required payments.[45] Only 56.5 percent of divorced, 36 percent of separated, and 47 percent of married custodial parents received the entire amount due.[46] This dismal picture had been the case since 1997.[47] The more that custodial parents need child support, the less likely they are to get it. For example, custodial parents with college degrees can generally obtain higher-paying jobs than those without high school diplomas. However, among those for whom the courts had ordered child support, 62 percent of the former got all the courts had promised, versus 30 percent of the latter.[48] Moreover, even if the fathers faithfully supply every bit of support that the courts require, what they contribute is obviously much less than if they were still married to their children's mother.[49]

Figure 12.1 shows the family income of females, who had at least one child in their households, by marital status in the National Survey of Family Growth for 2011 through 2015. Note how dramatically overrepresented at the low end, and underrepresented at the high end, divorced and separated custodial mothers are compared to married women.[50] Separated mothers were especially hard hit.

---

42. Fagan and Rector, "The Effects of Divorce on America," 12.
43. Cherlin, *Marriage, Divorce, Remarriage*, 73.
44. Ibid., 74.
45. Grall, "Custodial Mothers and Fathers and Their Child Support: 2013," 7.
46. Ibid.
47. Ibid., 9.
48. Ibid., 10.
49. Whitehead, *The Divorce Culture*, 155.
50. There were *no* significant differences between married women who were previously divorced versus those still in their first marriages.

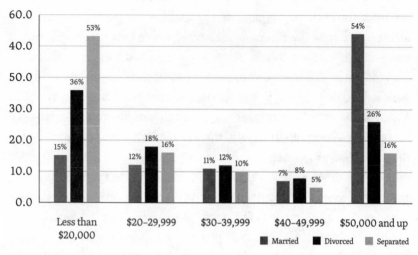

Figure 12.1: Percentage at Different Family Income Levels of Females With At Least One Child Under 18 in Their Households, by Marital Status (NSFG 2011-2015)

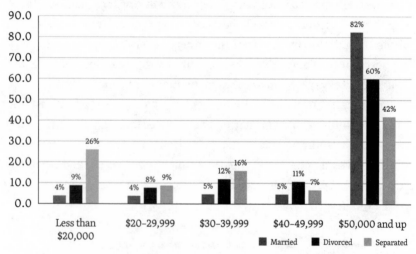

Figure 12.2: Percentage at Different Family Income Levels of Females With At Least One Child Under 18 in Their Households, Who Have College Degrees or Higher, by Marital Status (NSFG 2011-2015)[51]

---

51. "Separated" frequencies for income levels $20,000-29,999 through $40,000-49,999 ranged from three to seven and must be interpreted with caution.

Certainly, part of this is because poorer people are more likely to get divorced, as we saw in chapter 11. However, as we have also seen, divorce itself typically leads to serious financial repercussions. This is obvious in figure 12.2, which looks only at mothers with bachelor's degrees or higher. Even among these more educated women, divorced and separated are much worse off.

In one study, the household income of white married women who divorced and had teenage children dropped by 40 percent.[52] Moreover, for those who remain divorced, the impact upon retirement assets can be devastating.[53]

The fact is divorce creates two households from one. Economies of scale are lost, as it is simply cheaper and more efficient to care for, say, four people in one home than in two.[54] A reasonable estimate is that families need 30 percent more money to maintain the same standard of living if they split into two households.[55] Moreover, judges cannot set child support higher than the non-custodial parent can afford and still get on with a new marriage and family.

WHAT ABOUT REMARRIAGE?

In this *NSFG* data, those in first or remarriages were equally well off financially, however. This finding is consistent with a major analysis of US Census data comparing the family incomes of first versus remarried couples.[56] Thus, remarriage certainly helps to correct the financial difficulties of divorced women.

Most divorced women go on to remarry. One major study found that 54 percent of divorced women had remarried within five years, and 75 percent did so in ten years.[57] Including widows, a more recent study found that in 2014, overall, 52 percent of previously married women had remarried.[58] However, there are caveats here. First, women are much less

---

52. Waite and Gallagher, *The Case for Marriage*, 120.

53. Ibid.

54. Fagan and Rector, "The Effects of Divorce on America," 12; Waite and Gallagher, *The Case for Marriage*, 126.

55. Ibid., 118.

56. Pew Research Center, *Four-in-Ten Couples Are Saying "I Do," Again*, 17.

57. Bramlett and Mosher, "Cohabitation, Marriage, Divorce, and Remarriage in the United States," 22, 78.

58. Pew Research Center, *Four-in-Ten Couples Are Saying "I Do," Again*, 5. This is overall. It is likely that, over time, more of the women eventually remarry, as in the latter, Bramlett and Mosher study.

likely to remarry than men, or to wish to do so. The latter study found that 64 percent of previously married men had remarried, and that while 29 percent of divorced or widowed men were sure that they wanted to remarry, only 15 percent of divorced or widowed women wanted to.[59] Another study found that in 2010, the remarriage rate was almost twice as high for men as for women, though the difference was much smaller for younger folks.[60] The older divorced women are, the less likely they will remarry. Bramlett and Mosher found that 81 percent of women who divorced before age twenty-five remarried within ten years, compared to 68 percent of those who divorced when they were older than twenty-five.[61] On the other hand, evangelicals and those who identify as religious are more likely to remarry following divorce.[62]

Most importantly, as we briefly touched on in chapter 11, remarriages following divorce are much more likely than first marriages to end in divorce. In Bramlett and Mosher's study, 33 percent of first marriages for women ages fifteen to forty-four years of age had ended in divorce within ten years.[63] For second marriages, that percentage was 39 percent.[64] Among women who remarried prior to age twenty-five, 47 percent saw that remarriage ended by divorce within ten years.[65] Especially disconcerting is the fact that remarried women with children were much more likely to get divorced. Of remarried women with two or more children, 43 percent were divorced within ten years, compared to 41 percent who had only one child, and only 32 percent of those who were childless.[66] This latter, sad, finding is consistent with findings from another major study.[67]

Finally, stepparents are under no legal obligation to financially or otherwise care for their spouse's children unless they actually adopt

---

59. Ibid.

60. Cruz, "Remarriage Rate in the U.S., 2010." For example, among eighteen- to forty-five-year-olds, the remarriage rate per 1,000 in 2010 was eighty-five for males and seventy-three for females.

61. "Cohabitation, Marriage, Divorce, and Remarriage in the United States," 23.

62. Ibid., 78.

63. Ibid., 55.

64. Ibid., 83.

65. Ibid.

66. Ibid.

67. Teachman, "Complex Life Course Patterns and the Risk of Divorce in Second Marriages," 303.

them.[68] Where the divorced noncustodial parent remains involved in his children's lives, he is not likely to relinquish his own parental rights to enable this to happen. Many stepparents will care for their stepchildren as if they were their own anyway, but many will not, as I have personally observed many times.

PSYCHOLOGICAL WELL-BEING

There are many evidences that divorce is associated with poorer psychological health across a wide range of areas. Even for mental problems present before divorce, they worsen or at best fail to improve following divorce. Psychiatric difficulties also continue to be associated with divorce even after controlling for numerous other factors. These problems do not typically arise in most divorced people, nor are married folks immune to them. However, divorce does significantly increase the probability of having these problems.

A look at the percentages of married, divorced, or separated General Social Survey respondents who said they are "not happy" is revealing. Figure 12.3 includes the years 2006 through 2016, showing not only that divorced and separated adults are much more likely to say they are not happy, but that this is true even for those who are relatively better

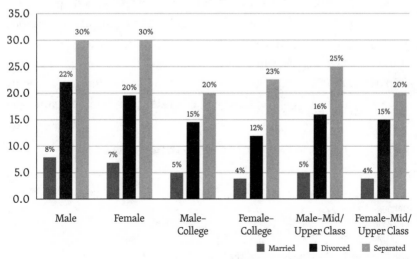

Figure 12.3: Percentage Who Said They Were "Not Happy," by Marital Status (GSS 2006-2016)

---

68. Whitehead, *The Divorce Culture*, 173.

off—those with college degrees or higher, and those who identify as middle or upper class. Not surprisingly, those suffering the most were separated. This is consistent with a long line of research on the relationship between divorce and unhappiness.[69]

A large amount of research confirms that divorced adults are less happy, experience more psychological suffering, and have lower self-esteem.[70] Problems include depression and alcohol abuse,[71] as well as other forms of substance abuse, and anxiety.[72] Augustine Kposowa found that divorce and separation more than doubled the risk of suicide among males.[73] Earlier research had found that divorce increased suicide more than that, and that it heightened the risk for both women and men.[74]

Andrew Cherlin notes that home life during separation and the early years of divorce is often very chaotic.[75] Meanwhile, the burdens and stress faced by single custodial parents is often crushing—being solely responsible for many decisions, having far more to do than time allows, and lacking emotional connection and support in these difficult times.[76]

In addition, divorcing couples often do not realize how much a judge's decisions are now going to intrude on their lives, and how hard that is going to be to live with.[77] Barbara Dafoe Whitehead observes, "The court's supervisory presence intrudes into the small, discretionary everyday matters that define the very conduct of private domestic life. Family courts rule on children's participation in religious holidays, birthdays, and special family occasions like weddings or reunions. They may be called upon to resolve conflicts over parents' participations in PTA meetings and school recitals; the mailing of report cards and medical reports; their choice of dentists, pediatricians, and

---

69. Waite and Gallagher, *The Case for Marriage*, 67–68, 70.

70. Starbuck and Lundy, *Families in Context*, 421; Amato, "The Consequences of Divorce for Adults and Children," 1274.

71. Ibid., 1274–75; Amato, "Research on Divorce," 658; Waite and Gallagher, *The Case for Marriage*, 57.

72. Ibid.

73. "Marital Status and Suicide in the National Longitudinal Mortality Study," 254.

74. Smith et al., "Marital Status and the Risk of Suicide," 78.

75. Cherlin, *Marriage, Divorce, Remarriage*, 72.

76. Ibid., 75.

77. Whitehead, *The Divorce Culture*, 165–68.

psychologists; even their decisions about music lessons or sports camp or religious education." This is beyond the obvious scheduling of the lives of parents and their children in and around custody arrangements. Who wants to live like that?

The Gallup organization has six sub-index scores that they combine into a "well-being index." Based on surveys of over 350,000 Americans in 2011, they found that, among respondents of different marital statuses, the lowest average scores overall, and on their indices for "life evaluation" and "emotional health," were those of separated people, followed by the divorced. Said their report, "Americans who are married have higher well-being than those who are not married, with those currently separated or divorced lagging far behind."[78] Gallup saw these differences by marital status in every year between 2008 and 2012.[79]

PHYSICAL HEALTH

Given the financial and psychological impacts of divorce and separation, including the increase in unhealthy behaviors such as substance abuse, we are not surprised to learn that divorce has negative impacts upon physical health as well. For example, divorce is associated with decreased immune functions, which in turn opens up the person to more health problems.[80] Overall, divorce is tied to increases in death rates and health problems.[81]

SOCIAL RELATIONSHIPS AND SUPPORT

One of the outcomes of divorce and separation is higher levels of social isolation.[82] Considering the disruption in kinship ties such as in-laws, relationships with "couple friends" or friends of the ex-spouses, and so on, this

---

78. Brown and Jones, "Separation, Divorce Linked to Sharply Lower Well-Being." The life evaluation measures their overall assessment of their current and future life, with the best scores labeled "thriving" and the worst "suffering." The emotional health index looks at smiling or laughter, learning or doing something interesting, being treated with respect, enjoyment, happiness, worry, sadness, anger, stress, and diagnosis of depression.

79. Ibid.

80. Waite and Gallagher, *The Case for Marriage*, 57.

81. Amato, "The Consequences of Divorce for Adults and Children," 1274; Amato, "Research on Divorce," 658; Starbuck and Lundy, *Families in Context*, 421.

82. Ibid.

is not surprising. Moreover, the time pressures on single, custodial parents often leaves little time for socializing.[83]

EFFECTS ON CHILDREN

While research suggests that children from high-conflict homes often do better following a divorce, as we have seen, that does not apply to most children of divorce.[84] Of course, this is assuming that the parents do not take effective measures to resolve their conflict, other than divorcing. As we have also seen, divorce may not resolve conflict between the parents.[85] Regardless, on average, children of divorce face a significant number of disadvantages compared to those from intact homes.

APPLYING WHAT WE ALREADY KNOW
Difficulties Tied to Financial, Health, and
Psychological Problems of Adults

As I indicated earlier, whatever impacts adults will usually affect their children. Pulling together what we have covered, consider these things. Following divorce, many children experience time in chaotic, disrupted households. They will usually experience a suddenly diminished standard of living, often to the point of moving from middle-class status to near poverty. Their larger social relationships, including ties to their non-custodial parents' families, may become weaker or even completely cut off. Older children especially often become aware that their biological fathers are not providing any, or adequate, child support, while they are instead funneling care to new marriages and families. They see their custodial parent, usually the mother, struggle with this. Conflict between their biological parents often continues, and too often they must endure prolonged legal battles, ones in which they are often the subject of, or are being used by their parents in, these court proceedings. Meanwhile, compared to children in intact homes, their parents are more likely to be physically sick, anxious, distressed, and unhappy.

---

83. Cherlin, *Marriage, Divorce, Remarriage*, 74.

84. Amato, "The Consequences of Divorce for Adults and Children," 1278; Waite and Gallagher, *The Case for Marriage*, 147.

85. Cf. Kelly and Emery, "Children's Adjustment Following Divorce," 353; Waite and Gallagher, *The Case for Marriage*, 144–45.

Adult Remarriage Realities Affect Children

Following divorce, a child's parents will likely go on to remarry. However, that often means even less time from the non-custodial parent than before he remarried, and the pain of seeing the latter devoting more resources to his new family than to his old one. As we have seen, the stepparent rarely has clear legal obligations to support his or her spouse's children. Meanwhile, given that remarriages are more likely to end in divorce, especially if there are children in the household, there is a strong likelihood that the custodial parent will get *another* divorce.

When we talk about the impact of divorce on children, we often fail to appreciate how often they experience more than one divorce. One of my research assistants of many years ago saw his parents divorce as he started college. Then his mother, with whom his primary residence remained, was married and divorced again before he graduated. I have seen this happen many times, often to much younger children. Frank Furstenberg and Andrew Cherlin estimated that half of all children whose parents remarried experienced a second divorce by their late teens, and 15 percent of all children whose parents got divorced had their custodial parent marry and divorce again before they reached age eighteen.[86] Another study in which Furstenberg was involved found, "Remarriage does not necessarily stabilize the child's family situation. Our results indicate that 37.3 percent of the children re-experience the disruption of their parents' marriage after entering a stepfamily situation."[87] Nicholas Wolfinger noted that 20 percent of the children born during the late 1970s have experienced more than one parental divorce.[88] Another study found that 10 percent of children whose parents divorce go on to experience *three or more* family breakdowns.[89] Scholars agree that a cycle of repeat divorces dramatically increases the negative impacts of marital dissolution upon children.[90]

Furstenberg and Cherlin recount the true story of a boy they named Vincent. His parents divorced when he was seven. After living with his mother and grandmother for a while, Vincent's mother moved in with her boyfriend, who eventually became his stepfather. That lasted four years

---

86. Furstenberg and Cherlin, *Divided Families*, 14.
87. Furstenberg et al., "The Life Course of Children of Divorce," 661.
88. Wolfinger, "Beyond the Intergenerational Transmission of Divorce," 1074.
89. Gallagher, *The Abolition of Marriage*, 76.
90. Chira, "Fractured Families: Dealing with Multiple Divorce."

until his mother's next divorce. At the time they wrote, Vincent's mother was in another, on-and-off, cohabiting relationship, unsure if she would marry the man or not.[91] Vincent's sad experience is similar to the one J. D. Vance recounted in his bestselling memoir, *Hillbilly Elegy*. As these experiences illustrate too, research on the effects of multiple divorces upon children typically underestimates the amount of disruption because it does not include cohabitations.

Pulling this together, Andrew Cherlin stated more recently that "the percentage of children experiencing three or more mother's partners today in the United States is probably higher than in any Western country at any time in the past several centuries."[92] We are disrupting children's lives more now through the voluntary actions of parents than centuries of short life expectancies and high mid-life death rates accomplished. That is incredibly sad.

Intergenerational Transmission of Divorce and Its Correlates

The reader may also recall that, in considering risk factors for divorce in premarital selection and preparation in chapter 6, we looked at the undisputed finding that adult children of divorce are more likely to get divorced themselves. In the General Social Survey for all ever-married respondents, from 2006 through 2016, 53 percent of those whose biological or adoptive parents had divorced or separated by the time they were age sixteen had gotten divorced or separated themselves, compared to 42 percent for those from intact homes. The picture does not change if we restrict the analysis only to those whose homes were at or above average income levels.

This appears to be partly because children from divorced homes are more likely to cohabit, marry at a young age, or have children out-of-wedlock.[93] They are also, on average, more likely to have serious marital conflict, poor communication skills, be less successful educationally and financially, be less committed to remaining married for life, more willing to consider divorce, and have weaker ties with their parents.[94] All these

---

91. Furstenberg and Cherlin, *Divided Families*, 13.

92. Cherlin, *The Marriage-Go-Round*, 183.

93. Kelly and Emery, "Children's Adjustment Following Divorce," 356.

94. Amato, "The Effects of Divorce and Marital Discord on Adult Children's Psychological Well-Being," 902–4. See also Whitton et al., "Effects of Parental Divorce on Marital Commitment and Confidence"; and Amato and Cheadle, "The Long Reach of Divorce," 191–92.

outcomes in turn increase their risk of divorce. Sadly, any sustained examination of how and why children from divorced homes are more likely to get divorced themselves uncovers numerous other ways in which they are at a disadvantage compared to those from intact families.[95]

We must consider two other grim realities. First, children who experience multiple marital disruptions are more likely to repeat that experience as adults.[96] Second, problems that can undermine marital quality, such as lower education achievements, weaker parental ties, and greater marital discord, are measurably greater out to the third generation.[97] Grandchildren suffer the effects of their grandparents' divorces, even when most occurred before they were born. Our failures can create consequences for those yet unborn (Num 14:18; Exod 20:5). Praise God that he can mitigate or reverse these for those who follow him.

WEAKENED PARENTAL BONDS

A great deal of research shows that children in divorced homes have, on average, weaker parental bonds than do those in intact families.[98] We are not surprised that this is the case with the non-custodial parent, usually the father. However, the evidence is that relationship with the custodial parent, usually the mother, also suffers. Following divorce, many fathers gradually disengage from their biological children, while many mothers display less emotional warmth, monitor their children less effectively, and are harsher and more erratic in their discipline.[99] Boys often fight with their mothers more following divorce.[100] Moreover, these eroded parental ties continue into the children's adulthood.[101]

Many children, especially boys, report wanting to spend more time with their fathers than the court orders.[102] Numerous studies have found

---

95. See also Wolfinger, "Beyond the Intergenerational Transmission of Divorce," 1063–64.

96. Wolfinger, "Beyond the Intergenerational Transmission of Divorce," 1075.

97. Amato and Cheadle, "The Long Reach of Divorce," 202.

98. Morrison and Coiro, "Parental Conflict and Marital Disruption," 627; Amato, "Research on Divorce," 657; Waite and Gallagher, *The Case for Marriage*, 128; Starbuck and Lundy, *Families in Context*, 423.

99. Amato and Cheadle, "The Long Reach of Divorce," 192; Kelly and Emery, "Children's Adjustment Following Divorce," 354.

100. Ibid.

101. Ibid.; Fagan and Rector, "The Effects of Divorce on America," 17–18.

102. Kelly and Emery, "Children's Adjustment Following Divorce," 354.

that children and young adults from divorced homes report that losing contact with the non-custodial parent, usually the father, was the hardest part of the experience.[103] Geographic moves are often necessary and can make this worse. Moves that separate children from their fathers by seventy-five or more miles radically diminish time and closeness between them.[104] When the father remarries, as is usually the case, this deepens the separation more.[105] Moreover a quarter or more of custodial mothers admit to sabotaging the father's visits with his children.[106]

A 2013 US Census report summarizes much of the current reality with regard to child custody overall. For children under twenty-one years of age who were in custody arrangements, fathers were the custodial parents only 17.5 percent of the time.[107] Forty-five percent of custodial parents had more than one child.[108] Fifty-four percent of custodial parents were either divorced, separated, or divorced and remarried; and, of these, the same percentage had been awarded child support.[109] Twenty-one percent of noncustodial parents lived in a different state and another 3 percent in a foreign country, and 31 percent had *no* contact with their child in the previous year.[110] Here is what Alison Clarke-Stewart and Cornelia Brentano said about father-child contact following divorce:

> Fathers have little contact with their children after divorce, and this contact decreases over time. The pattern of modest initial contact and sharp drop-off over time is strikingly similar across studies. According to the National Survey of Families and Households, nearly one-third of divorced fathers do not see their children, and only one-quarter see them as often as once a week. . . . Fathers disappear from their children's lives because they move, remarry or get involved in a new romantic relationship, lack financial resources,

103. Ibid.

104. Ibid.

105. Ibid.

106. Ibid.

107. Grall, "Custodial Mothers and Fathers and Their Child Support: 2013," 1.

108. Ibid.

109. I calculated this from frequencies in table 4, page 5, detailed tables that accompanied this report. Only 42 percent of never-married custodial single parents were awarded child support. "Custodial Mothers and Fathers and Their Child Support: 2013, Series P60-255, Detailed Tables."

110. Ibid., table 9, 41.

have strained relationships with their former spouse, or experience psychological pain caused by their diminished parental identity and status.[111]

LESS SUCCESSFUL ACADEMICALLY, SOCIALLY, FINANCIALLY

Numerous studies have found that, on average and all other things being equal, children from divorced homes have lower levels of academic achievement and success.[112] This includes being more likely to drop out of high school and less likely to attend college.[113] There are numerous reasons for this, including pushing kids into worse neighborhoods and schools due to reduced income, less parental supervision and help with homework, and more moving and school disruptions.[114] Figure 12.4 shows this clearly.

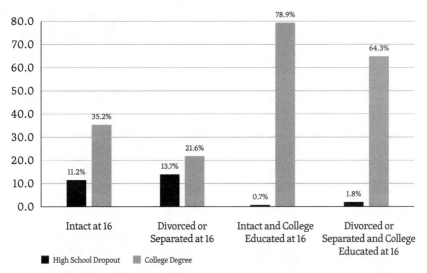

Figure 12.4: Percentage Over Age 23, High School Dropout versus College Degree, by Whether Parents Married or Divorced/Separated at Age 16, and Whether Parents Both Had College Degrees (GSS 2006–2016)

---

111. Clarke-Stewart and Brentano, *Divorce*, 136.

112. Amato, "The Consequences of Divorce for Adults and Children," 1277–78; Amato, "Research on Divorce," 653, 655; Amato and Cheadle, "The Long Reach of Divorce," 199, 201, 202; Kelly and Emery, "Children's Adjustment Following Divorce," 355–56; Fagan and Rector, "The Effects of Divorce on America," 8–10.

113. Ibid., 10–11; Amato and Cheadle, "The Long Reach of Divorce," 192; Kelly and Emery, "Children's Adjustment Following Divorce," 356; Waite and Gallagher, *The Case for Marriage*, 133.

114. Ibid., 134.

Among adults over twenty-three years of age in the General Social Survey for 2006 through 2016, those living with both parents at sixteen were more likely to complete college and less likely to drop out compared to those whose parents were divorced or separated at that age. This was even true among those whose parents both had college degrees.

Children from divorced homes are less likely to have strong social skills.[115] This includes and is partly due to their having less contact with adults in their communities, and fewer ties between their parents and the range of other important adults in their world—teachers, coaches, friends' parents, and so on.[116] Geographic moves necessitated by circumstances often disrupt their relationships with friends, schoolmates, teachers, and others.[117] With their finances likely moving downward, these changes often mean moving to less desirable, less hospitable areas.[118]

Overall, compared to folks raised in intact homes, adults whose parents divorced are also not as well off financially.[119] This is not surprising, given that their homes were more likely to move into lower income status, which can reduce sources of support. In addition, both academic achievement and social competency are critical to achieving financial success in the modern world. Besides, if they go on to get divorced or have children out-of-wedlock themselves, which they are at greater risk of, this will harm them financially.

PSYCHOLOGICAL WELL-BEING

The list of psychological problems that those raised in divorced homes are more likely to have, with all other things being equal,[120] is a long one. When preceded by high-conflict marriages, divorce can actually improve the picture for kids.[121] However, as we have seen, most divorces

---

115. Amato, "The Consequences of Divorce for Adults and Children," 1277; Amato, "Research on Divorce," 653; Kelly and Emery, "Children's Adjustment Following Divorce," 355–56; Starbuck and Lundy, *Families in Context*, 423.

116. Waite and Gallagher, *The Case for Marriage*, 129.

117. Ibid., 130.

118. Ibid.

119. Amato and Cheadle, "The Long Reach of Divorce," 192; "The Effects of Divorce on America," 11.

120. Waite and Gallagher, *The Case for Marriage*, 125.

121. Ibid., 132; Amato, "The Consequences of Divorce for Adults and Children," 1278; Amato, "Research on Divorce," 657; Starbuck and Lundy, *Families in Context*, 423.

do not. Many children suffer anxiety, depression, higher incidence of headaches, violent rage, difficulties sleeping, and excessive worry following divorce.[122] Children of divorce are more likely to suffer lower self-esteem.[123] Sadly, they are more likely to commit suicide.[124] Even when children from divorced homes escape clinical psychological problems, they often suffer disproportionately from psychological pain.[125] This includes difficulties such as worrying about whether both parents will be at their weddings or graduations, wondering if their fathers love them, feeling lonely, resenting the fact that circumstances forced them to prematurely take on adult responsibilities, finding family get-togethers to be unusually stressful, divided loyalties between mother and father, and so on.[126]

BEHAVIORAL PROBLEMS

Even controlling for other relevant factors, those raised in divorced homes are more likely to be involved in infractions in school, delinquency and adult criminality, incarceration, and substance abuse.[127] Sexually, they are on average more promiscuous and have elevated chances of having a child out-of-wedlock and cohabiting.[128] In the General Social Survey for 2006 through 2016, 38 percent of never-married respondents from intact homes reported three or more sex partners in the past five years, compared to 52 percent of those whose parents were divorced or separated at age sixteen. Among those who reported their childhood households enjoyed average to high family income, the difference was essentially the same—40 percent versus 55 percent.

---

122. Waite and Gallagher, *The Case for Marriage*, 132. See also Amato, "Research on Divorce," 655, on anxiety and depression; and Fagan and Rector, "The Effects of Divorce on America," 14.

123. Morrison and Coiro, "Parental Conflict and Marital Disruption," 627; Amato, "The Consequences of Divorce for Adults and Children," 1277; Amato, "Research on Divorce," 655; Starbuck and Lundy, *Families in Context*, 423.

124. Ibid.; Fagan and Rector, "The Effects of Divorce on America," 16; Amato, "Research on Divorce," 655.

125. Ibid., 656.

126. Ibid.; see also Fagan and Rector, "The Effects of Divorce on America," 13.

127. Ibid., 6, 8; Waite and Gallagher, *The Case for Marriage*, 134; Starbuck and Lundy, *Families in Context*, 423.

128. Fagan and Rector, "The Effects of Divorce on America," 23–25.

PHYSICAL HEALTH

Considering all that we have seen so far about the behavioral, psychological, and financial difficulties faced by children from divorced homes, we would expect that they would also have more health problems. That is precisely what the research shows.[129] One scientist tracking children before and after divorce discovered that their physical health problems increased by 50 percent.[130] Documented differences include hospitalization, asthma, heart problems, injuries, and convulsions.[131] It is harder for single mothers to monitor their children's health, prevent accidents, and the like.[132] Adults from divorced homes have shorter life expectancies and are more likely to die at relatively early ages.[133]

WHAT ABOUT REMARRIAGE?

For a child whose parents get divorced, remarriage of the custodial parent rarely solves their problems, and can make things worse, especially if preceded by cohabitation with the eventual stepparent, or someone else. One can imagine that this is especially problematic if the stepparent played a role in breaking up the parents' marriage, as in the case of an affair. We all know that this sad scenario is all too common. Andrew Cherlin points out that "children in stepfamilies show lower levels of well-being than children in two-biological-parent families. . . . In fact, some studies find no difference between children in stepfamilies and children in single-parent families. . . . The risk of having problems is higher in stepfamilies."[134]

Children in stepfamilies are far more likely to suffer abuse, usually at the hands of their stepparents.[135] Even worse are the mother's boyfriends or live-in lovers.[136] This includes all forms of serious abuse, including sexual and fatal abuse.[137]

---

129. Amato, "The Consequences of Divorce for Adults and Children," 1278; Amato, "Research on Divorce," 658.

130. Waite and Gallagher, *The Case for Marriage*, 130.

131. Ibid.; Fagan and Rector, "The Effects of Divorce on America," 16.

132. Waite and Gallagher, *The Case for Marriage*, 131.

133. Ibid.; Fagan and Rector, "The Effects of Divorce on America," 16.

134. Cherlin, *Public and Private Families*, 352.

135. Popenoe, *Life Without Father*, 71; Waite and Gallagher, *The Case for Marriage*, 135, 159.

136. "The Effects of Divorce in America," 7; *Life Without Father*, 70.

137. "The Effects of Divorce in America," 7–8. See also *Life Without Father*, 68

Moreover, bonding between stepparents and their spouse's biological children is often quite weak. David Popenoe reported one study in which only 53 percent of stepfathers said that they had "feelings" for their stepchildren, with even fewer indicating that they actually loved them.[138] Research suggests that stepparents provide less supervision, discipline, and nurture.[139] Children in stepfamilies leave home at an earlier age, either to marry or just be on their own.[140]

The degree to which the stepfamily relationships are a legal limbo is almost jarring. As Starbuck and Lundy observe, "The law is not particularly helpful in establishing stepfamily boundaries nor in defining the role of stepparents. . . . For the most part, the law ignores the stepparent-stepchild relationships."[141] For example, if the subsequent marriage ends in divorce, the stepparent usually has no standing for obtaining custody or visitation privileges.[142]

Beyond this, initially there is no shared family history.[143] Complex relationships, in addition to the obligations that one or both parents have to other families, cause stress and confusion.[144] Parents often have to negotiate many matters they would handle naturally in an intact family, such as who pays for a child's travel or college education, or for chores and allowances.[145]

Figure 12.5 shows some outcome differences for adult respondents who were living with both biological parents versus stepfamilies at age sixteen, combining the years 2006 through 2016.[146] Throughout, stepfamily outcomes were similar to those of single-parent homes. As with the problems of divorced adults, remarrying is not a panacea for children of divorce.

CONCLUSION

Scholars and pundits commonly argue that the negative effects I have outlined in this chapter, though well supported by a lot of solid research, are often on balance not that large. They assert that the seriousness of the

---

138. Ibid., 71.
139. Starbuck and Lundy, *Families in Context*, 430.
140. Cherlin, *Public and Private Families*, 352.
141. Starbuck and Lundy, *Families in Context*, 430.
142. Ibid.
143. Ibid., 428.
144. Ibid.
145. Ibid., 429.
146. Except for percentage married at twenty years of age or less. That item was not used after 1994, so I combined the years 1984 through 1994 here.

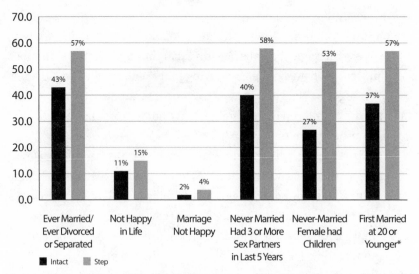

Figure 12.5: Respondents Raised in Average-Income to Wealthy Homes, Lived with Two Biological Parents versus Stepfamily at Age 16 (GSS, 2006–2016)

damage and difference between folks who did or did not experience divorce are real but slight. I disagree.

First, many of these differences, as we have seen, are not narrow. Second, some of these consequences are quite harmful. Third, given the sheer number of negative effects, it is highly unlikely that adults or children of divorce will escape all or even many of them. Fourth, we have to consider the increasingly common follow-ups to divorce—namely cohabitation, remarriage, subsequent break-ups in both types of relationship, and their cumulative impacts. Finally, these effects are often mutually reinforcing and interactive, as when diminished academic success can lead to lower incomes, higher risk of divorce, and diminished psychological well-being. We can easily multiply examples.

If we in the church want to experience more success in our battle against our divorce culture, we have to stop trying to explain away and excuse the damage it causes. At the same time, let us also hold out hope, comfort, and encouragement to divorced saints and their children. We ought to minister to them realistically without sugarcoating reality. Yet we should do so with all the optimism that the gospel of saving faith in a loving God, accomplished by Jesus Christ and lived out in the power of the Holy Spirit, guided by his inerrant and sufficient word, gives us. With God all things are possible (Matt 19:26; Mark 10:27).

PART 4

MARITAL HAPPINESS
AND SUCCESS

INTRODUCTION TO PART 4

There is much want of comfort then in solitude; much comfort in society. But there is no society more near, more entire, more needful, more kindly, more delightful, more comfortable, more constant, more continual, than the society of man and wife; the main root, source and original of all other Societies: Which of all others therefore man is naturally most inclined unto: And without which therefore even the heathen held the house and family half unfurnished and unfinished; and not fully happy, but half happy, though otherwise never so happy, till therewith it became complete.

Thomas Gataker[1]

In the last section, we looked at the human rending of God's own one-flesh marital covenant, something that is now almost as likely as death to end the journeys of husbands and wives together. It was necessary but hard to take up those topics. However, now, thankfully, in this last portion of the book I will consider more joyful subjects.

First, I will contemplate the *beauty* of Christian marriage in the blessings and joy of lifelong, happy, monogamous marriage between one man and one woman. In this book, we have considered matrimony's functions, specialness, irreplaceability, and many aspects of forming such unions with wisdom. We have also looked at foolish pathways to marriage, and some consequences of walking on those broad but harmful roads. In all this, we have touched on, but not really delved deeply into, the loveliness and deep-seated happiness expressed and found in matrimony and all it symbolizes, even in the midst of the difficulties, trials, and tribulations

---

1. "A Wife Indeed," 28–29.

that also certainly accompany all human marriages. In this chapter, I will do so.

In chapter 14, we will look at simple practices that people engage in, or avoid, to build and maintain marital satisfaction and happiness. From those obvious bits of common sense that "everyone knows" but not enough people practice, to things that perhaps go beyond that, we will consider helpful approaches from social science, experience, and the Bible.

Finally, chapter 15 considers what the church can do both to help build strong marriages and to foster a biblical marriage culture. The professing church has contributed to the decline of marriage through sins of both omission and commission. It has, however, also helped matrimony in many ways and can do much to help turn our current situation around. If the church is to protect and serve Christ's flock and also be salt and light to our larger culture, it must do better.

CHAPTER 13

THE BEAUTIFUL ORDER OF CHRISTIAN MARRIAGE

To recognize the estate of marriage is something quite different from merely being married. He who is married but does not recognize the estate of marriage cannot continue in wedlock without bitterness, drudgery, and anguish; he will inevitably complain and blaspheme like the pagans and blind, irrational men. But he who recognizes the estate of marriage will find therein delight, love, and joy without end.

Martin Luther[1]

To reach the full of earthly felicity a man must not be alone. A helpmeet was needed in Paradise, and assuredly she is not less necessary out of it. He that findeth a wife findeth a good thing. It is not every man that feareth the Lord who has a wife; but if he has, he shall share in his blessedness and increase it.

Charles Haddon Spurgeon[2]

THE PERFECT MARRIAGE

There will only ever be one perfect marriage in human history. Though the betrothal is unfolding as you read this, that holy wedding, which will bring together that faultless bride and groom, has not yet taken place. There would have been one such marriage already, but Adam and Eve's sin marred the excellence of their union, and that of every man and woman

---

1. "The Estate of Marriage," 368–69.
2. *The Treasury of David, Volume XII*, 47.

who have come together as husband and wife since that awful day. In even the best of all human marriages, sin tugs and twists, and we will not find perfection there.

No, the one perfect marriage speaks of the redemption that came millennia after the fall of Adam and Eve and all of their progeny, and awaits its full completion at the end of days, "already but not yet." As Francis and Lisa Chan remind us, of that glorious marriage mere human wedlock, lovely as it can be, "is a mere shadow."[3] All true believers, at the core of their being, long to be present at this glorious marriage, as the bride of Christ.

> Then I heard what seemed to be the voice of a great multitude, like the roar of many waters and like the sound of mighty peals of thunder, crying out, "Hallelujah! For the Lord our God the Almighty reigns. Let us rejoice and exult and give him the glory, for the marriage of the Lamb has come, and his Bride has made herself ready; it was granted her to clothe herself with fine linen, bright and pure"—for the fine linen is the righteous deeds of the saints. And the angel said to me, "Write this: Blessed are those who are invited to the marriage supper of the Lamb." (Rev 19:6–9a)

> Then I saw a new heaven and a new earth, for the first heaven and the first earth had passed away, and the sea was no more. And I saw the holy city, new Jerusalem, coming down out of heaven from God, prepared as a bride adorned for her husband. And I heard a loud voice from the throne saying, "Behold, the dwelling place of God is with man. He will dwell with them, and they will be his people, and God himself will be with them as their God. He will wipe away every tear from their eyes, and death shall be no more, neither shall there be mourning, nor crying, nor pain anymore, for the former things have passed away." (Rev 21:1–4)

> The Spirit and the Bride say, "Come." (Rev 22:17a)

The Bible often uses the reality of human relationships to describe the union of the redeemed to their God in terms that unpack the splendor and multi-faceted nature of that covenant unity with our triune God. We are

---

3. Chan and Chan, *You and Me Forever*, 42.

children of our heavenly Father, his sons and daughters (cf. Rom 8:14, 16; 9:8, 26; Gal 3:26; John 1:12; 11:52; 2 Cor 6:18; Heb 2:10, 13; 1 John 3:1-2, 10; Rev 21:7). Though we must be careful not to treat it flippantly, Christ regards us as his friends (John 15:13-15), and brethren (Mark 3:34; Rom 8:29; Heb 2:11). It is sublime and wonderful that God calls us to be his children, friends, and brethren. Yet the preeminent relationship, affirmed gloriously here in the book of Revelation and elsewhere (John 3:29; Matt 9:15; Mark 2:19-20; Luke 5:34-35), is our being collectively, along with all his saints (past, present, and future) betrothed to Jesus Christ to be his heavenly bride, the church. We are forgiven fully, redeemed completely, comforted intimately in his arms, accepted without reservation or hesitation, loved beyond all human loving, delighting and being delighted in, all filthiness washed away, radiant in purity, adoring her husband and wanting no thing and no one beside him. The perfected bride of the flawless groom entering into a perfect marriage for all eternity.

This then is the ultimate source of the beauty of human marriage, especially between believers who acknowledge, honor, and long for this greater heavenly reality. Flawed as our marriages are, as they are faithfully lived out here on earth, they partake of, reflect, and bear witness to that eternal marriage of the Lamb with those whom he was slain for. They are a living gospel proclamation embedded in the ordinary, everyday highs and lows, sufferings and joys, of husbands and wives living out their marriages in a mostly unbelieving world. Every marriage, whether it does so poorly or well, proclaims the relationship of Christ and his church.[4] Those things that make a marriage beautiful are the same things that God gives his people, by his Spirit, that make Christianity lovely—"love, joy, peace, patience, kindness, goodness, faithfulness, gentleness, self-control" (Gal 5:22-23).

This is why marriages can never be beautiful when we make them into idols, expecting them to deliver happiness and fulfillment as ends in themselves. All the purposes that God has given marriages are to help us, ultimately, to glorify and enjoy God, and to serve him. They point to the eternal, and help us as we walk, grow, and hope in Christ. God must be preeminent in all things, including our marriages.[5] In them, as in all else,

---

4. Wilson, *Reforming Marriage*, 12.

5. Ibid., 11.

we must hold loosely to the things of this world, looking ultimately to our eternal destiny and hope. Then and only then can we fully realize all that our marriages have to offer us, and the world, and be the kind of husbands or wives best suited to help our spouses find their truest fulfillment and joy.

BEAUTY IN THE ORDER OF MARRIAGE

I have maintained throughout this book, laying it out especially in the first several chapters, that God designed marriage with specific structure and purpose. There is room for flexibility in how people may fulfill this design across human cultures, religion, time periods, and marriages, but stepping outside God's framework entirely introduces chaos and destruction. Marriage is an objective, vital covenantal relationship given to the human race at creation to enable it to fulfill God's plan. The author of creation, and the natural laws he has made, witness to and enforce it. This belief opposes the conceit in our modern world that reality is what we say or believe it is, that we can ignore it and do what we want through the simple act of changing our social construction, or collective definition, of it. Like so many failed civilizations littering the landscape of history, modern humans have drunk deeply of the temptation to be gods to themselves, in understanding the nature and purposes of marriage as with so many other things. To appreciate marriage rightly, we must reject this thinking root and branch, and joyfully embrace and submit to his perfect plan as set forth in his inerrant word.

What God creates is not simply functional, and true, and necessary for our good. It is inherently lovely. To fully glorify and enjoy God in our marriages, as in everything else, we must take the time to appreciate the radiant splendor in its divine, ordinary, everyday created order. This is a delightful task, and we will never exhaust it.

The Preacher of Ecclesiastes gives us this wisdom: "He has made everything beautiful in its time. Also, he has put eternity into man's heart, yet so that he cannot find out what God has done from the beginning to the end" (Eccl 3:11). Here he is talking about our ordinary work. He later turns to the marriages within which we typically do our labor, "Enjoy life with the wife whom you love, all the days of your vain life that he has given you under the sun, because that is your portion in life and in your toil at which you toil under the sun" (Eccl 9:9). This reminds me of the wise counsel of "Old Fezziwig" to a young Ebenezer Scrooge, in the George C. Scott film version of *A Christmas Carol*, "What a difference it makes, Ebenezer, to travel the rough road of life with the right female to help bear the burden, eh?"

AN EXCLUSIVE UNION SO LONG AS BOTH SHALL LIVE

Young people contemplating the altar often ask themselves if they are prepared to go the distance. The more acutely aware they are of the vagaries of life and their own weaknesses, the more they will and ought to feel the weight of this commitment.

Yet there is sublime beauty in a man and wife who have suffered trials, weathered disagreements, learned to live with each other's often-irritating frailties, and still enjoy and rely upon one another. The love that endures and even grows as faithful couples experience the inevitable decline and indignities of age is like fine aged wine. The intimacy of their knowledge of each other, the history that they alone share, is a strong, deep river that, at the end of a good marriage, is immensely satisfying to the couple. It is also edifying and encouraging to others. Francis and Lisa Chan shared a friend's story about his parents, ninety-five and ninety-six years of age, married seventy-five years and in love since the sixth grade, and their thoughts about it.

> He proceeded to tell me that his mom's mind is slipping away, but his dad simply sits next to her for hours at a time with his hand resting gently on her arm. . . . I wonder what goes through his mind when he sits beside her. What must he think and feel when he reaches out and makes contact with that arm that has been beside him for 83 years? What would it be like to share 83 years of memories with another person? . . . Laughing together on a playground, falling in love, getting married, having kids, having grandkids, and having great-grandkids. The emotional depth must be intensified by scenes of arguments and tragedies, loss and heartbreak. I imagine them flipping the final pages leading up to the back cover, where scenes of these two finishing their life on earth side by side will finally be placed.[6]

---

6. Chan and Chan, *You and Me Forever*, 41–42.

Few of us have or will meet our husband or wife in elementary school, marry at twenty, and go on to live that long. Yet I think that most folks getting married for the first time hope that, should God grant them long life, the end will be as sweet as this. We will only get there by viewing our marriage as a treasure to protect at all costs, a covenant honored no matter what. Wine this fine is not fermented and aged without commitment, dedication, and trial. However, it is worth all it costs, not only for the spouses but also for those whom their lives touch, whom God has called them to serve and love. How many people have this couple blessed? How have their children's own marriages and parenting been enriched by their union, and in turn their grandchildren and great-grandchildren down through the generations? We have dealt with how three generations can taste the bitter fruits of a couple's divorce. Surely, a godly marriage can produce sweeter fruit that lasts at least that long. Consider the lasting blessing that was the marriage of Boaz and Ruth, King David's godly great-grandparents (Ruth 4:21–22).

There is beauty at each stage of courtship and married life. Much of this too, a husband and wife share specially. The montage of moments embedded into the history of a marriage and the memories of a man and woman, both good and bad, is uniquely theirs. There are elements about each marriage recognizable to almost every other, but no two are the same. There will never be another marriage exactly like this one, nor has there ever been one in the history of the world. At every point too, as believers should recognize, like Boaz and Ruth, God's grace and care have uniquely sustained and interacted with that marriage and will continue to do so. It is not only a marriage like no other, though not completely unlike or unrecognizable to others—God has woven his unique acts of providence toward that husband and wife into their story. Even though no marriage is perfect, they and all of us who have married or will do so should love each other and stand together, because this special and marvelous creation will never happen again.

One afternoon I was on my deer stand up in a tree after a cool mist had covered all of the branches and remaining leaves of late autumn with an infinity of tiny drops of dew. Suddenly, the sun broke through the trees and for just a few seconds every single bead was blazing, like diamonds. For a few seconds I found myself suspended in dazzling wonder beyond words, and then it was gone. Our lives are like that, our marriages too (Isa 40:8)—brief, fragile, yet also enduring and of immeasurable value, and worth preserving and protecting, like that memory.

A PUBLIC UNION

As over against modern ideals of individualized marriage or cohabitation— where folks make up their own parameters and decide what they will and will not promise one another, based on what they find personally fulfilling and meaningful and as long as it works for them—we have the sturdy, public institution of Christian marriage. This is God's covenant as it has existed since he created the human race, entered into before him and human witnesses who affirm that this couple has indeed met all of God's requirements for marriage and who can testify to the promises each has freely made to the other.

Marriage is both a private experience and a public reality. From the beginning, God made the man and woman husband and wife not only for each other, but also for others. That marriage is, after all, a means by which they are to glorify and enjoy God, and love their neighbor, not just their spouse.

Foremost will be their children, if God so chooses to bless them with offspring by birth or adoption. Through them across time, this humble couple will help to shape generations yet unseen. Was my salvation at least partially an answer to the prayer of my lay minister great-grandfather for his son, this man who died fifty years before I was born? Does your salvation have such a story embedded in it, hidden to all but God? How many generations have fathers and mothers been handing down the gospel in your family? If it has been several, then are not these forgotten men and women continuing, by their faithfulness, to bless your marriage and perhaps your children, and down the line? The apostle Paul told Timothy to pass his teachings on to faithful men who would in turn transmit them to others (2 Tim 2:2). He speaks of the church, but does not every godly parent hope that the echo of their faith will be shared, generation after generation, out to hundreds of years? If every parent follows the instruction of Deuteronomy 6:7 to teach his ways faithfully to their children, and God chooses to bless the hearing of it, will not this be the result? Surely, not all of our offspring and their descendants will follow Christ, but if we are faithful in the little things in how we raise our children, and do so within the framework of godly marriage, the blessings passed on over time will be substantial.

We see also that the homes that married people create are to be a blessing to many others, the great mystery of Christ's relationship with his bride, the church, embedded in each one (Eph 5:31–32). In a godly home, there are worship, prayer, Scripture study, witnessing, counseling, comfort, helping, and hospitality. Physical needs are cared for, including the care of many of the most vulnerable among us—infants, children, the sick, and the elderly. Meanwhile, the members of a sound family, rooted in godly marriage, serve and stabilize the larger community. As the *Westminster Confession of Faith* reminds us, if God chooses, married believers may increase the human race with legitimate offspring and the church with godly seed. Each faithful home creates its own unique mini-culture, its way of life, touching and enriching the larger culture in ever-enlarging spheres as its members go out, equipped, into their own respective callings. The requirement that God's elders be noted for hospitality, as well as being good husbands and fathers (1 Tim 2:2–5), is not an accidental add-on, but is central to what he is looking for from married saints. Christian marriages should be a source of great blessing to our larger world.

Now let us take what I have pointed out in this last paragraph, and the one before it, and think how they work together and reveal how God can use humble, faithful marriages to radiate blessings *simultaneously* across generations as they move outward into community, church, and society. We have all seen how quickly the family tree of a husband and wife branches out across decades and then centuries. In God's providence, the blessings of a godly husband and wife can carry out immeasurably across time and culture long after God takes them home. It can happen through their descendants and *their* spouses and all they touch, as well as others this couple has influenced and helped through their marriage and home with all *their* descendants and others that *they* influence. Only God knows what he can and intends to accomplish through that groom and bride as they simply live, love, and serve together across the span of their life, and the benefits of that spread across time and their social worlds. There is beauty in that, and quiet power, because it is not just about them, but about many whom their lives will touch.

Economists would describe the civil benefits of marriage partially as *public externality*, where individuals or groups produce benefits for others beyond what they are compensated. They might describe it as a *public good*, something that many experience the advantage of beyond those who sacrifice for it.[7] Yet no economist can capture the reach or richness of the blessings of a good marriage to the human race. They certainly cannot measure the degree to which God uses it, through biological propagation and faithful childrearing but many other ways as well, to populate heaven. Our civilization has forgotten this, and so, rather than rewarding godly marriage, our culture increasingly denigrates and even attempts to cripple it. This is of course ultimately because the evil one understands its place in God's plan, and seeks to destroy it, as he has done from the beginning. However, God also knows and loves his marital covenant and the human race for which he established it. He will protect both it and you over your lifespan however things seem in the short run. Let us cherish, appreciate, and defend it, as he does.

A SEXUAL UNION

Just as alcoholics can never truly and properly appreciate fine wine, those caught up in a sex-crazed culture with no regard for marital boundaries can never truly grasp the essence and joy of godly lovemaking. Like a drunk slugging down a bottle of expensive pinot noir, they might get the thrill of the drug but they will never know the wine's best depths and delights. Certainly, a porn-saturated culture cannot begin to comprehend the profound loveliness of a paunchy, middle-aged husband and wife finding comfort and reassurance in a brief erotic embrace at the end of a long day. Yet it is in everyday sexual love just like this that the one-flesh reality of marriage and all that it means before God is most often expressed and enjoyed. Notice this earthy recommendation from Scripture that fixes the delights of marital lovemaking beyond age or the vagaries of physical beauty and charm: "Let your fountain be blessed, and rejoice in the wife of your youth, a lovely deer, a graceful doe. Let her breasts fill you at all times with delight; be intoxicated always in her love" (Prov 5:18–19).

---

7. Andrew Cherlin ably applies these concepts to families in *Public and Private Families*, 6–7.

Puritan divine Thomas Hooker aptly compared marital love to the longing and communion each believer ought to have with Christ. His view of the proper love a man ought to have for his wife is profound. "The man whose heart is endeared to the woman he loves, he dreams of her in the night, hath her in his eye and apprehension when he awakes, muses on her as he sits at table, walks with her when he travels and parleys with her in each place where he comes."[8] It is within such tenderness and holy attention that sex between a husband and wife belongs and finds its best expression, having nothing to do with powerful sensation or striking physical attraction. C. S. Lewis pointed out that this kind of love between a man and a woman moves sexual fulfillment beyond animal need to something far richer, because the object is not to experience sensory gratification but to become one with the beloved.[9] Using the term "Eros" to mean "being in love," he sets forth the beauty of covenantal lovemaking. "Sexual desire, without Eros, wants it, the thing in itself; Eros wants the beloved. . . . In some mysterious but quite indisputable fashion the lover desires the Beloved herself, not the pleasure she can give . . . in Eros, a Need, at its most intense, sees the object most intensely as a thing admirable in herself, important far beyond her relation to the lover's need."[10]

Does this negate passion? Not at all; it actually liberates and directs it rightly. Here is the wise old Puritan William Gouge, describing an element of men's "domestic duties":

> Contrary is the disposition of such husbands as have no heat, or heart of affection in them: but Stoic-like delight no more in their own wives than in any other women, nor account them any dearer than others. A disposition no way warranted by the word. The faithful saints of God before mentioned, as also many other like to them, were no Stoics, without all affection: nor did they think it a matter unbeseeming them after a peculiar manner to delight in their wives (witness Isaac's sporting with his wife) for this is a privilege which appertains to the estate of marriage. But that I be not mistaken

---

8. *The Application of Redemption by the Effectual Work of the Word, and Spirit of Christ, for the Bringing Home of Lost Sinners to God*, 137–38. I updated spelling to improve readability.

9. Lewis, *The Four Loves*, 91.

10. Ibid., 94–95.

herein, let it be noted that the affection whereof I speak is not a carnal, sensual, beastly affection, but such an one as may stand with Christian gratitude and sobriety: having relation to the soul of a man's wife as well as to her body, grounded both on the near conjunction of marriage, and also on the inward qualities of his wife.[11]

Many souls around us are tired of empty sex. They are sick of using and being used, of performing and having their worth evaluated on how well they gratify another's sensual appetites, tired of wondering where they rank among the twenty or thirty who have come before them. As the Roman poet Lucretius pointed out, real love between a man and a woman is actually a distraction for those intent on experiencing sex as a mammalian rush.[12] The Hugh Hefners of this world know nothing about true marital lovemaking or its higher joys. As Christians, we can call our fellows out of this gilded trap into something as far beyond it as an ocean is to a puddle. We can celebrate sexual union that points ultimately to him who is the perfect fulfillment of every legitimate human desire.

TRUE COMPANIONS AND FRIENDS

How wonderful it is to have a companion for life, one with whom, as we have noted in chapter 2, we can simultaneously enjoy every level of friendship. We will find that a godly spouse well suited to us is pleasurable and useful but, best of all, that he or she delights in our highest moral good, is eager to grow in Christ with us, iron willing to be sharpened by iron (Prov 27:17). A husband and wife in a godly union are companions together, helping each other as each makes their own progress as pilgrims and aliens in this world, supporting and encouraging each other on the narrow way to the heavenly kingdom. Tim and Kathy Keller point out that to Adam, Eve was "the friend his heart had been seeking."[13] A godly spouse is our *alluph*, our "special confidant" (Prov 2:17).[14] How often we will find wisdom, comfort, refuge, and encouragement in this most

---

11. Gouge, *Of Domesticall Duties*, 362. I have taken liberty to modernize much of the spelling for clarity. I thank J. I. Packer for directing me to this text and the earlier one by Thomas Hooker; see Packer, *A Quest for Godliness*, 265.

12. Lewis, *The Four Loves*, 95.

13. Keller and Keller, *The Meaning of Marriage*, 117.

14. Ibid.

precious of all human companions who loves us at all times, even in the days of adversity (Prov 17:17).[15]

Consider again the wise words of the Preacher: "Two are better than one, because they have good reward for their toil. For if they fall, one will lift up his fellow. But woe to him who is alone when he falls and has not another to lift him up! Again, if two lie together, they keep warm, but how can one keep warm alone? And though a man might prevail against one who is alone, two will withstand him—a threefold cord is not quickly broken" (Eccl 4:9–12).

As Matthew Henry rightly notes about this passage, Solomon "designs hereby to recommend to us both marriage and friendship,"[16] which as we have seen are united in godly marriage. Two joined in marriage reward each other for the good they do, particularly regarding kindness and love. In Christian marriage, over time, there will be rewards deep and satisfying for the investments spouses pour into each other. As Matthew Henry also observed, reflecting upon this passage, two together, including a husband and wife, will help guard each other against temptation, pick up the other when he or she falls, and challenge one another. They will do more good for others than they would do apart.[17] When the world seems to be against a man or woman, his or her spouse is that ever-loyal friend. A husband and wife in a good marriage converse together, enjoy silence in each other's company, and can intimately communicate through a simple look or touch. They warm each other physically but more importantly in their affections for what is right and good, for the task ahead of them, helping to stoke fires that have grown cold, especially those that ought to burn for their Lord.[18]

Husbands and wives who have covenanted together to be bound in Christ are a threefold cord that is not easily broken. Again, Matthew Henry expresses the reality beautifully and succinctly: "Where two are closely joined in holy love and fellowship, Christ will by his Spirit come to them, and make the third, as he joined himself to the two disciples going to Emmaus, and then there is a threefold cord that can never be broken. They that dwell in love, dwell in God, and God in them."[19] Where a man

---

15. Ibid., 112.

16. *Commentary on the Whole Bible, Volume 3*, 826.

17. Ibid.

18. Ibid.

19. Ibid., 827.

and woman are joined organically not only in mutual love and their complementary selves, but also to Christ as individuals but also as one-flesh united, what God has created is radiant as the purest gold, strong as the hardest steel.

There are few faults more consistently seen in good marriages than when spouses simply fail to appreciate the wonderful gift their spouse is to them. King Lemuel's mother told him that an excellent wife is "far more precious than jewels" (Prov 31:10b), and then proceeded to explain numerous reasons why this is so, none of them having to do with mere charm or physical attractiveness. We husbands forget that far too often. The treasure in our spouse is not in the externals they bring to us, but in what they in essence *are* as the one God called to be our life partners, sharing the burdens and delights on our journey through this world. A good wife is a fruitful vine (Ps 128:3a), one that will remain fruitful. Here is what the Puritan divine Thomas Gataker, addressing men, had to say about finding such a wife:

> "'Oh could I but get a rich wife, a wealthy one,' says one; 'I would be well, I would be made for ever.' And, 'Let me have a fair one,' says another, 'and I care for no more.' 'Give me the woman,' says Sampson, 'for she pleases mine eye.' . . . But as that worthy Grecian once said, that he would rather have for his daughter, a man without money, than money without a man: So better were it for thee to have a wife without wealth or beauty, than to have wealth or beauty without a wife; and so be as far from having the comfort of a wife, as if thou had no wife at all."[20]

THE TWO AS ONE FLESH

Marriage, as I have touched on repeatedly and the Bible abundantly teaches, goes beyond even the deepest and most profound partnerships and friendships. The two become one flesh (Gen 2:23-24; Matt 19:4-6; Mark 10:6-8; Eph 5:28-31). This is the ultimate meaning of sexual intercourse in marriage, and points to the mystery by which marriage represents the union of Christ and his people (Eph 5:32). This then, in turn, informs how husbands

---

20. "A Wife Indeed," 23–24. I have taken the liberty to modernize the spelling and add quotation marks to his dialogue in order to improve readability, here and elsewhere.

and wives are to regard and treat one another (Eph 5:22–33). No other human relationship comes close. The mortal meets the divine, infused with holy grace, in marriage. The *Catechism of the Catholic Church* speaks rightly and elegantly about this:

> Holy Scripture affirms that man and woman were created for one another: "It is not good that the man should be alone." The woman, "flesh of his flesh," i.e., his counterpart, his equal, his nearest in all things, is given to him by God as a "helpmate"; she thus represents God from whom comes our help. "Therefore a man leaves his father and his mother and cleaves to his wife, and they become one flesh." The Lord himself shows that this signifies an unbreakable union of their two lives by recalling what the plan of the Creator had been "in the beginning": "So they are no longer two, but one flesh."[21]

Thomas Gataker sets forth the one-flesh union of a man and wife, rooted in the nature and order of the creation of Eve from Adam. His language is colorful and powerful. How any man could grasp this and subject his wife to abuse is beyond me—as the apostle Paul noted, "for no one ever hated his own flesh, but nourishes and cherishes it, just as Christ does the church, because we are members of his body" (Eph 5:29–30).

> Again, a wife is as a part, or a limb of her husband. As children are said to be part of their parents; because they have their being originally from them: so the woman may well be said to be a part or limb of man, because she had her beginning and her being originally from him. For the woman is of the man, says the Apostle; and not the man of the woman: as children are of their parents, and not their parents of them. The woman was made of the man's rib. She was at first taken out of man; and is therefore by creation as a limb wrest from him. And then was afterward joined again in marriage with man, that by nuptial conjunction becoming one flesh with him, she might be as a limb restored now and fastened again to him. Every wife should be then as a part of her husband; as a limb of him that hath her.[22]

---

21. 401.
22. "A Wife Indeed," 8–9.

The creation of Eve from Adam, and God rejoining her to him in the first marriage that ever was sets for us a divine pattern superior to every counterfeit concocted by mere mortals.[23] Hidden inside this historical moment are profound truths. Here is Douglas Wilson:

> Adam gave his wife two individual names. The first was *Ishshah*, or Woman, because she was taken out of man. The second was *Chavvah*—life-bearer—or as we say it in English, Eve. "And Adam called his wife's name Eve (*Chavvah*), because she was the mother of all living" (Gen. 3:20). Her two names reveal truth about her. The first reveals her dependence upon man—she was taken out of man. The second reveals man's dependence upon her—every man since is her son. . . . Each wife is an *Ishshah*, and each wife is a *Chavvah*. Each is woman, and each is Eve.[24]

This is of course the source of that part of the famous Noel Paul Stookey lyrics that I opened this book with, "As it was in the beginning, is now until the end, woman draws her life from man and gives it back again. And there is love."

"My beloved is mine, and I am his," exults the bride, "and his banner over me was love" (Song 2:16a, 4a). Perhaps every Christian husband needs to say to his wife, looking into her eyes and holding her hands, "You are bone of my bone, you are flesh of my flesh" (Gen 2:23a). Their hearts beat in each other's breasts for as long as they both live. She is part of him, he is part of her—they are one, no matter how many miles separate them, no matter what their condition. They depend on one another; each flows from the other, as it has been since the beginning. Two cords are now one knot. How does this not connect earth with heaven?

A GODLY SEED

Finally, though God does not bless every married couple with children, natural or adopted, the fruit of the womb is surely beautiful. Each little one is priceless, possessing an immortal soul. As C. S. Lewis pointed out, their lives make the life of a civilization like a gnat in comparison.[25] There

---

23. Wilson, *Reforming Marriage*, 14.
24. Ibid., 15.
25. Lewis, "The Weight of Glory," 274.

has never been another person exactly like them, and there will never be. When I gazed into the eyes of my firstborn at birth, I knew that the little one looking back, eyes hurt by the bright lights of the delivery room, would live forever. It was overwhelming.

This is a sacred trust God gives to parents, ideally setting this within the protection of marriage. For those unable to care for children within that covenantal framework, there ought to be married folks standing by to encourage and help.

We who worship the Father and the Son know that the bond of parent to child is holy and full of spiritual mystery. God uses our experience as parents to teach us about the nature of his care for us (cf. Luke 11:11–13; Heb 12:5–11).

Children are a wonderful blessing especially when—though they may proceed from marital love—they do not supersede that first and most important union between their married mother and father. Thomas Gataker reflects upon this: "Behold, children and the fruit of the womb, are the gift of God, says Solomon. Children are the gift of God; but the Wife is a more special gift of God: she comes in the first place, they in the second: And gifts are usually answerable to the greatness of the giver."[26]

Martin Luther's insights in "The Estate of Marriage" about how believers ought to view the difficult and even distasteful aspects of having children reflect his personal experience in the trenches with his wife through six children, and his pastoral insight. Responding to the understandable desire to look askance at the dirty diapers, nightly rocking, crying, rashes and sores of infant care while still having to look after the rest of the family and work all day,[27] he encourages us to see beyond the day-to-day drudgery to the glorious spiritual reality behind it all. Here is an excerpt addressed to husbands.

> What then does Christian faith say to this? It opens its eyes, looks upon all those insignificant and despised duties in the Spirit, and is aware that they are all adorned with divine approval as with the costliest gold and jewels. It says, 'O God, because I am certain that thou hast created me as a man and hast from my body begotten

---

26. "A Good Wife God's Gift," 12–13.

27. 369.

this child, I also know for a certainty that it meets thy perfect pleasure. I confess to thee that I am not worthy to rock the little babe
or wash his diapers, or to be entrusted with the care of the child
and its mother. How is it that I, without any merit, have come to
this distinction of being certain that I am serving thy creature and
thy most precious will? O how gladly will I do so, though the duties
should be even more insignificant and despised. Neither frost nor
heat, neither drudgery nor labor, will distress or dissuade me, for
I am certain that this is pleasing in thy sight.'[28]

Our little ones have a sin nature as we do. They belong to God, and he
calls us to steward them for him. Their time under our roof will be startlingly brief but profoundly important. This is an awesome responsibility.
The husband and wife who have become a family living under the protection and authority of God are a basic cell for earthly society and the church.
As the Westminster Larger Catechism teaches us, it is in learning to honor
their fathers and mothers that children acquire the ability to submit to
superiors and authorities in all realms of life.[29]

In children ideally, as in marriage and our response to God, love calls
forth love. Even with all our imperfections and failures, in both matrimony
and parenting, we experience that joyful comfort of love covering "a multitude of sins" (1 Pet 4:8). Here is William Gouge: "That love which naturally parents bear to their children, ought in equity to breed in children a
love to their parents. For love deserves love: and most unworthy are they
to be loved, who cannot love again. The love of parents above all others
is to be answered with love on children's part to the uttermost of their
power, because it is free, great, and constant."[30]

As fearful and difficult as this duty is, a godly marriage blessed by children is a wonderful thing. The man who fears the Lord, says the psalm-
ist, will have a wife like a "fruitful vine," and children "like olive shoots"
around his table, and if he is extra blessed, he will see his "children's

---

28. Ibid., 370. Note that Luther's view of the husband's role includes all the things that
we would often call "women's work," and he is quite explicit about this here and elsewhere.
He literally called those who denigrate washing diapers as effeminate, unfit for men,
"fools."

29. Q. 124, 81.

30. Gouge, *Of Domesticall Duties*, 429.

children" (Ps 128:3, 6). A husband and wife may live in a plain house on a tight budget in an ordinary town. However, if they love the Lord first and their spouse just behind, God has enriched them beyond reckoning. If he has also blessed them with children who honor and love them, no riches can possibly exceed what he has already given them.

CHAPTER 14

MARITAL SATISFACTION
AND HAPPINESS

Be sure that God be the ultimate end of your marriage, and that
you principally choose that state of life, that in it you may be most
serviceable to him; and that you may heartily devote yourselves and
your families unto God; that so it may be to you a sanctified condition. It
is nothing but making God our guide and end that can sanctify our state
of life. They that unfeignedly follow God's counsel, and aim at his glory,
and do it to please him, will find God owning and blessing their relation.

Richard Baxter[1]

In all nations the day of marriage was reputed the joyfullest day in all
their life, and is reputed still of all; as though the sun of happiness began
that day to shine upon us, when a good wife is brought unto us. Therefore
one saith, that marriage doth signify merry-age, because a play-fellow
has come to make our age merry, as Isaac and Rebekah sported together.

Henry Smith[2]

GOOD MARRIAGES START WITH GOD

PUTTING GOD FIRST

W hen I was a young college professor in my first faculty position, my college assigned me a course, required of all students, that critically overviewed major theories, concepts, and methods in the social sciences from the standpoint of basic orthodox Christianity. This meant starting with the building blocks of a biblical approach to understanding human society and culture, by which to evaluate other views. My first

---

1. Baxter, *A Christian Directory*, 404.
2. Smith, "A Preparative to Marriage," 11.

outline had me beginning the course with a detailed examination of what the Bible teaches about the basic nature of human beings and their condition. My department chair sent me back to the drawing board. He pointed out to me something along these lines, "Don't start with man. Start with God." Of course! How could I hope to understand the creation except in relation to its Creator and his attributes? I revised my syllabus, beginning the course not with humankind, but with God.

I have tried to do that in this book, to look at who God is and what he has designed marriage to *be* and to *do*. My aim has been to proceed from that foundation as we seek to understand the paths to true success in marriage, whether they are good practices, goals, and outcomes, or bad ones. All Christians should seek to do the same in their marriages. Start with God. Given that you are unique individuals with specific callings, situated in a particular social and cultural niche, how can your marriage be a vehicle to serve, worship, glorify, and enjoy God as he is revealed to you by his Spirit and through the Scriptures? How can your marriage be a means by which you will love the Lord your God with all your heart, soul, and mind, and your neighbor as much as you love yourselves (Matt 22:37–40), help your spouse to do this too, and raise your children to serve him likewise?

As someone who loves archery, I have learned that I tend to miss the target more often when I am most worried about hitting it. I am more likely to succeed when I simply focus instead on consistently carrying out the things I know I am supposed to do, in the right ways. Similarly, if we aim at achieving marital satisfaction and happiness as ends in themselves, we will often be disappointed. If our objective is to fulfill God's purposes for our union by his means, which includes pouring out our lives first to him and then through him for our spouse, our happiness will take care of itself. There will not always be joy in the short run. Life is hard, and there will be many dark times and trials on our journey through it. However, in the end those who seek the Lord in their marriage more than their own happiness will know that deep joy of Christian contentment that can only come from putting him first in all things.

C. S. Lewis's famous statement is pertinent here: "Aim at Heaven and you will get earth 'thrown in': aim at earth and you will get neither."[3] As

---

3. Lewis, *Mere Christianity*, 134. As Lewis noted here, this seems a "strange rule," but it works.

he noted elsewhere, when we think we want happiness, it is really God, to whom all true joy really points, that we are looking for.[4]

It is interesting that, immediately before giving the Colossians brief instructions about having godly marriages and homes, the apostle Paul reminded them, "whatever you do, in word or deed, do everything in the name of the Lord Jesus, giving thanks to God the Father through him" (3:17). Elsewhere he had said, "whatever you do, do all to the glory of God" (1 Cor 10:31). Those "whatever you do" phrases comprehend everything, including our marriages.

God has designed us to need God in order to serve God. As Saint Augustine famously prayed, "You have made us for yourself, and our heart is restless until it rests in you."[5] This should be obvious when we look at what kind of marriages we are aiming at, those that entail the depth of love and sacrifice that is a worthy representation of the relationship Christ has with his blood-purchased people. We want our marriages to be fruitful love calling forth life as does the Trinity. This is holy, wonderful, inspiring—but it is not within the ability of our natural selves to accomplish. Of course, we will need practical strategies and human help, counsel, admonition, and instruction at many points. This is a huge part of how God provides for our marriages. However, more than that, we also just need *him*. The center of every godly marriage is relationship with God. Praying, worshiping, pleading, trusting, abiding, meditating— seeking God continually in all the means by which he has given us to do so. As Paul David Tripp emphatically notes, in our marriages we can count on a God who is "faithful, powerful, and willing."[6] These words of Christ from the Gospel of John are as true for our marriages as they are for our individual walks, our churches, and everything else in God's kingdom:

> Abide in me, and I in you. As the branch cannot bear fruit by itself, unless it abides in the vine, neither can you, unless you abide in me. I am the vine; you are the branches. Whoever abides in me and I in him, he it is that bears much fruit, for apart from me you

---

4. Lewis, *Surprised by Joy*, 213.

5. *The Confessions of St. Augustine*, 43.

6. Tripp, *What Did You Expect?*, 25.

can do nothing. If anyone does not abide in me he is thrown away like a branch and withers; and the branches are gathered, thrown into the fire, and burned. If you abide in me, and my words abide in you, ask whatever you wish, and it will be done for you. By this my Father is glorified, that you bear much fruit and so prove to be my disciples. As the Father has loved me, so have I loved you. Abide in my love. If you keep my commandments, you will abide in my love, just as I have kept my Father's commandments and abide in his love. These things I have spoken to you, that my joy may be in you, and that your joy may be full. (John 15:4–11)

When I talk to sincere believers and ask them what they hope for their marriages, they talk about the kinds of blessings Jesus describes here. They want to be fruitful, to have God answer their prayers, to be secure in him, to know real love, and have lasting, abundant joy. There is nothing here about practical techniques, sufficient incomes, or nice houses in neighborhoods with great schools. Those who abide in him *will* bear fruit, experience his joy, and know his love to and from him as well as among each other. Moreover, as Jim Newheiser points out, to love as Christ loves, we must directly experience his love for us.[7] I like this expression by Francis and Lisa Chan, "Put simply: the Holy Spirit moves us from an impossible situation into a position where it is impossible to fail."[8] So long as husband and wife are truly alive in Christ, there is hope, but they point out, "A dead spouse cannot conjure up a living marriage."[9]

Some of the finest marriages I have seen are between saints living in awful circumstances but they abide in Christ day by day. When they fail to do so as they ought, by the power of the Holy Spirit they repent and then abide in him again. This is what that true word really means, said so often that it sometimes becomes a cliché and we miss its force—"keep Christ at the center of your marriage." When we do so, our marriages are organically part of that one perfect marriage our hearts yearn for even more than happiness here on earth. Regardless of what we are experiencing here in this troubled world, that remains secure.

---

7. Newheiser, *Marriage, Divorce, and Remarriage*, 79–80.
8. Chan and Chan, *You and Me Forever*, 51.
9. Ibid.

We also have strong research evidence that God-centered marriages are happier. In their "Survey of Marital Generosity" conducted in 2010–2011, researchers associated with the National Marriage Project asked married parents if they agreed that, "God is at the center of our marriage."[10] Where both partners did, they were 26 percent more likely to call their marriage "very happy" than if only one spouse, or neither, agreed with this statement.[11] They were also "at least 6 percentage points less likely to report that they are prone to separation or divorce."[12] From a social science perspective, much of this is because keeping God at the center is associated with other positive practices and beliefs.[13]

Of course, we know that the Lord himself also blesses those who confess and fear him (cf. 1 Sam 2:30). As Proverbs states, "In all your ways acknowledge him, and he will make straight your paths" (3:6).

THE MARRIAGE COVENANT IS FOR SINFUL PEOPLE

As we walk in relationship with Christ, we are acutely aware of our abiding sinfulness and our need for a Savior. We see that our spouse is a sinner as well, as are any children with which the Lord may choose to bless us. This knowledge will help us in many ways. As the Puritans often noted, our expectations will be more realistic when we remember that we marry not angels, but fallen human beings.[14] We will appreciate how much we need our partner as we seek to walk with Christ. The degree to which loving our spouse involves giving and receiving grace as we walk together will inform our perceptions and deepen our love. We ought to passionately covet fruits of the Spirit such as patience, kindness, faithfulness, gentleness, and self-control (Gal 5:22–23). Most believers recognize how valuable these gifts are in marital relationships. However, too often we forget why, as husbands and wives, we need them. It is because, as Paul David Tripp observes, we are sinners married to sinners living out our marriages in a fallen world.[15]

---

10. NMP, *State of Our Unions 2011*, 31.
11. Ibid., 31, 33.
12. Ibid., 31–33.
13. Ibid., 32.
14. Ryken, *Worldly Saints*, 51.
15. Tripp, *What Did You Expect?*, 21–25.

A Christ-centered marriage is, therefore, a gospel-centered marriage. Here is how Dave Harvey sets this out in his excellent book, *When Sinners Say "I Do"*:

> *By* the gospel we understand that, although saved, we remain sinners. *Through* the gospel we receive power to resist sin. Accurately understanding and applying the gospel *is* the Christian life. This also means that the gospel is an endless fountain of God's grace in your marriage. To become a good theologian and to be able to look forward to a lifelong, thriving marriage, you must have a clear understanding of the gospel. Without it, you *cannot* see God, yourself, or your marriage for what they truly are. The gospel is the fountain of a thriving marriage.[16]

This is related to something that the National Marriage Project called "marital generosity," which includes as one of its attributes being willing to forgive one's spouse for "mistakes and failings."[17] Generosity also includes showing respect, doing small acts of service, and showing regular affection.[18] Husbands and wives who both give and receive generosity are 36 percent more likely to say that they are "very happy in their marriage."[19] Believers who have a truly gospel-centered marriage, focused on that flawed partner whom they love, will be happier.

PRACTICAL BENEFITS OF CHRISTIAN DISCIPLINE
Church Involvement

In chapter 11, we saw how important regular involvement in local churches is to marital stability. Those who attend church services every week have dramatically lower risk of divorce. This is also associated with marital happiness and satisfaction. Being part of a strong church is vital to the health of Christian marriages.[20]

In the *GSS* for 2006–2016, married respondents who attended church weekly were a bit greater than 10 percent more likely than those who did

---

16. 25, emphasis in the original.
17. NMP, *State of Our Unions 2011*, 38.
18. Ibid.
19. Ibid., 38–39.
20. Cf. Newheiser, *Marriage, Divorce, and Remarriage*, 104.

not to indicate that their marriage was "very happy." This remained true for respondents in each self-identified social class except those who identified as "upper class," for each level of educational degree, and for both men and women. Church attendance made the biggest difference for respondents in the lower and middle classes, and for high school and two-year-degree graduates. Church attendance also made a much bigger difference for men than for women.

The National Marriage Project found that married women who attended church weekly were much more likely to indicate that they were very happy in their marriages. Controlling for the number of children that they had, for example, among those with four or more children, regular church attenders were 64 percent more likely to view their marriages as very happy compared to those who did not attend church weekly. For those with three children, regular church attenders were 24 percent more likely to say this. For married women with one or two children, regular church attenders were 25 percent more likely to call their marriages very happy, and childless women were 21 percent more likely to say this.[21]

There are numerous ways God blesses those who remain engaged in a local church, particularly as this goes beyond just regular attendance. Howard Markman and his colleagues identify a number of them.[22] In religious services and fellowship, couples' moral beliefs—including those about marital importance and commitment—are honed and strengthened.[23] Rituals establish connections between the spouses and others.[24] Numerous opportunities for service exist in every healthy local church. As these authors point out, "a whole body of research has emerged . . . showing that those who are happiest in life are those who take the time to give to others."[25] Active involvement in a local church builds all of these wonderful benefits into our lives, for married and single alike. Beyond all this, many churches provide regular opportunities for couples to develop their marriages.[26]

---

21. Calculated by author from data presented in NMP, *State of Our Unions 2011*, 55–56.
22. Markman et al., *Fighting for Your Marriage*, 301–2.
23. Ibid.
24. Ibid., 301.
25. Ibid.
26. Ibid., 302–3.

W. Bradford Wilcox also identifies all of these as positive effects of religious institutions upon marriage in his excellent book *Soft Patriarchs, New Men*.[27] He adds the important caveat that not all churches are equal when it comes to strengthening marriages. Our churches need to be vital; promote social connectedness among members; have strong, pro-family beliefs; and intentionally work on building strong marriages.[28] A Christian church that is uncertain about or unsupportive of biblical marriage is by definition not a sound church.

Spiritual Beliefs

In chapter 5, we saw how important shared religious beliefs are in choosing a spouse. This is certainly true for marital happiness. In their study of over fifty thousand couples, David Olson and his colleagues found that couples who shared and relied upon a similar set of spiritual beliefs, as measured by five survey items, were far more likely to be happy.[29] Happiness differences between those in agreement and those who disagreed on these items measuring the importance of shared spiritual beliefs in their relationship ranged from a low of 35 percent to a high of 53 percent.[30] Moreover, agreeing that spiritual beliefs were central in their relationship made a huge, positive difference on couples' scores in virtually every individual area known to be important to marital health and happiness: sex, money, communication and conflict resolution, closeness, even their leisure activities.[31] Marital satisfaction scores were a stunning two-and-a-half times higher for couples with high levels of spirituality agreement, compared to those with low levels of the latter.[32] Said the authors, "A shared spiritual relationship can provide a significant foundation for a growing marital relationship. In a real sense, God's unconditional love is a model for partnership. A couple's mutual faith helps them focus on the positive aspects of each other and encourage and respect one another. Their marriage is a sanctuary—a source of care, mutual protection, comfort, and refuge. *While feelings can*

---

27. Wilcox, *Soft Patriarchs, New Men*, 102–4.

28. Ibid.

29. Olson et al., *The Couple Checkup*, 151–53.

30. Calculated by author from data presented in ibid., 151.

31. Ibid., 150.

32. Ibid.

often vacillate, their faith provides the foundation for a commitment that sustains the relationship."[33]

Prayer

A "Marriage Oneness" survey of 3,850 couples found that praying together is a huge factor in marital happiness. Among couples who prayed together regularly, 68 percent were rated as highly connected, compared to only 21 percent of those who did not pray together much or at all.[34]

The normal Christian life involves prayer throughout the day, not just one dedicated time of prayer. This praying occurs in a number of situations both spontaneous and planned, including at meals, "lifting up" problems and people as needed, before meetings, at specifically religious gatherings, and so on. Praying should be almost as natural to believers as breathing, "praying without ceasing" (1Thess. 5:17).[35] The General Social Survey suggests that this type of praying is associated with happier marriages. Among married respondents between 2006 and 2016, 65 percent of those who said they prayed several times a day also claimed their marriages were "very happy," compared to 60 percent of those who prayed once a day only and about the same percentages for every other level of prayer. This takes us back to what Jesus said about abiding in him, which is a characteristic of praying Christians.

APPLYING INSIGHTS FROM PREMARITAL COUNSELING AND RESEARCH ON THE CAUSES OF DIVORCE

You may recall that good premarital preparation and education is rooted in understanding those things that tend to undermine marriage and lead to divorce. Many of them have to do with identifying habits and other practices that research has shown both help and hurt marriages, strengthening the former and correcting the latter. Since we have already addressed these thoroughly in chapter 9 and to a certain extent when we looked at causes for divorce in chapter 11, it will be sufficient to simply review those here and indicate how and why we can address those matters during the course of our marriages.

---

33. Ibid. (emphasis added).

34. Study conducted by PREPARE/ENRICH. Data presented in Feldhahn, *The Good News about Marriage*, 80–81.

35. Tripp, *What Did You Expect?*, 249.

BEING COMMITTED

A basic condition for marital success is to be radically committed to the union itself, in good times and bad. As Jim Newheiser says, "covenant love *endures*."[36] Tim and Kathy Keller liken the way we commit to our spouse to the manner in which we place Christ before idols: "Marriage won't work unless you put your marriage and your spouse first, and you don't turn good things, like parents, children, career, and hobbies, into pseudo-spouses."[37] Without commitment, couples will not make it through the hard times and do everything they can, in the Lord, to make their marriage the best it can be. It is the platform of marital happiness. Howard Markman and his colleagues point out that dedication to marriage involves "sacrifice, forgiveness, protecting priorities, and developing teamwork. . . . Commitment is knowing that you can count on each other to be there for one another and to support and help one another."[38] Husbands and wives enhance this by being solidly grounded in biblical teachings about marriage and divorce, involvement in a local church holding to sound doctrine in these areas, and being surrounded by family and friends who also have a high view of the marital covenant while avoiding those who are hostile or indifferent to marital commitment.[39] Where couples seek counseling, the counselor ought to be committed to helping the marriage succeed. Unfortunately, many marital counselors and attorneys believe that it is most ethical to be "value neutral" on divorce. Couples seeking help with their relationships should avoid such advisers.[40]

SEXUAL AND ROMANTIC FENCING OF THE MARRIAGE

Another absolute is avoiding anything that might lead to adultery—whether actual sex outside the marriage or any kind of romantic involvement with someone other than one's spouse. This means avoiding any thoughts and actions that could lead one to flirt with or otherwise place oneself in the way of temptation. There are the obvious, such as staying away from pornography or places and situations that actively encourage sexual lust and liaisons. At the time of this writing, current Vice President Mike Pence is being denigrated for

---

36. Newheiser, *Marriage, Divorce, and Remarriage*, 82 (emphasis added).
37. Keller and Keller, *The Meaning of Marriage*, 130.
38. Cf. Markman et al., *Fighting for Your Marriage*, 28.
39. NMP, *State of Our Unions 2011*, 29.
40. Waite et al., *Does Divorce Make People Happy?*, 29.

following what has been called the "Billy Graham rule." In general terms, this means avoiding spending time alone with members of the opposite sex and otherwise being careful of such relationships, while keeping all interactions entirely open before one's spouse. These are sound practices. Being involved in churches and friendships that foster transparency and accountability can also help husbands and wives avoid this heinous offense against God and their spouse. According to the GSS for 2006–2016, among those who have now reached their sixties, over three of ten ever-married men, and almost two of ten ever-married women, have committed sexual adultery at least once. This is a serious danger, and we do well to treat it with all the gravity, care, and attention it deserves. No one is immune but rather, as the apostle Paul said, "let anyone who thinks that he stands take heed lest he fall" (1 Cor 10:12).[41]

Today, social media is a major source of temptation to infidelity. We now even find a settled term for this: "Facebook infidelity."[42] Many married persons find themselves making strong emotional connections to those of the opposite sex on platforms such as Facebook that become romantic and eventually lead to sexual adultery. Encountering old lovers and rekindling relationships with them on Facebook appears to be increasingly common. These emotional ties can undermine marital satisfaction even if they do not become full-blown affairs, and even in unions that were previously solid and by all appearances happy.[43] Married men and women need to be exceedingly cautious on platforms such as Facebook, including being totally transparent with one another in their uses of it.

FINANCIAL HEALTH

I mentioned the importance of finances, which is a huge factor in marital success and failure.[44] Most couples will face financial pressures, but it is important they do as little as possible to inflict these on themselves unnecessarily through excessive debt, impulse buying, and idolatry of

---

41. See the excellent discussion of this in Newheiser, *Marriage, Divorce, and Remarriage*, 106–8.

42. Cf. Carter, "Facebook Infidelity." I am grateful for Pastor Nathan Devlin for urging me to include a warning about this powerful and growing threat to marriage.

43. Ibid.

44. *The Future of the American Family*, 73; McManus, *Marriage Savers*, 164; Olson et al., *The Couple Checkup*, 80; Markman et al., *Fighting for Your Marriage*, 409–410; Scott et al., "Reasons for Divorce and Recollections of Premarital Intervention," 134, 136, 141.

material goods and pleasure. Excessive consumer debt, especially when it climbs over about $10,000, has a significant negative impact upon wives, who appear to feel this burden more seriously than their husbands do.[45] For them, it is associated with lower marital happiness and a greater likelihood to contemplate divorce.[46]

Spouses should work together to establish godly financial priorities in their homes. A couple's budget and expenditures are a window into their hearts. Sound biblical and practical teaching on handling money, such as that provided by Dave Ramsey's excellent materials in *The Total Money Makeover* and his *Complete Guide to Money* tied to his nine-lesson "Financial Peace" series, has been an invaluable help to many thousands of Christian couples. *The Couple Checkup* by marriage expert David Olson and his colleagues has a fine overview of good and bad financial perspectives and practices as they relate to marital happiness and success.[47] There are of course other excellent materials targeted specifically to evangelicals, such as the works of Ron Blue, and an organization connected to the late Larry Burkett, Crown Financial Ministries. The key is to recognize the absolute importance of sound finances, not only for one's material welfare but also as a key element of marital peace, productivity, and happiness.

GOOD COMMUNICATION AND CONFLICT MANAGEMENT

Next, good communication and conflict management skills are essential, as I covered in detail in chapter 9.[48] They are the key to dealing with most other issues a couple will face, as well as just establishing and maintaining a warm, enjoyable, supportive, effective interpersonal relationship. Virtually every sound premarital or marital counseling program emphasizes these areas strongly, as we have seen.[49] No married couple will finish learning and growing in these areas. Ultimately, while there are many excellent techniques married couples can learn, so much rests upon being assertive, open, clear, and actively listening without defensiveness.[50]

---

45. NMP, *State of Our Unions 2011*, 22.

46. Ibid.

47. 79–104.

48. Besides reading the materials identified in the next footnote, and perhaps engaging in some directed training as provided in PREP and PREPARE/ENRICH programs we detailed in chapter 9, review this section in the latter for few more specifics of what good communication and approaches to conflict look like.

49. Cf. ibid., 33–77; Markman et al., *Fighting for Your Marriage*, 87–214.

Beyond that, in our marriages as in all our relationships we must meditate upon, and pray for, the fruit of the Holy Spirit: "love, joy, peace, patience, kindness, goodness, faithfulness, gentleness, self-control" (Gal 5:22–23). We ought to nurture godly love toward our spouses. That is, love that is "patient and kind . . . does not envy or boast . . . is not arrogant or rude . . . does not insist on its own way . . . is not irritable or resentful . . . does not rejoice at wrongdoing, but rejoices with the truth" and which "bears all things, believes all things, hopes all things, endures all things" (1 Cor 13:4–7). When angry moments come, as they inevitably will, we must not yield to sinful and destructive reactions such as withdrawal, brooding, seeking vengeance, losing control, physical or verbal abuse, and the like. Nor should we let the disagreement or hurt fester, but instead deal with the offending issue promptly.[51] As Paul taught, "Be angry and do not sin; do not let the sun go down on your anger, and give no opportunity to the devil" (Eph 4:26–27).

HONESTY

Spouses establish mutual trust by being consistently and mutually honest with each other.[52] At times, this may involve difficult confessions. This is something that requires hard things from both parties, the one opening up about his or her sins, the other making it possible for them to do so without condemning or blowing up at them.[53] Both will need to trust in God.[54] Paul told the Ephesians that because they are members of one body, they must tell each other the truth (Eph 4:25). How much more applicable is that to a man and woman joined as one flesh?[55]

SEXUAL RELATIONS

As discussed briefly in chapter 3, there is a powerful relationship between married couples having sex frequently and the happiness of their union. For example, in the General Social Survey, within every major age category, frequency of sex was positively associated with marital happiness.

---

50. Cf. Newheiser, *Marriage, Divorce, and Remarriage*, 110–18; Markman et al., *Fighting for Your Marriage*, 87–214; Olson et al., *The Couple Checkup*, 33–53.

51. Newheiser, *Marriage, Divorce, and Remarriage*, 105.

52. Ibid., 105.

53. Ibid., 106.

54. Ibid.

55. Ibid., 105.

For example, among those under forty, 68 percent of those who had sex at least every week said their marriages were "very happy," compared to 52 percent of those who had sex rarely. For those sixty and older, 72 percent of those who had sex at least weekly described their marriage as very happy, compared to 57 percent of those who had sex rarely. To be sure, for many reasons, couples have less lovemaking as they get older, as table 14.1 shows. This shapes couples' sexual expectations accordingly. Thus, among those sixty and older, those who had sex at least weekly were only 6 percent more likely than those who did so just one to three times a month to call their marriages very happy. Meanwhile, for those under forty, the difference was 17 percent. Still, shy of physical impediments, couples of any age who completely neglect sexual intimacy risk losing their marital happiness. Here we see again the wisdom of the apostle Paul's admonition that married people should not deprive one another sexually (1 Cor 7:5-6).

To be sure, we cannot say from data like this whether sexual frequency leads to greater marital happiness, or vice versa. For the purposes of personal action, I do not think that it makes that much difference. The fact is, the happier couples are, the more frequently they have sex, and given what the Scriptures teach as well, we do well to embrace the practice. Besides, research suggests that sex and relational quality both powerfully affect each other. For example, marital commitment is associated with sexual satisfaction.[56] In fact, as Waite and Gallagher note, "Sex is an integral part of the marital commitment," so much that "a sexless marriage is apt to be viewed as a 'lie' or as a 'pretense' or at best a divorce waiting to happen."[57]

Table 14.1: Frequency of Sex Within Last Year, Married Respondents Only (GSS 2000-2016)

Sexual Frequency	18–39	40–49	50–59	60–69	70–79	80–89
0–2 Times per Year	4%	8%	17%	30%	54%	68%
1–3 Times per Month	27%	36%	41.5%	44%	33%	27%
Weekly or More	69%	55.5%	41%	25.5%	13%	6%

56. Waite and Gallagher, *The Case for Marriage*, 94.
57. Ibid.

As David Olson and his colleagues point out, in sex "most obstacles stem from the quality of the relationship itself. In this way, a couple's sex life can reveal the heart of the relationship."[58] This works in two ways. Relationship problems can undermine the quality and frequency of sex. However, couples sometimes use frequent and "good" sex, consciously or not, to disguise, suppress, or avoid relational problems.[59] Either way, couples and those ministering to them should understand that sex is a kind of "barometer" of marital health.[60] Practically, improving sex can make for a happier and more satisfying marriage. Conversely, enhancing the overall quality of one's marital relationship, especially better communication, can improve sex.

Experts point out often that—more than frequency and other issues people commonly emphasize such as intensity, novelty, and technique—good communication about sexual issues contributes to a more satisfying sex life.[61] The main thing is that both partners feel the other person is open to them in this area, listens, and is responsive. Sexual issues and needs will change across the lifespan. For example, when partners are younger birth control is often a major topic to be resolved. There are pregnancy, childbirth, and adjustments afterward. With late middle age, the level of desire often diminishes, and women begin dealing with menopause. Physical injuries and conditions, medications, and many other matters will come into play. The fact is, there is no completely stable endpoint in a normal married couple's sex life, as life and circumstances create many changes, and they need to make adjustments often. This makes honest and open communication vital.

At least one partner in most marriages has one of five significant problems related to their sex lives and romantic intimacy, according to research by David Olson and his colleagues. About two-thirds say they are dissatisfied with the amount of affection they receive, that their partner's level of interest in sex differs from theirs, and that sex has become "less interesting and enjoyable."[62] Over half complain that their "sexual relationship is

---

58. Olson et al., *The Couple Checkup*, 107. See also Newheiser, *Marriage, Divorce, and Remarriage*, 147.

59. Olson et al., *The Couple Checkup*, 107.

60. Ibid.

61. Starbuck and Lundy, *Families in Context*, 330.

62. Olson et al., *The Couple Checkup*, 108.

not satisfying or fulfilling" and that they are dissatisfied with "the level of openness in discussing sexual topics."[63]

Note how amenable issues such as this are to correction, if partners would learn to communicate more about these things and be open to making adjustments to serve their partners.[64] Learning to appreciate and account for differences between men and women is also critical.[65] For example, men tend to be more visually aroused. On average, they are also more able to separate sexual desire from emotional and relational realities, while women tend to associate these three things.[66] I have seen and experienced how hard it is for husbands to understand how much their wives typically need to unite "emotional, relational, and sexual intimacy" in order to be fully responsive to their husband's advances.[67]

Couples can often improve their sex lives a great deal just by learning about and doing those actions that create intimacy—using touch, romantic talk, setting, compliments, small "tokens of affection," serving.[68] For the majority of couples who complain that the partners differ in their level of desire for sex, it is because the man wants to have sex more often.[69] Addressing this generally means some kind of mutual adjustment, with neither partner begrudging the other. Meanwhile, men need to understand that the fact they initiate sex more than their wives is normal. This just reflects typical sex differences, and does not necessarily indicate that their wife is unwilling or lacks affection for them.[70] Not allowing conflict or tension to linger is critical to being able to enjoy sex in marriage.[71] Next, the key to sexual wholeness in marriage is focusing on *giving*, rather than receiving, pleasure.[72] Finally, setting aside time and private space for special times of sexual union is important.[73] It is too easy for busy couples to let

---

63. Ibid., 108.

64. Markman et al., *Fighting for Your Marriage*, 281–85.

65. Olson et al., *The Couple Checkup*, 111–13.

66. Ibid., 113.

67. Ibid.

68. Ibid., 113–16; see also Markman et al., *Fighting for Your Marriage*, 271–74.

69. Olson et al., *The Couple Checkup*, 117.

70. Ibid.

71. Markman et al., *Fighting for Your Marriage*, 278.

72. Keller and Keller, *The Meaning of Marriage*, 233.

73. Markman et al., *Fighting for Your Marriage*, 275.

everything else come first rather than, as the old Puritan ministers so often advised, making sure that lovemaking is not neglected, but is a priority.[74]

Regardless, it is important for Christian husbands and wives not to be deceived or seduced by the confused, sex-crazed, and morally relativistic culture they live in. Being biblically grounded, protecting their interior lives from filth, and drawing on the insights and experiences of fellow believers will help a great deal in walking by a different, godly set of expectations and standards in marital sex.

Newly married people sometimes find that their sexual pleasure is short of expectations they had before they were married. This is quite common. It is important that they remember that sex is a skill and, as such, will get better with practice. Good communication, the desire to please one's partner, and simple time in the doing of it will bring better sex over time.[75]

Our God delights in husbands and wives coming together sexually, as they do so under the banner of mutual, covenant-honoring, sacrificial love. The Song of Songs presents a narrative of a man and woman anticipating the full delights of all their senses as they come together in the marital bed. Believers should make this as much an object of prayer and seeking wisdom as every other area of their marital relationship. Our God is not stingy.

OTHER WAYS TO ENHANCE MARRIAGES
BEING REALISTIC ABOUT THE EFFECT OF CHILDREN ON MARITAL RELATIONS

Most people want children. In most of the years since 1972 that the General Social Survey has been done, they have asked people how many children it is ideal for a family to have. Among those who answered the question, the percentage saying "none" has ranged between 1.2 percent and 3.6 percent. Among those who have ever married, that range is 0.5 percent to 1.8 percent. For those eighteen to twenty-nine years of age, combining 2006–2016, 75 percent thought the ideal was two or three, less than 1 percent wanted none, and only a little over 2 percent thought an only child was best. Even for those who had never had children, the picture was very much the same.

---

74. Ibid., 286–87. Many of the points from this paragraph are also addressed very well in Newheiser, *Marriage, Divorce, and Remarriage*, 152–53.

75. I am grateful to Pastor Nathan Devlin for pointing this out.

Meanwhile, despite the constant stereotyping of "carefree" singles versus "trapped" married mothers and fathers, in the *GSS* for this same time period, the latter were almost twice as likely to say that they were "very happy" than childless singles. This remained true even among those under thirty years of age. In addition, married couples with children are much more likely than those without to say that their life "has an important purpose."[76] National Marriage Project researchers also found that those who value children more—what they call "pro-natalism"—are much more likely to say that their marriages are very happy, and much less prone to divorce.[77]

Despite all this, for married couples having children is a major adjustment and stressor, more than most parents-to-be fully appreciate until they are in the middle of it. Disruption in sex lives and private time, hormonal changes and even post-partum depression for many mothers, sleepless nights followed by long days at work, financial demands, and more can be quite difficult. Though over the long run the quality of marriage for childless couples and those who have had children is the same, upon the birth of a child both marital satisfaction and happiness can dip quite a bit.[78] In 2006–2016, for married couples under forty, 75 percent of those without children said that their marriages were "very happy," compared to 64 percent of those with one child, and 59.5 percent of those with two to three. This is not because they have greater conflict, nor are they more prone to divorce during this time.[79] Meanwhile, the *overall* happiness of married respondents was not appreciably different whether they had no children or three. They just face more stress, demands, and disruption that directly reduce their *marital* bliss.

It is important for married people to expect these changes in their marriage when their first child arrives. Children can be hard to care for, at all the stages of their lives. At the same time, the marital situation will smooth out over time. In those same *GSS* years, among married respondents sixty and older, the percentages saying their marriages were "very

---

76. NMP, *State of Our Unions 2011,* 13, 16.

77. Ibid., 34–35.

78. Ibid., 12–13; Cowan and Cowan, "Interventions to Ease the Transition to Parenthood," 412.

79. NMP, *State of Our Unions 2011,* 13.

happy" were not appreciably different whether they had no, one, two, or three children.[80] Meanwhile, there are wonderful benefits, such as having a larger sense of purpose. As researchers at the National Marriage Project point out, "Yes, parents have to put up with the stresses of sleepless nights, toddler temper tantrums, and teenage sullenness, not to mention the time and money spent on their kids, but they also get to enjoy their infant's first smile, their two-year-old's bedtime caresses, their son's bar mitzvah, and their daughter's tournament-winning soccer goal. When suffering, sacrifice, toil, and treasure are expended on some great and valued purpose—including the bearing and rearing of children—difficult tasks can take on a positive meaning."[81] We could add that God calls us to have this mindset whether or not we marry or have children. Our goal as believers is to serve, honor, glorify, and live for him in whatever he calls us to, not pursue our own immediate comfort and subjective happiness.

In fact, having children is a powerful tool that God uses in the lives of married people to reveal hidden areas of selfishness and help them learn to place others before themselves. When a couple has children, care for their spouse and offspring calls them to higher levels of demanding service and sacrifice than marriage alone may require. As they grow through this, and serve one another by caring for their children, this will ultimately strengthen their marriages.[82]

DECISIONS ABOUT PAID WORK

One debate that too many people have politicized in recent years is whether married women, particularly mothers, should maintain employment outside the home even if it is not financially necessary that they do so. Researchers have long agreed, contrary to feminist or traditionalist claims, that it really boils down to the aspirations, desires, and callings of the women. When women are full-time homemakers, or employees outside the home, against their will, they will tend to be less happy.[83]

Couples will also need to consider what they believe is the best arrangement for their children. Regardless of what they personally want, these

---

80. 66 percent, 65.5 percent, and 62.5 percent, respectively.
81. NMP, *State of Our Unions 2011*, 13–15.
82. I am grateful to Pastor Nathan Devlin for suggesting this.
83. Starbuck and Lundy, *Families in Context*, 328.

decisions must place the needs of their families' most vulnerable members first.

Beyond this, they also need to look honestly at the degree to which masculine and feminine, the natures of men versus those of women, legitimately and profoundly differ. It is God, after all, who made humans male and female (Gen 1:27; 2:22–23). They should not expect to want or need the same things in relationship to domestic duties and paid employment outside the home, as they are complementary parts of a whole rather than two humans, united as one but essentially the same in their basic natures. Thus, it is not surprising that, in the GSS for 2000 through 2016, only 44 percent of married women between 25 and 35 years of age with children were working full-time, and only 37 percent of those with more than two children were doing so. Among those who identified as middle or upper class and had a spouse working full time, only 40 percent of married women in this age group with at least one child were working full time, and that percentage dropped to 25 percent if they had more than two children. The fact is, most couples with children, where the husband is able to provide for the family, opt for the wife to focus more on homemaking, especially when the children are young.

There are also many arrangements and types of jobs, and this is going to matter a good deal. Women working excessive work hours, holding traditionally male jobs, who do work requiring graduate education, or who make considerably higher incomes than their husbands all tend to be more prone, on average, to divorce.[84] This does not mean that a married couple should not be comfortable having these kinds of arrangements, but if they do, they ought to look for other ways to strengthen their marriage against these risks.

Table 14.2 shows the percentages of married respondents in the 2000–2016 GSS that identified their marriage, and their overall life, as "very happy," by employment status. Obviously, there are not significant differences between those who worked full-time and those who were full-time homemakers. Though there were over fourteen times more women than men who stayed home and kept house, the few men who did so were as happy as those who worked full-time. Being involuntarily unemployed

---

84. Ibid.

Table 14.2: Percentage "Very Happy" in Marriage and Overall, by Sex and Employment, Married Respondents Only (GSS 2000–2016)

Employment	Males "Very Happy" Marriage	Females "Very Happy" Marriage	Males "Very Happy" Overall	Females "Very Happy" Overall
Full-Time	65%	61%	41%	42%
Part-Time	58%	58%	39%	41%
Temporarily Not Working	63%	63%	30%	43%
Laid Off / Unemployed	51%	46%	29%	24%
Retired	64%	59%	43%	44%
School	72%	66%	48%	46%
Keeping House	66%	59%	39%	42%

was hard for both husbands and wives, though being temporarily unemployed was harder for men.

Regardless, from the standpoint of marital and general happiness for married people, table 14.2 certainly shows that many options can work. There is no one-size-fits-all. Chances are this is also going to shift for many couples across their lifespan. What couples do when their children are young, for example, may be quite different than will be the case when they are all in school full-time or the spouses go into the empty-nest period. Moreover, as flexible scheduling and working from home continue rapidly growing, the distinctions between full-time working parent and homemaker will continue to blur, as they already have.[85] Right now, at least 38 percent of those in managerial, business, and professional arenas already work from home for most or all of their employment.[86] Experts predict this will continue to spread.

---

85. Cf. Shin, "Work From Home in 2017."
86. Ibid.

SHARING WORK AROUND THE HOUSE

One reality that is beyond dispute is that both husbands and wives are happier in their marriages when they equally share the work around the house. This does not mean they have to do the same things in some kind of enforced gender egalitarianism. Nor does it mean some kind of traditional division into "men's and women's work." It means that each carries an equitable part of the load in keeping the house clean and functional. National Marriage Project researchers found that though wives benefited from this more than husbands, both were better off when they were equal contributors.[87] Wives who said that they and their husband did housework equally were 22 percent more likely to identify their marriage as "very happy" compared to women who did not enjoy such a marriage. Husbands who shared work equitably with their wives were 15 percent more likely to say their marriage was very happy.[88]

SUPPORTIVE SOCIAL NETWORKS

It is important to have friends and family behind one's marriage. National Marriage Project researchers note that, "husbands and wives with high levels of social support for their marriage are at least 23 percentage points more likely to report that they are very happy, or almost 50 percent more likely to be very happy in their marriages, when family and friends are invested in their marriages. Moreover, a high level of support from family and friends is one of the top five predictors of marital quality and stability for married mothers."[89]

It is critically important for young married couples especially, however, to gravitate to *positive* friends and family members. As we have mentioned earlier, those who have a more jaundiced view of marriage in general, or *this* marriage in particular, can actually do a lot of damage.[90] My wife and I have seen too many situations over the years where spouses had their marriages eaten by canker worms, in the form of "friends" who encouraged wives or husbands in being critical of their spouses, or who counseled divorce as a quick solution to trivial problems. All social contacts have the

---

87. NMP, *State of Our Unions 2011*, 23–24.
88. Ibid., 24.
89. Ibid., 28–29.
90. Ibid., 28, 30.

potential to do great good or terrible harm. As the apostle Paul counseled, "Do not be deceived: 'Bad company ruins good morals'" (1 Cor 15:33).

SPENDING TIME WITH ONE'S FAMILY

It is critical that husbands and wives have private time together. This becomes more of a challenge in those periods of life when children are coming along and job demands can be intense, but that just means there needs to be more intention, effort, and creativity put into having such time. Wilcox and Dew found that young couples who maintained their private time together when their first baby arrived were far less likely to experience a decline in the quality of their marriages than those who let that time diminish.[91] It is in such time together that couples engage in so many of the positive activities we have discussed in this chapter, such as communication, handling conflict, sexual intimacy, and so on. For example, finding time to spend alone together is vital to maintaining a quality marriage in the face of kid pressure.[92]

Moreover, once children are in the picture, it is important to spend time with them as well, as a family, and perhaps with the kids individually. Interestingly, National Marriage Project researchers showed that, for married parents, regularly spending time *both* together and with children significantly enhanced marital happiness and reduced the risk of divorce.[93] In fact, husbands who spent time with their children daily or almost daily were almost twice as likely to say that their marriages were very happy versus those who did not.

These researchers uncovered something that echoes God's order in a deep, wonderful way: "There does not seem to be a zero-sum relationship between time devoted to parenthood and marriage. Fathers and mothers who spend lots of time with their children in activities such as playing, talking, or working on projects together also enjoy significantly higher levels of marital happiness and lower divorce proneness (and also enjoy more couple time with one another)."[94] Jesus said, "Give, and it will be given to you. Good measure, pressed down, shaken together, running over,

---

91. Wilcox and Dew, *The Date Night Opportunity*, 10.

92. Ibid., 3.

93. NMP, *State of Our Unions 2011*, 44–47.

94. Ibid., 45–46.

will be put into your lap. For with the measure you use it will be measured back to you" (Luke 6:38). Remember too these words of Christ regarding children: "Whoever receives one such child in my name receives me" (Matt 18:5). We mentioned earlier the importance of husbands and wives engaging in regular, small acts of generosity toward one another. When they become parents, they should serve their children liberally as well. Taken together, loving both our children and our spouses in regular, usually small, ways, we have not only happy marriages, but also healthy families.

SOME ADVICE FOR THE UNEQUALLY YOKED

As we saw in chapter 5, ideally the husband and wife should share the same commitment to serving the Lord, submitting to biblical teaching, prayer and worship, and other elements of spiritual belief and practice. This is not always the case. Typically, such religiously mixed marriages exist because one partner converted and the other did not, one departed from the faith and the other remained, or a believer chose to marry a non-Christian despite what the Scriptures teach about that. Regardless, a marriage between a believer and an unbeliever is a covenant marriage before the Lord, and God's blessings and grace are in it (1 Cor 7:13–14).

Quite often, advice to believers in these situations focuses heavily on praying for and otherwise seeking, through example and action, the turning of the unbelieving spouse to Christ in true repentance and faith (1 Pet 3:1–2). This is obviously something that faithful Christian partners will do for their spouses, a sacrifice of love rooted in gospel revelation. Meanwhile, believers should seek to live according to their callings as children of God, including attending public worship, prayer and Bible reading, and all other means of growing in grace and understanding, in ways sensitive to and considerate of their spouses' needs and feelings. Believing spouses should also make raising their children in the Lord a major priority.

Both partners should pursue a happy, satisfying, fruitful marriage together as well, applying all the normal practical wisdom, including the advice in this chapter, in doing so. The believing partner should expect the church to help in this, as with any other marriage. Unbelieving spouses often welcome good marital support from the church.

Beyond this, however, for both the believing and unbelieving spouse there are going to be significant and unique marital and familial challenges in every area of life, because our beliefs in or about God influence every aspect of our existence. For example, a believing parent will want his or her children to express faith in Christ, but how will this influence the children's view of the other parent? How will a non-Christian react to his or her spouse directing some family finances to support the work of the church? Will he or she want to attend worship services with his or her family? If so, how will strong messages on sin and the need for salvation affect him or her?

As I relayed in chapter 5, I grew up with a Roman Catholic mother and an agnostic father but was raised Catholic, and thus experienced a religiously mixed marriage directly. I have also had opportunity to see some of the same dynamics and difficulties that our family experienced played out in the lives of unequally yoked evangelicals. I attended services with my siblings and mother every week while my father stayed at home or went golfing, seeing so many of the other kids in the pews with both of their parents. At times that was hard. Yet I also saw my parents' marriage last fifty-three years, my mother never denigrated my father's lack of faith or complained to us about it, and I benefited from the support of both of them.

For those in unequally yoked marriages, I strongly recommend the book *Surviving a Spiritual Mismatch in Marriage* by Lee and Leslie Strobel. It is rooted in the authors' experiences following Leslie's conversion to evangelical Christianity while Lee remained a non-believing journalist until he eventually came to faith in Christ as well. The book excellently communicates the experience, fears, and concerns of both partners and provides practical advice.[95] Here, I will share some of their most important advice for the believing partner. Beyond that, every such marriage has its own unique wrinkles, challenges, and opportunities. Nothing here can replace the ongoing support and counsel of faithful Christian pastors and friends, and further reading of quality Christian works addressing this matter, for those in this situation.

---

95. The Strobels also provide a good resource list on page 269 for believers married to unbelievers. In addition to the list, consider these resources: Deborah L. McCarragher, *Mission Possible: Spiritual Covering* (Fleming Island, FL: Alabaster Box Publishing, 2007); Jeri Odell, *Spiritually Single: Living With an Unbelieving Husband* (Kansas City: Beacon Hill Press, 2002); Nancy Kennedy, *When He Doesn't Believe: Help and Encouragement for Women Who Feel Alone in Their Faith* (Colorado Springs: WaterBrook Press, 2001); Lynn Donovan and Dineer Miller, *Winning Him Without Words: 10 Keys to Thriving in Your Spiritually Mismatched Marriage* (Grand Rapids: Baker, 2010).

First, it is important that, regardless of one's faith and spiritual fellowship, while keeping God first in everything, that, for believers, their husbands or wives should be the most important human person in their life.[96] As Lee says about Leslie, "Over time, I developed the unmistakable feeling that I was still the Number One person in her life—just as she was in mine."[97] This means that, assuming that the unbelieving partner is and remains a loving husband or wife, appreciating, respecting, needing, and relying upon them.[98] All the acts of simple service and kindness that one should expect from any good spouse to the other ought to be there in abundance.[99] Believing spouses should never compare their mate unfavorably to Christian husbands or wives.[100] Moreover, religiously mixed marriage or not, there is still plenty of common ground spouses share.[101] Perhaps most importantly, in all of this giving and receiving love, the point is not to do these things to win the other to Christ, as if they are a "project," but simply because they are life partners whom believing spouses love and appreciate for themselves.[102]

Next, it is important for the believer to display true empathy, looking at their faith, and perhaps their children's, from the point of view of their spouse, and really listening to them.[103] How do they feel knowing that their spouse does not believe that they have assurance of eternal life? What do they think when commitment to Sunday services prevents their husband or wife from joining them in some treasured excursion? Are they afraid that their partner respects their pastor's advice more than their own? To minister to such concerns, we must first comprehend and empathize with them. Most of us who are believers experience some of this in our relationship with those who do not share our faith but are close to us. Reading the Strobel book, I was aware that I have encountered similar reactions to my beliefs from unbelieving siblings and friends, for example, and even from my father.

---

96. *Surviving a Spiritual Mismatch*, 68.

97. Ibid.

98. Ibid., 68–69, 71.

99. Ibid., 70.

100. Ibid., 72–73.

101. Ibid., 71–72.

102. Ibid., 73.

103. Ibid., 42–55, 90.

Third, it will often be necessary, as the Strobels put it, for the believer to keep some of their prayer, Bible study, fellowship, and so on "under the radar."[104] That is, not pushing it, wittingly or unwittingly, into the faces of their partners, unnecessarily creating conflict.[105] This does not mean being dishonest, but rather sensitive and loving even as one seeks to follow God and grow in grace. For example, Leslie Strobel made small adjustments in when she scheduled prayer and Bible study, and turned down various church activities that might have alienated her husband or otherwise gotten in the way of their marriage.[106]

Next, believing spouses need to have at least one close friend, also Christians, who will provide them with support, guidance, understanding, and a listening ear.[107] In the absence of a believing spouse, this is critical. These friends should be faithful prayer partners, able to maintain confidences. The Strobels suggest that in such situations, it is important that those supportive friends be able to instruct and guide in the Christian life, be a good role model who is also transparent and genuine, that they be kind and committed, and that they are able to provide honest counsel firmly but in love.[108]

Children bring special challenges. It is an important calling on every Christian parent to instruct their children in the faith and impart to them biblical morals. In unequally yoked situations, parents may agree that this is best for the children, or they may not. They may agree on particular moral rules, for example about premarital sex or dating, or they may not. There are no easy answers here. Often, as was true in my home, the unbelieving parent is comfortable with their children getting religious training and being grounded in moral values they hold in common with their spouse, such as honesty, integrity, and self-control.[109] When we lived in the Bronx, many unbelievers were happy to have their kids attend our Sunday school or Vacation Bible School. Normal opportunities for instruction abound in the home, including

---

104. Ibid., 66.
105. Ibid., 67.
106. Ibid., 66–67.
107. Ibid., 73–74.
108. Ibid., 73–78.
109. Ibid., 109–110.

movies, bedtime stories, and the like, that do not disrupt the rhythm of the household.[110]

Meanwhile, it is important to allow children to ask honest questions and raise legitimate doubts, including about the differences in the religious beliefs and practices of Mommy and Daddy.[111] Finally, by consistently demonstrating love and respect for the unbelieving spouse, and upholding them in ways big and small, the believer in such situations ought to avoid turning their children against the other parent.[112] This can be as simple as a loving goodbye and then hello when going to and coming from church.[113]

None of this guarantees a good outcome. Unbelieving spouses may have varying levels of hostility to the Christian faith or particular elements about it. As a child, I sometimes found it hard to pray when my father, whom I looked up to, openly maintained that the benefits of it, if any, were purely psychological. The Strobels point out that there will be moments where handling disagreements on faith issues involving children will require a great deal of tact and patience.[114] Sometimes, the going can get quite tough. They note, "There are non-Christian spouses whose hostility toward Christianity is so extreme that they don't want their children to have any Christian influence. In those rare cases, the Christian partner must rely on prayer for her children and implement these ideas only so far as she can without causing ongoing arguments in the home."[115]

PARTING THOUGHTS

The covenant of marriage is wonderful. Trusting completely in the Lord and being devoted single-mindedly to him has to be the bedrock of every element of our lives, including our marriages. Even if both partners passionately love the Lord and seek to apply, prayerfully and by God's grace, every element of earthly wisdom to their union and their lives, they will still fall short more often than they would like.

---

110. Ibid., 111–12.
111. Ibid., 112–13.
112. Ibid., 115–16.
113. Ibid., 115.
114. Ibid., 115–16.
115. Ibid., 116.

A daunting challenge I have experienced when writing about Christian marriage, and caring about it as much as I do, has been to marvel at its essential goodness, order, and beauty; identify and applaud its accomplishments and benefits; and help people to live out and uphold all the covenantal obligations of matrimony, but without transforming it into an idol. Marriage does not save; Jesus Christ does. Being an amazing wife or a steadfast and loving husband is great and honorable, but it does not grant us eternal life. Only the blood and imputed righteousness of Christ, received as a helpless sinner, can do that. The bride in her dazzling raiment surrounded by family and friends should thrill the heart of her groom, and he should delight in becoming one with her. However, this is nothing compared to the radiant Son of God sitting on his throne surrounded by hosts upon hosts of angels and saints redeemed by his sacrifice.

Most of us will be or already are married. Many are not and some will never participate in that estate. The latter will include some who want to be married but it just never comes together for them. Some will remain celibate due to same-sex attraction or some other infirmity, while others will do so because that is their calling. Some will have wonderful marriages that last many decades, while others will face tragedy or endure troubled unions. Saints who love the Lord, and who have fully devoted their lives to him, may experience any of these outcomes.

It is the delightful responsibility of every believer who is called by God to enter into the marital covenant to pray, work, and study to enjoy a godly, happy marriage in and through every season of life. Every church should make it a high priority to promote such marriages among and in their churches. This is a blessing to the married and single alike. However, the ultimate good is to rely on, glorify, enjoy, and serve our creator God. Without that it is all sinking sand but with that, we will be able to endure and even be fruitful in whatever life brings (Matt 7:24–27).

CHAPTER 15

RECOMMENDATIONS
FOR THE CHURCH

*In creating man and woman, God instituted the human family and
endowed it with its fundamental constitution. . . . 'The Christian
family constitutes a specific revelation and realization of ecclesial
communion, and for this reason it can and should be called a domestic
church.' It is a community of faith, hope, and charity; it assumes
singular importance in the Church, as is evident in the New Testament.*

Catechism of the Catholic Church[1]

*Besides, a family is a little Church, and a little commonwealth, or at
least a lively representation thereof, whereby trial may be made of
such as are fit for any place of authority, or of subjection in Church or
commonwealth. Or rather it is as a school wherein the first principles
and grounds of government and subjection are learned: whereby men
are fitted to greater matters in Church or commonwealth. Whereupon
the Apostle declareth, that a Bishop that cannot rule his own house, is
not fit to govern the Church. So we may say of inferiors that cannot be
subject in a family; they will hardly be brought to yield such subjection
as they ought in Church or commonwealth.*

William Gouge[2]

A s the above quotes illustrate, conservative Protestants and Catholics
agree that marriage is the proper foundation for families and that

---

1. 532. The section in quotes is taken from Pope John Paul II's apostolic exhortation
"Familiaris Consortio."

2. Gouge, *Of Domesticall Duties*, 18. Spelling updated for clarity.

the latter are domestic churches. We could say that Christian families are therefore, at least in significant respects, churches in miniature within the larger church, carrying out many of the same functions, including teaching the truths and disciplines of their faith to their members. It starts with marriage. As the *Westminster Confession of Faith* notes, godly marriages also normally provide the church "with an holy seed."[3] Healthy families require sound marriages, and both contribute to, and strongly benefit from, churches that are doctrinally solid, vigorous, and effectual.

Thus the church, in promoting godly marriages and through them the families they generate and sustain, benefits itself enormously as it seeks to carry out its mission. William Gouge said that a believing family rooted in covenant marriage is a "seminary" and a "beehive" of the church, propagating and training Christians.[4] He also pointed out that, "A bad husband, wife, parent . . . is no good Christian."[5] Believers who are not faithful spouses will not be solid church members able to serve well. The apostle Paul highlights that in his stipulations for appointing elders (1 Tim 3:2, 4; Titus 1:6).[6] Pope John Paul II, noting some of these very things, but also the widespread confusion and difficulty of Christian marriage and family in the modern world, called on the church to recognize the fundamental importance of both marriage and family, and that a church at its best teaches, serves, supports, and encourages godly marriage and family life.[7] Focusing on marriage specifically—marriage and the church need each other to stay healthy and strong, and even more so as our culture increasingly rebels against God-ordained marital design.

Yet, as Michael McManus has sadly observed, there is a great deal of evidence that, when it comes to strengthening and upholding marriage, much of the church has been "missing in action."[8] Certainly, we have seen depressing statistics in various parts of the present book that help us to understand why he would say that. Many of us have seen that the willingness of church leaders to address biblical doctrine and practical

---

3. 80.
4. Gouge, *Of Domesticall Duties*, 18.
5. Ibid., 17.
6. More on this below.
7. "Familiaris Consortio."
8. McManus, *Marriage Savers*, 49.

consequences of various sins such as premarital sex, cohabitation, unbiblical divorce, and even abuse declines in proportion to how many "people
whose feathers might get ruffled sit in the pews."[9] This is particularly scandalous since the Bible addresses these types of matters clearly and repeatedly. Beyond what pastors tackle in preaching and teaching, we also see that
too many churches do not do the basic things that help people form and
maintain strong marriages, while neglecting many practices that would
help every member, married or not.

In this chapter, I will apply much that has been considered throughout
this book to finding ways that churches can help members who are married
or seeking it form and sustain strong, happy, godly marriages. This will
include developing healthy pro-marriage cultures within the church, and
taking a biblical, prophetic, and courageous stance, rooted in love, toward
our mostly unbelieving and openly pagan modern society.

NORMAL CHRISTIANITY

Most of the weaknesses of modern marital understanding, formation, and
practice in the church today simply reflect that so much Christian living
and church life is sub-normal. If we take our cues not from the culture
around us, but from the Bible, in defining "normal," that becomes clear.
Normal Christianity means being part of a biblical church that teaches and
preaches solid truth week in and week out. It means being accountable to
the leaders of that church, while in turn holding the latter responsible for
being the kind of people with whom we can entrust our souls. It means
that those leaders deal with problem areas with compassion, tact, patience,
kindness, humility, love, and so on, but also with honesty and courage,
rooted in Scripture, as dealing with people precious to God, bought by the
blood of his Son, whose spiritual welfare has eternal significance.

The leaders of healthy churches know that they are responsible to teach
the whole counsel of God, not just the convenient or popular parts. After
all, the souls of those whom the Lord has entrusted them are on the line,
and the enemy is deceptive, attractive, and unrelenting. In the modern
West, nowhere is this truer than in doctrine and practice related to marriage, divorce, fornication, homosexuality, male and female identity,

---

9. Ibid., 50.

cohabitation, dating, and the like. In fact, destructive lies in these areas have become a major spear tip that the evil one is using, aggressively and skillfully, to confuse, undermine, and ultimately destroy the church and Christians. The culture today is also, in the main, on the side of darkness more than light with regard to these things, and increasingly militant in its pressure and advocacy. If God's gospel ministers have a fear of man rather than of God, trusting their safety and security more to pleasing people than in honoring God (Prov 29:25; Isa 8:11–13; Luke 12:4–5; Heb 13:6) and refusing to preach his truth in these hotly contested areas, their congregants will end up weak and ignorant, easy prey for false teaching.

Every person given a role as an overseer over any portion of Christ's flock ought to be in full agreement with what the apostle Paul lovingly relayed in his farewell to the Ephesian elders, and they should strive to live up to the high demands he makes upon those who would shepherd his flock. Every believer ought to desire such leaders, knowing of course that we live in a fallen world in which every church and minister is far from perfect. We should seek out and submit to such leaders even knowing that at times they will tell us what in our flesh we do not want to hear, and will ask us to do things that in our sin nature we will not wish to do.

> But I do not account my life of any value nor as precious to myself, if only I may finish my course and the ministry that I received from the Lord Jesus, to testify to the gospel of the grace of God. And now, behold, I know that none of you among whom I have gone about proclaiming the kingdom will see my face again. Therefore I testify to you this day that I am innocent of the blood of all, for *I did not shrink from declaring to you the whole counsel of God.* Pay careful attention to yourselves and to all the flock, in which the Holy Spirit has made you overseers, to care for the church of God, which he obtained with his own blood. I know that after my departure fierce wolves will come in among you, not sparing the flock; and from among your own selves will arise men speaking twisted things, to draw away the disciples after them. Therefore be alert, remembering that for three years I did not cease night or day to admonish every one with tears. And now I commend you to God and to the word of his grace, which is able to build you up and to give you the inheritance among all those

who are sanctified. I coveted no one's silver or gold or apparel. You yourselves know that these hands ministered to my necessities and to those who were with me. In all things I have shown you that by working hard in this way we must help the weak and remember the words of the Lord Jesus, how he himself said, "It is more blessed to give than to receive." (Acts 20:24-35, emphasis added)

Normal Christianity also means that we will be mutually supportive of, and accountable to, our brothers and sisters in Christ. This will require, quite often, stepping outside our comfort zones in service and in telling the truth. Paul encouraged the Galatians to "bear one another's burdens, and so fulfill the law of Christ" (Gal 6:2). He told the Ephesians that they should be "speaking the truth in love" (4:15). He emphasized this further: "Therefore, having put away falsehood, let each one of you speak the truth with his neighbor, for we are members one of another" (Eph 4:25). The whole, glorious content of this fourth chapter of Ephesians helps us to see what godly ends this loving truthfulness serves. It helps to protect us from, and correct, doctrinal error (v. 14). Contrary to the constant modern refrain that truth is divisive, it actually fosters Christian unity and peace (vv. 1-6), though in the long run it will separate those who love the truth from those bent on pursuing delusions and lies. If telling the truth harmed the unity of true believers, Paul would not have encouraged it in the context of fostering a church yoked together in the common pursuit of God marked by tenderness and love. Next, honesty is necessary for us to grow, individually and corporately, into Christian maturity, undergoing sanctification and becoming more like our Lord (vv. 13-16). Finally, truthful confrontation is part of God's solution for sin (vv. 25-32).

When our churches and spiritual leaders strive, in the grace of God and by the power of the Holy Spirit, to embrace normal Christianity as the word of God describes it, we will have healthy Christians. They will not have already obtained perfection, but they will strive toward their highest calling in Christ (Phil 3:12-14), be constantly growing and maturing, increasingly exhibiting the fruits of the Spirit and their particular gifts within the church as a whole (Rom 12:4-8; 1 Cor 12:4-31). Such people will ultimately be prepared to be godly husbands and wives, fathers and mothers. Many will even become worthy counselors and mentors to those pursuing marriage, or to betrothed or married couples.

HIGH STANDARDS FOR SPIRITUAL LEADERS

Whatever differences of interpretation exist among those who take the authority of the Bible seriously, serious students of the Scriptures can agree that the apostle Paul's list of qualifications for church elders and deacons (1 Tim 3:2–13; Titus 1:5–9) requires that they be model husbands and fathers, should they be married and have children. These qualities directly correspond to their ability to oversee the church (1 Tim 3:5). That is not surprising for many reasons, including that they ought to be providing effective instruction and oversight to those in their congregations leading the "domestic churches" within which a lot of instruction, training, and discipleship is also occurring. Given how much practical Christian teaching and training actually occurs with the family, including those directly related to marriage,[10] churches do well to have leaders able to model and credibly instruct those overseeing families in their midst.

However, sadly, many churches are not scrupulous in appointing their spiritual leaders, including their ordained pulpit ministers. This includes many in ordained ministry or overseeing Christian organizations whose marriages and families are a mess, and even who have been involved in heinous sins against their marital covenant and spouses. I have seen men in Christian leadership who left their wives for other men's wives, married their lovers, and continued in their ministries with barely any interruption. That is hardly taking adultery and unbiblical divorce seriously and gravely undermines those churches' witness to the world and their members. I have seen men continue in ordained ministry despite complete alienation from their spouses, or perpetrating continuing, serious domestic abuse. How do these kinds of realities, which many Christians witness over their years of living in the church, help the people of God learn to take their own marital covenants seriously?

Startlingly, the man and woman who hold the Guinness World Record for largest numbers of recorded divorces are the late Glynn Wolfe, a Baptist minister divorced and remarried twenty-nine times, and his last wife, Linda, who had done so twenty-three times.[11] A study of about 4,500 Protestant clergy conducted in 1993 and 1994 found that their percentages

---

10. Cf. McManus, *Marriage Savers*, 55–58 on the vital roles the "little churches" of Christian families play.

11. "Glynn 'Scotty' Wolfe; World's Most Married Man."

of divorce were the same as the national average.[12] Some denominations were far worse, and others—such as the Southern Baptists, who have resisted putting divorced persons in ordained ministry—had very low percentages divorced. Still, the overall picture is depressing.

This is not the place to get into thorny questions about restoration for spiritual leaders who gravely violate their marital covenants, have seriously troubled marriages, who have obtained unbiblical divorces, been guilty parties in divorce action, and so on. On the one hand, all of us sin and we each rely, ultimately, on the mercy of God, not our own righteousness. It is also true that the "husband of one wife" qualification for elder (1 Tim 3:2; Titus 1:6) does not clearly rule out divorced men as church leaders.[13] On the other hand, as we saw in King David's life following the awful crimes he committed in his affair with Bathsheba, forgiveness does not include the right to be free from consequences.[14] Moreover, someone who is truly repentant is grateful for freedom and restoration of access to communion with God and the means of grace, and will not demand an imagined "right" to keep his pulpit or other Christian leadership role. The key is that Christians take these matters very seriously, and that those leaders who fall into serious sin at least submit to rigorous rehabilitative ministry and correction prior to any return to official ministry work. Though circumstances vary and wisdom is needed, leaders with ongoing serious marital problems should often be asked to step down at least until those issues are resolved and well behind them. Churches should not ignore or pass over such matters lightly, as is so often the case. This is as much for their welfare as for the health and witness of the church. Holding our leaders to high standards in their marital conduct would do much to strengthen the church internally and recover its public witness.

REGULAR CHURCH ATTENDANCE AND SERVICE

Throughout this book we have repeatedly seen the importance of regular church participation in every area of married life, premarital sexuality, marital preparation, and so on. This literally leaps out of the statistics.

---

12. Associated Press, "Study Shows Average Divorce Rate among Clergy."

13. See the solid, brief discussion in Cherlin, *Marriage, Divorce, Remarriage*, 292–94.

14. The careful student of the Bible, starting with 1 Samuel 11, will find the downstream consequences of David's actions were staggering, despite the mercy God extended to him.

Most church leaders would also say, officially or otherwise, that encouraging members' regular attendance and service in church is a key part of their responsibilities. It also makes sense that no amount of good teaching and ministry helps people who are rarely there to receive it, members or not. Yet in over four decades of being a committed believer, I have been involved in a couple of churches in which leaders rarely if ever confronted members who frequently absented themselves from church services. The fruit of this, contrasted with those congregations where leaders always spoke in a pastoral manner to members who became lax in their commitments, was obvious.

In the GSS for 2006 through 2016, among those who identify as conservative Protestant believers, only 47 percent stated that they attend church at least about weekly, while over one-third stated that they did so never or rarely. Those who further said that they believe the Bible is the inerrant word of God, did better, but still less than 60 percent attended church about weekly or more, while one-quarter rarely or never did so. Meanwhile, studies repeatedly show that Americans overestimate church attendance on surveys, such that the true percentages attending church may be literally half of what polls such as the GSS capture.[15] Percentages are better for conservative Protestants, but not by much.[16] For example, two prominent researchers estimated that only about 25 percent of Southern Baptists are in church on any given Sunday.[17]

Spiritual leaders must demonstrate faithful church participation, and churches should not appoint anyone to offices such as vestry-person, elder, or deacon who is not a model of regular commitment. Moreover, church leaders need to follow up with members who neglect weekly church services. This is critically important for their souls (Heb 10:24–25). Using whatever biblical means are at their disposal, in love, they ought to admonish such persons to repentance and recommitment, in their church or in some other biblical congregation. For true believers, regular attendance in a faithful church is not optional.

---

15. Hadaway and Marler, "How Many Americans Attend Worship Each Week? An Alternative Approach to Measurement," 307; Cox et al., *I Know What You Did Last Sunday*.

16. "How Many Americans Attend Church Each Week?" 314.

17. Ibid.

MINISTERING TO HEADS OF FAMILIES

Those leading domestic churches within our congregations need to be equipped for their important work of caring for their marriages and families. They will then be better able, for example, to lead their own children after them in vital areas such as sexual purity, courtship, and mate selection, as well as in developing the characteristics of godly future husbands and wives. Too few churches provide meaningful oversight or accountability for household heads, who are most typically husbands. Materials and other help with such important activities as leading family devotions, catechizing, talking to kids about sex and dating, and so forth can be extremely helpful. Most married men I know, and this includes myself, really struggle with establishing godly practices such as these in our homes. Protestant leaders in the past made equipping household heads a major priority, and churches today need to follow their example.

DIRECTLY FOCUSING ON MARRIAGE

LONG BEFORE THEY MARRY

Churches need to address sexual issues accurately and honestly, in age-appropriate ways, with their young people. This must start not with rules or practical warnings, but with a biblically sound theology of sex. That should in turn be rooted in a clear understanding of what marriage is and what its purposes are. From here, how and why God only regards sexual activity as legitimate or holy when it occurs within the framework of covenantal marriage between one man and one woman, and why he is both loving and wise to do so, is clear.

Teaching Holistic Biblical Chastity

As Dale Kuehne has observed, in matters of sexuality our culture has moved from an ethic of covenant to one of consent,[18] what he calls the *iWorld*. Confronted with essential questions such as whether any sex between consenting adults can be forbidden and whether we deny full completion and relational intimacy to millions by restricting sex to marriage between one man and one woman for life,[19] professing Christians are increasingly

---

18. Kuehne, *Sex and the iWorld*, 21.
19. Ibid., 20.

choosing consent and tolerance over a consistent biblical ethic. Premarital sex, cohabitation, serial divorce, and homosexuality are now entrenched, while incest and polyamory appear to be part of the rapidly approaching future of acceptance. The professing church has been flat-footed, clumsy, and even hypocritical in responding to this sexual "liberation" juggernaut. Given the rich teachings of Scripture on marriage, sexuality, and maleness and femaleness, buttressed by centuries of profound doctrine and reflection upon the same as well as a great cloud of historical witness of faithful lives lived in the past, this is inexcusable. We can help the people in our pews to see that, as Keuhne has put it, "orthodox Christian teaching about human sexuality and relationships can lead us to a life with more fulfillment than the iWorld offers."[20] We can do so much more, so much better.

Getting into "don't do this and don't do that," just cherry-picking Scripture texts to denounce different types of acts, is not sufficient. Our young people need to see that God's plan for chastity is inextricably part of his plan for the human race from creation, including the natural order, and we must never lose sight of that. They should see that sexual chastity is not something believers are to endure until they marry. Rather, as the Puritans so often said, it should be a *lifelong* blessing, including virginity before marriage and faithfulness after it.[21]

Based on this straightforward but rich understanding, questions about different types of sexual activity outside marriage, and any actions that might naturally lead to it, are plainly resolved. Nothing outside the legitimate marriage of a man and woman is permissible. Moreover, biblical chastity enables relational connectedness, meaning and purpose, human welfare and flourishing, that no modern alternative lifestyle can hope to achieve.

Only after this is established does it make sense to talk to young people, typically those who are a bit older, about the facts surrounding different types of sexual activities and the consequences thereof. Folks who expect to use condoms, other contraception, or sexual activities other than intercourse, such as anal or oral sex, to escape the negative results of violating God's moral order will be disappointed. Those teaching younger people, either directly or through instruction to their parents, need to address the

---

20. Ibid., 149.
21. Ryken, *Worldly Saints*, 46.

full spectrum of risks, remaining honest to the information we have and never going beyond or sensationalizing it. We who care about our young people and want to see them become fruitful citizens of God's kingdom need to teach them about the real risks of various forms of sex outside marriage. These include pregnancy, sexually transmitted diseases, relational violence including rape, emotional scarring from repeated lovers, abortion, and undermining their chances of forming happy future marriages.

Housed within the larger theological framework we have discussed above, such devastating results should be understandable, because this is what happens when human beings rebel against the boundaries of a loving God. Like the young woman who fell to her death at Niagara Falls because she insisted on climbing on the fence despite the warnings, there are reasons those rules exist.[22] They are not detached entities that exist for their own sake; "they are there because they are there." Their purpose is to help us live and love well.

In doing so, being a finger-wagger, censorious, or judgmental is counterproductive and ungodly. It is especially critical in such discussions to hold forth the gospel of repentance, faith, forgiveness, restoration, and healing continually. On the one hand, we do not want young believers to be presumptuous about sexual sin. The attitude of "I can always ask God to forgive me later" is a dangerous presumption. On the other hand, we do not want them to feel hopeless in the face of their failures and sins past, present, and future. They should be able to confess their sexual sins, and we ought to be able to forgive and minister to them with real compassion when they do so.

Churches determined to teach about sexuality and chastity have many fine materials to draw upon. I hope this includes using content from various sections of chapters 3, 7, and 8 in this book. The key is to start with the big theological picture—with God, creation, and covenant—and proceed to the details and consequences from there.

Teaching Sound Practices of Dating and Mate Selection

Church leaders should expose young believers and their parents to reliable wisdom from the Scriptures and human experience related to forming relationships with potential marital partners and making godly mate-selection

---

22. *Huffington Post Canada*, "Ayano Tokumasu Niagara Falls Death."

choices. The latter should include those general qualities that must be true of all suitable spouses such as we addressed in chapter 5, and those practical issues of particular suitability that we overviewed in chapter 6.

Again, this must be rooted in a sound understanding of God's definition of, and purposes for, marriage. Following our current culture in thinking about marriage in terms of individual self-fulfillment and romance will ultimately not lead to godly orientation to dating and courtship. Single believers must first comprehend that marriage is an institution with a particular structure meant to provide legitimate and fruitful sexual fulfillment, mutual help, and procreation and rearing of godly offspring. This makes a huge difference in how one approaches the calling to seek and secure a marriage partner. For example, substituting sound judgment and the experience of caring, older saints with romantic feelings and raw physical attraction makes no sense to someone who grasps a biblical understanding of marriage's nature and ends. Coupled with the need to protect and uphold each other's chastity, this will tend to promote wise and godly practices, including avoiding early and serial dating, pursuing unbelievers, and the like.

All this appears more relevant in light of the real dangers of divorce and unhappy marriage. Seeing wise premarital actions tied to good marriages and foolish ones associated with the opposite will help singles understand why we do not want them to stumble emotionally into marriage. Here too, getting across to singles the truth about cohabitation and directly challenging the false beliefs about it, are extremely important.

Excellent Premarital Counseling and Education

I have provided premarital counseling for two couples who were required, by the churches conducting their weddings, to show they had successfully completed such an approved Christian program. These churches displayed solid wisdom. In my opinion, no pastor should officiate at the wedding of any couple who has not done so. Unfortunately, it appears that most churches have no such requirement.[23] In many, premarital counseling is brief and not in any sense deep, or directed, based on evidence, to the key areas necessary for marital success. When my wife and I got married,

---

23. McManus, *Marriage Savers*, 128.

for example, we had a single one-hour session with the officiating pastor, talking about a few Bible verses and praying together.[24] One officiating pastor rejected my strong advice that a particular couple receive at least six weeks of counseling prior to marriage. Within a month of their marriage, this pastor was dealing with the fact that the new husband had a serious drug-addiction problem that he hid until after the wedding. Michael McManus sadly observes that, when it comes to marriage, "Clearly, most churches are little more than 'blessing machines.'"[25]

Premarital intervention is particularly important for those who are previously divorced, particularly if there are children involved and both partners are pursuing remarriage. Given the number of special issues involved, the best premarital counselors and systems tailor their content and approaches for those becoming remarried and forming blended families.

The same is generally true for cohabiting couples—premarital counseling for them means handling distinct sets of issues. Those who take the Bible and requirements of true repentance seriously must address the sin issue with the gravity it deserves, not treating it lightly (Jer 6:14). I agree with John Piper, whose position is that he will only officiate the wedding for a cohabiting couple if they repent, live apart, and refrain from sexual intimacy for a while before getting married.[26] That time apart should include premarital counseling, which also enables the couple to focus on preparing for lifelong marriage while growing in Christian knowledge and holiness. Beyond this, pastors will often encounter complicating factors, such as the couple having children, limited income that precludes maintaining two residences for a time, and so on. There is no one-size-fits-all solution. Church leaders tackling these kinds of conundrums will need sanctified wisdom. However, so long as the time period is not too long and both partners remain actively involved with them, children will benefit by seeing their parents take sin seriously. In addition, most churches have the resources to provide short-term help to a couple needing to live apart until they marry, so that in doing so they can prepare better for matrimony and honor God with their obedience to him.

---

24. The pastor who conducted Michael McManus's wedding did even less. See ibid., 129.
25. Ibid., 128.
26. "Will You Marry a Couple Already Living Together?"

Where possible, churches should have at least one member of the pastoral staff trained to do thorough, systemic premarital education and counseling. If not, churches may identify suitable counselors through local networks, and where necessary, meet them in order to carefully vet them.

Mentor Couples

One powerful but frequently overlooked practice is mentoring, where older couples with successful, well-established marriages spend significant time with younger engaged couples as advisers, counselors, models, and often eventually, trusted friends.[27] Michael McManus calls this one of the "greatest untapped resources to save marriages."[28] Mentoring can also occur in conjunction with using premarital inventories and counseling.[29] As McManus notes, "Mentoring is a deeply biblical concept"[30] (cf. 2 Tim 2:2; Titus 2:2-4). A good mentoring program requires pastoral oversight, selecting mentor couples wisely, and then equipping them through such means as reading basic books on premarital preparation, training by pastoral staff, or going through basic training in one of the premarital counseling systems. Mentors can round out what pastors can provide while also lifting some of the burden of helping engaged couples prepare for marriage.[31] I would advise any church launching a formal premarital mentoring program to contact and visit other churches that are doing this to glean practical insights. Churches that have them will typically feature them on their websites, and contacts through denominations and minister networks will often bear fruit.

STRENGTHENING EXISTING MARRIAGES

Mentor Couples (Again)

Properly selected and trained mentor couples can also be invaluable for helping those with troubled marriages.[32] Some can even focus on that especially high-risk group, those who are divorced and remarried and

---

27. Smalley, "Invest in Your Marriage with Mentors."

28. McManus, *Marriage Savers*, 319.

29. Ibid., 319–20.

30. Ibid., 320.

31. Ibid., 323.

32. Ibid., 320. For a good overview of what to look for in mentor couples, and to help interested couples see if they would be good mentors, see McDonald, "Are You Ready to Be a Mentor?"

particularly those who have formed stepfamilies.[33] One effective strategy, in addition to establishing mentor relationships, is to have such couples lead weekend retreats, such as those done after the models of "Marriage Encounter" and "Retrouvaille."[34] An excellent program to train mentor couples is provided through Focus on the Family, created and overseen by Drs. Les and Leslie Parrot.[35] Almost every church would find this effective and reasonably priced program to be useful and affordable.

Programs and Classes on Marriage

Churches can use Sunday school classes, small groups, and other means to provide biblically sound marriage instruction. Often this is as simple as selecting a quality book, particularly one designed for such use, and having discussion and lessons based on it led by someone qualified to do so. Special weekend retreats or seminars can supplement this. The Christian Counseling and Education Foundation (CCEF) provides a treasure trove of fine resources, in numerous media formats, dealing with many areas of marital relationships.[36] Another fine option is FamilyLife's *The Art of Marriage* curriculum, which draws on forty solid biblical teachers in sets designed for different length classes and formats.[37] Since 2011, over 700,000 couples have participated in classes based on this.[38] Tim and Kathy Keller's popular *The Meaning of Marriage* is a fine choice. A six-session study guide that instructors may use along with it is available with and without DVD.[39] The series is appropriate for singles as well, not just married folks. Dave Harvey's *When Sinners Say "I Do,"* a great choice as well, also has a study guide available. Francis and Lisa Chan's *You and Me Forever* and Paul David Tripp's *What Did You Expect?* are helpful as well. Obviously, many churches will find the present book useful. Of course, these suggestions only scratch

33. McManus, *Marriage Savers*, 320. Cf. Westover Church, "Step-Families," for an example of one such ministry.

34. McManus, *Marriage Savers*, 320. Different Marriage Encounter options, and contact information with overview, are provided in ibid., 333. Retrouvaille was started by Roman Catholics, but is available to couples from all denominations and uses mentor couples powerfully. Information about it can be obtained at https://retrouvaille.org.

35. Focus on the Family, "Marriage Mentoring."

36. At https://www.ccef.org/topic/marriage.

37. http://www.familylife.com/theartofmarriage/about.

38. Ibid.

39. *The Meaning of Marriage Study Guide*.

the surface of fine Christian materials available to help believers understand marriage as God has designed it to strengthen their own unions.

When Encountering Problems beyond Church Expertise

Every church will eventually encounter problems that are outside the ministry experience of its spiritual leaders. This does not mean that they will
be matters in which the Bible does not provide a foundation. However, with
little or no experience and the risk of negative effects of well-intentioned
but misguided ministry and counseling, it is generally best not to try to
tackle some situations without outside help. Abuse, serious drug or pornography addictions, homosexuality, gender identity confusion, sexual
dysfunctions that are harming a marriage, trauma from having abortions,
complex financial problems, incest—these kinds of things are going
to come to the attention of every pastor eventually. Unfortunately, most
churches will not have the expertise and experience needed to handle them
adequately. The spiritual leaders in these congregations can certainly oversee, guide, and even establish general frameworks and boundaries for care,
but will need outside assistance.

This is where it is critical that every church have access to such help
when necessary or at least know where to look for such assistance. This can
mean fellow pastors or elders who have experience and specialized training
in particular areas, such as solid Christian counseling services, supportive medical professionals, or social workers who are believers, and so on.
For example, in our region, Harvest USA supports churches and families
dealing with a range of problems associated with sexual brokenness and
gender identity.[40] There are professors specializing in counseling in conservative seminaries and Christian colleges. A fine, trained biblical counselor serves many churches in our area by providing intervention, under
the oversight of the local church leaders, in areas such as substance abuse
and domestic violence.

The early seventeenth-century English poet John Donne is famous for
the line "no man is an island."[41] This is certainly true for churches as well,
each local church being an expression of that great "holy catholic church"

---

40. See https://harvestusa.org.

41. From *Devotions upon Emergent Occasions*, Meditation XVII.

of the Apostles' Creed. Unfortunately, too many local churches try to minister to serious issues that are beyond their training experience without relying on all that God has provided for his people outside those walls. I have seen great harm done by such "do-it-yourself" ministry. Over time, most churches will want to have, maintain, and expand sound external support and referral networks to cope with such matters.

As our culture continues to degenerate in the areas of marriage and sexuality, it will get harder, not easier, for churches to minister to the brokenness they will encounter. How many pastors are ready to deal with repentant former lesbians leaving same-sex marriages with children, and negotiating shared custody with their former "spouses"? What about young men addicted to virtual-reality sex systems, or husbands having "affairs" with sexual robots such as those already being openly sold and continually refined? How many churches are prepared to minister to broken men repenting of gender reassignment surgery they had in vain attempts to try to become female, or to women trying to break free from polyamorous relationships? What about that young woman who went forward with marrying a wonderful guy who is compatible in every way except that he is same-sex attracted? I point these things out not to shock or be sensationalistic, but because these situations are here now, and increasing.

There is a lot of confusion and plenty of false teaching and destructive "ministry," and such are easier to find than competent, godly, biblical ministry. These are not times for churches to try to serve the marriages and married men and women in our midst without drawing on all God has provided them outside the walls of their own local congregations.

CONCLUSION

At the beginning of the human race, God made the first man, the first woman, and the first marriage. In that moment he embodied elements of his Trinitarian love and personhood, his sacred image, his plan for redemption and the relationship through which he would enter space-time history as the Incarnate Son of God parented by a carpenter and his young peasant bride, pointing to the culmination of human history in the marriage of the Lamb. The auto mechanic and his wife raising their children in some forgotten corner of Staten Island imperfectly, as with all marriages, represent and embody that. So does the Chinese couple operating a grocery store in

Nanjing and the petroleum company executive and her lawyer husband in Moscow. Like so many other wonders in God's created order, marriage is part of his natural order but is in so many ways beyond it, pointing us constantly to his rich, boundless, covenant love even as it provides a structure that meets many of our most basic needs. From the beginning of time, man has taken woman and God has made of them one flesh, and from that, he has brought forth precious fruit for the furtherance of humankind and the increase of his church.

We as the church of Christ must, by the grace of God, love, defend, and strengthen Christian marriage regardless of the cost. We must use the natural wisdom and means he gives us and also the supernatural weapons—prayer, the sacraments, the gathering of his people and the faithful preaching of his inerrant, perfect Scripture by honest, sincere, committed ministers of his gospel. This does not begin in grand conferences or in elaborate, well-funded political initiatives. It starts with caring for the people around us every Lord's Day, helping them to see, understand, embrace, and experience the beautiful order of God's holy covenant of matrimony.

For the glory of God, the welfare of his people, and the reinvigorating of our Christian witness in the face of an increasingly hostile, post- and even anti-Christian culture, the hour is late and the need is great to restore and strengthen Christian marriage. Let the church of Jesus Christ rededicate itself to this task, tying it first and preeminently to the Son of God, who embraces lost and helpless sinners and makes of them his own spotless, radiant bride.

BIBLIOGRAPHY

Adams, Jay E. *Marriage, Divorce, and Remarriage in the Bible: A Fresh Look at What Scripture Teaches*. Grand Rapids: Zondervan, 1980.

Adams, Thomas. *An Exposition upon the Second Epistle General of St. Peter*. Revised and corrected edition by James Sherman. 1633. Reprint, London: Henry G. Boyn, 1848.

Allen, Douglas W., Catharine Pakaluc, and Joseph Price. "Nontraditional Families and Childhood Progress through School: A Comment on Rosenfeld." *Demography* 50, no. 3 (2013): 955–61.

Amato, Paul R. "The Consequences of Divorce for Adults and Children." *The Journal of Marriage and Family* 62, no. 4 (2000): 1269–87.

———. "Research on Divorce: Continuing Trends and New Developments." *The Journal of Marriage and Family* 72, no. 3 (2010): 650–66.

Amato, Paul R., and Alan Booth. *A Generation at Risk: Growing Up in an Era of Family Upheaval*. Cambridge, MA: Harvard University Press, 1997.

Amato, Paul R., and Jacob Cheadle. "The Long Reach of Divorce: Divorce and Child Well-Being across Three Generations." *The Journal of Marriage and Family* 67, no. 1 (2005): 191–205.

Amato, Paul R., and Denise Previti. "People's Reasons for Divorcing: Gender, Social Class, the Life Course, and Adjustment." *Journal of Family Issues* 24, no. 5 (2003): 602–26.

Amato, Paul R., and Stacey J. Rodgers. "Do Attitudes toward Divorce Affect Marital Quality?" *The Journal of Family Issues* 20, no. 1 (1999): 69–86.

Amato, Paul R., and Juliana M. Sobolewski. "The Effects of Divorce and Marital Discord on Adult Children's Psychological Well-Being." *American Sociological Review* 66, no. 6 (2001): 900–921.

American College of Pediatricians. "Mental Health." *Facts about Youth* (website). http://factsaboutyouth.com/posts/mental-health.

———. "Physical Health." *Facts about Youth* (website). http://factsaboutyouth.com/posts/physical-health.

———. "Promiscuity." *Facts about Youth* (website). http://factsaboutyouth.com/posts/promiscuity.

American Culture and Faith Institute. "Where Born Agains Are Missing the Mark." https://www.culturefaith.com/where-born-agains-are-missing-the-mark/.

American Psychological Association. *Answers to Your Questions for a Better Understanding of Sexual Orientation and Homosexuality*. Washington, DC: The American Psychological Association, 2008.

———. "APA on Children Raised by Gay and Lesbian Parents." http://www.apa.org/news/press/response/gay-parents.aspx.

Anderson, Jane. "The Impact of Family Structure on the Health of Children: Effects of Divorce." *The Linacre Quarterly* 81, no. 4 (2014): 378–87.

Anderson, Lydia. "Divorce Rate in the United States: Geographic Variation, 2015." *Bowling Green State University National Center for Marriage and Family Research* (website), December 1, 2016. https://www.bgsu.edu/ncfmr/resources/data/family-profiles/anderson-divorce-rate-us-geo-2015-fp-16-21.html.

Arendell, Terry. *Mothers and Divorce: Legal, Economic, and Social Dilemmas.* Berkeley: University of California Press, 1986.

Aristotle. *Nicomachean Ethics: Books VIII and IX.* Translated by Michael Pakaluk. Oxford: Clarendon Press, 1998.

Associated Press. "Study Shows Average Divorce Rate Among Clergy: Couples: National Survey Refutes Belief That Pressures of Ministry Cause More Marital Breakups." *Los Angeles Times*, July 1, 1995. http://articles.latimes.com/1995-07-01/local/me-19084_1_divorce-rate.

Association of Reproductive Health Professionals. "Choosing a Birth Control Method: Male Condom." Updated June 2014. https://www.arhp.org/quick-reference-guide-for-clinicians/choosing-a-birth-control-method/barrier-methods/male-condom.

Aughinbaugh, Alison, Omar Robles, and Hugette Sun. "Marriage and Divorce: Patterns by Gender, Race, and Educational Attainment." *Monthly Labor Review*, October 2013. https://doi.org/10.21916/mlr.2013.32.

Augustine. *The Confessions of Saint Augustine.* Translated by John K. Ryan. New York: Doubleday, 1960.

Austen, Jane. *Pride and Prejudice.* New York: Alfred E. Knopf, 1991.

Ayers, David J. "Abortion's Slippery Slope: The 'Two-Minus-One Pregnancy.'" *The Center for Vision and Values*, August 17, 2011. http://www.visionandvalues.org/2011/08/abortion-s-slippery-slope-the-two-minus-one-pregnancy.

Bailey, Sarah Pulliam. "Here Are the Key Excerpts on Religious Liberty from the Supreme Court's Decision on Gay Marriage." *The Washington Post*, June 26, 2015. https://www.washingtonpost.com/news/acts-of-faith/wp/2015/06/26/here-are-the-key-excerpts-on-religious-liberty-from-the-supreme-courts-decision-on-gay-marriage.

Barna, George. *The Future of the American Family.* Chicago: Moody, 1993.

Barna Group. "Born Again Christians Just as Likely to Divorce as Are Non-Christians." Blog entry, September 8, 2004. https://www.barna.com/research/born-again-christians-just-as-likely-to-divorce-as-are-non-christians.

———. "Porn in the Digital Age: New Research Reveals 10 Trends." Blog entry, April 6, 2016. https://www.barna.com/research/porn-in-the-digital-age-new-research-reveals-10-trends.

———. "Majority of Americans Now Believe in Cohabitation." Blog entry, June 24, 2016. https://www.barna.com/research/majority-of-americans-now-believe-in-cohabitation.

Baxter, Richard. *Baxter's Practical Works, Volume 1, A Christian Directory: or, A Sum of Practical Theology and Cases of Conscience.* 1673. Reprint, Ligonier, PA: Soli Deo Gloria, 1990.

Bellah, Robert, Richard Madsen, William M. Sullivan, Ann Swidler, and Steven M. Tipton. *Habits of the Heart: Individualism and Commitment in American Life*. New York: Harper & Row, 1985.

Bersamin, Melina M., Deborah A. Fisher, Samantha Walker, Douglas L. Hill, and Joel W. Grube. "Defining Virginity and Abstinence: Adolescents' Interpretations of Sexual Behaviors." *Journal of Adolescent Health* 41, no. 2 (2007): 182–88.

BibleInfo.com. "What Does the Bible Say about Interracial Marriage?" http://www .bibleinfo.com/en/questions/what-does-bible-say-about-interracial-marriages.

Bingham, Scott. "Only One in Four Couples Living Together Plan to Marry." *The Telegraph*, January 10, 2014. http://www.telegraph.co.uk/women/mother-tongue/ 10561849/Only-one-in-four-couples-living-together-plan-to-marry.html.

Binstock, Georgina, and Arland Thornton. "Separations, Reconciliations, and Living Apart in Cohabiting and Marital Unions." *Journal of Marriage and Family* 65, no. 2 (2003): 432–43.

Binzer, Larson. "Millennial Children of Divorce: Fear, Anxiety and Determination to End the Cycle." *Genyu* (website), December 9, 2014. http://genyu.net/2014/12/09/ millennial-children-of-divorce-fear-anxiety-and-determination-to-end-the-cycle.

Blankenhorn, David. *Fatherless America: Confronting Our Most Urgent Social Problem*. New York: Basic Books, 1995.

Blasser, William N. "How Long Does Child Support Last?" *Blasser Law* (website), August 23, 2013. https://www.blasserlaw.com/how-long-does-child-support-last.

Blott, Unity. "Happily Married Couple Who Share a Girlfriend Reveal They Are Divorcing after 12 Years So That One of Them Can Marry Her—and Give Her Legal Rights to Their Three Children." *Daily Mail Online,* April 25, 2017. http://www.dailymail .co.uk/femail/article-4443102/Happily-married-couple-pan-marry-girlfriend.html.

Boehi, David, Brent Nelson, Jeff Schulte, and Lloyd Shadrach. *Preparing For Marriage: Discover God's Plan for a Lifetime of Love*. Revised and updated ed. Bloomington, MN: Bethany House, 2010.

———. *Preparing for Marriage Leader's Guide*. Revised and updated ed. Bloomington, MN: Bethany House, 2010.

Boice, James Montgomery. *Romans*. Volume 2, *The Reign of Grace (Romans 5–8)*. Grand Rapids: Baker, 1992.

The Book of Common Prayer. Introduction by James Wood, New York: Penguin, 2012.

Booth, Alan, John N. Edwards, and David R. Johnson. "Social Integration and Divorce." *Social Forces* 70, no. 1 (1991): 207–24.

Bowcott, Owen. "Gay Marriage: Some Legal Inequalities Will Remain." *The Guardian*, February 5, 2013. https://www.theguardian.com/society/2013/feb/05/gay-marriage -some-inequalities-remain.

Bowlus, Audra J., and Shannon Seitz. "Domestic Violence, Employment, and Divorce." *International Economic Review* 47, no. 4 (2006): 1113–49.

Bramlett, Matthew D., and William D. Mosher. "First Marriage Dissolution, Divorce, and Remarriage: United States." *Centers for Disease Control*. https://www.cdc.gov/ nchs/data/ad/ad323.pdf.

———. "Cohabitation, Marriage, Divorce, and Remarriage in the United States: Data from the National Survey of Family Growth." *Vital Health Statistics* 23, no. 22 (July 2002): 1–93.

Braver, Sanford L. "The Gender Gap in Standard of Living after Divorce: Vanishingly Small?" *Family Law Quarterly* 33, no. 1 (1999): 111–36.

Brown, Alyssa, and Jeffrey M. Jones. "Separation, Divorce Linked to Sharply Lower Well-Being." *Gallup News*, April 20, 2012. http://news.gallup.com/poll/154001/separation-divorce-linked-sharply-lower-wellbeing.aspx.

Brown, Susan L., and I-Fen Lin. "The Gray Divorce Revolution: Rising Divorce among Middle-Aged and Older Adults, 1990–2010." *The Journals of Gerontology: Series B* 67, no. 6 (2012): 731–41.

Browning, Don S. *Marriage and Modernization: How Globalization Threatens Marriage and What to Do about It.* Grand Rapids: Eerdmans, 2003.

Brownson, James V. *Bible, Gender, Sexuality: Reframing the Church's Debate on Same-Sex Relationships.* Grand Rapids: Eerdmans, 2013.

Burke, Edmund. *The Works of the Right Hon. Edmund Burke.* Volume 2. London: Holdsworth and Ball, 1834.

Burns, Jim, and Doug Fields. *Getting Ready for Marriage: A Practical Guide for Your Journey Together.* Colorado Springs, CO: David C. Cook. 2014.

———. *Getting Ready for Marriage Workbook.* Colorado Springs, CO: David C. Cook, 2015.

Calvin, John. *Commentary on the First Book of Moses Called Genesis.* Volume 1. Translated by John King. Grand Rapids, Eerdmans, 1948.

———. *Sermons on the Ten Commandments.* Edited and translated by Benjamin W. Farley. Grand Rapids: Baker, 1980.

———. "The Commentaries of John Calvin on the Prophet Malachi." In *Commentaries on the Twelve Minor Prophets: Volume 9,* translated by John Owen, 456–632. Grand Rapids: Baker, 1993.

Carroll, Jason S., and William Doherty. "Evaluating the Effectiveness of Premarital Prevention Programs: A Meta-Analytic Review of Outcome Research." *Family Relations* 52, no. 2 (2003): 105–18.

Carson, D. A. "Matthew." In *The Expositor's Bible Commentary*, vol. 9, rev. ed., edited by Tremper Longman III and David E. Garland, 23–670. Grand Rapids: Zondervan, 2010.

Carter, Zack. "Facebook Infidelity: Ten Safeguards Your Marriage Needs Today." *Psychology Today*, July 18, 2017. https://www.psychologytoday.com/blog/clear-communication/201707/facebook-infidelity-10-safeguards-your-marriage-needs-today.

Cassiday-Shaw, Aimee K. *Family Abuse and the Bible: The Scriptural Perspective.* New York: Routledge, 2012.

Catalano, Shannan. *Intimate Partner Violence, 1993–2010.* Revised ed. Washington, DC: Bureau of Justice Statistics, 2015.

Catechism of the Catholic Church. 2nd ed. Washington, DC: The United States Catholic Conference, 2000.

Centers for Disease Control and Prevention. "Condoms and STDs: Fact Sheet for Public Health Personnel." https://www.cdc.gov/condomeffectiveness/docs/condoms_and_stds.pdf.

———. *Sexually Transmitted Disease Surveillance, 2014.* Atlanta: US Department of Health and Human Services, 2015.

———. "Reported Cases of STDs on the Rise in the U.S." November 17, 2015. https://
www.cdc.gov/nchhstp/newsroom/2015/std-surveillance-report-press-release.html.

———. "Mental Health." Gay and Bisexual Men's Health. https://www.cdc.gov/
msmhealth/mental-health.htm.

———. "For Your Health: Recommendations for A Healthier You." Gay and Bisexual
Men's Health. https://www.cdc.gov/msmhealth/for-your-health.htm.

———. "STD Risk and Oral Sex: CDC Fact Sheet." Sexually Transmitted Diseases (STDs).
https://www.cdc.gov/std/healthcomm/stdfact-stdriskandoralsex.htm.

———. "How Effective Are Birth Control Methods?" Contraception. https://www.cdc
.gov/reproductivehealth/contraception/index.htm.

———. "Syphilis: CDC Fact Sheet (Detailed)." Sexually Transmitted Diseases (STDs).
https://www.cdc.gov/std/syphilis/stdfact-syphilis-detailed.htm.

The Center for Marriage and Family Studies and Life Innovations. *Bible Verses for the
PREPARE/ENRICH Program.* Minneapolis: Life Innovations, 2004.

Central Intelligence Agency. "Country Comparison: Total Fertility Rate." The World
Factbook. https://www.cia.gov/library/publications/the-world-factbook/rankorder/
2127rank.html.

Challies, Tim. "Ten Common but Illegitimate Reasons to Divorce." Blog entry, August
21, 2017. https://www.challies.com/articles/10-common-but-illegitimate-reasons
-to-divorce.

Chan, Francis, and Lisa Chan. *You and Me Forever: Marriage in Light of Eternity.* San
Francisco: Claire Love, 2014.

Cherlin, Andrew J. "Demographic Trends: A Review of Research in the 2000s." *Journal
of Marriage and Family* 72, no. 3 (2010): 403–19.

———. *Marriage, Divorce, Remarriage.* 2nd ed. Cambridge, MA: Harvard University
Press, 1992.

———. *The Marriage-Go-Round: The State of Marriage and the Family in America Today.*
New York: Alfred Knopf, 2009.

———. *Public and Private Families: An Introduction.* 8th ed. New York: McGraw-Hill,
2016.

Chira, Susan. "Fractured Families: Dealing with Multiple Divorce—A Special Report."
New York Times, March 19, 1995. http://www.nytimes.com/1995/03/19/us/
fractured-families-dealing-with-multiple-divorce-special-report-struggling-find
.html?pagewanted=all.

Clarke, Sally C. "Advance Report of Final Divorce Statistics, 1989 and 1990." *Monthly
Vital Statistics Report* 43, no. 9 (1995): 1–32.

Clarke-Stewart, Alison, and Cornelia Brentano. *Divorce: Causes and Consequences.* New
Haven, CT: Yale University Press, 2006.

Clements, Jonathan. "Getting Married Has Its Financial Benefits." *The
Wall Street Journal,* May 25, 2014. http://www.wsj.com/articles/
SB10001424052702304652804579571931962914924.

Coontz, Stephanie. "Divorce, No-Fault Style." *The New York Times,* June 16, 2010. http://
www.nytimes.com/2010/06/17/opinion/17coontz.html.

———. *Marriage, a History: From Obedience to Intimacy or How Love Conquered Marriage.* New York: Viking, 2005.

Copen, Casey E., Kimberly Daniels, Jonathan Vespa, and William D. Mosher. "First Marriages in the United States: Data from the 2006–2010 National Survey of Family Growth." *National Health Statistics Reports*, no. 49 (March 22, 2012): 1–21.

Copen, Casey E., Kimberly Daniels, and William D. Mosher. "First Premarital Cohabitation in the United States." *National Health Statistics Reports*, no. 64 (April 4, 2013): 1–16.

Cowan, Carolyn Pape, and Philip A. Cowan. "Interventions to Ease the Transition to Parenthood: Why They Are Needed and What They Can Do." *Family Relations: An Interdisciplinary Journal of Applied Family Studies* 44, no. 4 (1995): 412–23.

Cox, Daniel, Robert P. Jones, and Juhem Navarro-Rivera. *I Know What You Did Last Sunday: Measuring Social Desirability Bias in Self-Reported Religious Behavior, Belief, and Identity.* Washington, DC: Public Religion Research Institute, 2014.

Cranford, James A. "DSM-IV Alcohol Dependence and Marital Dissolution: Evidence from the National Epidemiologic Survey on Alcohol and Related Conditions." *Journal of Studies on Alcohol and Drugs* 75, no. 3 (2014): 520–29.

Cruz, Julissa. "Remarriage Rate in the U.S., 2010." National Center for Marriage and Family Research, 2012. https://scholarworks.bgsu.edu/cgi/viewcontent.cgi?article=1024&context=ncfmr_family_profiles.

Cui, Ming, Frank D. Fincham, and Jared A. Durtschi. "The Effect of Parental Divorce on Young Adults' Romantic Relationship Dissolution: What Makes a Difference?" *Personal Relationships* 18, no. 3 (2011): 410–26.

Daly, Jim. "Is Intentional Childlessness Biblical?" *Focus on the Family*, August 19, 2013. http://jimdaly.focusonthefamily.com/is-intentional-childlessness-biblical.

Deal, Ron L., and David H. Olson. *The Remarriage Checkup: Tools to Help Your Marriage Last a Lifetime.* Minneapolis: Bethany House, 2010.

DeBoer, Fredrik. "It's Time to Legalize Polygamy: Why Group Marriage Is the Next Horizon of Social Liberalism." *Politico*, June 26, 2015. https://www.politico.com/magazine/story/2015/06/gay-marriage-decision-polygamy-119469.

Deffinbaugh, Robert L. "The Qualities of a Godly Mate." *The Way of the Wise: Studies in the Book of Proverbs* (blog). Bible.org, June 2, 2004. https://bible.org/seriespage/12-qualities-godly-mate

DeParle, Jason, and Sabrina Tavernise. "For Women under 30, Most Births Occur outside Marriage." *New York Times*, February 17, 2012. http://www.nytimes.com/2012/02/18/us/for-women-under-30-most-births-occur-outside-marriage.html.

DeRose, Laurie, Mark Lyons-Amos, W. Bradford Wilcox, and Gloria Huarcaya. "The Cohabitation-Go-Round: Cohabitation and Family Instability across the Globe." In *World Family Map 2017: Mapping Family Change and Child Well-Being Outcomes*, 3–21. New York: Social Trends Institute, 2017.

DeRouchie, Jason. "If Your Right Hand Causes You to Sin: Ten Biblical Reflections on Masturbation." *Desiring God*, December 3, 2016. http://www.desiringgod.org/articles/if-your-right-hand-causes-you-to-sin.

Dever, Mark. "Christian Hedonists or Religious Prudes? The Puritans on Sex." In *Sex and the Supremacy of Christ*, edited by John Piper and Justin Taylor, 245–70. Wheaton, IL: Crossway, 2005.

DeYoung, Kevin. *What Does the Bible Teach about Homosexuality?* Wheaton, IL: Crossway, 2015.

Doss, Brian D., Galena K. Rhoades, Scott M. Stanley, Howard J. Markman, and Christine A. Johnson. "Differential Use of Premarital Education in First and Second Marriages." *Journal of Family Psychology* 23, no. 2 (2009): 268–73.

Dreher, Rod. *The Benedict Option: A Strategy for Christians in a Post-Christian Nation.* New York: Sentinel, 2017.

Eason, Gary. "Bitter Divorcees 'Using Children.'" *BBC News,* November 16, 2009. http://news.bbc.co.uk/2/hi/uk_news/england/8361684.stm.

Eastwick, Paul W., Laura B. Luchies, Eli J. Finkel, and Lucy L. Hunt. "The Predictive Validity of Ideal Partner Preferences: A Review and Meta-Analysis." *Psychological Bulletin* 140, no. 3 (2014): 623–65.

Edgar, Thomas. "Divorce & Remarriage for Adultery or Desertion." In *Divorce and Remarriage: Four Christian Views,* edited by H. Wayne House, 151–96. Downers Grove, IL: InterVarsity Press, 1990.

Elliott, Sinikka. *Not My Kids: What Parents Believe about the Sex Life of Their Teenagers.* New York: New York University Press, 2012.

Emling, Shelley. "A Happy Marriage Leads to Better Health, Study Finds." *The Huffington Post,* February 14, 2013. http://www.huffingtonpost.com/2013/02/14/married-couples-healthier-than-singles-study_n_2686051.html.

Engle, Gigi. "Anal Sex: What You Need to Know, How to Do It the *Right* Way." *Teen Vogue,* July 7, 2017. http://www.teenvogue.com/story/anal-sex-what-you-need-to-know.

Everitt, Lauren. "Ten Key Moments in the History of Marriage." *BBC News Magazine,* March 14, 2012. http://www.bbc.com/news/magazine-17351133.

Fagan, Patrick F., and Robert Rector. "The Effects of Divorce on America." *The Heritage Foundation Backgrounder,* no. 1373. (2000): 1–32.

Fee, Gordon D. *The First Epistle to the Corinthians.* Revised ed. Grand Rapids: Eerdmans, 2014.

Feldhahn, Shaunti. *The Good News about Marriage: Debunking Discouraging Myths about Marriage and Divorce.* Colorado Springs: Multnomah, 2014.

Fields, Jason. *Living Arrangements of Children, 1996: Current Population Reports P-70–74.* Washington, DC: US Census Bureau, 2001.

Find Law. "Marriage Requirements Basics: Consent, Age, and Capacity." http://family.findlaw.com/marriage/marriage-requirements-basics-consent-age-and-capacity.html?version=2.

Finer, Lawrence B. "Trends in Premarital Sex in the United States, 1954–2003." *Public Health Reports,* 122, no. 1 (2007): 73–78.

Fischer, David Hackett. *Albion's Seed: Four British Folkways in America.* New York: Oxford University Press, 1989.

Fisher, Daniel. "Does a Victory for Gay Marriage Lead to Polygamy? It Depends on Your Reasoning." *Forbes,* April 24, 2015. http://www.forbes.com/sites/danielfisher/2015/04/24/does-a-victory-for-gay-marriage-lead-to-polygamy-depends-on-the-reasoning/#5681197647ee.

Flavel, John. *The Whole Works of the Reverend Mr. John Flavel.* Vol. 8. London: Paisley, 1770.

Florensky, Pavel. *The Pillar and Ground of the Truth: An Essay in Orthodox Theodicy in Twelve Letters.* Translated and annotated by Boris Jakim. 1914. Reprint, Princeton, NJ: Princeton University Press, 1997.

FOCCUS. "FOCCUS Pre-Marriage Inventory." http://www.foccusinc.com/foccus -inventory.aspx.

———. "Evidence of Reliability and Validity for FOCCUS Fourth Edition Pre-Marriage Inventory." http://www.foccusinc.com/Resources/1.pdf.

Forhan, Sara, Sami L. Gottlieb, Maya R. Sternberg, Fujie Xu, Deblina Datta, Geraldine M. McQuillan, Stuart Berman, and Lauri E. Markowitz. "Prevalence of Sexually Transmitted Infections among Female Adolescents Aged 14 to 19 in the United States." *Pediatrics* 124, no. 6 (2009): 1505–19.

Francis-Tan, Andrew, and Hugo M. Mialon. "'A Diamond Is Forever' and Other Fairy Tales: The Relationship between Wedding Expenses and Marriage Duration." *Economic Inquiry* 53, no. 4 (2015): 1919–30.

Full Marriage Equality. "Consensual Incest FAQ" (blog). http://marriage-equality .blogspot.com/p/consensual-incest-faq.html.

Furstenberg, Frank F., Jr., and Andrew Cherlin. *Divided Families: What Happens to Children When Parents Part.* Cambridge, MA: Harvard University Press, 1991.

Furstenberg, Frank F., Jr., Christine Winquist Nord, James L. Peterson, and Nicholas Zill. "The Life Course of Children of Divorce: Marital Disruption and Parental Contact." *American Sociological Review* 48, no. 5 (1983): 656–68.

Futris, Ted G., Allen W. Barton, Tiffiany M. Aholou, and Desiree M. Seponski. "The Impact of PREPARE on Engaged Couples: Variations by Delivery Format." *The Journal of Couple and Relationship Therapy* 10, no. 1 (2011): 69–86.

Garber, Megan. "For a Lasting Marriage, Try Marrying Someone Your Own Age." *The Atlantic*, November 9, 2014. https://www.theatlantic.com/health/archive/2014/11/ why-to-marry-someone-your-own-age/382520.

Gallagher, Maggie. *The Abolition of Marriage: How We Destroy Lasting Love.* Washington, DC: Regnery, 1996.

Garrett, William R. "The Protestant Ethic and the Spirit of the Modern Family." *Journal for the Scientific Study of Religion* 37, no. 2 (1998): 222–33.

Gataker, Thomas. *A Good Wife God's Gift and, A Wife Indeed.* London, 1623. https:// quod.lib.umich.edu/e/eebo/A01534.0001.001?view=toc.

Gates, Gary J. "How Many People Are Lesbian, Gay, Bisexual and Transgender?" *The Williams Institute*, April, 2011. http://williamsinstitute.law.ucla.edu/research/census-lgbt -demographics-studies/how-many-people-are-lesbian-gay-bisexual-and-transgender.

———. "In U.S., More Adults Identifying as LGBT." Gallup, January 11, 2017. http://www .gallup.com/poll/201731/lgbt-identification-rises.

Gehring, René. *The Biblical "One Flesh" Theology as Constituted in Genesis 2:24: An Exegetical Study of This Human-Divine Covenant Pattern, Its New Testament Echoes, and Its Reception History throughout Scripture Focusing on the Spiritual Impact of Sexuality.* Eugene, OR: Wipf & Stock, 2013.

The Geneva Bible: A Facsimile of the 1560 Edition. Introduction by Lloyd E. Berry. Madison, WI: University of Wisconsin Press, 1969.

Gibbons, Judith L., Randy R. Richter, Deane C. Wiley, and Deborah A. Stiles. "Adolescents' Opposite-Sex Ideal in Four Countries." *Journal of Social Psychology* 136, no. 4 (1996): 531–37.

Gill, John. *Exposition of the Old and New Testament.* 1746–1763. http://www.sacred-texts.com/bib/cmt/gill.

Girgis, Sherif, Ryan T. Anderson, and Robert P. George. *What Is Marriage? Man and Woman: A Defense.* New York: Encounter, 2012.

Glass, J. D. "Two Studies That Prove Domestic Violence Is an LGBT Issue." *The Advocate,* September 4, 2014. http://www.advocate.com/crime/2014/09/04/2-studies-prove-domestic-violence-lgbt-issue.

Glick, Paul C. "Marriage, Divorce and Living Arrangements: Prospective Changes." *Journal of Family Issues* 5, no. 1 (1984): 7–26.

Gouge, William. *Of Domesticall Duties: Eight Treatises.* London, 1622. https://quod.lib.umich.edu/e/eebo/A68107.0001.001?view=toc.

Grall, Timothy. "Custodial Mothers and Fathers and Their Child Support: 2013." *Current Population Reports.* Washington, DC: US Census Bureau, 2016. https://www.census.gov/content/dam/Census/library/publications/2016/demo/P60-255.pdf.

Gregg, Samuel. "A Father's Love: The Story of Charles and Anne." *The Catholic World Reporter,* April 26, 2017. http://www.catholicworldreport.com/Item/5594/a_fathers_love_the_story_of_charles_and_anne.aspx.

Grenz, Stanley J. *Sexual Ethics: An Evangelical Perspective.* Louisville: Westminster John Knox, 1990.

Grubbs, Judith Evans. "Infant Exposure and Infanticide." In *The Oxford Handbook of Childhood and Education in the Classical World,* edited by Judith Evans Grubbs and Tim Parkin, 83–107. New York: Oxford University Press, 2013.

Guttmacher Institute. "Induced Abortion in the United States." January 2017. https://www.guttmacher.org/fact-sheet/induced-abortion-united-states?gclid=Cj0KEQiAuonGBRCaotXoycysvIMBEiQAcxV0nIUtBCnuupr2YkOEZX83qemA0PRpf8J-r-u3yqqga30aAo4K8P8HAQ.

Haas, Harold. *Marriage.* Philadelphia: Muhlenberg Press, 1960.

Hadaway, C. Kirk, and Penny Long Marler. "How Many Americans Attend Worship Each Week? An Alternative Approach to Measurement." *The Journal for the Scientific Study of Religion* 44, no. 3 (2005): 307–22.

Haque, Fahlma. "Meet the World's First Gay Married Throuple." *New York Post,* February 27, 2015. http://nypost.com/2015/02/27/thai-throuple-believed-to-be-worlds-first-gay-married-trio.

Harris, Joshua. *Boy Meets Girl: Say Hello to Courtship.* Sisters, OR: Multnomah, 2000.

Harrison, Everett F., and Donald A. Hagner. "Romans." In *The Expositor's Bible Commentary,* vol. 11, rev. ed., edited by Tremper Longman III and David E. Garland, 19–237. Grand Rapids: Zondervan, 2008.

Harvey, Dave. *When Sinners Say "I Do": Discovering the Power of the Gospel for Marriage.* Wapwallopen, PA: Shepherd Press, 2007.

Healthwise Incorporated. "Assisted Reproductive Technology." *WebMD*, May 22, 2015. http://www.webmd.com/hw-popup/assisted-reproductive-technology.

Henry, Matthew. *Commentary on the Whole Bible: New Modern Edition Complete and Unabridged in Six Volumes.* Vols. 1 and 3. Peabody, MA: Hendrickson, 1991.

The Heritage Foundation. "Four in Ten Children Are Born to Unwed Mothers." http://familyfacts.org/charts/205/four-in-10-children-are-born-to-unwed-mothers?utm_medium=newsletter&utm_campaign=culturewatch.

Heth, William A. "Remarriage for Adultery and Desertion." In *Remarriage after Divorce in Today's Church*, edited by Mark L. Strauss et al., 59–83. Grand Rapids: Zondervan, 2006.

Hersch, Patricia. *A Tribe Apart: A Journey into the Heart of American Adolescence.* New York: Ballantine, 1998.

Higgins, Liz. "Three Reasons Millennials Are Waiting to Get Married." *The Gottman Institute*, April 3, 2017. https://www.gottman.com/blog/3-reasons-millennials-are-waiting-to-get-married.

Hobbes, Michael. "Together Alone: The Epidemic of Gay Loneliness." *The Huffington Post*, March 2, 2017. http://highline.huffingtonpost.com/articles/en/gay-loneliness.

Hodge, A. A. *The Westminster Confession: A Commentary.* 1869. Reprint, Carlisle, PA: Banner of Truth, 2002.

Hodge, Charles. *1 and 2 Corinthians.* 1857 and 1859. Reprint, Carlisle, PA: Banner of Truth, 1974.

Holley, Paul, Scott Yabiku, and Mary Benin. "Outwitting Divorce: How Intelligence Can Keep Couples Together." Paper presented at Population Association of America Annual Meeting, Boston, MA, April 2004.

Hooker, Thomas. *The Application of Redemption by the Effectual Work of the Word, and Spirit of Christ, for the Bringing Home of Lost Sinners to God.* London: Peter Cole, 1656.

Horn, Wade F. "Wedding Bell Blues: Marriage and Welfare Reform." *The Brookings Institution*, June 1, 2001. https://www.brookings.edu/articles/wedding-bell-blues-marriage-and-welfare-reform.

Huffington Post Canada. "Ayano Tokumasu Niagara Falls Death: Student's Last Moments Caught On Camera, Couple Says." *HuffPost*, October 17, 2011. https://www.huffingtonpost.ca/2011/08/17/ayano-tokumasu-niagara-falls-japanese-student-last-moments-camera_n_929003.html.

Hugenberger, Gordon P. *Marriage as a Covenant: Biblical Law and Ethics as Developed from Malachi.* Eugene, OR: Wipf & Stock, 1994.

Hundley, Tom, and Ana P. Santos. "The Last Country in the World Where Divorce Is Illegal." *Foreign Policy*, January 19, 2015. http://foreignpolicy.com/2015/01/19/the-last-country-in-the-world-where-divorce-is-illegal-philippines-catholic-church.

Hunt, Lucy L., Paul W. Eastwick, and Eli J. Finkel. "Leveling the Playing Field: Longer Acquaintance Predicts Reduced Assortative Mating on Attractiveness." *Psychological Science* 26, no. 7 (2015): 1046–53.

Hymowitz, Kay. "Divorce Rates Are Falling—But Marriage Is Still on the Rocks." *Time*, December 3, 2014. http://time.com/3616569/divorce-rates-are-falling-but-marriage-is-still-on-the-rocks.

Instone-Brewer, David. *Divorce and Remarriage in the Bible: The Social and Literary Context*. Grand Rapids: Eerdmans, 2002.

———. *Divorce and Remarriage in the Church: Biblical Solutions for Pastoral Realities*. Downers Grove, IL: InterVarsity Press, 2003.

Jacquet, Susan E., and Catherine A. Surra. "Parental Divorce and Premarital Couples: Commitment and Other Relationship Characteristics." *Journal of Marriage and Family* 63, no. 3 (2001): 627–38.

Jao, Ariel. "U.S. Cities With the Highest Rate of Same-Sex Married Couples." *NBC News*, March 5, 2018. https://www.nbcnews.com/feature/nbc-out/u-s-cities-highest-rate -same-sex-married-couples-n852716.

Jerman, Jenna, Rachel K. Jones, and Tsuyoshi Onda. "Characteristics of U.S. Abortion Patients in 2014 and Changes since 2008." *Guttmacher Institute*, 2016. https://www .guttmacher.org/report/characteristics-us-abortion-patients-2014.

Jesus Is Lord. "Divorce and Remarriage: Profaning the Covenant of Marriage," June 5, 2004. https://www.jesus-is-lord.com/profaning.htm.

Johnson, Sherman E., and George A. Buttrick. "The Gospel according to St. Matthew." In *The Interpreter's Bible*, vol. 7, edited by George Arthur Buttrick et al., 229–625. Nashville: Abingdon Press, 1951.

Johnstone, Ronald L. *Religion in Society: A Sociology of Religion*. 8th ed. New York: Routledge, 2016.

Jones, Beth Felker. *Faithful: A Theology of Sex*. Grand Rapids: Zondervan, 2015.

Jones, Jeffrey M. "In U.S., 10.2% of LGBT Adults Now Married to Same-Sex Spouse." *Gallup Daily*. https://www.gallup.com/poll/212702/lgbt-adults-married.sex.spouse.aspx.

Jones, Rachel K., Lawrence B. Finer, and Susheela Singh. "Characteristics of U.S. Abortion Patients, 2008." *Guttmacher Institute*. https://www.guttmacher.org/report/ characteristics-us-abortion-patients-2008.

Jourard, Sidney M. *The Transparent Self*. Revised ed. New York: Van Nostrand Reinhold, 1971.

JRKM. "Elton John's Canadian Husband David Furnish in Tabloid Sex Tale." *Pop Goes the News*, April 8, 2016. https://popgoesthenews.com/2016/04/08/elton-johns -canadian-husband-david-furnish-in-tabloid-sex-tale.

Kass, Amy A., and Leon R. Kass. "Proposing Courtship." *First Things*, no. 96 (October 1999): 32–41.

Kann, Laura, Tim McManus, William A. Harris, Shari L. Shanklin, Katherine H. Flint, Barbara Queen, Richard Lowry, David Chyen, Lisa Whittle, Jemekia Thornton, Connie Lim, Denise Bradford, Yoshimi Yamakawa, Michelle Leon, Nancy Brener, Kathleen A. Ethier. "Youth Risk Behavior Surveillance: United States, 2017," *Morbidity and Mortality Weekly Report: Surveillance Summaries* 67, no. 8 (2018): 1–479.

Kaufman, Edward, and Marianne R. M. Yoshioka. *Substance Abuse Treatment and Family Therapy: A Treatment Improvement Protocol*. Rockville, MD: US Department of Health and Human Services, 2004.

Keener, Craig S. *. . . And Marries Another: Divorce and Remarriage in the Teaching of the New Testament*. Peabody, MA: Hendrickson, 1991.

———. *Matthew*. IVP New Testament Commentary. Downers Grove, IL: InterVarsity Press, 1997.

———. "Remarriage for Circumstances Other Than Adultery and Desertion." In *Remarriage after Divorce in Today's Church*, edited by Mark L. Strauss et al., 103–119. Grand Rapids: Zondervan, 2006.

Keller, Kathy. "Don't Take It from Me: Reasons You Should Not Marry an Unbeliever." *The Gospel Coalition*, January 22, 2012. https://www.thegospelcoalition.org/article/dont-take-it-from-me-reasons-you-should-not-marry-an-unbeliever.

Keller, Timothy, and Kathy Keller. *The Meaning of Marriage: Facing the Complexities of Commitment with the Wisdom of God*. New York: Dutton, 2011.

Kelly, Joan B., and Robert E. Emery. "Children's Adjustment Following Divorce: Risk and Resilience Perspectives." *Family Relations* 52, no. 4 (2003): 352–62.

Kennedy, Sheela, and Larry L. Bumpass. "Cohabitation and Children's Living Arrangements: New Estimates from the United States." *Demographic Research* 19, no. 47 (2008): 1663–92.

Kennedy, Sheela, and Steven Ruggles. "Breaking Up Is Hard to Count: The Rise of Divorce in the United States, 1980–2010." *Demography* 51, no. 2 (2014): 587–98.

Klaus, Hanna. "Reproductive Technology (Evaluation and Treatment of Infertility): Guidelines for Catholic Couples." *United States Conference of Catholic Bishops*, 2009. http://www.usccb.org/issues-and-action/marriage-and-family/natural-family-planning/resources/upload/Reproductive-Technology-Evaluation-Treatment-of-Infertility-Guidelines-for-Catholic-Couples.pdf.

Kline, Galena H., Scott M. Stanley, Howard J. Markman, P. Antonio Olmos-Gallo, Michelle St. Peters, Sarah W. Whitton, and Lydia M. Prado. "Timing Is Everything: Pre-Engagement Cohabitation and Increased Risk for Poor Marital Outcomes." *Journal of Family Psychology* 18, no. 2 (2004): 311–18.

Kosciw, Joseph G., and Elizabeth M. Diaz. *Involved, Invisible, Ignored: The Experiences of Lesbian, Gay, Bisexual, and Transgender Parents and Their Children in Our Nation's K–12 Schools*. New York: Gay, Lesbian, and Straight Education Network, 2008.

Köstenberger, Andreas J., and David W. Jones. *God, Marriage, and Family: Rebuilding the Biblical Foundation*. 2nd ed. Wheaton, IL: Crossway, 2010.

Kposowa, Augustine J. "Marital Status and Suicide in the National Longitudinal Mortality Study." *Journal of Epidemiology and Community Health* 54, no. 4 (2000): 254–61.

Kramer, Rita. *In Defense of the Family: Raising Children in America Today*. New York: Basic Books, 1983.

Kreider, Rose M., and Renee Ellis. "Number, Timing, and Duration of Marriages and Divorces: 2009." *Current Population Reports*. Washington, DC: US Census Bureau, 2011. https://www.census.gov/prod/2011pubs/p70-125.pdf.

Kuehne, Dale S. *Sex and the iWorld: Rethinking Relationship beyond an Age of Individualism*. Grand Rapids: Baker, 2009.

Kurtzleben, Danielle. "If You Grew Up Far Richer Than Your Spouse, It Will Likely Change Your Marriage." *Vox*, March 23, 2015. https://www.vox.com/2015/3/23/8267675/rich-poor-marriage-class.

LaMance, Ken. "The Evolution of Same-Sex Marriage Laws." *Legal Match*, 2014. https://www.legalmatch.com/same-sex-marraige-history.html.

Landau, Elizabeth. "Commitment for Millennials: Is It OK, Cupid?" *The Scientific American,* February 8, 2016. https://blogs.scientificamerican.com/mind-guest-blog/commitment-for-millennials-is-it-okay-cupid.

Laney, J. Carl. *The Divorce Myth.* Bloomington, MN: Bethany House, 1987.

———. "No Divorce and No Remarriage." In *Divorce and Remarriage: Four Christian Views,* edited by H. Wayne House, 15–54. Downers Grove, IL: InterVarsity Press, 1990.

Lang, Nico. "Gay Open Marriages Need to Come Out of the Closet." *The Daily Beast,* January 1, 2016. http://www.thedailybeast.com/articles/2016/01/01/gay-open-marriages-need-to-come-out-of-the-closet.html.

Larson, Peter J., and David J. Olson. "Cohabitation Reduces Relationship Quality for Dating and Engaged Couples." *Life Innovations,* 2010. https://www.prepare-enrich.com/pe/pdf/research/cohab_relat_qual.pdf.

Laughlin, Lynda. "A Child's Day: Living Arrangements, Nativity, and Family Transitions: 2011." United States Census Bureau (website), December 9, 2014. https://www.census.gov/newsroom/blogs/random-samplings/2014/12/a-change-in-circumstances-family-and-household-transitions-and-child-well-being.html.

Leman, Kevin. *Sheet Music: Uncovering the Secrets of Sexual Intimacy in Marriage.* Carol Stream, IL: Tyndale, 2003.

Lemmons, Emilie. "Ecumenical and Interfaith Marriages." *For Your Marriage* (blog). http://www.foryourmarriage.org/catholic-marriage/church-teachings/interfaith-marriages.

LeWine, Howard. "HPV Transmission during Oral Sex a Growing Cause of Mouth and Throat Cancer." *Harvard Health Publishing,* November 29, 2016. http://www.health.harvard.edu/blog/hpv-transmission-during-oral-sex-a-growing-cause-of-mouth-and-throat-cancer-201306046346.

Lewis, C. S. *The Four Loves.* New York: Harcourt Brace, 1960.

———. *Mere Christianity.* San Francisco: HarperSanFrancisco, 2001.

———. *Surprised By Joy: The Shape of My Early Life.* New York: Harcourt Brace, 1955.

———. "The Weight of Glory." *Theology* 43, no. 257 (1941): 263–74.

Lewis, Ruth, Clare Tanton, Catherine H. Mercer, Kirstin R. Mitchell, Melissa Palmer, Wendy Macdowall, and Kaye Wellings. "Heterosexual Practices among Young People in Britain: Evidence from Three National Surveys of Sexual Attitudes and Lifestyles." *The Journal of Adolescent Health* 61, no. 6 (2017): 694–702.

Li, David K. "Married Lesbian 'Throuple' Expecting First Child." *New York Post,* April 23, 2014. http://nypost.com/2014/04/23/married-lesbian-threesome-expecting-first-child.

Lightfoot, Gordon. "If You Could Read My Mind" (song lyrics). http://gordonlightfoot.com/ifyoucouldreadmymind.shtml.

Lim, Sol, Cheol E. Han, Peter J. Uhlhass, and Marcus Kaiser. "Preferential Detachment during Human Brain Development: Age- and Sex-Specific Structural Connectivity in Diffusion Tensor Imaging (DTI) Data." *Cerebral Cortex* 25, no. 6 (2013): 1477–89.

Livingston, Gretchen. "Tying the Knot Again? Chances Are, There's a Bigger Age Gap Than the First Time Around." *Pew Research Center,* December 4, 2014.

http://www.pewresearch.org/fact-tank/2014/12/04/tying-the-knot-again-chances
-are-theres-a-bigger-age-gap-than-the-first-time-around.

Lofquist, Daphne, Terry Lugaila, Martin O'Connell, and Sarah Feliz. "Households and Families: 2010." 2010 Census Briefs, April 2012. https://www.census.gov/prod/cen2010/briefs/c2010br-14.pdf.

Longfellow, Henry Wadsworth. *The Courtship of Miles Standish: And Other Poems.* Boston: Ticknor and Fields, 1859.

Los Angeles Times. "Glynn 'Scotty' Wolfe: World's Most Married Man" (obituary). *Los Angeles Times,* June 20, 1997. http://articles.latimes.com/1997-06-20/local/me-5329_1_linda-essex-wolfe-glynn-scotty-wolfe-longest-seven-years.

Luoma, Jason B., and Jane L. Pearson. "Suicide and Marital Status in the United States, 1991–1996: Is Widowhood a Risk Factor?" *American Journal of Public Health* 92, no. 9 (2002): 1518–22.

Luther, Martin. *A Compend of Luther's Theology.* Edited by Hugh Thomson Kerr. Philadelphia: Westminster Press, 1943.

———. "The Estate of Marriage." In *The Book of Marriage: The Wisest Answers to the Toughest Questions,* edited by Dana Mack and David Blankenhorn, 367–73. 1522. Reprint, Grand Rapids: Eerdmans, 2001.

Lynd, Robert S., and Helen Merrell Lynd. *Middletown: A Case Study in American Culture.* New York: Harcourt Brace, 1929.

MacArthur, John F. *1 Corinthians.* The MacArthur New Testament Commentary. Chicago: Moody Press, 1984.

Mack, Wayne. *Preparing for Marriage God's Way: A Step-by-Step Guide for Marriage Success Before and After the Wedding.* 2nd ed. Phillipsburg, NJ: P&R, 2013.

MacMillan, Amanda. "Teenagers Today Are Having More of This Type of Sex." *Time,* November 21, 2017. http://time.com/5032544/teen-sex-health/?utm_source=time.com&utm_medium=email&utm_campaign=thebrief&utm_content=2017112117pm&xid=newsletter-brief.

Manning, Wendy D., Marshal Neal Fettro, and Esther Lamidi. "Child Well-Being in Same-Sex Parent Families: Review of Research Prepared for American Sociological Association Amicus Brief." *Population Research Policy Review* 33, no. 4 (2014): 485–502.

Marin, Barbara VanOss, Douglas B. Kirby, Esther S. Hudes, Karin K. Coyle, and Cynthia A. Gómez. "Boyfriends, Girlfriends, and Teenagers' Risk of Sexual Involvement." *Perspectives on Sexual and Reproductive Health* 38, no. 2 (2006): 76–83.

Markman, Howard J., Scott M. Stanley, and Susan L. Blumberg. *Fighting for Your Marriage.* 3rd ed. San Francisco: Jossey Bass, 2010.

Martin, Joyce A., Brady E. Hamilton, Michelle J. K. Osterman, Anne K. Driscoll, and T. J. Mathews. "Births: Final Data for 2015." *National Vital Statistics Reports* 66, No. 1 (2017): 1–69.

Martin, Joyce A., Brady E. Hamilton, Michelle J. K. Osterman, Anne K. Driscoll, and Patrick Drake. "Births: Final Data for 2016." *National Vital Statistics Reports* 67, No. 1 (2018): 1–54.

Mascie-Taylor, C. G. N. "Spouse Similarity for IQ and Personality and Convergence." *Behavioral Genetics* 19, no. 2 (1989): 223–27.

McDermott, Rose, James H. Fowler, and Nicholas A. Christakis. "Breaking Up Is Hard to Do, Unless Everyone Else Is Doing It Too: Social Network Effects on Divorce in a Longitudinal Sample." *Social Forces* 92, no. 2 (2013): 491–519.

McDonald, Sabrina Beasley. "Are You Ready to Be a Mentor?" *FamilyLife*, 2005. http://www.familylife.com/articles/topics/faith/essentials/reaching-out/are-you-ready-to-be-a-mentor.

McManus, Michael J. *Marriage Savers: Helping Your Friends and Family Avoid Divorce.* Revised ed. Grand Rapids: Zondervan, 1995.

Mendle, Jane, K. Paige Harden, Eric Turkheimer, Carol A. Van Hulle, Brian M. D'Onofrio, Jeanne Brooks-Gunn, Joseph L. Rodgers, Robert E. Emery, and Benjamin B. Lahey. "Associations between Father Absence and Age of First Sexual Intercourse." *Child Development* 80, no. 5 (2009): 1463–80.

Merrill, Eugene H. *Deuteronomy.* The New American Commentary. Nashville: Broadman & Holman, 1994.

Merritt, Jonathan. "Christian Rock Star Comes Out as Gay: Here's the Letter He Wrote to the World." *Religion News Service*, May 5, 2016. http://religionnews.com/2016/05/31/christian-rockstar-comes-out-as-gay-heres-the-letter-he-wrote-to-the-world.

Miller, Claire Cain, and Quoctrung Bui. "Equality in Marriage Grows, and So Does Class Divide." *New York Times*, February 27, 2016. https://www.nytimes.com/2016/02/23/upshot/rise-in-marriages-of-equals-and-in-division-by-class.html.

Milton, John. *The Prose Works of John Milton: With A Biographical Introduction.* Vol. 1. Edited by Rufus Wilmot Griswold. New York: Wiley and Putnam, 1847.

Mohler, Albert R., Jr. "Can Christians Use Birth Control?" *Albert Mohler* (blog), May 8, 2006. http://www.albertmohler.com/2006/05/08/can-christians-use-birth-control.

———. "Deliberate Childlessness: Moral Rebellion with a New Face." *Albert Mohler* (blog), October 13, 2003. http://www.albertmohler.com/2003/10/13/deliberate-childlessness-moral-rebellion-with-a-new-face-4.

———. "Deliberate Childlessness Revisited." *Albert Mohler* (blog), August 15, 2005. http://www.albertmohler.com/2005/08/15/deliberate-childlessness-revisited.

Moisse, Katie, and Jessica Hopper. "Pat Robertson Says Alzheimer's Makes Divorce OK." *ABC News*, September 15, 2011. http://abcnews.go.com/Health/AlzheimersCommunity/pat-robertson-alzheimers-makes-divorce/story?id=14526660.

Moldenhauer, Aaron. "The Babylonian Captivity of the Church." *Lutheran Reformation*, January 12, 2016. http://lutheranreformation.org/history/the-babylonian-captivity-of-the-church.

Monto, Martin A., and Anna G. Carey. "A New Standard of Sexual Behavior? Are Claims Associated with the 'Hookup Culture' Supported by General Social Survey Data?" *The Journal of Sex Research* 51, no. 6 (2014): 605–15.

Montoya, R. Matthew, Robert S. Horton, and Jeffrey Kirchner. "Is Actual Similarity Necessary for Attraction? A Meta-Analysis of Actual and Perceived Similarity." *Journal of Social and Personal Relationships* 25, no. 6 (2008): 889–922.

Moore, Russell D. *Onward: Engaging the Culture without Losing the Gospel.* Nashville: B&H, 2015.

———. "Should Christians Adopt Embryos?" *The Christian Post*, September 21, 2012. http://www.christianpost.com/news/should-christians-adopt-embryos-81992.

Morgan, Edmund S. *The Puritan Family: Religion and Domestic Relations in Seventeenth-Century New England*. New York: Harper & Row, 1966.

Morin, Rich. "Is Divorce Contagious?" *Pew Research Center,* October 21, 2013. http://www.pewresearch.org/fact-tank/2013/10/21/is-divorce-contagious.

Morrison, Donna Ruane, and Mary Jo Coiro. "Parental Conflict and Marital Disruption." *The Journal of Marriage and Family* 61, no. 3 (1999): 626–37. http://www.radford.edu/~junnever/articles/divorce2.pdf.

Murray, Charles. *Coming Apart: The State of White America, 1960–2010*. New York: Crown Forum, 2012.

Murray, John. *Divorce*. Phillipsburg, NJ: P&R, 1961.

National Center for Health Statistics. "100 Years of Marriage and Divorce Statistics, United States, 1867–1967." *Data from the National Vital Statistics System* 12, no. 4 (1973): 1–61. https://stacks.cdc.gov/view/cdc/12831.

———. "2013–2015 National Survey of Family Growth: Public Use Data Files, Codebooks, and Documentation." *Centers for Disease Control and Prevention*, October 26, 2017. https://www.cdc.gov/nchs/nsfg/nsfg_2013_2015_puf.htm.

———. "About the National Survey for Family Growth." *Centers for Disease Control and Prevention*, June 23, 2016. https://www.cdc.gov/nchs/nsfg/about_nsfg.htm.

———. "Births, Marriages, Divorces, and Deaths for 1996." *Monthly Vital Statistics Report* 45, no. 12 (1997): 1–20. https://www.cdc.gov/nchs/data/mvsr/mv45_12.pdf.

———. "Births, Marriages, Divorces, and Deaths for 1997." *Monthly Vital Statistics Report* 46, no. 12 (1998): 1–20. https://www.cdc.gov/nchs/data/mvsr/mv46_12.pdf.

———. *Health, United States, 2015: With Special Feature on Racial and Ethnic Health Disparities*. Washington, DC: US Government Printing Office, 2016.

———. *Report to Congress on Out-of-Wedlock Childbearing*. Washington, DC: US Government Printing Office, 1995.

National Institutes of Health. "Director's Message: Sexual and Gender Minorities Formally Designated as a Health Disparity Population for Research Purposes." October 6, 2016. https://www.nimhd.nih.gov/about/directors-corner/message.html.

The National Marriage Project. *The State of Our Unions 2009: Money and Marriage*. Edited by W. Bradford Wilcox. Charlottesville, VA: The National Marriage Project and the Institute for American Values, 2009.

———. *The State of Our Unions 2011: When Baby Makes Three: How Parenthood Makes Life Meaningful and How Marriage Makes Parenthood Bearable*. Edited by W. Bradford Wilcox. Charlottesville, VA: The National Marriage Project and the Institute for American Values, 2011.

———. *The State of Our Unions 2012: The President's Marriage Agenda*. Edited by Elizabeth Marquardt, David Blankenhorn, Robert I. Lerman, Linda Malone-Colon, and W. Bradford Wilcox. Charlottesville, VA: The National Marriage Project and the Institute for American Values, 2012.

National Right to Life. "Abortion Statistics: United States Data and Trends." 2017. http://www.nrlc.org/uploads/factsheets/FS01AbortionintheUS.pdf.

New Geneva Study Bible. Nashville: Thomas Nelson, 1995.

Newheiser, Jim. *Marriage, Divorce, and Remarriage: Critical Questions and Answers*. Phillipsburg, NJ: P&R, 2017.

New York State Department of Health. "Frequently Asked Questions (FAQs) about Condoms." January 2014. https://www.health.ny.gov/diseases/aids/consumers/ condoms/faqs.htm.

Olasky, Marvin. "Rosaria Butterfield: No Free Passes." *World Magazine*, July 22, 2016. https://world.wng.org/2016/07/rosaria_butterfield_no_free_passes.

Olson, David, Amy Olson-Sigg, and Peter J. Larson. *The Couple Checkup: Find Your Relationship Strengths*. Nashville: Thomas Nelson, 2008.

———. "PREPARE/ENRICH Program: Overview and New Discoveries about Couples." *The Journal of Family and Community Ministries* 25, no. 1 (2012): 30–44. https:// www.prepare-enrich.com/pe/pdf/research/newdiscoveries.pdf.

Olson, Randal S. "What Makes for a Stable Marriage? Part 2." *Randal S. Olson* (blog), November 6, 2014. http://www.randalolson.com/2014/11/06/what-makes-for-a -stable-marriage-part-2.

Ortberg, John. "Leader's Insight: There's Something about Joseph." *CT Pastors*, 2006. http://www.christianitytoday.com/pastors/2006/november-online-only/cln61127 .html.

Orthodox Church in America. "Marriage." *The Orthodox Faith, Volume 2, Worship: The Sacraments* (website). https://oca.org/orthodoxy/the-orthodox-faith/worship/the -sacraments/marriage.

———. "Marriage to a Non-Christian." *The Orthodox Faith, Questions and Answers* (website). https://oca.org/questions/sacramentmarriage/marriage-to-a-non-christian.

Owens, Eric. "Leftist Law Professor Says Gay Marriage Likely to Lead to Legalized Incest, Polygamy." *The Daily Caller*, July 19, 2013. http://dailycaller.com/2013/07/ 19/leftist-law-professor-admits-gay-marriage-likely-to-lead-to-legalized-incest -polygamy.

Packer, James I. *Knowing God*. Downers Grove, IL: InterVarsity Press, 1973.

———. *A Quest for Godliness: The Puritan Vision of the Christian Life*. Wheaton, IL: Crossway, 1990.

———. "Is Systematic Theology a Mirage? An Introductory Discussion." In *Doing Theology in Today's World: Essays in Honor of Kenneth S. Kantzer*, edited by John D. Woodbridge and Thomas Edward McComiskey, 17–38. Grand Rapids: Zondervan, 1991.

Pan, Yue, and Ke-Sheng Wang. "Spousal Concordance in Academic Achievements and IQ: A Principal Component Analysis." *Open Journal of Psychiatry* 1, no. 2 (2011): 15–19.

Pappas, Stephanie. "Genetic Match? People Marry Those with Similar DNA." *Live Science* (website), May 19, 2014. https://www.livescience.com/45674-genetic-match -marriage.html.

Parrott, Les, and Leslie Parrott. "Marriage Mentoring." *Focus on the Family*. http://www .marriagementoring.com/focus.

Parliament of the United Kingdom. "Marriage (Same Sex Couples) Act 2013." *The National Archives of the United Kingdom* (website), July 27, 2013. http://www .legislation.gov.uk/ukpga/2013/30/enacted.

———. "Matrimonial Causes Act 1973." *The National Archives of the United Kingdom* (website). http://www.legislation.gov.uk/ukpga/1973/18/contents.

PBS. "Hooking Up." *Religion and Ethics Newsweekly* (website), May 8, 2009. http://www
.pbs.org/wnet/religionandethics/2009/05/08/may-8-2009-hooking-up/2896.

Perls, Frederick S. *The Gestalt Therapy Verbatim*. Compiled and edited by John O. Ste-
vens. Moab, UT: Real People Press, 1969.

Pew Research Center. "America's Changing Religious Landscape." *Religion and Public
Life* (website), May 12, 2015. http://www.pewforum.org/2015/05/12/americas
-changing-religious-landscape.

———. "The Decline of Marriage and Rise of New Families." *Pew Social Trends* (website),
November 18, 2010. http://www.pewsocialtrends.org/2010/11/18/the-decline-of
-marriage-and-rise-of-new-families.

———. "Four-in-Ten Couples Are Saying 'I Do' Again: Growing Number of Adults Are
Remarried." *Pew Social and Demographic Trends* (website), November 14, 2014.
http://www.pewsocialtrends.org/2014/11/14/four-in-ten-couples-are-saying-i-do
-again.

———. "Millennials in Adulthood." *Social and Demographic Trends* (website), March 7,
2014. http://www.pewsocialtrends.org/2014/03/07/millennials-in-adulthood.

———. "Most Millennials Resist the 'Millennial' Label." *U.S. Politics and Policy* (website),
September 3, 2015. http://www.people-press.org/2015/09/03/most-millennials
-resist-the-millennial-label.

———. "Parenting in America: Outlook, Worries, Aspirations Are Strongly Linked to
Financial Situation." *Social and Demographic Trends* (website), December 17, 2015.
http://www.pewsocialtrends.org/2015/12/17/parenting-in-america.

———. "The U.S. Hispanic Population Has Increased Sixfold Since 1970." *Factank: News
in the Numbers* (website), February 26, 2014. http://www.pewresearch.org/fact
-tank/2014/02/26/the-u-s-hispanic-population-has-increased-sixfold-since-1970.

Pickhardt, Carl E. "Adolescent Breakups." *Psychology Today* (website), October 11,
2010. https://www.psychologytoday.com/blog/surviving-your-childs-adolescence/
201010/adolescent-break-ups.

Piper, John. "Divorce and Remarriage: A Position Paper." *Desiring God* (blog). July 21,
1986. http://www.desiringgod.org/articles/divorce-remarriage-a-position-paper.

———. "Racial Harmony and Interracial Marriage." *Desiring God* (blog). January 16,
2005. http://www.desiringgod.org/messages/racial-harmony-and-interracial
-marriage.

———. "Will You Marry a Couple Already Living Together?" *Desiring God* (blog), June
17, 2014. https://www.desiringgod.org/interviews/will-you-marry-a-couple-already
-living-together.

———. *Preparing for Marriage: Help for Christian Couples*. Minneapolis: Desiring God, 2015.

Polling Report. "Values." *PollingReport.com*, May 3–7, 2017. http://www.pollingreport
.com/values.htm.

Pope Benedict XVI. "Angelus: Feast of the Holy Family." *Vatican.va*, December 27, 2009.
http://w2.vatican.va/content/benedict-xvi/en/angelus/2009/documents/hf_ben-xvi
_ang_20091227.html.

Pope Francis. "General Audience on Christian Marriage." *Zenit: The World Seen
from Rome* (website), May 6, 2015. https://zenit.org/articles/general-audience-on
-christian-marriage.

Pope John Paul II. "Familiaris Consortio: Apostolic Exhortation of Pope John Paul II." *Vatican.va*, November 22, 1981. http://w2.vatican.va/content/john-paul-ii/en/apost _exhortations/documents/hf_jp-ii_exh_19811122_familiaris-consortio.html.

Popenoe, David. *Life Without Father: Compelling New Evidence That Fatherhood and Marriage Are Indispensable for the Good of Children and Society.* New York: Martin Kessler, 1996.

Popenoe, David, and Barbara Dafoe Whitehead. *Should We Live Together? What Young Adults Need to Know about Cohabitation and Marriage: A Comprehensive Review of Recent Research.* 2nd ed. Piscataway, NJ: The National Marriage Project, 2002.

———. *Cohabitation, Marriage, and Child Well-Being: A Cross-National Perspective.* Piscataway, NJ: The National Marriage Project, 2008.

Potter, Daniel. "Same-Sex Parent Families and Children's Academic Achievement." *Journal of Marriage and Family* 74, no. 3 (2012): 556–71.

PREPARE/ENRICH: Workbook for Couples. Minneapolis: Life Innovations, 2008. https://www.prepare-enrich.com/prepare_enrich_content/reference/couples _workbook.pdf.

PREPARE/ENRICH: Sample Facilitator Report. Minneapolis: Life Innovations, 2015. https://www.prepare-enrich.com/pe/pdf/counselor/sample_facilitator_report.pdf.

Ptacek, Kerry. *Family and Government in Puritan New England.* Hoover, AL: Covenant Family Fellowship, 1995.

Rainey, Dennis, and Barbara Rainey. *Preparing for Marriage Devotions for Couples: Discover God's Plan for a Lifetime of Love.* Revised and updated. Ventura, CA: Regal, 2013.

Ramsey, Dave. *Complete Guide to Money.* Brentwood, TN: Ramsey Press, 2012.

———. *The Total Money Makeover: The Proven Plan for Financial Fitness.* Nashville: Thomas Nelson, 2013.

Redding, Richard E. "Politicized Science." *Society* 50, no. 5 (2013): 439–46.

Regnerus, Mark. *Cheap Sex: The Transformation of Men, Marriage, and Monogamy.* New York: Oxford University Press, 2017.

———. *Forbidden Fruit: Sex & Religion in the Lives of American Teenagers.* New York: Oxford University Press, 2009.

———. "How Different Are the Adult Children of Parents Who Have Same-Sex Relationships? Findings from the New Family Structures Study." *Social Science Research*, 41, no. 4 (2012), 752–70.

———. "New Research on Same-Sex Households Reveals Kids Do Best With Mom and Dad," *The Witherspoon Institute: Public Discourse*, February 10, 2015. http://www .thepublicdiscourse.com/2015/02/14417.

———. "Parental Same-Sex Relationships, Family Instability, and Subsequent Life Outcomes for Adult Children: Answering Critics of the New Family Structures Study with Additional Analyses." *Social Science Research*, 41, no. 6 (2012), 1367–77.

Regnerus, Mark, and Jeremy Uecker. *Premarital Sex in America: How Young Americans Meet, Mate, and Think about Marrying.* New York: Oxford University Press, 2011.

Regnerus, Mark, Naomi Schaefer Riley, and Russell Moore. "Is Interfaith Marriage Always Wrong, Given That the Bible Teaches Us Not to Be 'Unequally Yoked'? Experts Weigh In on Biblical Bonding." *Christianity Today*, July 10, 2013.

http://www.christianitytoday.com/ct/2013/june/is-interfaith-marriage-always
-wrong-given-that-bible-teache.html.

Reilly, Robert R. *Making Gay Okay: How Rationalizing Homosexual Behavior Is Changing Everything*. San Francisco: Ignatius, 2014.

Relate Institute. "The Relate Assessment." *Relate Institute* (website), undated. https://
relateinstitute. com/the-relate-assessment.

Richards, Larry. "Divorce and Remarriage under a Variety of Circumstances." In
Divorce and Remarriage: Four Christian Views, edited by H. Wayne House, 215–48.
Downers Grove, IL: InterVarsity Press, 1990.

Rheinstein, Max. "Trends in Marriage and Divorce Laws of Western Countries." *Law
and Contemporary Problems* 18, no. 1 (1953): 3–19.

Rhoades, Galena K., and Scott M. Stanley. *Before "I Do": What Do Premarital Experiences Have to Do with Marital Quality among Today's Young Adults?* Charlottesville,
VA: The National Marriage Project, 2014.

Rhoades, Galena K., Scott M. Stanley, and Howard J. Markman. "The Pre-Engagement
Cohabitation Effect: A Replication and Extension of Previous Findings." *Journal of
Family Psychology* 23, no. 1 (2009): 107–11.

———. "Couples' Reasons for Cohabitation Associations with Individual Well-Being and
Relationship Quality." *Journal of Family Issues* 30, no. 2 (2009): 233–48.

Rieff, Philip. *The Triumph of the Therapeutic: Uses of Faith After Freud*. New York:
Harper & Row, 1966.

Riley, Naomi Schaefer. *'Til Faith Do Us Part: How Interfaith Marriage Is Transforming
America*. New York: Oxford University Press, 2013.

Robards, James, Maria Evandrou, Jane Falkingham, and Athina Vlachantoni. "Marital
Status, Health, and Mortality." *Maturitas* 73, no. 4 (2012): 295–99.

Robinson, Christy K. "Letter from John Winthrop to Mary Tyndal." *Mary Barrett Dyer*
(blog), February 8, 2014. https://marybarrettdyer.blogspot.com/2014/02/john
-winthrops-love-letter-to-his.html. Original written April 4, 1618. [David J. Ayers
modernized the spelling and grammar to improve readability.]

Rocca, Francis X. "Pope Francis Opens New Phase in Church's Debate on Divorce." *The
Wall Street Journal*, April 8, 2016. https://www.wsj.com/articles/pope-francis-calls
-for-leniency-toward-divorced-catholics-1460109702.

Romano, Lois. "Bob Bauman, After the Fall." *The Washington Post*, August 6,
1986. https://www.washingtonpost.com/archive/lifestyle/1986/08/06/bob
-bauman-after-the-fall/8dbf0791-1cf3-4aa2-87eb-2f5e1339bbf2/?utm_term=
.13894e0098d2.

Rosenfeld, Michael J. "Nontraditional Families and Childhood Progress through
School." *Demography* 47 No. 3 (2010): 755–75.

———. "Reply to Allen et al." *Demography* 50, no. 3 (2013): 963–69.

Ryken, Leland. *Worldly Saints: The Puritans as They Really Were*. Grand Rapids:
Zondervan, 1986.

Saint-Jacques, Marie-Christine, Caroline Robitaille, Élisabeth Godbout, Claudine
Parent, Sylvie Drapeau, and Marie-Helene Gagne. "The Processes Distinguishing
Stable from Unstable Stepfamily Couples: A Qualitative Analysis." *Family Relations*
60, no. 5 (2011): 546–47.

Sawhill, Isabel. "Twenty Years Later, It Turns Out Dan Quayle Was Right about Murphy Brown and Unmarried Moms." *The Washington Post*, May 25, 2012. https://www.washingtonpost.com/opinions/20-years-later-it-turns-out-dan-quayle -was-right-about-murphy-brown-and-unmarried-moms/2012/05/25/gJQAsNCJqU _story.html?utm_term=.29aa3c8f98f2.

Schaeffer, Francis A. *The Church before the Watching World: A Practical Ecclesiology.* Downers Grove, IL: InterVarsity Press, 1971.

———. *Letters of Francis Schaeffer.* Edited with introductions by Lane T. Dennis. Westchester, IL: Crossway, 1985.

Schoen, Robert, and Vladimir Canudas-Romo. "Timing Effects on Divorce: Twentieth-Century Experience in the United States." *The Journal of Marriage and Family* 68, no. 4 (2006): 749–58.

Scott, Shelby B., Galena K. Rhoades, Scott M. Stanley, Elizabeth S. Allen, and Howard J. Markman. "Reasons for Divorce and Recollections of Premarital Intervention: Implications for Improving Relationship Education." *Couples and Family Psychology* 2, no. 2 (2013): 131–45.

Semega, Jessica L., Kayla R. Fontenot, and Melissa A. Kollar. "Income and Poverty in the United States: 2016." *United States Census Bureau*, September, 2017. https://www .census.gov/content/dam/Census/library/publications/2017/demo/p60-259.html.

Singh, Gopal K., T. J. Matthews, Sally C. Clarke, Trina Yannikos, and Betty L. Smith. "Annual Summary of Births, Marriages, Divorces, and Deaths: United States, 1994." *Monthly Vital Statistics Report* 43, no. 13 (1995): 1–44.

Shain, Benjamin, and AAP Committee on Adolescence. "Suicide and Suicide Attempts in Adolescents." *Pediatrics* 138, no. 1 (2016): 669–676.

Shin, Laura. "Work from Home in 2017: The Top 100 Companies Offering Remote Jobs." *Forbes*, January 31, 2017. https://www.forbes.com/sites/laurashin/2017/01/31/work -from-home-in-2017-the-top-100-companies-offering-remote-jobs/#38a44bf42d8a.

Shorter, Edward. *The Making of the Modern Family.* New York: Basic Books, 1975.

Slattery, Juli. "Masturbation: Is It Wrong?" *Today's Christian Woman*, May, 2014. http:// www.todayschristianwoman.com/articles/2014/may/masturbation-is-it-always-sin .html?start=1.

Smalley, Erin. "Invest in Your Marriage with Mentors." *Focus on the Family*. https:// www.focusonthefamily.com/marriage/preparing-for-marriage/invest-in-your -marriage-with-mentors.

Smith, Henry. "A Preparative to Marriage." In *The Sermons of Henry Smith: The Silver-Tongued Preacher*, edited by John Brown, 9–35. London: Cambridge University Press, 1908.

Smith, Jack C., James A. Mercy, and Judith M. Conn. "Marital Status and the Risk of Suicide." *American Journal of Public Health* 78, no. 1 (1988): 78–80.

Smith, Tom W., Peter Marsden, Michael Hout, and Jibum Kim. "General Social Surveys, 1972–2016." *National Science Foundation*. http://gss.norc.org/get-the-data.

South, Scott J., and Glenna Spitze. "Determinants of Divorce over the Marital Life Course." *American Sociological Review* 51, no. 4 (1986): 583–90.

Sproul, R. C. *The Intimate Marriage: A Practical Guide to Building a Great Marriage.* Phillipsburg, NJ: P&R, 1975.

Spurgeon, Charles Haddon. *The Treasury of David.* Volume 7. 1869. Reprint, Pasadena, TX: Pilgrim Publications, 1983.

———. "The Relationship of Marriage." In *The Metropolitan Tabernacle Pulpit,* vol. 13, 409–20. 1867. Reprint, Pasadena, TX: Pilgrim Publications, 1986.

Stacey, Judith. "Good Riddance to 'The Family': A Response to David Popenoe." *Journal of Marriage and Family* 55, no. 3 (1993): 545–47.

Stanley, Scott M., Paul R. Amato, Christine A. Johnson, and Howard J. Markman. "Premarital Education, Marital Quality, and Marital Stability: Findings from a Large, Random Household Survey." *Journal of Family Psychology* 20, no 1 (2006): 117–26.

Stanley, Scott M., and Galena Kline Rhoades. "The Perils of Sowing Your Wild Oats." *Psychology Today* 49, no. 4 (2016): 40–42.

Stanley, Scott M., Galena Kline Rhoades, and Howard J. Markman. "Sliding Versus Deciding: Inertia and the Premarital Cohabitation Effect." *Family Relations* 55, no. 4 (2006): 499–509.

Stanley, Scott M., Daniel Trathan, Savanna McCain, and B. Milton Bryan. *A Lasting Promise: The Christian Guide to Fighting for Your Marriage.* New and rev. ed. San Francisco: Jossey-Bass, 2014.

Stanton, Glenn. "Premarital Sex and Greater Risk of Divorce." *Focus on the Family.* https:// www.focusonthefamily.com/about/focus-findings/marriage/premarital-sex -and-divorce.

Starbuck, Gene H., and Karen Saucier Lundy. *Families in Context: Sociological Perspectives.* 3rd ed. Boulder, CO: Paradigm Publishers, 2015.

Stein, Joseph. "Fiddler on the Roof." In *Fifty Best Plays of the American Theater,* edited by Clive Barnes, 463–97. New York: Crown, 1970.

Stephens, William N. *The Family in Cross-Cultural Perspective.* 1963. Reprint, Lanham, MD: University Press of America, 1982.

Stepler, Renee. "Number of U.S. Adults Cohabiting with a Partner Continues to Rise, Especially among Those 50 and Older." *Pew Research Center,* April 6, 2017. http:// www.pewresearch.org/fact-tank/2017/04/06/number-of-u-s-adults-cohabiting -with-a-partner-continues-to-rise-especially-among-those-50-and-older.

———. "Led by Baby Boomers, Divorce Rates Climb for America's 50+ Population." *Pew Research Center,* March 9, 2017. http://www.pewresearch.org/fact-tank/2017/03/ 09/led-by-baby-boomers-divorce-rates-climb-for-americas-50-population.

Stewart, Rebecca Felsental. "Does a Better Relationship Mean Better Health? The Perks of Marriage and Long-Term Relationships." *WebMD,* January 26, 2012. http://www .webmd.com/sex-relationships/guide/relationships-marriage-and-health?page=1.

Stith, Sandra M. "Domestic Violence." *American Association of Marriage and Family Therapy* (website), undated. http://www.aamft.org/iMIS15/AAMFT/Content/ Consumer_Updates/Domestic_violence.aspx.

Stone, Lawrence. *Road to Divorce: England 1530–1987.* Oxford: Oxford University, 1990.

Strauss, Mark L. "Conclusions: Three Questions for You to Answer." In *Remarriage after Divorce in Today's Church,* edited by Mark L. Strauss et al., 137–41. Grand Rapids: Zondervan, 2006.

Streib, Jessi. *The Power of the Past: Understanding Cross-Class Marriages.* New York: Oxford University Press, 2015.

Strong, Bryan, Christine DeVault, and Theodore Cohen. *The Marriage and Family Experience: Intimate Relationships in a Changing Society.* 10th ed. Belmont, CA: Thomson Learning, 2008.

Stookey, Paul. "Wedding Song (There Is Love)." Milwaukee: Hal Leonard Music, 2008.

Szwedo, David E., Joanna M. Chango, and Joseph P. Allen. "Adolescent Romance and Depressive Symptoms: The Moderating Effects of Positive Coping and Perceived Friendship Competence." *Journal of Clinical Child and Adolescent Psychology* 44, no. 4 (2015): 538–50.

Sullins, Donald Paul. "Emotional Problems among Children with Same-Sex Parents: Difference by Definition." *British Journal of Education, Society and Behavioural Science* 7, no. 2 (2015): 99–120.

Swanson, Ana. "The Real Reason Some People End Up with Partners Who Are Way More Attractive." *The Washington Post,* May 3, 2016. https://www.washingtonpost .com/news/wonk/wp/2016/05/03/the-real-reason-some-people-end-up-with -partners-who-are-way-more-attractive/?utm_term=.8b8950f6368a.

Sweeney, Megan M. "Remarriage and Stepfamilies: Strategic Sites for Family Scholarship in the Twenty-first Century." *Journal of Marriage and Family* 72, no. 3 (2010): 667–84.

Teachman, Jay. "Complex Life Course Patterns and the Risk of Divorce in Second Marriages." *The Journal of Marriage and Family* 70, no. 2 (2008): 294–305.

———. "Premarital Sex, Premarital Cohabitation, and the Risk of Subsequent Marital Dissolution among Women." *The Journal of Marriage and Family* 65, no. 2 (2003): 444–55.

Tiglao, Getsy. "Do What All the World Does: Have a Divorce Law." *Manila Bulletin,* July 14, 2017. http://news.mb.com.ph/2017/07/14/do-what-all-the-world-does -have-a-divorce-law.

Tjaden, Patricia, and Nancy Thoennes. *Extent, Nature, and Consequences of Intimate Partner Violence: Findings from the National Violence against Women Survey.* Washington, DC: US Department of Justice, 2006.

Towner, Philip H. *1–2 Timothy and Titus.* Downers Grove, IL: InterVarsity Press, 1994.

Tripp, Paul David. *What Did You Expect? Redeeming the Realities of Marriage.* Wheaton, IL: Crossway, 2010.

Troeltsch, Ernst. *The Social Teaching of the Christian Churches: Volume 1.* Translated by Olive Wyon. Louisville: John Knox, 1992.

United States Census Bureau. "Custodial Mothers and Fathers and Their Child Support: 2013, Series P60–255, Detailed Tables." *Current Population Survey,* April 2014. https://www2.census.gov/programs-surveys/demo/tables/families/2013/chldsu13.pdf.

———. "The Majority of Children Live with Two Parents, Census Bureau Reports." *Newsroom,* November 17, 2016. https://www.census.gov/newsroom/press-releases/2016/ cb16-192.html.

———. *Statistical Abstract of the United States: 2012.* Washington, DC: US Census Bureau, 2012.

———. "Table C3: Living Arrangements of Children under 18 Years and Marital Status of Parents, by Age, Race, Sex and Hispanic Origin and Selected Characteristics of the Child for All Children: 2017." *Current Population Survey: America's Families and Living Arrangements: 2017*, May 4, 2018. https://www.census.gov/data/tables/2016/demo/families/cps-2016.html.

———. "Table FG3: Married Couple Family Groups, by Presence of Own Children under 18, and Age, Earnings, Education, and Race and Hispanic Origin of Both Spouses: 2017." *Current Population Survey: America's Families and Living Arrangements: 2017*, May 4, 2018. https://www.census.gov/data/tables/2017/demo/families/cps-2017.html.

———. "Table MS-2: Estimated Median Age at First Marriage: 1890 to Present." *Family: Historical Marital Status Tables*, November 2016. https://www.census.gov/data/tables/time-series/demo/families/marital.html.

———. "Table UC3: Opposite Sex Unmarried Couples by Presence of Biological Children under 18, And Age, Earnings, Education, and Race And Hispanic Origin of Both Partners: 2018." *America's Families and Living Arrangements: 2017*. May 4, 2018. https://www.census.gov/data/tables/2016/demo/families/cps-2016.html.

UNC Carolina Population Center. "The National Longitudinal Study of Adolescent Health (Add Health)." *Life Course Studies Program* (website). http://lifecourse.web.unc.edu/research_projects/add_health.

United States Conference of Catholic Bishops. "About Catholic Marriage: FAQs." *For Your Marriage* (website). http://www.foryourmarriage.org/catholic-marriage/faqs.

———. "Annulment." *Marriage* (website). http://www.usccb.org/issues-and-action/marriage-and-family/marriage/annulment.

The University of Texas at Austin. "University of Texas at Austin Completes Inquiry into Allegations of Scientific Misconduct." *UT News,* August 29, 2012. https://news.utexas.edu/2012/08/29/regnerus_scientific_misconduct_inquiry_completed.

Vaillancourt, C. "God Made Marriage." *Catholic Missions Leaflets* (website). http://www.catholicmissionleaflets.org/marriage.htm.

Vance, J. D. *Hillbilly Elegy: A Memoir of a Family and Culture in Crisis*. New York: HarperCollins, 2016.

VanderWeele, Tyler J. "What *The New York Times* Gets Wrong about Marriage, Health, and Well-Being." *Institute for Family Studies*, May 30, 2017. https://ifstudies.org/blog/what-the-new-york-times-gets-wrong-about-marriage-health-and-well-being.

Veith, Gene. "Exploding Myths about Cohabitation." *Patheos* (blog), April 5, 2017. http://www.patheos.com/blogs/geneveith/2017/04/exploding-myths-about-cohabitation-draft/?utm_source=facebook.

Verbrugge, Verlyn D. "1 Corinthians." In *The Expositor's Bible Commentary*, vol. 11, rev. ed., edited by Tremper Longman III and David E. Garland, 239–414. Grand Rapids: Zondervan, 2008.

Waite, Linda J., Don Browning, William J. Doherty, Maggie Gallagher, Ye Luo, and Scott M. Stanley. *Does Divorce Make People Happy? Findings from a Study of Unhappy Marriages*. New York: Institute for American Values, 2002.

Waite, Linda J., and Maggie Gallagher. *The Case for Marriage: Why Married People Are Happier, Healthier, and Better Off Financially*. New York: Broadway Books, 2000.

Wallerstein, Judith S., and Julia M. Lewis. "The Unexpected Legacy of Divorce: Report of a 25 Year Study." *Psychoanalytic Psychology* 21, no. 3 (2004): 353–70.

Walters, Mikel L., Jieru Chen, and Matthew J. Breiding. *The National Intimate Partner and Sexual Violence Survey (NISVS): 2010 Findings on Victimization by Sexual Orientation*. Atlanta: Centers for Disease Control and Prevention, 2013.

Wang, Wendy. *The Rise of Intermarriage: Rates, Characteristics Vary by Race and Gender*. Washington, DC: Pew Social & Demographic Trends, 2012.

Wang, Wendy, and Kim Parker. "Record Share of Americans Have Never Married." *Pew Research Center Social & Demographic Trends*, September 24, 2014. http://www.pewsocialtrends.org/2014/09/24/record-share-of-americans-have-never-married/.

Wang, Wendy, and Paul Taylor. "For Millennials, Parenthood Trumps Marriage." *Pew Research Center Social and Demographic Trends*, March 9, 2011. http://www.pewsocialtrends.org/2011/03/09/for-millennials-parenthood-trumps-marriage.

Ward, Brian W., James M. Dahlhamer, Adena M. Galinsky, and Sarah S. Joestl. "Sexual Orientation and Health among U.S. Adults: National Health Interview Survey, 2013." *National Health Statistics Reports* no. 77, July 15, 2014. https://www.cdc.gov/nchs/data/nhsr/nhsr077.pdf.

Wells, Jonathan. "The Eight Surprising Health Benefits of Getting Married." *The Telegraph*, April 11, 2016. http://www.telegraph.co.uk/men/health/the-eight-surprising-health-benefits-of-getting-married.

Wenham, Gordon J. "No Remarriage after Divorce." In *Remarriage after Divorce in Today's Church*, edited by Mark L. Strauss et al., 19–47. Grand Rapids: Zondervan, 2006.

Westermarck, Edward. "The Future of Marriage in Western Civilization." In *The Book of Marriage: The Wisest Answers to the Toughest Questions*, edited by Dana Mack and David Blankenhorn, 19–33. Grand Rapids: Eerdmans, 2001.

The Westminster Confession of Faith, Together with the Larger Catechism and Shorter Catechism, with Scripture Proofs. 3rd ed. Atlanta: Committee for Christian Education & Publication, 1990.

Weston, Ruth, Lixia Qu, and David de Vaus. "Premarital Cohabitation and Marital Stability." Paper presented at the HILDA Conference, Melbourne, Australia, March 2003.

Westover Church. "Step-Families." *Westover Church* (website). https://www.westoverchurch.com/ministries/care-support/step-families.

Whitehead, Barbara Dafoe. "Dan Quayle Was Right." *The Atlantic Monthly*, 271, no. 4 (1993): 47–84.

———. *The Divorce Culture*. New York: Alfred A. Knopf. 1996.

Whitton, Sarah W., Galena K. Rhoades, Scott M. Stanley, and Howard J. Markman. "Effects of Parental Divorce on Marital Commitment and Confidence." *Journal of Family Psychology* 22, no. 5 (2008): 789–93.

Wiederman, Michael. "Premarital Sex." In *Sex and Society*, vol. 3, 636–66. New York: Marshall Cavendish, 2010.

Wilcox, W. Bradford. "Don't Be a Bachelor: Why Married Men Work Harder, Smarter, and Make More Money." *The Washington Post*, April 2, 2015. https://www.washingtonpost.com/news/inspired-life/wp/2015/04/02/dont-be-a-bachelor-why-married-men-work-harder-and-smarter-and-make-more-money.

———. "How Focused On the Family? Evangelical Protestants, the Family, and Sexuality." In *Evangelicals and Democracy in America: Volume 1, Religion and Society*, edited by Steven Brint and Jean Reith Schroedel, 251–75. New York: Russell Sage Foundation, 2009.

——. *Soft Patriarchs, New Men: How Christianity Shapes Fathers and Husbands.* Chicago: University of Chicago Press, 2004.

Wilcox, W. Bradford, and Jeffrey Dew. *The Date Night Opportunity: What Does Couple Time Tell Us About the Potential Value of Date Nights?* Charlottesville, VA: The National Marriage Project, 2012.

Wilcox, W. Bradford, and Elizabeth Marquardt. *When Baby Makes Three: How Parenthood Makes Life Meaningful and How Marriage Makes Parenthood Bearable.* Charlottesville, VA: The National Marriage Project, 2011.

Wilcox, W. Bradford, and Nicholas H. Wolfinger. "Then Comes Marriage? Religion, Race and Marriage in Urban America." *Social Science Research* 36, no. 2 (2007): 569–89.

Wilcox, W. Bradford, and Wendy Wang. *The Marriage Divide: How and Why Working Class Families Are More Fragile Today.* Washington, DC: American Enterprise Institute, 2017.

Wildsmith, Elizabeth, Megan Barry, Jennifer Manlove, and Brigitte Vaughn. "Dating and Sexual Relationships." *Adolescent Health Highlights* 2013, no. 4 (2013): 1–10.

Williamson, Hanna C., Thomas E. Trail, Thomas N. Bradbury, and Benjamin R. Karney. "Does Premarital Education Decrease or Increase Couples' Later Help-Seeking?" *The Journal of Family Psychology* 28, no. 1 (2014): 112–17.

Wilson, Douglas. "Gresham and Emily." *Blog and Mablog,* undated. https://dougwils.com/the-church/gresham-and-emily.html.

——. *Reforming Marriage: Gospel Living for Couples.* Moscow, ID: Canon, 1995.

——. *Her Hand in Marriage: Biblical Courtship in the Modern World.* Moscow, ID: Canon, 1997.

Wilson, James Q. *The Marriage Problem: How Our Culture Has Weakened Families.* New York: HarperCollins, 2002.

Wingerd, Daryl, Jim Eliff, Jim Chrisman, and Steve Burchett. *Divorce and Remarriage: A Permanence View.* Kansas City: Christian Communicators Worldwide, 2009.

Winthrop, John. *Some Old Puritan Love-letters: John and Margaret Winthrop, 1618–1638.* Edited by Joseph Hopkins Twichell. New York: Dodd, Mead & Company, 1894.

Witte, John, Jr. "Marriage and Family Life." In *The Calvin Handbook,* edited by Herman J. Selderhuis, 455–65. Grand Rapids: Eerdmans, 2009.

——. "The Reformation of Marriage Law in Martin Luther's Germany: Its Significance Then and Now." *Journal of Law and Religion* 4, no. 2 (1986): 293–351.

Wright, H. Norman, and Wes Roberts. *Before You Say "I Do": A Marriage Preparation Guide for Couples.* Eugene, OR: Harvest House, 2015.

Wolfinger, Nicholas H. "Beyond the Intergenerational Transmission of Divorce: Do People Replicate the Patterns of Marital Instability They Grew Up With?" *Journal of Family Issues* 21, no. 8 (2000): 1061–86.

——. "Counterintuitive Trends in the Link between Premarital Sex and Marital Stability." *Institute for Family Studies,* June 6, 2016. https://ifstudies.org/blog/counterintuitive-trends-in-the-link-between-premarital-sex-and-marital-stability.

Zebrowitz, Leslie A., and Robert G. Franklin, Jr. "The Attractiveness Halo Effect and the Babyface Stereotype in Older and Younger Adults: Similarities, Own-Age

Accentuation, and Older Adult Positivity Effects." *Experimental Aging Research* 40, no. 3 (2014): 375–93.

Zhang, Yuanting, and Jennifer Van Hook. "Marital Dissolution among Interracial Couples." *Journal of Marriage and Family* 71, no. 1 (2009): 95–107.

Zill, Nicholas, Frank F. Furstenberg, James Peterson, and Kristin Moore. "National Survey of Children: Wave 1, 1976, Wave 2, 1981, and Wave 3, 1987." Ann Arbor, MI: Inter-university Consortium for Political and Social Research [distributor], 1990. https://doi.org/10.3886/ICPSR08670.v3.

Zylstra, Sarah. "Are Evangelicals Bad for Marriage? A New Study Says Protestants Are More Likely Than Non-religious Americans to Divorce, but Some Disagree." *Christianity Today*, February 14, 2014. http://www.christianitytoday.com/ct/2014/february-web-only/are-evangelicals-bad-for-marriage.html.

SUBJECT INDEX

Y

NAME INDEX

SCRIPTURE INDEX